The Rise and Fall of the U.S. Mortgage and Credit Markets

The Rise and Fall of the U.S. Mortgage and Credit Markets

A Comprehensive Analysis of the Market Meltdown

James R. Barth
Tong Li
Wenling Lu
Triphon Phumiwasana
Glenn Yago

WILEY

John Wiley & Sons, Inc.

For general information on our other products and services or for technical support, please contact our Customer Care Department within the United States at (800) 762-2974, outside the United States at (317) 572-3993 or fax (317) 572-4002.

Wiley also publishes its books in a variety of electronic formats. Some content that appears in print may not be available in electronic books. For more information about Wiley products, visit our web site at www.wiley.com.

ISBN 978-0-470-47724-3

Printed in the United States of America.

10 9 8 7 6 5 4 3 2 1

For
Rachel, Yiping and Keneng, Mei Yun and Sheng Fu,
Valaiporn, and Stephanie

Contents

List of Illustrations

List of Tables

Acknowledgments

This book could not have been completed without the help of the following Milken Institute staff members: editors Lisa Renaud and Dinah McNichols, who offered many insightful comments; intern Shelly Shen, who provided excellent research assistance; librarians Lisa Montessi and Jorge Velasco, who accommodated numerous requests for data and literature with great patience; Jared Carney, director of marketing and program development, who saw the potential for this research to become a Wiley & Sons book; and Michael Klowden, president and CEO, and Skip Rimer, director of programs and communications, who provided valuable support and suggestions.

Chapter 1

Overleveraged, from Main Street to Wall Street

I have great, great confidence in our capital markets and in our financial institutions. Our financial institutions, banks and investment banks, are strong.

—Treasury Secretary Henry Paulson
March 16, 2008
CNN

but just six months later:

The financial security of all Americans . . . depends on our ability to restore our financial institutions to a sound footing.

—Treasury Secretary Henry Paulson
September 19, 2008
Press release

and after another two months:

We are going through a financial crisis more severe and unpredictable than any in our lifetimes.

—Treasury Secretary Henry Paulson
November 17, 2008
"Fighting the Financial Crisis, One Challenge at a Time"
The New York Times

For generations, the home mortgage market has efficiently and successfully extended credit to more and more families, enabling millions of Americans to own their own homes. Indeed, the homeownership rate reached a record high of 69.2 percent in the second quarter of 2004. The growth of subprime mortgages that contributed to this record, moreover, meant that many families or individuals deemed to be less creditworthy were provided with greater opportunities to purchase homes.

But, unfortunately, a system borne of good intentions veered horribly off track, derailed by several factors, including poor risk-management practices, too many assets funded with too little homeowner-contributed equity capital, and lax regulatory oversight.

In the past, the vast majority of mortgages were more carefully vetted by well-capitalized neighborhood savings and loans, institutions that held and serviced these loans throughout their lifetimes. In recent years, however, the mortgage industry increasingly moved toward securitization (that is, packaging mortgages into securities and selling them in the secondary market).

This sweeping change in the marketplace was a positive innovation that provided the mortgage industry with greater liquidity, helping make new loans accessible to more Americans, at different levels of income, than ever before. This structure worked fairly well (with a few notable exceptions), producing a reasonable widening of consumers' access to credit. But by 2004, it was becoming ever more apparent credit was expanding too rapidly, and too many market participants at every level were taking on dangerous levels of leverage. What began as healthy growth in mortgage originations and housing starts swiftly became a home price bubble.

Ironically, it was the demise of *another* bubble that set the stage for the initial run-up in real estate. In the late 1990s, Internet stocks were sizzling; investors poured millions into start-ups that had never turned a dime of profit. When the dot-coms cratered in 2000 and 2001, they sent the broader stock markets tumbling. This crash, combined with the effects of the 9/11 terrorist attacks, sent the United States into a mild recession. To stimulate the economy and prevent deflation, the Federal Reserve slashed interest rates to historic lows—and suddenly, to borrowers and lenders alike, home mortgages looked too tempting to pass up. Having just been burned by one bubble, the nation wasted no time creating another in its wake.

Real estate was a real, tangible asset, and it seemed to be a safe haven in comparison to those high-flying, hard-crashing technology stocks. Unlike the dot-com boom, the housing expansion drew in millions of middle-class and lower-income families. There had been previous boom-and-bust cycles in real estate, of course, but caution was cast aside in the rush to get in on a "sure bet" with rapidly rising home prices—and nothing had ever before rivaled the recent housing market in terms of sheer scale and reach.

At the height of the boom, home prices were rising at a torrid pace in overheated markets like Southern California. Backyard barbecues were filled with talk of instant housing wealth, and anyone sitting out the party in a rental unit was regarded with bemused pity. Inland from Los Angeles, McMansions were sprouting in the desert, as developers raced to keep up with demand.

Today many of those same Southern California communities are dotted with abandoned properties and foreclosure signs. Countless families no doubt thought they had landed a piece of the American dream, only to see it slip through their fingers just a few years later.

California was by no means the only place where many dreams went sour. Variations on these stories played out from coast to coast. Unable to resist the many tempting deals being offered and lured in by the popular wisdom of the moment, home buyers rushed in, convinced that investing in real estate was the chance of a lifetime. Cable TV introduced average Americans to the concept of flipping houses for profit and encouraged them to tap their newfound equity for pricey renovations.

As home values escalated, many borrowers were unable to obtain loans on the basis of traditional standards. Mortgage brokers and lenders were able to keep churning out seemingly profitable mortgages in such an environment by casting their nets even wider, and borrowers were eager to accommodate them. Soon many loans were being written on such loose terms that they were clearly unsustainable unless home prices continued rising. Real estate agents and those originating mortgages who felt they had next to nothing to lose if things went bad allowed buyers with shaky credit histories and modest incomes to dive in. In the reach for yield, many financial institutions made loans to such home buyers, either holding on to them or packaging the loans for sale to investors. With the upside gain seeming limitless, it was hardly surprising that many were eager to participate, with the regulatory authorities taking no early and strong steps to slow things down to a more normal pace.

A host of new loan products offered buyers the chance to own a home with no money down or with temporarily low introductory payments. These products can have perfectly legitimate uses in the right circumstances but can prove dangerous in the wrong hands. All lenders and borrowers needed to know was that if prices kept rising, everyone would be happy. There would be plenty of time to refinance later, and in the process borrowers would be improving their credit records.

When home prices did come plunging back to earth, the outcome was much the same across the nation: too many homeowners found themselves in way over their heads, and too many home builders found themselves with an excess inventory of unsold homes. But this is not solely a tale of home buyers who overreached and home builders who overbuilt. The damage quickly grew and spread far beyond the scope of the actual mortgage defaults and foreclosures.

Not only did financial institutions suffer losses on mortgages they held, but so too did investors who bought mortgage-backed securities in the secondary market. These investments in essence themselves became a giant bubble, resting on the wobbly foundation of risky loans. Investors from around the world were clamoring for a piece of the action and got it with mortgage-backed securities—and even new securities *backed* by mortgage-backed securities. After all, ratings agencies essentially blessed by the regulatory authorities handed out AAA ratings on many of these investment vehicles. Some observers have tied this situation to the fact that these agencies were paid by the very parties who issued the securities.

In addition to the vast market for mortgage-backed securities, billions of dollars were soon at stake because insurance was available to cover losses on any defaults; coverage came in the form of newer derivatives known as credit default swaps that were issued on these securities. Some firms were even trading large amounts of these swaps on debt in which they had no ownership stake at all. Because these swaps were traded over the counter and not on a central exchange with member-contributed capital available to cover losses, concern grew regarding the ability of counterparties to fulfill their contractual agreements, heightening investors' sense of unease.

What initially appeared to be nothing more than a routine retrenchment in home prices soon morphed into a many-headed hydra. Throughout 2008, increasing losses and write-downs were announced by various financial firms (worldwide losses had reached $685 billion through October 31, 2008). Some venerable names were ultimately acquired or outright failed due to the enormity of their losses.

From Main Street to Wall Street, one common thread runs through all facets of this story: leverage. Homeowners and major financial firms alike had taken on too much risk and too much debt in their quest for gains. Whenever leverage is excessive, or too many assets are supported with too little owner-contributed equity capital, a decline in the value of the assets can leave the owner of those assets without the capital to cover losses. In short, an excessively leveraged nation is nothing more than a bubble nation.

As of this writing, the U.S. economy is engaged in a massive wave of deleveraging, a scramble to reduce debt and sell assets as well as an attempt to obtain new capital from any willing source, including the government. Unfortunately, this process has caused a major credit crunch and sent asset prices further downward. Even solid companies with no connection to the real estate and finance sectors have been affected as credit markets seized up. In the process, a rush to liquidity has created severe difficulties for individuals, small businesses, large corporations, and even state and local governments as they try to obtain short-term funding simply to meet payrolls and cover ongoing operating expenses.

In many cases, the government has now become the buyer of last, if not first, resort, intervening in the market in ways not seen since the New Deal. (See Appendix Figure A.1 and Table A.1 for a historical overview of the government's role in the banking sector.) To contain the damage, the government invoked some existing but seldom-used powers and created others out of whole cloth. As the financial sector continued to lurch from crisis to crisis in 2008, the government's response has been marked by an improvisational quality that has failed to restore confidence in the financial system.

The first truly startling intervention came about in March 2008, when the Federal Reserve provided a $29 billion loan to help JPMorgan Chase acquire Bear Stearns in the wake of that firm's sudden collapse. But months later, the Fed refused to bail Lehman Brothers out of similar straits, and the firm was forced to file for bankruptcy in September 2008. Just two days later came another flip-flop, when the Federal Reserve extended an $85 billion loan to the faltering insurance giant American International Group (AIG) in exchange for equity warrants that would give it a 79 percent ownership stake. A month later, the Fed agreed to extend AIG another lifeline of up to $37.8 billion in cash collateral in exchange for investment-grade, fixed-income securities. Then again in the following two months, it was announced that AIG was getting another $20.9 billion loan from the Fed and $40 billion in capital from Treasury.

The government has also attempted to shore up mortgages directly. In July 2008, the Housing and Economic Recovery Act authorized the Federal Housing Authority to guarantee up to $300 billion in new 30-year fixed-rate mortgages for subprime borrowers. But the guarantees were conditional on lenders voluntarily writing down principal loan balances to 90 percent of current appraisal value; there are indications that the program has not met with much initial success as of this writing. The Act also provided temporary authority to the Treasury Secretary to purchase any obligations and other securities in any amounts issued by Fannie Mae and Freddie Mac, the two big government-sponsored enterprises that hold and guarantee most of the nation's mortgages. But by September 7, 2008, both institutions had deteriorated sufficiently that they were placed into conservatorship, or effectively nationalized, to ensure that they would remain solvent. At the same time, the Treasury announced a temporary program to purchase Fannie Mae and Freddie Mac mortgage-backed securities to help make more mortgage financing available to home buyers.

When all of these government interventions failed to stem the growing crisis, even bolder action was undertaken in October 2008. At the request of the Bush administration, Congress passed the Emergency Economic Stabilization Act, granting the Treasury unprecedented powers to use up to $700 billion to stabilize the financial sector. The bailout plan also raised the limit on bank deposits secured by the Federal

Deposit Insurance Corporation (FDIC) from $100,000 to $250,000 per depositor, attempting to reassure depositors that their cash was safe in the banking system. Furthermore, the government announced it was insuring individual investors against losses in money market mutual funds, instruments that had for decades been regarded as safe havens before one such fund "broke the buck." The SEC also temporarily barred investors from taking any short positions in selected companies, in an effort to stop the bleeding in the stock market.

By late November 2008, Treasury had injected $179 billion in capital into 30 financial institutions. The FDIC had also extended unlimited insurance coverage to all noninterest-bearing transaction accounts. The Fed, in addition to several other new and historic programs, in the same month took steps to force down home mortgage rates by agreeing to buy up to $600 billion of housing-related securities issued and guaranteed by Fannie Mae, Freddie Mac, Ginnie Mae, and Federal Home Loan Banks as well as creating a $200 billion program to lend money against securities backed by car loans, student loans, credit card debt, and small-business loans.

The sheer size of the bailout, with $7.5 trillion or more committed as of late November 2008, provoked a storm of controversy. Many critics have cried foul about the government's lack of transparency; others fume that by rescuing firms and individuals that took on too much leverage, the government has created thorny new problems of moral hazard (the concept that shielding parties from the full consequences of their risk taking actually encourages them to take even greater risks in the future). Still others complained that insufficient effort and funds have thus far been devoted to halting the rising tide of home foreclosures. It is ironic to note that the United States has essentially been nationalizing its financial institutions while China has embarked on privatizing many of its own.

From its very outset, the Obama administration has been faced with the daunting task of quelling a crisis that has metastasized throughout the financial sector and into the real economy. Housing markets need to be stabilized, and the wave of foreclosures must be stemmed. But more than that, confidence in the nation's basic financial institutions and regulatory authorities must be restored, and reforms must be undertaken to better assure financial stability in the future.

The government has taken on additional debt in an attempt to shore up the financial system, which only worsens the nation's already staggering deficit. Future administrations will be grappling with the ramifications of those decisions for years to come.

In a very real sense, the bill for this bubble has now been handed to taxpayers.

Chapter 2

Overview of the Housing and Mortgage Markets

I t has been a long-standing public policy to promote homeownership for all socioeconomic and racial groups across the nation. To facilitate the purchase of homes, a variety of financial instruments and institutions have come into existence over the years. The myriad types of housing units and mortgage products available in the marketplace have opened the door to homeownership for millions of families, offering them the chance to steadily build wealth over a lifetime.

Owning a home can bestow a sense of security and autonomy—but today, in a cruel twist, many Americans now regard their homes as the source of worry and dashed expectations. How did everything change so suddenly and dramatically?

Before we examine the factors that led up to the mortgage meltdown and its spread throughout the financial sector and into the real economy, a bit of historical context is in order.

Housing Units, Mortgage Debt, and Household Wealth

There were 130.4 million housing units in the United States at the end of the third quarter of 2008, as shown in Figure 2.1. To put this number in perspective, the nation's total population was 304 million, and there

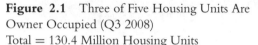

Figure 2.1 Three of Five Housing Units Are Owner Occupied (Q3 2008)
Total = 130.4 Million Housing Units

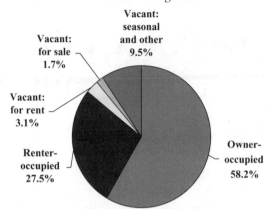

SOURCES: U.S. Census Bureau, Milken Institute.

were 111 million households, or 2.7 persons per household.[1] There were 18.9 million more vacant housing units than households. (See Appendix Table A.2 for further detail.)

Most housing units (58 percent) are owner occupied.[2] Renter-occupied units account for 28 percent of the total, while vacant units account for the remaining 14 percent. Some of the vacant units are for sale or rent, while others are used on weekends or similar short periods by their owners or seasonally by vacationers. The mere fact that some housing units are vacant is not a cause for alarm. However, when the number of vacant units rises significantly above the normal level, this does become a warning signal that home prices may be in for a tumble and home construction may be headed for a slowdown.

The vast majority of buyers cannot possibly pay the full price for a home all at once,[3] so obtaining a mortgage is their key to achieving the American dream. Mortgage debt has made homeownership a reality for a greater number of households and allowed for an expansion in the number of housing units. Moreover, in the process of using mortgages as a tool to purchase homes, individuals are able to accumulate wealth; as they make payments on interest and principal, they build equity in their homes and increase their net worth. Because mortgage interest is tax deductible, they also enjoy significant tax benefits along the way.

Figure 2.2   Mortgage Debt Enables Homeownership and Leads to Wealth Accumulation (Quarterly, 1952–Q2 2008)

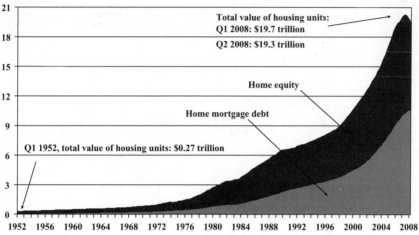

SOURCES: Federal Reserve, Milken Institute.

Figure 2.2 shows the increase in the total value of housing units from the first quarter of 1952 to the second quarter of 2008—a more than 71-fold increase, from $270 billion to $19.3 trillion.[4] Both home equity and mortgage debt have risen right along with the total value of all housing units over the past half century.

In recent years, however, home mortgage debt has grown faster than accumulated equity. As shown in Figure 2.3, mortgage debt accounted for slightly more than half the value of all housing units as of June 2008. Its share increased fairly rapidly and steadily following World War II and the Korean War, from 19 percent in 1952 to 37 percent in 1965, then declined somewhat and fluctuated within a fairly narrow range until the early 1990s. The share of housing debt to the total value of housing units again rose fairly rapidly, to 43 percent in 2001, and continued rising to a record high of 55 percent in the second quarter of 2008. The recent rise in the share reflects the fact that a lending boom produced record highs in both the total value of housing units and the homeownership rate. (See Figure A.2 in the Appendix for more information on the relatively close and positive relationship between the homeownership rate and the mortgage debt-to-GDP ratio.)

Figure 2.3   In 2008, Mortgage Debt Accounts for More than 50 Percent of the Value of Housing Stock (Quarterly, 1952–Q2 2008)

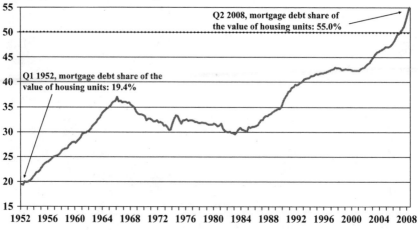

SOURCES: Federal Reserve, Milken Institute.

Figure 2.4 illustrates the relationship between the housing and mortgage markets. It shows the total value of all housing units broken down by the types of mortgages supporting them (prime or subprime) and by the share of those mortgages that have been securitized in the capital markets (i.e., bundled into pools and used to back securities that are sold to investors). The figure also shows that $10.6 trillion of the total value of all housing units consists of mortgage debt; the remaining $8.7 trillion is homeowner equity.

What makes up this $10.6 trillion universe of mortgage debt? Prime mortgage loans account for 91.6 percent of the debt outstanding, while subprime mortgage loans account for the other 8.4 percent. Of the total amount of mortgages outstanding, 59 percent have been securitized. (See Appendix, Figure A.2, for empirical evidence on the relationship between securitization and the homeownership rate.) The remaining 41 percent are held as assets in the portfolios of financial firms and therefore funded with the firms' own equity capital and outstanding debt (or deposits). Moreover, this figure shows that as a result of actions in response to the spreading financial crisis, the federal government controlled 46 percent of the total value of outstanding mortgage debt as of September 2008.

Figure 2.4   Value of Housing Units: How Much Has Been Borrowed, Who Are the Borrowers, and Who Funds Them? (Q2 2008)

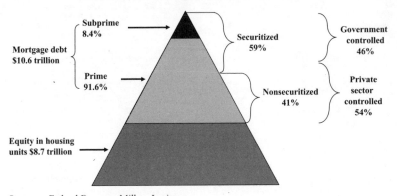

SOURCES: Federal Reserve, Milken Institute.

NOTE: The share of mortgage debt that is controlled by the government and by the private sector is based on Q3 2008 data.

Figure 2.5 provides a more detailed picture of the different funding sources of mortgages outstanding for single-family homes, residential units (single- and multifamily), and commercial properties. Total residential and commercial mortgages amounted to $14.7 trillion at the end of the second quarter of 2008. Just 5 percent of that total comes to roughly $700 billion, which is coincidentally the upper limit of the amount provided to the U.S. Treasury Department under the Emergency Economic Stabilization Act of 2008.

Figure 2.5 shows more specifically that home mortgages are the dominant share of all residential mortgages outstanding, accounting for 93 percent of the total. Even when adding in commercial mortgages, the share of home mortgages is nearly 80 percent.

The biggest asset owned by the typical American family is their home, which represents substantially more than their net worth (their assets minus their debts). Indeed, as Table 2.1 shows, for all families except those in the top 20 percentiles of income, the median value of their primary residence is greater than the median value of their net worth. For those families in the bottom 20th percentile of income, the median value of the primary residence is more than nine times the median value of their net worth. More generally, the ratio of these two measures is inversely related to the median value of household net worth.

Figure 2.5   Sources of Funding for Residential and Commercial Mortgages (Q2 2008)

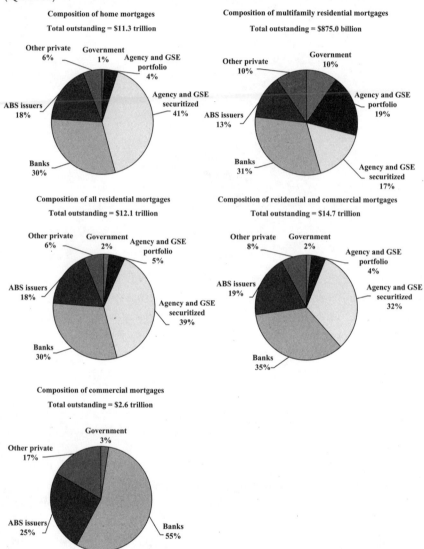

SOURCES: Federal Reserve, Milken Institute.
NOTE: *ABS* refers to asset-backed securities. *GSE* refers to Fannie Mae and Freddie Mac (each is a government-sponsored enterprise). *Agency* refers to Ginnie Mae.

Table 2.1 Homes Are an Important Component of Household Wealth, Especially for Lower-Income Families (2004)

Percentile of Income	Median Value of Primary Residence (US$ Thousands)	Median Value of Household Assets (US$ Thousands)	Median Value of Household Net Worth (US$ Thousands)	Median Value of Primary Residence/ Median Value of Household Net Worth
Less than 20	70	17.0	7.5	9.3
20–39.9	100	78.2	33.7	3.0
40–59.9	135	154.6	72.0	1.9
60–79.9	175	289.2	160.0	1.1
80–89.9	225	458.5	313.3	0.7
90–100	450	1,157.7	924.1	0.5

SOURCES: Federal Reserve, Milken Institute.
NOTE: See the Appendix, where Table A.3 provides information about different characteristics of homeowners, and Figure A.3 illustrates the role of real estate in household wealth.

Tracking this relationship emphasizes a simple point: homes represent a more crucial component of net worth for lower-income families than for higher-income families.

Types of Home Mortgages

Prime and subprime loans are broad categories of home mortgages, but they are only a small part of the story. The universe of mortgage loans is much more complex. The main types are illustrated in the bottom row of Figure 2.6.

Figure 2.6 Types of Loans Available in the Home Mortgage Market

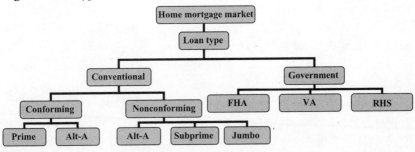

SOURCES: LoanPerformance, Milken Institute.

Both the government and private firms play large roles in the home mortgage market. The government is directly involved through the granting of Federal Housing Administration (FHA) loans, as well as loans through the Department of Veterans Affairs (VA) and the Rural Housing Service of the Department of Agriculture. FHA and VA loans must meet the requirements set by each of these government agencies. If they do, the loans are guaranteed by the agencies and securitized by the Government National Mortgage Association (Ginnie Mae).

The mortgage loans offered by private firms (those not insured by government agencies) are referred to as *conventional mortgage loans*. Some conventional mortgage loans conform to the requirements for purchase by the Federal National Mortgage Association (Fannie Mae) and the Federal Home Loan Mortgage Corporation (Freddie Mac); these *conforming loans* can be either securitized by those entities or held in their portfolios. By buying mortgage loans, these two government-sponsored enterprises (GSEs) create liquidity for lenders, freeing up capital so they can make more loans and thus better support the credit market. The access to funding from the capital markets on fairly generous terms by Fannie Mae and Freddie Mac has historically generated a steady demand for conforming loans, and in the process allowed lenders to offer somewhat more favorable terms on these home mortgages. Nonconforming loans can be securitized by private-label securitizers or held in the portfolios of financial institutions.

Conforming loans are further broken down into two categories that describe the creditworthiness of the borrower: prime and Alt-A loans. Nonconforming loans are subdivided into Alt-A, subprime, and jumbo loans. *Jumbo loans* are those exceeding the maximum loan amounts set for purchase by Fannie Mae and Freddie Mac, while *Alt-A loans* are those issued to borrowers whose creditworthiness is deemed to be slightly below prime but slightly better than subprime (the Alt-A category frequently includes loans made to borrowers who do not fully, if at all, document their income). We will fully describe subprime borrowers and the subprime market in Chapter 3.

Figures 2.7 and 2.8 show the proportion of conventional and government home mortgages originated and outstanding for selected years. Total loan originations (new loans issued) increased from $500 billion in 1990 to $2.4 trillion in 2007 before declining to $900 billion in the

Figure 2.7   Conventional and Government Home Mortgage Originations (Selected Years)

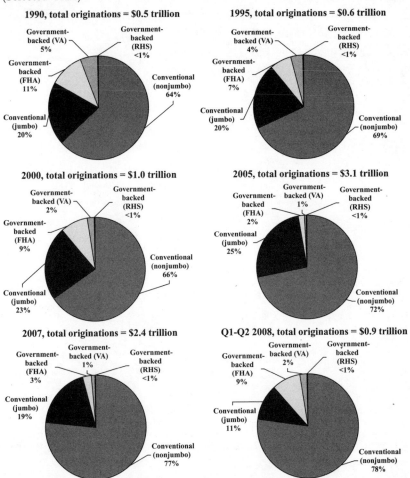

SOURCES: Office of Federal Housing Enterprise Oversight, Milken Institute.
NOTE: The Office of Federal Housing Enterprise Oversight (OFHEO) was replaced on July 30, 2008, with the Federal Housing Finance Agency (FHFA) upon enactment of the Federal Housing Finance Regulatory Reform Act of 2008. See Appendix Table A.4 for data for every year from 1990 to Q2 2008.

first half of 2008, while the total amount outstanding increased from $2.6 trillion to $11.3 trillion over the same period. But notably, the government share of mortgage originations declined from 16 percent in 1990 to less than 4 percent in 2007, falling slightly more than 12 percentage points, before rebounding to 11 percent in the first half of 2008.

Figure 2.8   Conventional and Government Home Mortgages Outstanding (Selected Years)

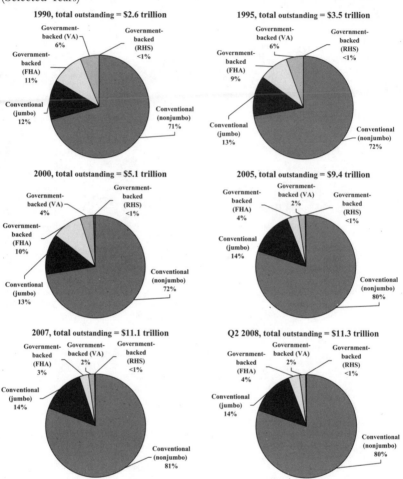

SOURCES: Office of Federal Housing Enterprise Oversight, Milken Institute.
NOTE: OFHEO was replaced on July 30, 2008, with the Federal Housing Finance Agency (FHFA). See Appendix Table A.5 for data for every year from 1990 to Q2 2008.

Meanwhile, the conventional share increased from 84 to 96 percent, growing slightly more than 12 percentage points, before declining to 89 percent in the first half of 2008. The reversals in the recent shares reflect the impact of the financial crisis on mortgage markets.

A similar shift can be seen in the figure illustrating mortgages outstanding. The private sector became an increasingly important funding source for home mortgages in recent years, but this trend is reversing itself in the wake of the meltdown.

Another key characteristic of a mortgage is the type of interest rate that is charged. For many years, the vast majority of home loans were *fixed-rate mortgages* (FRMs), in which the interest rates stays constant over the entire life of the loan, so monthly payments stay the same. But *adjustable-rate mortgages* (ARMs) take a different approach, allowing the rate to rise or fall in concert with a benchmark index. Figures 2.9 and 2.10 show the growing importance of ARMs over time. From 1990 to 2000, their originations almost tripled, from $127.6 billion to $311.3 billion, and then more than tripled *again,* topping $1.1 trillion in 2004 and 2005, before declining sharply to $106.7 billion in the first half of 2008. Their outstanding amounts grew 10-fold. ARMs also accounted for an increasing share of mortgages outstanding, rising from 9 percent

Figure 2.9   Originations of Conventional and Government ARMs (Selected Years)

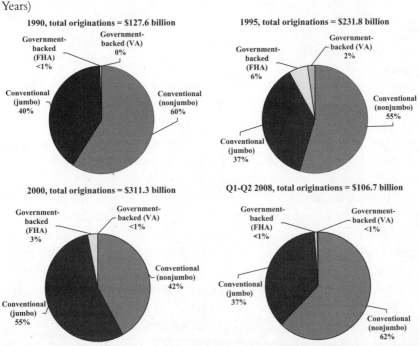

SOURCES: Office of Federal Housing Enterprise Oversight, Milken Institute.
NOTE: OFHEO was replaced on July 30, 2008, with the Federal Housing Finance Agency (FHFA). See Appendix Tables A.6 and A.7, which list data for every year from 1990 to Q2 2008.

Figure 2.10   Conventional and Government ARMs Outstanding (Selected Years)

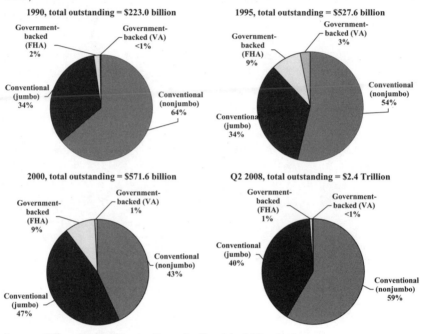

SOURCES: Office of Federal Housing Enterprise Oversight, Milken Institute.
NOTE: OFHEO was replaced on July 30, 2008, with the Federal Housing Finance Agency (FHFA). See Appendix Tables A.8 and A.9, which list data for every year from 1990 to Q2 2008.

to 23 percent over the same period. While there have been many media accounts of subprime ARMs gone bad, it is worth noting that many prime borrowers have taken out these loans as well.

These two figures also provide information about the relative share of conventional and government mortgages originated and outstanding from 1990 to the first half of 2008. The vast majority of ARMs originated and outstanding over this period were conventional mortgages, not government-backed home loans.

The share of conventional jumbo ARM originations rose from 40 percent of all home mortgages in 1990 to 55 percent in 2000, before dropping to 37 percent in the first half of 2008, with the collapse of the housing bubble. The share of conventional jumbo ARMs outstanding rose from 34 percent in 1990 to 47 percent in 2005 and then fell to 40 percent in the first half of 2008.

Figure 2.11 Subprime and Alt-A Shares of Mortgage Originations Spike between 2001 and 2006 and Then Fall (Selected Years)

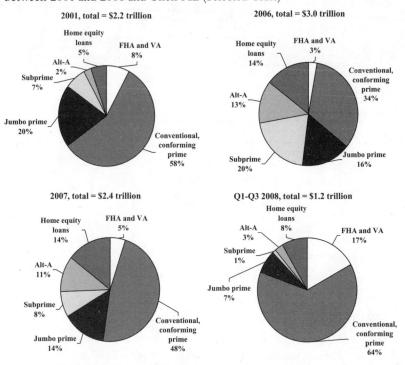

SOURCES: Inside Mortgage Finance, Milken Institute.

To provide a fuller understanding of the complexity of housing and mortgage markets, Figure 2.11 breaks down mortgage originations by product for selected years. Total originations of all different types of loans increased by $800 billion from 2001 to 2006, from $2.2 trillion to $3.0 trillion, but then declined by $600 billion, to $2.4 trillion, in 2007. Originations declined still further in the first three quarters of 2008, by $780 billion on an annualized basis.

It is important to note that FHA and VA mortgage originations declined sharply as a share of all loans, shrinking from 8 percent in 2001 to 3 percent in 2006. But then they reversed course and increased to 5 percent in 2007, spiking to 17 percent in the first three quarters of 2008.

Mortgage originations to less creditworthy borrowers (in the form of subprime and Alt-A loans) displayed similar sharp increases during the boom, followed by big drops in their shares.

Figure 2.12   Types and Purposes of Loans Available in the Home Mortgage Market

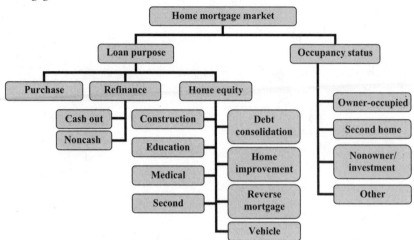

SOURCES: LoanPerformance, Milken Institute.

Figure 2.12 provides yet another perspective on the home mortgage market. Mortgage loans are not only taken out for the initial purchase of a home. They may also be used to refinance an existing loan, obtaining better terms. But in addition, borrowers can tap into the equity in their homes, taking out cash for tuition payments, medical expenses, home improvements, consolidation of credit card debt, or the purchase of another home for investment or speculative purposes. Indeed, Figure 2.11 shows that nearly 15 percent of all mortgage originations in both 2006 and 2007 were home equity loans, up sharply from only about 5 percent in 2001. During the housing boom, consumers increasingly came to view their homes as ready sources of credit. In fact, some borrowers were using their home equity to juggle debt or finance a lifestyle they could not truly afford.

Two Housing Finance Models: Originate-to-Hold vs. Originate-to-Distribute

It is important to understand how the mortgage market has evolved over the past three decades and how some of the major changes (occurring behind the scenes, as far as consumers were concerned) contributed to the current market deterioration.

Prior to 1980, the vast majority of all home mortgage loans were made by savings and loan associations. These institutions originated, serviced, and held mortgage loans in their portfolios, in what is widely referred to as an *originate-to-hold model*. Then, as early as 1970, the model began to change as single institutions no longer provided all three functions. Home mortgage loans were increasingly *securitized* (i.e., put into pools and packaged into securities backed by the individual loans), which is referred to as the *originate-to-distribute model*.

In 1970, Ginnie Mae was the first to issue a new type of security: a mortgage pass-through, a vehicle through which monthly payments of interest and principal on a pool of FHA and VA home mortgage loans were literally "passed through" to investors. Subsequently, Ginnie Mae, Fannie Mae, and Freddie Mac became the primary securitizers of home mortgages.[5] Other financial firms, beginning with Bank of America (which issued the first private-sector mortgage pass-through backed by conventional mortgages in 1977), also became participants in this market[6] and are commonly referred to as *private-label securitizers*.

The advent of securitization brought about dramatic changes. Savings institutions, which accounted for 49 percent of outstanding home mortgages in 1980, saw their share decline to only 8 percent by the second quarter of 2008 (see Figure 2.13 and also Appendix Table A.12).

Figure 2.13 Changing Funding Sources for Home Mortgages (Selected Years)

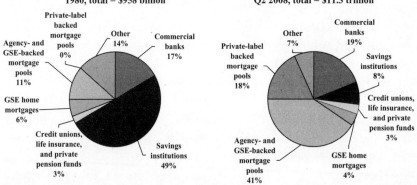

SOURCES: Federal Reserve, Milken Institute.

NOTE: *Agency* refers to Ginnie Mae; *GSE* refers to Fannie Mae and Freddie Mac.

Figure 2.14   The Mortgage Model Switches from Originate-to-Hold to Originate-to-Distribute (Selected Years)

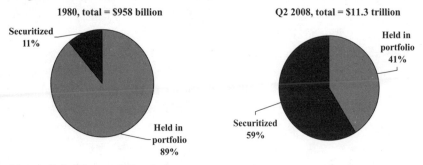

SOURCES: Federal Reserve, Milken Institute.

Commercial banks, meanwhile, became twice as important as savings and loans as a funding source for home mortgage loans over the same period.

At the same time, securitized home mortgages increased from 11 percent to 59 percent of the total share of home mortgages, while the share of home mortgages following the originate-to-hold model dropped from 89 percent to 41 percent (see Figure 2.14 and Appendix Table A.13).

Securitization was a financial innovation that contributed in a monumental way to the development of the mortgage market by tapping into a broader base for funding. The securitization process also brought about an "unbundling" of the three sources of revenue derived from home mortgages. Savings and loans no longer had to hold these mortgages in their portfolio for the long term; they could decide to forgo the associated interest payments they once received over the term of the loan in favor of selling the loan to investors. These transactions would generate origination fees and free up capital so more new loans could be made. The investors who bought the securities backed by the mortgages would receive the interest and principal payments for funding the underlying loans (which were collected, for a fee, by a servicer and then passed on to the investors).

The unbundling of the home mortgage process into these three separate functions (funding, origination, and servicing) meant there were distinct sources of revenue that could be earned by different financial

Figure 2.15   By 2006, Mortgage Brokers Accounted for a Majority of
Home Mortgage Originations (Selected Years)

1987, total number of brokers = 7,000   **2006, total number of brokers = 53,000**

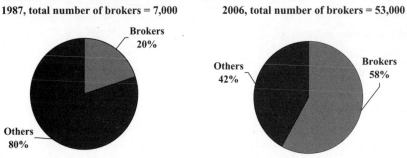

SOURCES: Wholesale Access, Milken Institute.
NOTE: *Others* includes retailer productions.

firms. Savings and loans could opt to use outside servicing firms, and they
could also turn to outside vendors (in the form of mortgage brokers)
to handle the origination function. In 1987, there were only 7,000
mortgage brokers, but that figure had increased to 53,000 by 2006 as loan
originations surged. Brokers' share of mortgage originations increased
from 20 percent in 1987 to 68 percent in 2003 before declining to
58 percent in 2006 (see Figure 2.15 and also Figures A.4 and A.5 in
the Appendix). The advantage for brokers of specializing in origination
(and focusing only on origination fees as their source of revenue) is that
the associated credit risk of the loans was passed on to the holder of
the mortgages or to the investor who ultimately bought the securities
backed by those loans.[7] This business model would eventually prove
to have major ramifications, as it opened the door to an acceptance of
riskier loans by originators, because the risk was borne by others.

Not only had the savings and loans historically performed all three
functions in the loan process, but they had also provided mortgages
to customers purchasing homes in their immediate vicinity—and they
had fairly extensive knowledge about market conditions in their own
backyards. By contrast, investors who purchased securities based on pools
of home mortgage loans could be located halfway around the world from
the homes that served as collateral.

Because they were so removed from the origination process, investors in mortgage-backed securities relied on lenders—and even more

heavily on rating agencies—to evaluate the quality of the underlying loans. Just as credit scores became commonly used as a measure of the creditworthiness of the individuals taking out home mortgages, credit ratings for mortgage-backed securities were supposed to provide accurate information for investors to gauge risk.

Agencies like Moody's Investors Service, Standard & Poor's, and Fitch Ratings benefited from this new process. They were now weighing in to far-flung investors, earning revenue by rating the credit quality of securities based on collateralized pools of home mortgage loans. It was a long way—both literally and figuratively—from the old savings and loan model.

Over time, the issuance of mortgage-backed securities became less dominated by Ginnie Mae, Freddie Mac, and Fannie Mae. Before 2007, the share of all home mortgage security issuance by private-label mortgage issuers increased from just 2 percent in 1985 to 56 percent in 2006 (see Figure 2.16 and Appendix Table A.10). In terms of outstanding home mortgage securities, the share accounted for by private-label issuers increased from 6 percent to 37 percent over the same period (see Figure 2.17 and Appendix Table A.11). Indeed, their share of issuance more than doubled, from an average of 21 percent in the years 2000 to 2003 to an average of 49 percent in 2004–2007. Their share of the outstanding securities similarly doubled, from an average of 15 percent in 2000–2003 to an average of 31 percent in 2004–2007. But in the first three quarters of 2008, in the wake of the meltdown, the origination

Figure 2.16 Share of Private-Label Mortgage Issuance Increases by 36 Percentage Points in Two Decades

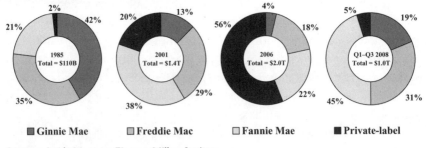

Sources: Inside Mortgage Finance, Milken Institute.

Figure 2.17 Private-Label Mortgage Issuers Account for a Larger Share of Outstanding Home Mortgage Securities (Selected Years)

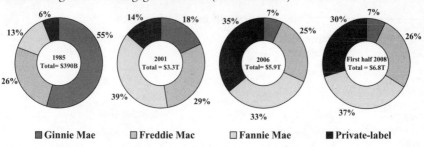

◼ Ginnie Mae   ☐ Freddie Mac   ☐ Fannie Mae   ◼ Private-label

SOURCES: Inside Mortgage Finance, Milken Institute.

share of the private-label mortgage issuers fell back to just 5 percent, as parts of the country were left with a huge increase in the inventory of unsold homes.

Home mortgages securitized by Ginnie Mae, Fannie Mae, and Freddie Mac enjoy an advantage over other securitized mortgages: the interest and principal payments on the securities backed by these mortgages are guaranteed by these firms (in the case of Ginnie Mae, the securities are actually backed by the FHA and VA). This means that the purchasers of the securities issued by these entities are guaranteed that they will receive the promised interest and principal payments, even if there are defaults on the underlying mortgages. Fannie Mae and Freddie Mac must purchase any loans that have been securitized if the borrowers fail to make mortgage payments on a timely basis. These two GSEs, moreover, require private mortgage insurance when loan-to-value ratios exceed 80 percent.

There is an important distinction to make regarding these three entities: Ginnie Mae is a government agency, while Fannie Mae and Freddie Mac are government-sponsored enterprises. Although Fannie and Freddie are publicly traded corporations, this unique status was interpreted by nearly everyone to imply that they would never be allowed to fail. And while that promise was never made explicit, the federal government indeed made good on it in September 2008, when the two institutions were placed into conservatorship run by the Federal Housing Finance Agency (FHFA); their stockholders and debt holders were not wiped out.

Figure 2.18 Guarantees of Asset-Backed Securities by Monoline Insurers Dominate Those for Municipal Securities (December 2006)

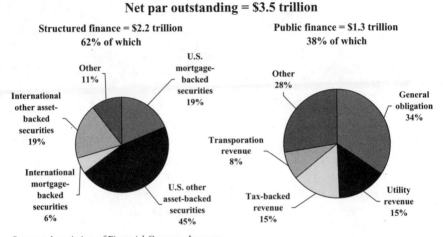

Net par outstanding = $3.5 trillion

Structured finance = $2.2 trillion
62% of which

Public finance = $1.3 trillion
38% of which

Other 11%

U.S. mortgage-backed securities 19%

Other 28%

International other asset-backed securities 19%

General obligation 34%

Transporation revenue 8%

International mortgage-backed securities 6%

U.S. other asset-backed securities 45%

Tax-backed revenue 15%

Utility revenue 15%

SOURCE: Association of Financial Guaranty Insurers.

The case of home mortgages that are securitized by private-label issuers is different. Instead of receiving real or implied government backing, these securities have typically been guaranteed by *monoline insurers* (so called because they provide insurance coverage only for securities available in the capital market). In 2006, these monoline insurance firms had insured $543 billion in mortgage-backed securities worldwide, which represented 25 percent of their total guarantees (see Figure 2.18). The deterioration in the value of mortgage-backed securities in 2007 and 2008 raised concerns about their ability to honor their guarantees for not only these securities but also for municipal and other securities.

Although securitization initially involved only home mortgage loans, it has spread to many other types of loans, including automobile, home equity, and credit card loans. Total outstanding securities backed by various assets more than doubled from $4.2 trillion in 1999 to $10.1 trillion in the second quarter of 2008. The share of securities backed by assets other than home mortgages increased by 5 percentage points over the same period, from 21 to 26 percent (see Figure 2.19 and Appendix Figure A.6).

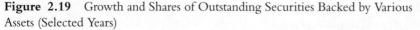

Figure 2.19   Growth and Shares of Outstanding Securities Backed by Various Assets (Selected Years)

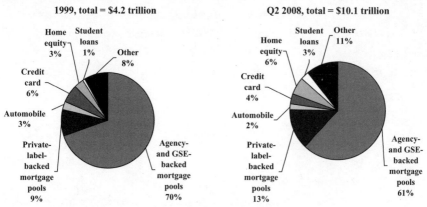

SOURCES: Securities Industry and Financial Markets Association, Milken Institute.
NOTE: *Agency* refers to Ginnie Mae; *GSE* refers to Fannie Mae and Freddie Mac.

Low Interest Rates Contribute to Credit Boom and Record Homeownership Rates

The government has always stressed the virtues of homeownership and taken steps to promote it over the years. But while homeownership may be a worthwhile goal in and of itself, providing credit in excessive amounts to the home mortgage market leads to housing booms and busts. The increases in homeownership may therefore last only as long as the housing bubble does—and the broader financial sector and economy may suffer tremendously when the bubble bursts.

An important contributing factor to the most recent credit boom and the record high homeownership rate it produced were the low interest rates that prevailed from 2001 to the end of 2004, as the Federal Reserve took steps to combat the 2001 recession and prevent deflation.[8] Figure 2.20 shows the sharp decline in mortgage rates that occurred during this period.

A second factor contributing to the era of easy credit was a global savings glut. Foreign investors, flush with cash, made record purchases of U.S. securities. Indeed, the United States was the largest importer of

Remarks on Homeownership...
One of the great successes of the United States in this century has been the partnership forged by the national government and the private sector to steadily expand the dream of homeownership to all Americans. ... Since 1993, nearly 2.8 million new households have joined the ranks of America's homeowners, nearly twice as many as in the previous 2 years. But we have to do a lot better. The goal of this strategy, to boost homeownership to 67.5 percent by the year 2000, would take us to an all-time high, helping as many as 8 million American families across that threshold. ...When we boost the number of homeowners in our country, we strengthen our economy, create jobs, build up the middle class, and build better citizens.
    President Bill Clinton
    Remarks on the National Homeownership Strategy
    University of California, Santa Barbara
    June 5, 1995

[D]uring the past few years, ... low mortgage rates have supported record levels of home construction and strong gains in housing prices. Indeed, increases in home values, together with a stock-market recovery that began in 2003, have recently returned the wealth-to-income ratio of U.S. households to 5.4, not far from its peak value of 6.2 in 1999 and above its long-run (1960–2003) average of 4.8. ... The depth and sophistication of the country's financial markets have allowed households easy access to housing wealth.
    Remarks by Governor Ben S. Bernanke
    "The Global Saving Glut and the U.S. Current Account Deficit"
    Virginia Association of Economists, Richmond, Virginia
    March 10, 2005

capital in the world in 2007 (see Figure 2.21). This influx of capital contributed to lower rates, particularly longer-term rates, than would otherwise have occurred. China, in particular, accumulated massive foreign exchange reserves and invested heavily in the United States. According

Figure 2.20   Did the Fed Lower Interest Rates Too Much and for Too Long? Federal Funds Rate vs. Rates on FRMs and ARMs (Weekly, January 1991–November 1, 2008)

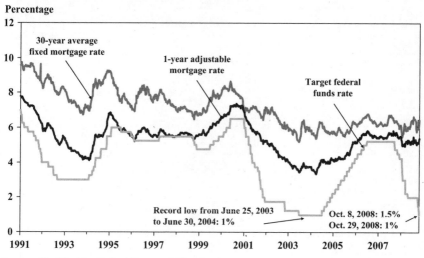

SOURCES: Freddie Mac, Federal Reserve, Milken Institute.

to Bardhan and Jaffee (2007), "the need to maintain a somewhat under-valued Chinese yuan has caused China to make extensive investments in U.S. Treasury and Agency securities, with the likely result that U.S. mortgage rates have been at least 50 [basis points] lower; indeed a case could be made that U.S. mortgage rates are a full percentage point lower as a result." (See the Appendix, Figures A.7 and A.8.)

As Figure 2.22 shows, the inflow of capital into the United States as a share of GDP increased beginning in 2001, from 3.3 percent to a high of 5.3 percent in 2006, and then declined to 4.5 percent in 2007. Despite even that decline, the United States was the largest importer of capital in the world in 2007, as illustrated in Figure 2.21.

The low interest rate environment from 2001 to 2004 had another effect on many home buyers: they increasingly opted for adjustable-rate mortgages (ARMs) over fixed-rate mortgages (FRMs). As Figure 2.23 shows, the ARM share of total mortgage applications tends to move inversely with the one-year ARM rate—which in turn tends to move positively with the target federal funds rate. In other words, because the

Figure 2.21 The United States Is the Largest Importer of Capital (2007)
Total Worldwide Capital Inflows = $1.4 Trillion

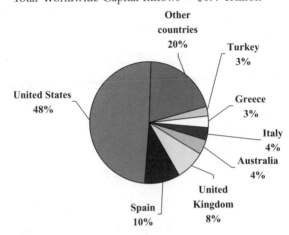

SOURCES: International Monetary Fund, Milken Institute.

typical adjustable rate on a home mortgage is initially set below fixed rates, many individuals choose to fund home purchases with ARMs during periods of declining interest rates and avoid them during periods of rising interest rates.[9]

Figure 2.22 Capital Inflows to the United States (1983–2007)

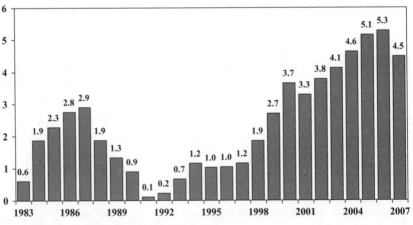

SOURCES: International Monetary Fund, Milken Institute.

Figure 2.23   On a Roughly Similar But Inverse Track: ARM Share of Total Mortgage Applications and the One-Year ARM Rate (Weekly, 1990–November 3, 2008)

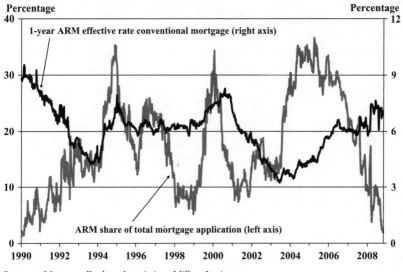

SOURCES: Mortgage Bankers Association, Milken Institute.
NOTE: The weekly correlation of the ARM share and ARM rate between 1990 and November 3, 2008 is −0.3915.

It is instructive to briefly review how ARMs first gained nationwide attention and then came to play such a prominent role in the current home mortgage market turmoil. They first became important in the wake of the savings and loan collapse in the early 1980s. When the Federal Reserve changed its operating policy to combat inflationary pressures in the late 1970s, short-term interest rates rose more rapidly than long-term rates, and the yield curve inverted (i.e., short-term rates exceeded longer-term rates).

As we discussed earlier, savings and loans were heavily involved in the mortgage market at that time, holding about half of all the home mortgage loans in the United States in their portfolios. The vast majority of these mortgages were traditional fixed-rate, 30-year mortgages. The inverted yield curve meant nearly all savings and loans would be insolvent if their mortgage portfolios were marked-to-market (i.e., priced at their current market value rather than their book value) because the interest rates on these loans were lower than the rates on newly issued loans.

Indeed, the approximately 4,000 savings and loans that made up the industry at the time were estimated to be insolvent by roughly $150 billion (or $399 billion in 2008 dollars).

How did savings and loans get into such a dire situation? Until that time, they were largely prohibited from offering ARMs or using hedging instruments to reduce their interest rate risk. Congress responded to the savings and loan crisis by broadening the powers of savings and loans so they could operate more like commercial banks, which held more diversified portfolios and thus largely avoided the same plight as more specialized institutions. Savings and loans were subsequently allowed to offer adjustable-rate mortgages and to hedge their interest rate risk with various derivative instruments.

Adjustable-rate mortgages accounted for less than 5 percent of originations in 1980, but that share increased substantially, although it also fluctuated fairly widely thereafter (see Appendix Table A.14). But the low interest rates of 2001 to 2004, combined with the increased popularity of ARMs, contributed to a surge in home mortgage originations and a record-high homeownership rate of 69.2 percent in the second quarter of 2004 (see Figure 2.24). Conversely, the rental rate declined to an all-time low of 30.8 percent over the same period (see Figure 2.25).

ARMs held a clear attraction for lenders. When lending institutions offer fixed-rate mortgages and hold them in portfolio, the lender bears the interest rate risk, but when they offer and hold ARMs, that risk is shifted to the borrower.

During the housing boom—an era of easy credit and limitless optimism regarding prospects for home price increases—many borrowers happily took on that risk, considering only their ability to manage the low initial payments. They assumed they would have no difficulty in refinancing when their rates reset and their monthly payments went up, because the prices of their homes would be higher. That strategy did work for a time, but it could not be sustained indefinitely. Many consumers either did not understand or did not adequately appreciate the interest rate risk they were assuming and did not stop to consider that home prices do not rise indefinitely.

Homeownership rates for all races and ethnic groups reached record highs by 2005 and then declined somewhat, with African Americans

Figure 2.24   Credit Boom Pushes Homeownership Rate to Historic High
(Quarterly, 1965–Q3 2008)

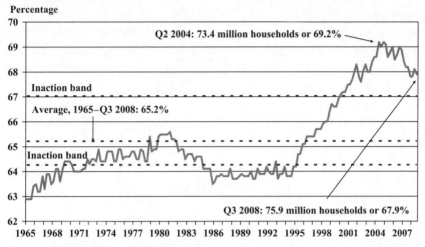

SOURCES: U.S. Census Bureau, Milken Institute.

NOTE: The homeownership rate is calculated as the ratio of owner-occupied housing units divided by all occupied housing units. Also, we consider the transition of the homeownership rate between the unit root regime and a stationary regime. The inaction bands show that only when the homeownership rate is below (or above) the bands does it switch over to the stationary process. Within the bands, the homeownership rate is governed by the unit root process. More detailed information is available from the ongoing research in this area by James R. Barth, Triphon Phumiwasana, and Hyeongwoo Kim (Auburn University).

Figure 2.25   Rental Rate Hits an All-Time Low in 2004
(Quarterly, 1965–Q3 2008)

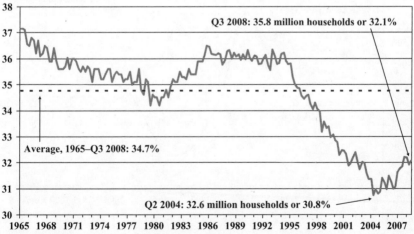

SOURCES: U.S. Census Bureau, Milken Institute.

experiencing the biggest drop (see Appendix Table A.15). The erosion in the overall homeownership rate (which fell to 67.9 percent in the third quarter of 2008) was accompanied by the same percentage point increase in the rental rate. Some renters became homeowners but then found themselves renting again in a relatively short period of time as they defaulted on their loans. It is important to keep in mind, however, that there is nothing inherently wrong with being a renter rather than a homeowner.

Mortgage Originations, Home Prices, and Sales Skyrocket

The low-interest environment from 2001 to 2004, as discussed, un-leashed a tsunami of demand for home mortgages. Figure 2.26 shows a decline in the one-year ARM rate, from 7.04 percent in 2000 to 3.76 percent in 2003, and a corresponding surge in the credit available for home purchases. Home mortgage originations increased from $1.0 trillion in 2000 to a high of $3.9 trillion in 2003. They then fell to $2.9 trillion in 2004 and increased to $3.1 trillion in 2005. They

Figure 2.26 Low Interest Rates and Credit Boom (1994–Q3 2008)

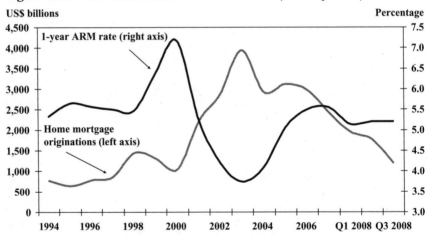

SOURCES: Inside Mortgage Finance, Federal Reserve, Milken Institute.
NOTE: Home mortgage originations for Q1-Q3 2008 are annualized.

Figure 2.27   Home Price Bubble and Credit Boom (1994–Q3 2008)

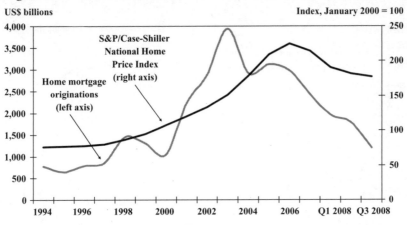

SOURCES: Inside Mortgage Finance, S&P, Milken Institute.

NOTE: Home mortgage originations for Q1–Q3 2008 are annualized.

declined once again to $3.0 trillion in 2006 and still further to $2.4 trillion in 2007 as the mortgage market meltdown occurred. In the first three quarters of 2008, originations totaled only $490 billion, $445 billion, and $300 billion, respectively. During the surge in home mortgage originations, some lenders began soliciting hard for new loans and relaxing their underwriting standards to keep the party going.

Accompanying the surge in home mortgage originations was, of course, a corresponding surge in home prices in the early and mid-2000s. Home mortgage originations shot up by 276 percent from 2000 to 2003, and home prices increased by 41 percent over the same period, as shown in Figure 2.27. This thriving market also pushed homeownership to a new high, as shown in Figure 2.28.

Home prices can be tracked by using different indices or concentrating on different geographical regions. Figure 2.29 shows that the annual growth rate of prices from January 1987 to December 2006 was 5.16 percent, based on the national home price index from the Office of Federal Housing Enterprise Oversight (OFHEO), and 6.52 percent, based on S&P/Case-Shiller's 10-metro composite home price index (see Appendix Table A.16 for a discussion of the differences in these two indices). Regardless of the measurement used, from 2000 to 2006 most of the arrows were pointing in one direction: straight up.

Figure 2.28   Home Price Bubble and Homeownership Climb (1990–Q2 2008)

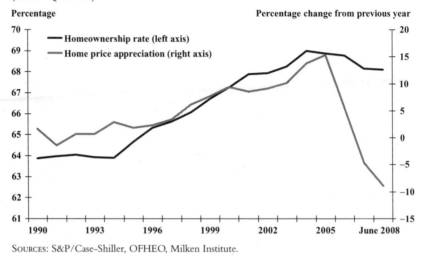

SOURCES: S&P/Case-Shiller, OFHEO, Milken Institute.

While home prices rose steadily across most of the nation, they were absolutely skyrocketing in certain hot markets. Appendix Table A.17 tracks prices in the 20 individual metropolitan statistical areas covered by S&P/Case-Shiller's home price index. It shows that from 2000 to 2006, Miami posted an average annual home price increase of 17.1 percent. During that same period, prices in Los Angeles rose by an average of 16.1 percent per year, while in Las Vegas, the average annual jump was 14.0 percent. At the height of the boom, bidding wars often broke out between buyers in these markets, and many sellers closed deals well above their initial asking prices. Desirable properties might be snapped up at their first showings.

But what goes up must come down, and that was especially true in the most overheated markets. From August 2007 to August 2008, prices in Miami, Los Angeles, and Las Vegas plummeted by 28.1 percent, 26.7 percent, and 30.6 percent, respectively. Figure 2.29 also shows that home prices collapsed after 2006.

Not surprisingly, the surge in home mortgage originations indicated briskly rising home sales. Both new and existing homes saw record-high sales in the fall of 2005 (see Figure 2.30). New developments sprouted around the nation as home builders raced to keep up with demand. But

Figure 2.29   Home Price Bubble Peaks in 2006
(Monthly, January 1987–September 2008)

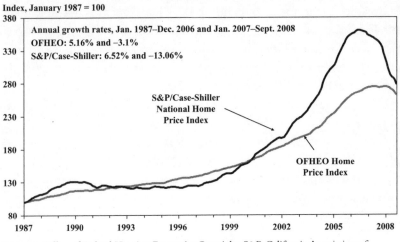

Index, January 1987 = 100

Annual growth rates, Jan. 1987–Dec. 2006 and Jan. 2007–Sept. 2008
OFHEO: 5.16% and –3.1%
S&P/Case-Shiller: 6.52% and –13.06%

S&P/Case-Shiller
National Home
Price Index

OFHEO Home
Price Index

SOURCES: Office of Federal Housing Enterprise Oversight, S&P, California Association of
Realtors, Moody's Economy.com, Milken Institute.

Figure 2.30   Home Sales Peaked in Fall 2005, Then Plummeted
(Monthly, 1968–September 2008)

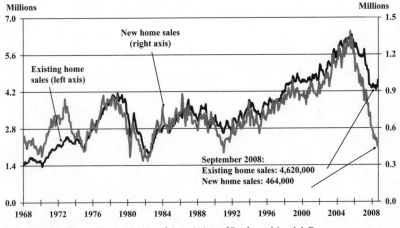

Millions   Millions

New home sales
(right axis)

Existing home
sales (left axis)

September 2008:
Existing home sales: 4,620,000
New home sales: 464,000

SOURCES: U.S. Census Bureau, National Association of Realtors, Moody's Economy.com,
Milken Institute.

as the chart indicates, the bursting of the bubble led to a plunge in sales of both new and existing homes.

Steadily rising prices and home sales had kept the housing market aloft for quite some time, but once the reversal began, it set a chain reaction in motion. Those who bought their homes near the end of the boom suddenly found that their properties were not worth what they paid. Borrowers could not rely on market conditions to keep increasing their equity—and many found themselves with ARMs they could not refinance.

The subprime market was the first area to show cracks in the foundation. In Chapter 3, we will examine how subprime lending grew, how it melted down, and why tremors in this one particular market ultimately sent shock waves through the entire financial system.

Chapter 3

Buildup and Meltdown of the Mortgage and Credit Markets

After 2006, it became practically impossible to turn on the TV without seeing another increasingly gloomy report about "the subprime crisis." Even as trouble spread far beyond this particular corner of the housing market, the word *subprime* was being used as shorthand for the cause of the nation's financial woes. But does the entire concept of subprime lending really deserve the stigma that has been attached to it by the media's coverage?

It is true that subprime borrowers were the first to show signs of stress when housing prices ceased their upward trajectory. When the bubble burst, a wave of defaults and foreclosures began sweeping through the subprime market. These were undeniably painful losses, but even so, how did they cause such outsized reverberations throughout the financial system?

To truly grasp the story behind the mortgage meltdown, it is helpful to step back and take an in-depth look at the growth of subprime lending, examining how the system was used and abused and how the securitization trend discussed in Chapter 2 magnified the losses in this market.

What Is a Subprime Mortgage and Who Is a Subprime Borrower?

How Do Regulators Characterize Subprime Borrowers?
By providing loans to borrowers who do not meet the credit standards for borrowers in the prime market, subprime lending can and does serve a critical role in the nation's economy. These borrowers may have blemishes in their credit record, insufficient credit history or non-traditional credit sources. Through the subprime market, they can buy a new home, improve their existing home, or refinance their mortgage to increase their cash on hand.

> "Unequal Burden: Income and Racial Disparities in Subprime Lending in America"
> U.S. Department of Housing and Urban Development
> April 2000

Subprime borrowers typically have weakened credit histories that include payment delinquencies, and possibly more severe problems such as charge-offs, judgments, and bankruptcies. The borrowers may also display reduced repayment capacity as measured by credit scores, debt-to-income ratios, or other criteria that may encompass borrowers with incomplete credit histories.

> OCC, FRB, FDIC, and OTS
> *Federal Register*
> July 12, 2002

The term *subprime* generally refers to borrowers who do not qualify for prime interest rates because they exhibit one or more of the following characteristics: weakened credit histories typically characterized by payment delinquencies, previous charge-offs, judgments, or bankruptcies; low credit scores; high debt-burden ratios; or high loan-to-value ratios.

> Roger T. Cole, Director, Division of Banking Supervision and Regulation
> Board of Governors of the Federal Reserve System
> March 22, 2007

Given the intense media coverage of the subprime mortgage market, it may come as a surprise to learn that the distinction between prime and subprime borrowers is not clear-cut. Economists at the Federal Reserve Bank at San Francisco define *subprime* as "a lender-given designation for borrowers with low credit scores (FICO scores less than 620, for example), with little credit history, or with other types of observable credit impairment."[1] But it is misleading to think that lenders rely solely on FICO scores for distinguishing between the two types of borrowers. Individuals can be considered prime borrowers with FICO scores below 620, and they can be considered subprime borrowers with scores above that cutoff.

A FICO score can range from a low of 300 to a high of 850.[2] Higher scores represent greater creditworthiness; the median score is about 720. And while we tend to treat FICO scores as an appropriate measure of a borrower's creditworthiness, Figure 3.1 shows that roughly one-fifth of the population would be in the subprime borrower category based on a cutoff of 620 alone—meaning that, conversely, four-fifths of the population would be considered prime borrowers. The fact that such an enormous portion of the population would classified in the prime

Figure 3.1 National FICO Scores Display Wide Distribution

Percentage of population

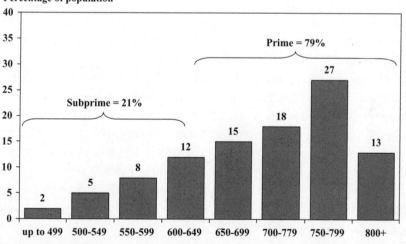

SOURCE: myFICO (2007).

NOTE: FICO scores range from 300 to 850.

Figure 3.2 What Goes into a FICO Score?

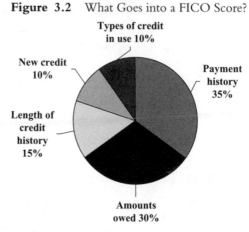

SOURCE: myFICO (2007).

borrower category on the basis of just their FICO scores may not be fully appreciated in the constant bombardment of news stories about problems in the mortgage market.

Figure 3.2 illustrates the components that make up a FICO score. Although a score captures a great deal of useful information, it clearly omits certain factors that could be critical to lenders in making credit decisions—most notably salary and employment history. Lenders may also consider criteria such as the loan-to-value ratio (whether the borrower is able to contribute a significant down payment) and the income-to-debt ratio (whether the borrower can reasonably be expected to handle the required monthly loan payments given their income). Figure 3.3 shows the distribution of prime and subprime borrowers by FICO score. It is interesting to note that prime borrowers may have FICO scores below 400, while subprime borrowers may score above 820.

Figure 3.3 shows that 55 percent of the borrowers who received mortgage loans in 2006 had FICO scores above 620 yet were considered subprime by lenders. Indeed, most importantly, there is no standard industrywide definition for a subprime borrower. This means each lender makes its own determination about which customers are subprime.[3] To the extent that appropriate risk-based pricing (setting higher interest rates for borrowers deemed to be riskier) was used, moreover, the

Figure 3.3 Prime and Subprime Mortgage Originations by Borrower FICO Score Reveal Substantial Overlaps (2006)

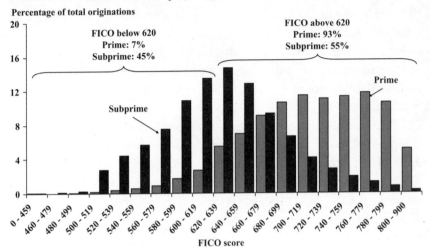

SOURCES: LoanPerformance, Milken Institute.

distinction between prime and subprime lending becomes somewhat artificial.

Just as prime and subprime borrowers cannot be distinguished on the basis of FICO scores alone, it is similarly misguided to categorize them based on the mortgage products they choose. Over the past decade, most (if not all) of the products offered to subprime borrowers have also been offered to prime borrowers. In fact, from January 1999 through July 2007, prime borrowers chose 31 of the 32 types of available mortgage products (including fixed-rate, adjustable-rate, and hybrid mortgages, including those with balloon payments) chosen by subprime borrowers. (See Appendix Tables A.18 and A.19 for an exact breakdown.)

There are clear differences in the *extent* to which certain types of loans were chosen by prime and subprime borrowers, but both groups have had access to a wide range of mortgage products. Some of the products criticized for being inappropriate have not been marketed to or chosen by subprime borrowers exclusively. Furthermore, regulatory authorities have noted that "subprime lending is not synonymous with predatory lending."[4]

If the product itself, such as the adjustable-rate mortgage, was the problem in the subprime market, one might expect *all* borrowers using that product to be facing foreclosure. But this is not the case. Foreclosure rates are rising, but the rates differ widely by type of product and borrower. No single product accounts for all foreclosures, though certain loans (such as hybrid mortgages and pay-option ARMs, which will be addressed later) posed greater problems than other types of mortgage products.

Rather than barring the use of a certain product by *all* borrowers, it is important to question whether individuals are being matched with the appropriate products for their financial circumstances. An adjustable-rate mortgage with a low initial teaser rate may be a wonderful tool for a medical student who expects her income to grow substantially in the near future, for example, but it may not be the best choice for borrowers who lack similar prospects—and it is definitely a poor choice for any borrower who does not fully understand how the payments may change over time. Mortgage products with perfectly legitimate uses should not be used in ways for which they were not designed.

Subprime Lending Grows Rapidly and New Products Gain Acceptance

The rapid growth of subprime lending is a relatively recent phenomenon, even though such mortgages have been around for some time. Figures 3.4 and 3.5, respectively, show that subprime home mortgage originations increased dramatically, from $160 billion in 2001 to $625 billion in 2005. Over the same period, subprime home mortgages outstanding rose from $479 billion to $1.2 trillion. (Both originations and the amount outstanding declined sharply when the housing bubble burst: only $16 billion in subprime mortgages were originated during the first three quarters of 2008.)

As Table 3.1 and Figure 3.6 show, subprime mortgages accounted for less than 5 percent of total originations in 1994. In 2000, their share increased to 13 percent and eventually topped 20 percent in both 2005 and 2006. (Their share then dropped to 7.9 percent in 2007 and shrank to less than 1 percent in the third quarter of 2008.)

Figure 3.4   Subprime Home Mortgage Originations Increase Rapidly before
Big Decline (2001–Q3 2008)

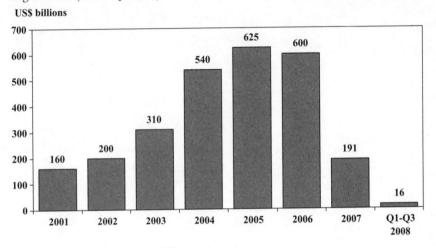

SOURCES: Inside Mortgage Finance, Milken Institute.

Figure 3.5   Subprime Home Mortgages Outstanding Increase Rapidly before
Big Decline (1995–Q2 2008)

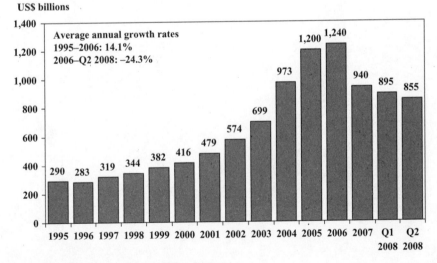

SOURCES: Inside Mortgage Finance, Milken Institute.

Table 3.1 Subprime's Importance for Home Mortgage Originations (1994–Q3 2008)

Year	Share of Total Mortgage Originations (%)		Top 25 Subprime Originators	Total Mortgage Originations (US$ Billions)	Subprime MBS Share of Total Mortgage Originations	Subprime MBS Share of Total Subprime Originations
	Prime	Subprime				
1994	95.5	4.5	n.a.	773	1.4	31.6
1995	89.8	10.2	4.0	639	2.9	28.4
1996	87.7	12.3	5.8	785	4.5	36.4
1997	85.5	14.5	8.7	859	7.3	50.0
1998	89.7	10.3	6.5	1,450	5.7	55.1
1999	87.8	12.2	8.1	1,310	4.6	37.9
2000	86.8	13.2	9.8	1,048	5.3	40.5
2001	92.2	7.8	5.7	2,215	4.3	55.2
2002	92.6	7.4	6.8	2,885	4.2	57.1
2003	91.6	8.4	8.1	3,945	5.1	61.0
2004	81.8	18.2	16.7	2,920	13.7	75.7
2005	78.7	21.3	19.4	3,120	16.3	76.3
2006	79.9	20.1	18.2	2,980	16.2	80.5
2007	92.1	7.9	7.0*	2,430	9.0	114.0
Q1 2008	97.9	2.1	1.8 **	490	0.4	20.9
Q2 2008	99.1	0.9	0.9 **	445	0.04	4.3
Q3 2008	99.3	0.7	n.a.	300	0.0	0.0

SOURCES: Inside Mortgage Finance, Milken Institute.
NOTE: *and **indicate the share of top 20 and top 10, respectively.

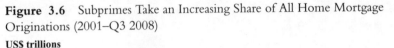

Figure 3.6 Subprimes Take an Increasing Share of All Home Mortgage Originations (2001–Q3 2008)

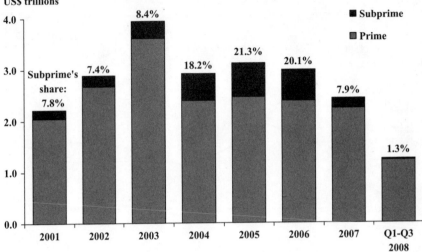

SOURCES: Inside Mortgage Finance, Milken Institute.

As subprime lending grew, more and more of these loans were packaged into mortgage-backed securities (MBS). In 1994, some 31.6 percent of subprime mortgage were securitized, but by 2006, that share had more than doubled to 80.5 percent of all subprime loans. The top 25 subprime mortgage originators accounted for 90 percent or more of all subprime originations after 2001.

Relatively low interest rates, both nominal and real, fueled this tremendous growth. In a low-interest rate environment, when credit is readily available, efforts to increase returns on equity can be accomplished through increased leverage, acquisition of higher-risk assets, or both. (But the troubling flip side to this situation is the eventual need to unwind excessive leverage and rush into lower-risk assets, including cash.)

The 10-year Treasury note rate had fallen from 6 percent in 2000 to 4 percent in 2003; it then stayed flat for another two years before rising to 4.8 percent in 2006 and remaining relatively unchanged until the crisis started in 2007. With little to be gained in Treasuries, investors were searching for higher yields in other fixed-income vehicles. Mortgage-

Figure 3.7   Subprime Share of Home Mortgages Grows Rapidly before Big
Decline (1995–Q2 2008)

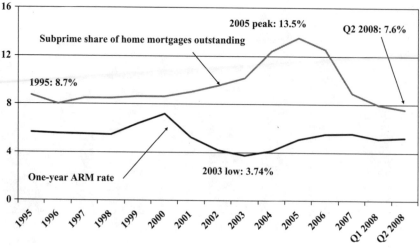

SOURCES: Inside Mortgage Finance, Federal Reserve, Milken Institute.
NOTE: The correlation between the subprime share of home mortgages and the one-year ARM rate is
−0.3683.

backed securities promised the returns they were seeking—and the
riskier the mortgages used as collateral, the higher the yields.

At the borrower's end of the equation, interest rates on mortgages
were hitting lows not seen for decades—and adjustable-rate mortgages
were especially tantalizing. Figure 3.7 shows that as the one-year ARM
rate declined from 2001 to 2004, the share of subprime home mortgages
spiked.

The seemingly insatiable demand for residential real estate naturally
caused prices to rise, with price bubbles forming in certain markets. After
rising at an average annual rate of slightly less than 3 percent during the
1990s, home prices jumped nationally by an average of nearly 9 percent
per year from 2000 to 2006. Stated another way, a home worth $150,000
in 2000 was worth $251,565 in 2006.

This environment fueled unbridled optimism on the part of lenders,
borrowers, and investors. The prevailing attitude was that real estate was
an investment that couldn't miss. Many borrowers made their financial
moves with the assumption that prices would go on climbing indefinitely.

It was an era of easy credit, and subprime lenders stepped up their marketing efforts. It was simple to obtain a mortgage loan that required little or no down payment. Some borrowers opted for no-money-down, interest-only loans that were little better than renting—but did leave them positioned to profit if home prices continued rising, creating instant equity in the homes. Average Americans from coast to coast were suddenly buying houses and condos to flip for profit. Furthermore, lenders were writing loans that allowed borrowers to tap the equity in their homes for consumption purposes. This flurry of demand, in turn, pushed housing prices even higher.

Mortgage brokers found subprime loans attractive because they could earn fees while passing along the credit risk to those who ultimately funded the loans. In hindsight, many participants in the housing market who should have known better nonetheless clearly underestimated the risks associated with subprime loans—and many unethical players chose to purposefully ignore those risks and exploit the situation for short-term gain.

Table 3.2 shows a significant shift in the composition of mortgage originations when interest rates were at their lows. The share of subprime loans nearly tripled from 2001 to 2006, going from 7.2 percent to 20.1 percent. Also, the share of Alt-A loans (those made to borrowers whose creditworthiness was considered to be somewhere between prime and subprime) increased to a high of 13.4 percent in 2006, up from only 2.5 percent in 2001. While home prices surged, owners began to think of their homes as a convenient and growing source of cash to be tapped like an ATM; home-equity loans tripled in amount from 2001 to 2006–2007.

Of course, while the shares of subprime and Alt-A loans were increasing, the share of conventional, conforming prime loans declined by nearly 25 percentage points from 2001 to 2006 (falling from 57.1 percent to 33.2 percent). At the same time, FHA and VA shares also fell, from 7.9 percent to 2.7 percent. The pendulum swung back again with the collapse in home prices and the surge in foreclosures. The conventional, conforming prime, FHA, and VA shares had increased to nearly 80 percent of all mortgage originations by the third quarter of 2008.

The subprime mortgage industry developed a number of innovative products that fueled its continued growth during the mid-2000s. These

Table 3.2 Mortgage Originations by Product (2001–Q3 2008)

Year	FHA and VA	Conventional, Conforming Prime	Jumbo Prime	Subprime	Alt-A	Home Equity Loans	Total US$ Billions
			Share of Total (%)				
2001	7.9	57.1	20.1	7.2	2.5	5.2	2,215
2002	6.1	59.1	19.8	6.9	2.3	5.7	2,885
2003	5.6	62.4	16.5	7.9	2.2	5.6	3,945
2004	4.6	41.4	17.6	18.5	6.5	11.3	2,920
2005	2.9	34.9	18.3	20.0	12.2	11.7	3,120
2006	2.7	33.2	16.1	20.1	13.4	14.4	2,980
2007	4.9	47.3	14.3	7.9	11.3	14.4	2,430
Q1 2008	9.6	66.5	8.0	2.0	4.3	9.6	490
Q2 2008	16.0	66.3	6.5	0.9	2.2	8.1	445
Q3 2008	30.1	55.7	6.3	0.7	1.0	6.3	300

SOURCES: Inside Mortgage Finance, Milken Institute.

Figure 3.8 ARM Share Grows, Following Low Interest Rates (Quarterly, 2001–Q2 2008)

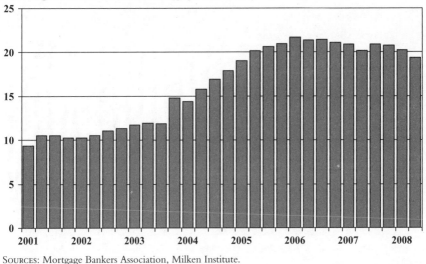

Percentage of all number of home mortgages outstanding

SOURCES: Mortgage Bankers Association, Milken Institute.

products were variations on adjustable-rate mortgages, which had been around for a long time. As Figure 3.8 shows, the ARM share of all outstanding home mortgages rose from about 10 percent in 2001 to a high of about 21 percent in 2006. But as Figure 3.9 indicates, this figure conceals the importance of ARMs for subprime loans. ARMs almost always accounted for 40 to 50 percent of subprime loans, whereas they always accounted for less than 20 percent of prime loans and less than 10 percent of FHA loans.

In contrast to prime and FHA borrowers, a greater proportion of subprime borrowers wound up with loans that exposed them to substantial interest-rate risk. Furthermore, as Figure 3.10 shows, most of the subprime loans were *hybrids* (loans that begin with a low fixed rate for an initial period, then reset to higher, variable rates for the remainder of the term of the loan). For example, 2/28 hybrid loans offered low fixed interest ("teaser") rates for two years, then reset semiannually or annually to an index value plus a certain margin (subject to periodic and lifetime interest rate caps) during the remaining 28 years of the loan. The 3/27 hybrids offered initial fixed rates for the first 3 years and then resets for the remaining 27 years of the loan. (There are also hybrid

Figure 3.9   Largest Share of ARMs Go to Subprime Borrowers
(Quarterly, 2001–Q2 2008)

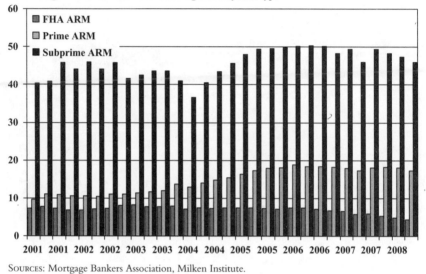

Percentage of total number of outstanding ARM by loan type

□ FHA ARM
□ Prime ARM
■ Subprime ARM

Sources: Mortgage Bankers Association, Milken Institute.

option ARM loans, which are a combination of option ARMs and
hybrid ARMs. See the glossary for explanations of different types of
mortgage loans.) In 2006, such hybrids accounted for nearly two-thirds
of all subprime mortgage loans and almost half of all Alt-A loans. Clearly,
subprime borrowers with these types of loans were bearing substantial
interest-rate risk.

Figure 3.10   Hybrids Dominate Subprime Home Purchase Loan
Originations (2006)

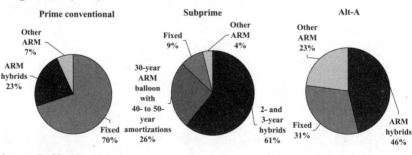

Source: Freddie Mac.

Certain product variations increased this risk, and the *option ARM* (also called the "pay-option ARM" or the "pick-a-payment" loan) became especially notorious in this regard. During the initial period, borrowers can choose their payment each month: a low minimum payment, an interest-only payment, or a fully amortizing 15- or 30-year fixed-rate payment. Because the minimum payment is actually less than the interest due, it can result in *negative amortization* (an actual *increase* of the loan balance on the back end) and large monthly payments in later years. The complexity and potential pitfalls of these loans made it essential that they be reserved for exactly the right type of financially savvy borrower, but unfortunately, in the heady days of the housing boom, prudence was in short supply.

Many subprime borrowers with ARMs simply intended to refinance their mortgages before the rates went higher—and that strategy did work for a time. As long as home prices continued to rise, even buyers who put no money down would find themselves with equity in two to three years, and that equity made it possible to obtain a new loan. Borrowers and lenders alike tended to focus only on the borrower's ability to carry the low initial payments, and loans were written for increasingly large amounts.

As for the risks being incurred by lenders, some seem to have operated under the assumption that in the event of a default, the home could be sold for more than the loan amount. This required the optimistic expectation that home prices would continue rising—or that the mortgage loan would simply be securitized, shifting the credit risk to another party.

Table 3.3 provides detailed information on the share of 2/28 and 3/27 hybrids among subprime and prime originations. The 2/28 hybrid share of subprime originations peaked at 28 percent in 2004, for example, before declining to 12 percent in 2007. The 3/27 hybrid share was 12 percent in 1999; it slid for several years before bouncing back to 9 percent in 2004, then falling all the way to 1.6 percent in 2007. The 2/28 hybrid share of prime originations was always less than 0.1 percent, while the 3/27 hybrid share reached a peak of 1.3 percent in 2004 before declining to 0.13 percent in 2007. Hybrid ARMs clearly played a much bigger role in the subprime market than in the prime market.

Table 3.3   Growth of Hybrids in Home Mortgage Originations (1999–2007)

Year	Share of Annual Subprime Origination (%)		Share of Annual Prime Origination (%)	
	2/28 Hybrid	3/27 Hybrid	2/28 Hybrid	3/27 Hybrid
1999	6.05	12.36	0.01	0.06
2000	13.74	7.54	0.02	0.14
2001	24.28	5.08	0.01	0.34
2002	25.38	3.84	0.01	0.79
2003	25.26	5.34	0.01	0.86
2004	27.58	8.83	0.05	1.34
2005	24.08	7.96	0.09	0.55
2006	17.11	2.79	0.05	0.27
2007	11.98	1.63	0.00	0.13

SOURCES: LoanPerformance, Milken Institute.

Subprime Mortgages Enable More Widespread Homeownership

Words of Praise from Regulators for Subprime Lending
Subprime mortgage lending provides credit to borrowers with past credit problems, often at a higher cost or less favorable terms than loans available in the conventional prime market. In most cases, these lenders offer credit to borrowers who would not qualify for a loan in the prime market, thus expanding access to credit and helping more families to own their own homes. The higher costs of these loans may serve to offset the increased risk that these lenders assume in lending to these borrowers.

"Unequal Burden in Baltimore: Income and Racial Disparities in Subprime Lending"
U.S. Department of Housing and Urban Development
May 2000

(*Continued*)

This should be a time of great satisfaction for the advocates of low-income and minority borrowers. As a result of the good economy, various technological changes, and innovative financial products, credit to low-income and minority borrowers has exploded in recent years . . . . A significant portion of this expansion of low-income lending appears to be in the so-called subprime lending market. This market has expanded considerably, permitting many low-income and minority borrowers to realize their dreams of owning a home and have a chance for acquiring the capital gains that have so increased the wealth of upper-income households.
Remarks by Federal Reserve Governor Edward M. Gramlich
Fair Housing Council of New York, Syracuse, New York
April 14, 2000

Expanded access to mortgage credit has helped fuel substantial growth in homeownership. The national rate of homeownership increased from 1995 through mid-2006, reaching nearly 69 percent of all households this year. All major racial and ethnic groups have made gains in homeownership, but in percentage terms the largest increases have been made by minority households.
Remarks by Federal Reserve Chairman Ben S. Bernanke
Opportunity Finance Network's Annual Conference, Washington, D.C.
November 1, 2006

Overall, the emergence of risk-based subprime lending should produce positive social welfare effects.
J. Michael Collins, Eric S. Belsky, and Karl E. Case
"Exploring the Welfare Effects of Risk-based Pricing in the Subprime Mortgage Market"
Joint Center for Housing Studies Working Paper Series
April 2004

Given the widely documented abuses by brokers, lenders, investors, and borrowers alike—and especially given the heartbreaking wave of foreclosures experienced by families across the country—it is hardly surprising that the entire subprime lending industry has come under scrutiny. But acting to curtail it too hastily, based on opinions rather than supporting evidence, could ultimately block millions more from homeownership.

It is important to remember that subprime lending is not problematic in and of itself. It arose out of good intentions, and when deployed with full disclosure and a proper appreciation of risk, it can open the door of opportunity to millions of lower-income Americans, including those who are working in good faith to overcome past financial problems. It would be a shame to close off that opportunity altogether rather than simply acting to rein in abuses of the system. For all the tales of irresponsible borrowing and lending, millions of families are now in their own homes thanks to subprime mortgages—and millions of those loans are being paid on time.

One of the most vocal critics has been the Center for Responsible Lending (CRL), which issued a report in 2007 stating that the subprime mortgage market has resulted in a net ownership loss of 854,674 units.[5] CRL suggested that subprime loans have been a bad development for individuals, despite the fact that approximately 1.3 million loans were granted to first-time home buyers from 2000 to 2006.

But following the basic approach taken by CRL, we found that even with rising foreclosure rates over the period, the nation has actually seen a net gain in homeownership of 434,683 units.[6] To arrive at this estimate, we used CRL assumptions, with one important exception. CRL assumed that 25 percent of all loans for home purchases were made to first-time home buyers. But it calculated the number of subprime foreclosures based on *all* first-lien, owner-occupied subprime loans. This would include not only purchases of homes by first-time purchasers but also purchases of second homes and purchases by investors. Rather than using CRL's calculation, we compared all purchase-loan foreclosures to the same types of loans to first-time home buyers. Because CRL's data are proprietary, we relied on LoanPerformance (LP) data for our calculations and were able to nearly duplicate the results obtained by CRL.

Table 3.4 shows our calculations along with those of CRL. CRL found a net homeownership loss in every year over the period

Table 3.4 Net Homeownership Gain or Loss Due to Subprime Mortgage Lending: Center for Responsible Lending (CRL) Calculations vs. Calculations Based on LoanPerformance (LP) Data

Year	CRL Calculations			LP Data/Calculations			Memo	
	Estimated Number of First-Time Home Buyers Using Subprime Mortgages[1] a	Foreclosures on Subprime Mortgages[2] b	Net Homeownership Gain (Loss)[3] c = a-b	Estimated Number of First-Time Home Buyers Using Subprime Mortgages[4] d	Foreclosures on Subprime Mortgages[5] e	Net Homeownership Gain (Loss)[6] f = d-e	Nationwide Net Homeownership Gain (Loss)[7] g = f/42%	CRL Foreclosure Rates Used in Calculations[8] h
2000	87,651	133,126	(45,475)	30,726	17,944	12,782	30,433	14.6
2001	80,856	105,464	(24,608)	26,953	12,398	14,554	34,653	11.5
2002	85,883	102,252	(16,369)	33,920	13,297	20,623	49,103	9.8
2003	120,807	181,464	(60,657)	71,306	34,512	36,794	87,604	12.1
2004	219,180	348,345	(129,165)	115,657	72,632	43,024	102,439	15.7
2005	324,361	632,302	(307,941)	141,314	109,660	31,654	75,368	19.4
2006	354,172	624,631	(270,459)	103,282	80,146	23,135	55,083	19.4
Total	**1,272,910**	**2,127,584**	**(854,674)**	**523,156**	**340,589**	**182,567**	**434,683**	**16.3**

SOURCES: LoanPerformance, Center for Responsible Lending, Milken Institute.

[1] Applying CRL assumption that 25 percent of purchase, first-lien, owner-occupied subprime originations are for first-time homebuyers to CRL proprietary data.
[2] CRL foreclosures on first-lien, owner-occupied subprime mortgages.
[3] Number of first-time homebuyers minus number of foreclosures, using CRL proprietary data.
[4] Applying CRL assumption that 25 percent of purchase, first-lien, owner-occupied subprime originations are for first-time home buyers, using LP data.
[5] Foreclosures on purchase, first-lien, owner-occupied subprime mortgages, using LP data.
[6] Number of first-time home buyers minus number of foreclosures, using LP data.
[7] Nationwide net homeownership gain (loss) is based on the assumption that LP data are a sample that captures 42 percent of all subprime mortgage loans.
[8] These are the foreclosure rate used in CRL's calculations and the LP-data calculations.

2000–2006, totaling almost 854,700 units for the entire period. In contrast, we found a net homeownership gain in every year, or 434,683 units nationwide, for the period. We obtained the nationwide figure by adjusting the LP data, which accounts for between 40 percent and 50 percent of all subprime mortgage loans, by 42 percent. (Comparing LP data with national aggregate data from Inside Mortgage Finance, we arrived at the 42 percent figure.)

CRL asserted that the subprime market generated more than $2 trillion in home loans and that those loans "will lead to a net loss of homeownership for almost 1 million families." However, we found that by matching the same kinds of loans, the result is a net gain of nearly half a million units. These analyses, however, do not take into account subprime mortgage loans made before 2000 or those made after 2006.

The point of this exercise is not to unduly question the analysis of CRL but to inject a note of caution. Before regulators rush to prohibit subprime mortgage loans or certain mortgage products, it is important to be sure that these actions will do more good than harm. Continued access to credit (that is, to subprime mortgage loans) does help those home buyers who would otherwise have trouble obtaining credit to realize their dreams of homeownership. Without the subprime loan market, it is clear that many individuals—perhaps 1 million or more—would have been denied access to the credit they needed to become first-time homeowners over the period we examined. While foreclosure rates among first-time buyers with subprime mortgages may be high, they are not 100 percent, so *some* borrowers are benefiting from such loans. It is worth noting the words of former Federal Reserve Governor Edward M. Gramlich:

> *One of the important stories of the 1990s was the huge growth in subprime lending. . . . One visible outcome has been an increase in home ownership rates for low-income and minority borrowers. This represents a welcome extension of home mortgage and other credit to previously underserved groups—a true democratization of credit markets. Millions of low and moderate-income families now have a chance at owning a home and building wealth.*[7]

So what rate of foreclosure on subprime mortgages is socially optimal? That is a thorny question, and obviously the number of families who have lost their homes in the past few years is nothing short of tragic. But it is impossible to eliminate *all* risk in an uncertain world. Attempting to regulate with the goal of achieving a foreclosure rate of zero would come with a cost: restricting the privilege of homeownership only to those with sterling credit.

Securitization Facilitates the Funding of Subprime Mortgages

As chronicled in Chapter 2, mortgage lending has undergone a sea change in recent years: the switch from the originate-to-hold model to the originate-to-distribute model. This was especially true in the case of subprime loans. At the height of the housing boom, investors were clamoring to put their money into mortgage-backed securities (MBS)—particularly those backed by subprime loans, which offered big returns. The process of securitizing and selling the loans gave lenders a source of funding and liquidity to make additional loans.

As Figure 3.11 shows, beginning with the onset of record low interest rates in 2001, the cumulative share of subprime mortgage originations

Figure 3.11   Securitization Becomes the Dominant Funding Source for Subprime Mortgages (1994–Q3 2008)

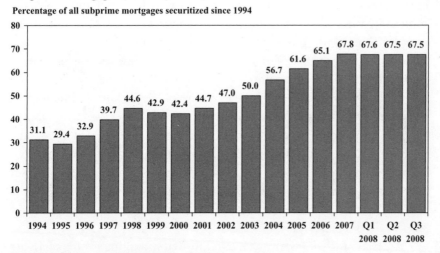

Percentage of all subprime mortgages securitized since 1994

Sources: Inside Mortgage Finance, Milken Institute.
Note: Each bar represents the cumulative share of all subprime mortgage originations securitized starting in 1994 and continuing through the third quarter of 2008.

that were securitized steadily increased, from 44.7 percent to 67.8 percent in 2007, before declining to 67.5 percent in the third quarter of 2008. Although the most recent decline appears to be quite small, the percentage of subprime mortgage loans originated in the first quarter of 2008 was at its lowest level (2.1 percent) over the entire period. This means, roughly speaking, that two-thirds of the credit risk associated with subprime loans has been shifted through the capital markets, from lending institutions to investors, in the form of securities backed by those loans.

Issuers of securities backed by subprime mortgage loans know that these investments are quite risky. To enhance the creditworthiness of the securities and attract more investors, they have turned to monoline insurers (firms that provide guarantees only in the capital markets), among others, to cover potential losses on some of these investment vehicles. (Most of these monoline insurers also guarantee municipal securities. In fact, until their recent ventures in guaranteeing subprime and other asset-backed securities, their primary business had been insuring municipal securities.)

These private insurers play the same role for subprime loans that Ginnie Mae, Freddie Mac, and Fannie Mae play for conforming loans: they guarantee the timely payment of interest and principal on the securities they issue. (The home mortgages securitized by Ginnie Mae are insured by the Federal Housing Authority, the Veterans Administration, and the Rural Housing Service.) Monoline insurers do not, however, have backing from the federal government and must rely on their own capital to honor the guarantees.

Table 3.5 shows the subprime exposure of selected monoline insurers for several recent years. It also shows how the exposure has changed over time and the total exposure of each firm as compared to its capital position in 2006. In addition, the credit ratings of the firms by S&P are provided as of October 31, 2008. The subprime mortgage market meltdown and, more generally, the problems spreading throughout the financial sector have clearly cast a pall over all of these firms, and for some, raised serious questions about their financial viability.

A weakening in the financial condition of monoline insurers has dire implications, not only for their ability to fulfill their commitments regarding existing municipal securities but also for their ability to guarantee

Table 3.5 Subprime Exposure of Selected Monoline Insurers (Selected Years, US$ Millions)

	Total Stockholders' Equity, as of 2006	Total Insured Subprime Mortgage Portfolio, as of 2006	Insured Subprime Mortgage Portfolio by Origination Year (at par)					Credit Rating by S&P, as of October 31, 2008
			2006	2005	2004	2003	Prior to 2003	
Ambac Assurance	6,190	10,448	1,214	1,948	1,027	2,891	3,369	AA/Negative
Assured Guaranty	1,651	4,683	3,651	66	343	557	67	AAA/Stable
CIFG Guaranty	na	2,035	609	1,296	130	0	0	B/Watch Dev
FGIC	2,079	7,468	381	4,379	2,104	0	604	B/Watch Neg
Financial Security Assurance	2,722	4,932	259	1,068	2,540	165	900	AAA/Negative
MBIA Assurance	7,204	5,777	1,152	483	1,038	1,496	1,609	AA/Negative
XL Capital Assurance	10,131	1,416	0	388	915	3	110	n.a.
ACA Financial Guaranty	640	9	0	9	0	0	0	BBB+/Negative
Radian Asset Assurance	2,649	567	63	61	213	164	67	CCC/Watch Dev

SOURCES: S&P; Milken Institute.

new issuance. It also can lead to a downgrading in the credit ratings of the outstanding municipal securities already guaranteed by these firms, which may reduce the ability or willingness of investors to hold such securities.

Aside from the monoline insurers, other firms that have guaranteed MBS have also been hit by the deterioration in the mortgage market—including most notably the insurance giant American International Group (AIG), which received an $85 billion emergency loan from the Federal Reserve on September 16, 2008, in exchange for equity warrants giving it a majority ownership stake in the firm. Shortly thereafter, in the first week of October, the Federal Reserve extended an additional loan of almost $38 billion. Just a month later, on November 10, 2008, AIG received an additional $40 billion capital injection from the Treasury.

Not surprisingly, the issuance of securities by private-label issuers has steadily declined over the past year, given the widening and deepening of the recent mortgage market problems. Figure 3.12 shows that from July to August 2008, private-label issuers have offered virtually no such

Figure 3.12 Private-Label Mortgage-Backed Security Issuance Dries up in 2008

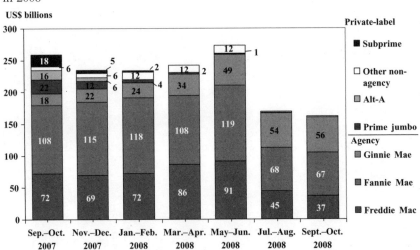

SOURCES: Inside Mortgage Finance, Milken Institute.

securities. In contrast, Ginnie Mae is the only securitizer reporting an increase, going from $18 billion from September–October 2007 to $56 billion in September–October 2008. This is due to the increase in the origination of FHA home mortgage loans and Ginnie Mae's securitization of them. (For a longer-term perspective on the relative importance of different mortgage-backed securities issuers, see the Appendix, Table A.10 and Figure A.10.) Because the FHA and Ginnie Mae are part of the federal government, they have full access to the capital markets for loans they originate and securitize. Borrowers can put down 3 percent (3.5 percent after January 1, 2009) on an FHA-insured mortgage; maximum loan amounts on the more expensive East and West coasts were set at $729,750 through December 2008 and then dropped to $625,000 in January 2009.

The Housing Bubble
Reaches the Breaking Point

Starting to Face the Possibility of Losses

The very large flows of mortgage funds over the past two years have been described by some analysts as possibly symptomatic of an emerging housing bubble, not unlike the stock market bubble whose bursting wreaked considerable distress in recent years. Existing home prices (as measured by the repeat-sales index) rose by 7 percent during 2002, and by a third during the past four years. Such a pace cannot reasonably be expected to be maintained. And recently, price increases have clearly slowed. . . . But any analogy to stock market pricing behavior and bubbles is a rather large stretch.

Remarks by Federal Reserve Chairman Alan Greenspan
Annual Convention of the Independent Community Bankers of America, Orlando, Florida
March 4, 2003

(Continued)

These loans (subprime) represent roughly $370 billion in outstandings, or 4.3 percent of all mortgages, and may ultimately result in just $110 billion in net loan losses for the mortgage industry. In addition, it is likely that any foreclosures associated with these troubled mortgages will be spread over a number of years, and losses will be borne not just by banks, but also by investors in privately-issued mortgage-backed securities.

>Economic Conditions and Emerging Risks in Banking
>Report to the FDIC Board of Directors, p. 14
>Federal Deposit Insurance Corporation
>May 9, 2006

We know from data . . . that a significant share of new loans used to purchase homes in 2005 were nonprime (subprime or near-prime), . . . [and] the share of securitized mortgages that are subprime climbed in 2005 and in the first half of 2006. [But] we believe the effect of the troubles in the subprime sector on the broader housing market will likely be limited, and we do not expect significant spillovers from the subprime market to the rest of the economy or to the financial system.

>Remarks by Federal Reserve Chairman Ben S. Bernanke
>Federal Reserve Bank of Chicago's 43rd Annual Conference on Bank Structure and Competition
>Chicago, Illinois
>May 17, 2007

Now that we are in a crisis, it is instructive to look back and examine whether there were ample signs of a housing bubble—and whether heeding these warning signs could have mitigated the damage.

As discussed earlier, the Federal Reserve created a low-interest rate environment, which was further fueled by an inflow of funds from investors based in other countries with savings gluts. Low interest rates set off a surge in home sales, prices, and housing starts, and the whole system was kept well oiled with liquidity by investors searching far and wide for higher yields. There were plenty of telling indicators along

Figure 3.13   The Recent Run-up of Nominal Home Prices Was
Extraordinary (1890–Q2 2008)

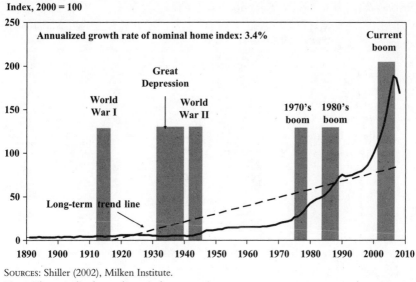

Index, 2000 = 100

SOURCES: Shiller (2002), Milken Institute.
NOTE: The annualized growth rate is the geometric mean.

the way that these trends had converged to produce a bubble that was
reaching dangerous proportions.

It is useful to begin by placing recent housing prices in a broader
context. Figures 3.13 to 3.16 show what happened to both nominal
and real (adjusted for inflation) home prices from 1890 to the second
quarter of 2008. Over this long period, nominal home prices rose at an
annualized rate of 3.4 percent (just 0.57 percent in real terms). It is clear
from these figures that the recent run-up in prices quickly outstripped
historical norms. Figures 3.14 and 3.16, moreover, contain another important lesson: they show that home prices do not just rise in a steady
trajectory—they can undergo fairly wide swings, both positive and negative. But amid the heady days of the housing boom, many market
participants chose to ignore the fact that housing prices can drop and
that booms are often followed by busts. Taken together, these figures
make a compelling case that the recent home price bubble was simply
not sustainable as it continued to grow with each passing day.

Table 3.6 shows the real returns on U.S. stocks, bonds, and homes
from 1890 to 2007—and as it happens, stocks and bonds have been

Figure 3.14   Home Prices Don't Go up Forever: Change in Nominal Home Prices in 100-Plus Years (1890–Q2 2008)

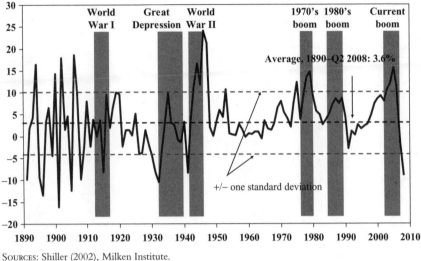

SOURCES: Shiller (2002), Milken Institute.
NOTE: The average growth rate is the arithmetic mean.

Figure 3.15   The Recent Run-up of Real Home Prices Was Extraordinary (1890–Q2 2008)

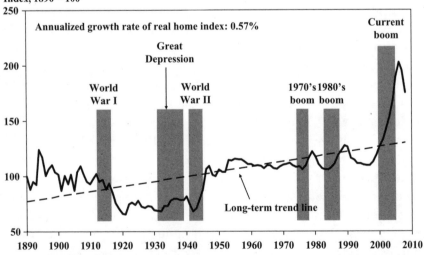

SOURCES: Shiller (2002), Milken Institute.
NOTE: The annualized growth rate is the geometric mean.

Figure 3.16   Home Prices Don't Go up Forever: Change in Real Home Prices in 100-Plus Years (1890–Q2 2008)

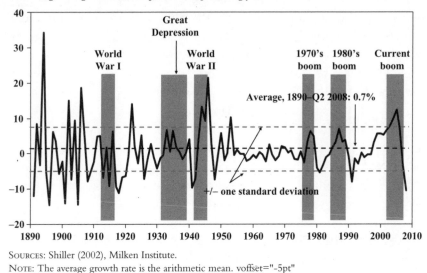

Percentage change in real home prices from preceding year

Sources: Shiller (2002), Milken Institute.
Note: The average growth rate is the arithmetic mean. voffset="-5pt"

better investments than homes over time (providing real returns of 6.3 and 4.7 percentage points, respectively, while the real return on homes totaled only 0.6 percent over this long period). Only from 1997 to 2007, a period that encompasses a collapse in stock prices due to the dot-com implosion and the growth of a major housing price bubble in its place, did homes deliver higher real returns than stocks and bonds.

Table 3.6   Real Returns on Stocks, Bonds, and Homes

Average Return (%)	Stocks	Bonds	Homes
1890–1925	5.4	3.8	−0.7
1926–1945	6.8	2.8	1.0
1946–1970	9.5	3.7	0.2
1971–1996	6.5	8.5	0.0
1997–2007	1.5	4.9	6.0
1890–2007	6.3	4.7	0.6

Sources: Robert Shiller, Milken Institute.
Note: The percentages are based on geometric means and the real return for homes is based on home price appreciation.

The fact that homes have typically produced low returns over long periods underscores why lenders traditionally made mortgage loans to individuals with "skin in the game" (i.e., a down payment that gave them a significant equity stake from the outset). Borrowers with equity have more cushion against financial stress and will fight to stay in their homes and protect their initial investment. Those with very little (or even negative) equity are not as well positioned to maneuver when times are tough and are more likely to lose (or walk away from) their homes if their personal circumstances deteriorate.

For many years, a 20 percent down payment was considered standard, and regarded as some evidence of the borrower's financial stability. In other words, lenders preferred to grant mortgages with a *loan-to-value ratio* (the outstanding mortgage balance as a percentage of the price of the home) closer to 80 percent than to 90 percent or higher. Maintaining that ratio was also considered in applications for second mortgages and home equity loans. (See Appendix Figure A.11 for information on bank home loans, including the breakdown of those secured by first liens, junior liens, and home equity loans, as well as those that are financed with ARMs.)

Lenders traditionally took these steps to manage risk because in most cases they have no recourse to the borrower's other assets or income in the event of default and because they frequently get no more than 50 percent to 75 percent out of foreclosures. But at the height of the boom, these standards were abandoned. Lenders were churning out mortgages that required little or no money down—knowing they could pass that increased risk on to investors.

A comparison of the nominal return on homes to other selected assets is provided in Figure 3.17. It shows what $1 invested in each of the assets in 1890 was worth at year-end 2007. Homes slightly outperformed gold after 1988 but distantly trailed the returns on stocks, bonds, and CDs.

Figure 3.18 provides a much shorter but equally revealing look at what was happening to home prices both nationwide and in California from 1979 to September 2008. The peak median home price nation-wide was about 90 percent higher than the average median price over that period, while California's peak exceeded its average by more than 150 percent. The peak price nationwide was $229,093 (virtually the

Figure 3.17   Nominal Returns on Selected Assets (1890–2007)

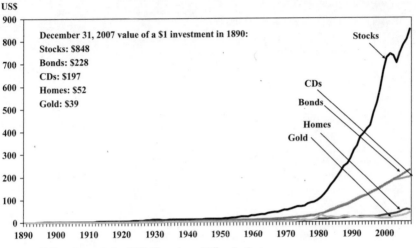

SOURCES: Shiller, Guggenheim, IMF, Bloomberg, Milken Institute.

Figure 3.18   California and National Median Home Prices Reach Record Highs (Monthly, January 1979–September 2008)

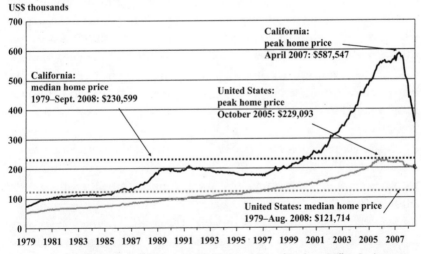

SOURCES: National Association of Realtors, California Association of Realtors, Milken Institute.
NOTE: Median home prices for the U.S. updated to August 2008.

Figure 3.19   Ratio of Median Home Price to Median Household Income Increases Rapidly (1968–2007)

Median home price/median household income

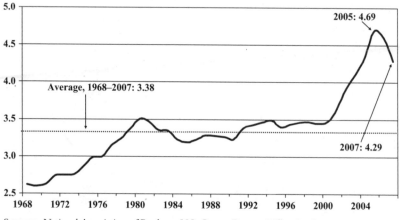

SOURCES: National Association of Realtors, U.S. Census Bureau, Milken Institute.

same as the average median California home price over the period 1979 to September 2008), while in California that figure soared to $587,547. Home prices in different regions clearly rose at varying rates and reached varying peaks. But in some overheated markets, prices were setting record highs that were out of whack with anything seen during the previous 30 years. In Southern California, which became something of a poster child for the housing boom, there were tales of bidding wars, of modest bungalows with million-dollar price tags, and of houses in new developments being snapped up even before construction was completed.

More alarming, as Figure 3.19 shows, the median price of a home also rose sharply in the early and mid-2000s relative to median household income, climbing well above the average ratio maintained from 1968 through 2007. This should have been a red flashing light, warning that homes were becoming less affordable. Of course, home buyers were accommodated with mortgages tailored to their circumstances but with a corresponding increase in risk. Borrowers were stretching further and further to buy homes.

Another sign of overheating in the housing sector was the precipitous decline in the rent-to-price ratio in the early and mid-2000s. As

Figure 3.20   Rent–Price Ratio Reached Historic Low in 2006 But Has Slightly Rebounded (Quarterly, 1960–Q1 2008)

Annual rents as percentage of home prices

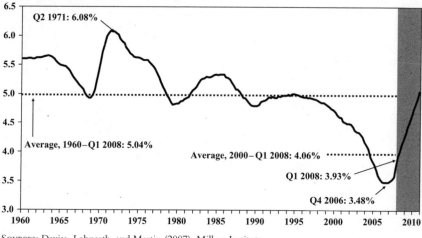

SOURCES: Davisa, Lehnertb, and Martin (2007), Milken Institute.
NOTE: The average rental price growth rate from 1960 to Q1 2008 is 5.52 percent.

Figure 3.20 shows, the average ratio was 5 percent over the period from 1960 to the first quarter of 2008. But from 2000 to the first quarter of 2008, the average declined to 4 percent. The ratio reached a record low of just below 3.5 percent in the fourth quarter of 2006. The substantial decline in this ratio through 2006 suggests that a bubble in home prices was occurring, especially in those areas with the biggest declines in the ratio. With the burst of housing bubble, however, the ratio has since been rising but is still substantially below its average value from the first quarter of 1960 to the first quarter of 2008. The shaded area in Figure 3.20 shows a possible path for the rent-to-price ratio to return to its long-term norm.

Figure 3.21 shows a substantial jump in both existing and new homes for sale, beginning in 2001. Once the housing bubble began to burst, new homes for sale began their downward path, but existing homes for sale—including those in foreclosure—continued to climb.

Market participants were profiting from these sharply rising home prices during the boom, so it is unsurprising that many ignored the signs that the market was becoming unsustainable. But it is fair to ask why

Figure 3.21   Recent Jump in Homes for Sale: Existing and New Homes (Monthly, 1989–September 2008)

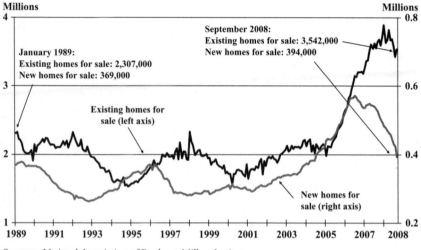

SOURCES: National Association of Realtors, Milken Institute.

regulators and government officials failed to take action that might have discouraged lenders from taking tremendous risks.

The Collapse Begins

By mid-2007, it was clear that the housing market had fallen into real distress. The most obvious sign, illustrated in Figure 3.22, was a long, steep plunge in home prices, as chronicled by the two S&P/Case-Shiller home price indexes.

Falling prices unleashed a cascade of consequences. Many homeowners—especially those who bought near the end of the boom—now found themselves under water (owing more than their home's current market value). Without equity, borrowers with ARMs were unable to refinance before their rates reset. Faced with higher monthly payments, many households fell into default. Foreclosures rose sharply—in fact, RealtyTrac reported that more than 573,000 properties nationwide were in some stage of foreclosure in the first half of 2007.[8] Multiple subprime lenders filed for bankruptcy.

Figure 3.22   2005: The Collapse in Home Prices Begins
(Quarterly, Q1 1988–Q2 2008)

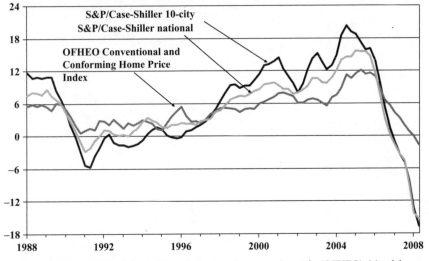

Home price indexes, percentage change on a year earlier

SOURCES: S&P/Case-Shiller, Office of Federal Housing Enterprise Oversight (OFHEO), Moody's Economy.com, Milken Institute.

In August 2007, the problems reached a crescendo with the collapse of two Bear Stearns hedge funds that invested heavily in subprime-related securities. Many investors grew increasingly concerned about declining asset values and excessive leverage at other financial firms. Moreover, money markets were freezing up; the interbank lending market was charging loan rates at spreads reaching 21-year highs over Treasury securities; and the flight to safety pushed the Treasury rate to its lowest daily level since 1952. Suddenly, the crisis on Main Street had arrived on Wall Street's doorstep. As the timeline in Figure 3.23 illustrates, a torrent of events unfolded in rapid succession as the Dow Jones U.S. Financial Index continued its downward trend.

The credit crunch was on: Figure 3.24 shows that the spread between LIBOR (the London Interbank Offered Rate, reflecting what banks charge for short-term lending to other banks) and the overnight index swap rate jumped from less than 14 basis points in July 2007 to 48 basis points in the second week of August and still higher to 364 points on October 10, 2008. Since August 2007, the average spread was 89 basis

Figure 3.23 Timeline for the Subprime Mortgage Market Meltdown and Credit Market Freeze (December 2006–October 31, 2008)

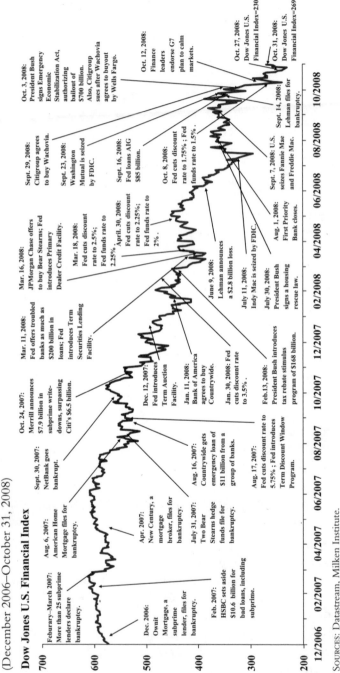

Dow Jones U.S. Financial Index

SOURCES: Datastream, Milken Institute.

Figure 3.24   Liquidity Freeze: Spread between Three-Month LIBOR and
Overnight Index Swap Rates (Weekly, 2001–October 31, 2008)

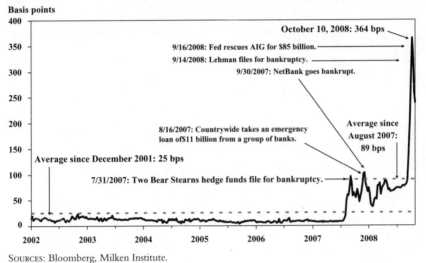

SOURCES: Bloomberg, Milken Institute.

points, compared to an average of 25 basis points from December 2001
to October 10, 2008.

The TED spread (the gap between the three-month LIBOR rate and
the three-month Treasury bill rate; "T" for Treasury bill rate and "ED"
for Eurodollars) is another measure of liquidity, reflecting the extent to
which banks are willing to lend to one another; a widening TED spread
indicates an increased risk of credit defaults in the marketplace. As Figure
3.25 shows, this indicator stood at an average of 86 basis points over the
period from December 2005 to October 15, 2008, but on August 20,
2007, it jumped to 240 basis points. It widened still further to 464 basis
points on October 10, 2008. The previous high was 255 basis points in
November 1987.

In addition, the market for commercial paper (short-term debt, rou-
tinely issued by corporations to cover operating expenses) was showing
signs of stress. Figure 3.26 shows that the rate firms have to pay on asset-
backed commercial paper rose sharply in early September 2007 and then
again in December 2007 as compared to the rates paid on comparable
rated financial and nonfinancial commercial paper.

Clearly, the meltdown of the mortgage market had produced a
widespread shortage of liquidity in the financial system. Firms with

Figure 3.25   Widening TED Spread: Spread between Three-Month LIBOR and T-Bill Rates (Daily, December 31, 2005–October 31, 2008)

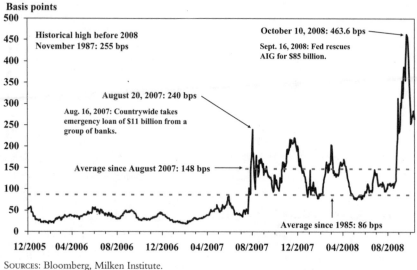

SOURCES: Bloomberg, Milken Institute.
NOTE: The TED spread is calculated as the difference between the three-month LIBOR and three-month T-bill interest rate.

Figure 3.26   Market for Liquidity Freezes
(Daily, May 1, 2007–October 31, 2008)

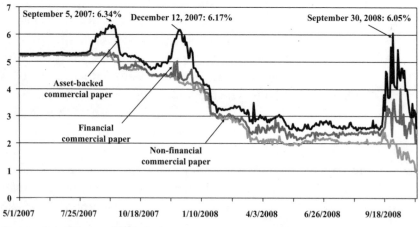

SOURCES: Federal Reserve, Milken Institute.

cash were holding onto it, and other firms were rebuilding their capital, making them reluctant to lend.

These multifaceted problems soon spilled over to the real economy. Even beyond the financial sector, credit spreads widened and stock prices declined. The unemployment rate rose as recessionary effects set in. Efforts to help the credit markets toward recovery became critical.

Overwhelming uncertainty in the marketplace bracketed these problems: uncertainty about the value of assets ultimately collateralized by homes and, therefore, uncertainty about the financial condition of the firms holding or guaranteeing these assets. And looming over it all was worry over the murkiness hidden in the form of outstanding credit default swaps, which had grown to enormous sums and could be triggered if the markets worsened and the underlying securities fell in value. Little information was available about the counterparties to these credit derivatives and their exact risk exposures and financial conditions.

Meanwhile, home prices now seemed to be in freefall. As Figure 3.27 shows, home prices had fallen a few times before October 2005 but had never plunged so abruptly and so deeply as they did after that month. In August 2008, the median home price had fallen 9.8 percent from the previous year. The declines were even steeper in once-overheated regions.

Figure 3.27 Median Existing Home Price: Too Good to Last (Monthly, 1969–August 2008)

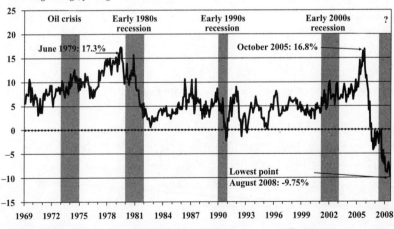

SOURCES: National Association of Realtors, Moody's Economy.com, Milken Institute.

Figure 3.28   Forty-Six States Report Falling Prices in Q4 2007

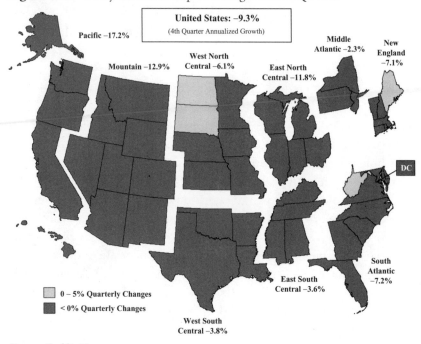

SOURCE: Freddie Mac.

Figure 3.28 shows that 46 states saw home prices fall in the fourth quarter of 2007, while only four states experienced price increases over the period. Home values deflated in all nine regions of the country, with the biggest decline (17.2 percent) posted in the Pacific region (the West Coast). The problem clearly was national in scope, unlike the savings and loan crisis of the 1980s, which was largely concentrated in Texas.

More detailed information on home prices in 20 metropolitan areas over four different periods is provided in Figures 3.29 to 3.32 and Appendix Figures A.12 to A.15. Figures 3.29 to 3.32 show the price changes using S&P/Case-Shiller indexes, while the figures in the Appendix track Office of Federal Housing Enterprise Oversight (OFHEO) indexes.

The figures based on the S&P/Case-Shiller indexes are quite revealing: individuals who purchased homes one year prior to August 2008 experienced a decline in home price in all 20 metropolitan areas.

Figure 3.29 One-Year Home Price Changes for Selected Metropolitan Areas (August 2007–August 2008)

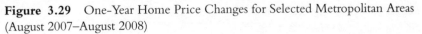

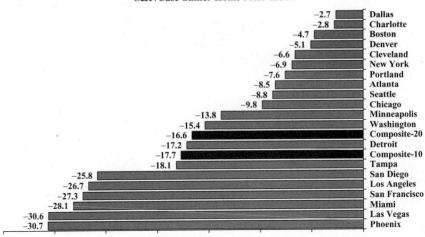

SOURCES: S&P/Case-Shiller, Milken Institute.

Figure 3.30 Two-Year Home Price Changes for Selected Metropolitan Areas (August 2006–August 2008)

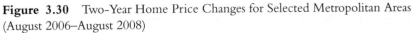

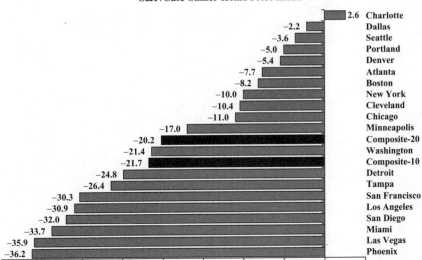

SOURCES: S&P/Case-Shiller, Milken Institute.

Figure 3.31   Four-Year Home Price Changes for Selected Metropolitan Areas (August 2004–August 2008)

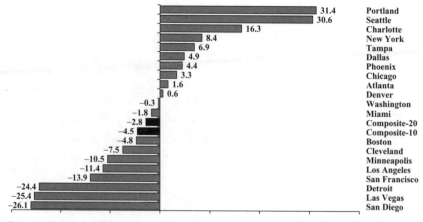

SOURCES: S&P/Case-Shiller, Milken Institute.

Figure 3.32   Five-Year Home Price Changes for Selected Metropolitan Areas (August 2003–August 2008)

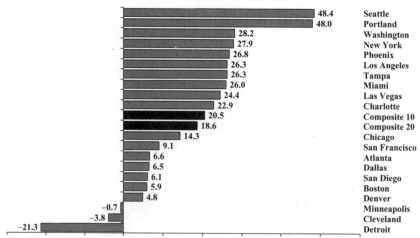

SOURCES: S&P/Case-Shiller, Milken Institute.

However, if you go back in time and take a longer-term view, the declines in home prices eventually turn into gains for all the metropolitan areas except three: Detroit, Cleveland, and Minneapolis. In contrast, Appendix Figures A.12 to A.15, based on the OFHEO indexes, paint a similar picture, but with smaller price declines (which may be explained by the fact that the OFHEO indexes include only conforming loans, whereas the S&P/Case-Shiller indexes also include subprime and jumbo loans).

In the figures, it is worth noting that neither Detroit nor Cleveland (both located in Rust Belt states with struggling economies) rank among the top two metropolitan areas experiencing the biggest declines in home prices over the past one or two years, but they do come out worst over the four-year period. Home prices in Las Vegas and Miami, in contrast, continue to post price gains when measured over the longer time period. How long this will continue to be the case is uncertain, given the continued deteriorating economy.

As home prices declined, housing starts also cratered, as shown in Figure 3.33. After reaching a record high of 1.8 million units in January 2006, they plummeted to only 544,000 units in September 2008. This

Figure 3.33 Housing Starts Hit Record in 2006 But Then Drop 64 Percent (Monthly, 1959–September 2008)

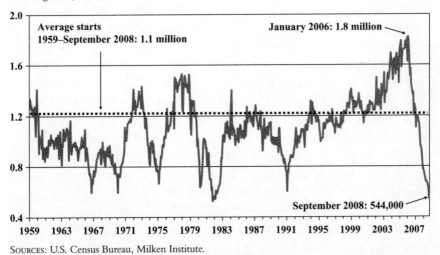

Housing units, millions

SOURCES: U.S. Census Bureau, Milken Institute.

Figure 3.34 Private Construction Spending on Residential Property Declines since the Peak of 2006 (Monthly, 1993–September 2008)

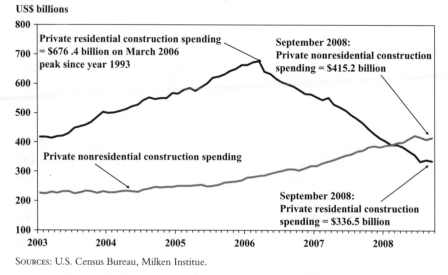

SOURCES: U.S. Census Bureau, Milken Institue.

is nearly half the average over the past 30 years. (Compared to a year earlier, the decline was 42 percent, far greater than the mean change of 1.15 percent over the same period, as shown in Appendix Figure A.16.)

More generally, Figure 3.34 shows that residential private construction spending declined steadily after reaching a peak in March 2006. In September 2008, such spending was less than half the value at the peak and even below the 2003 level. This clearly creates extra hardships for those employed in this sector of our economy.

In addition to the drop in housing starts, existing home sales fell nationwide by 29 percent from the fourth quarter of 2005 to the fourth quarter of 2007. Figure 3.35 shows that even though all states experienced declines in sales, they ranged from less than 20 percent in some states to more than 40 percent in several others. Nevada posted the biggest plunge, at 65 percent, over the two-year period. The incredible flood of homes sales posted just a few years earlier had slowed to a trickle.

As Figure 3.36 illustrates, declining home sales are associated with homes sitting on the market for longer periods of time. The length of time it took to sell both new and existing homes stretched out rapidly

Figure 3.35 Existing Home Sales Are Down Everywhere over the Past Two Years (Percentage Change, Q4 2005–Q4 2007)

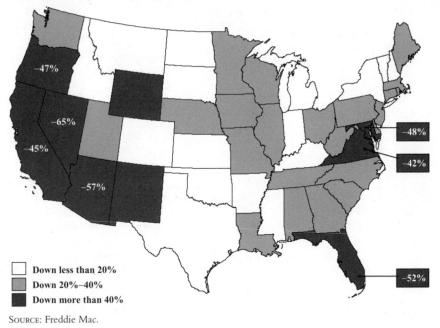

SOURCE: Freddie Mac.

Figure 3.36 Homes Sit Longer on the Market (Monthly, 1989–September 2008)

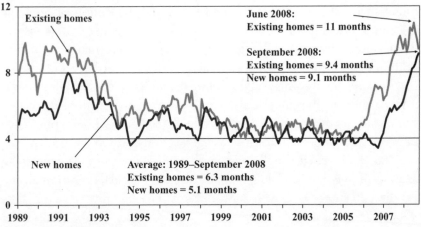

SOURCES: National Association of Realtors, Moody's Economy.com, Milken Institute.

Figure 3.37   Homes Stay Longer on the Market as Home Appreciation Slows (Monthly, 1989–September 2008)

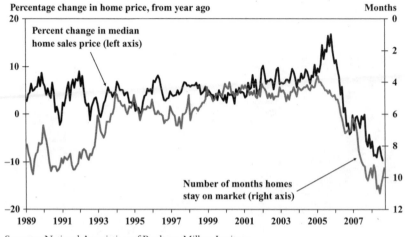

SOURCES: National Association of Realtors, Milken Institute.
NOTE: The correlation between the percentage change in median home sales price and the number of months homes stay on market, using monthly data for 1989 through September 2008, is −0.5986.

beginning in 2006, reaching 20-year record highs in June 2008. Homes sat longer on the market because home appreciations were dropping, as shown in Figure 3.37. The simple correlation between these two variables was −0.60 over the period 1989 to September 2008. Many sellers were unwilling to face the reality that the boom was over. A home might sit for months while the owner resisted the notion of reducing the asking price. It was now a buyer's market. No longer worried about being outbid, buyers could afford to be choosy—and many decided to postpone purchases, believing that prices had even further to fall.

As mentioned earlier, falling home prices have left many borrowers under water (in the uncomfortable position of owing more than their homes are worth). Figure 3.38 shows the percentage of homes purchased between 2001 and 2006 that have negative equity as of the second quarter of 2008. The average for all the areas shown is 45 percent. The worst-hit areas were in Arizona, California, Florida, and Nevada. (For more details on the percentage of buyers with negative home equity, see Appendix Table A.22.)

Many homes were sold at a loss between the third quarter of 2007 and the second quarter of 2008. In fact, that was the case with one-third

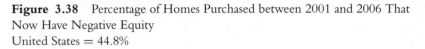

Figure 3.38   Percentage of Homes Purchased between 2001 and 2006 That
Now Have Negative Equity
United States = 44.8%

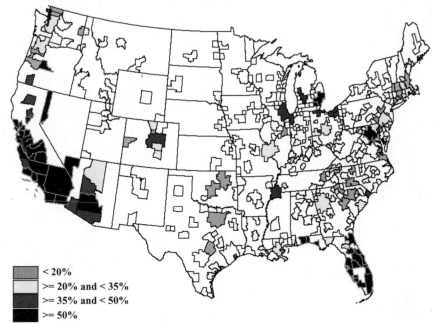

     < 20%
     >= 20% and < 35%
     >= 35% and < 50%
     >= 50%

SOURCES: Zillow.com, Milken Institute.

of homes sold in the areas indicated in Figure 3.39. Once again, the states
in greatest distress were Arizona, California, and Florida; Nevada and
Michigan also showed widespread losses. But the rest of the country was
not immune; many other areas suffered as well. Perhaps not surprisingly,
many of the homes that did manage to sell were foreclosures. Figure
3.40 shows that nearly 20 percent of home sold in a recent period were
foreclosures, with the highest concentration of these sales in California
and Nevada. (For details on the percentage of homes recently sold for a
loss, see Appendix Table A.23; for information on foreclosure sales, see
Appendix Table A.24.)

The presence of so many heavily discounted foreclosed properties
on the market causes prices to spiral down even further. Furthermore,
lenders typically incur substantial losses when homes are foreclosed.

Taking a longer view of the mortgage market, both prime and subprime loans have fallen into delinquency and foreclosure in the past, and

Figure 3.39   Percentage of Homes Sold at a Loss between
Q3 2007 and Q2 2008
United States = 32.7 %

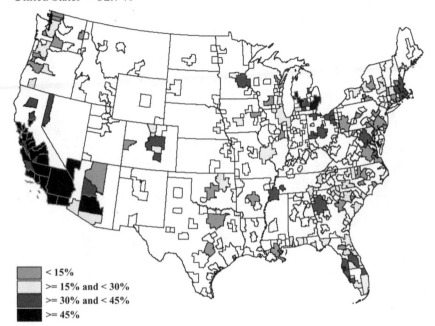

< 15%
>= 15% and < 30%
>= 30% and < 45%
>= 45%

SOURCES: Zillow.com, Milken Institute.

there have been spikes in these rates at various points in earlier decades. In
the past few years, these numbers have hit record highs. Figures 3.41 and
3.42 show that subprime delinquencies reached nearly 20 percent and
foreclosures rose to almost 5 percent in the second quarter of 2008. Although prime loans remain in much better shape, prime delinquency and
foreclosure rates have more than doubled over the past 10 years to highs
of 2.35 percent and 0.67 percent, respectively. (Appendix Tables A.25 to
A.27 contain more information on delinquencies and foreclosure rates.)

Figure 3.43 shows that subprime ARMs are particularly likely to default (i.e., become delinquent or fall into foreclosure). These mortgages,
with their potential for escalating monthly payments, reached a default
rate of 33.4 percent in the second quarter of 2008—triple the rate for
defaults on subprime fixed-rate mortgages. Prime fixed-rate mortgages
performed best, even better than FHA and VA loans. (See Appendix
Table A.28 for more information on delinquencies and foreclosures.)

Figure 3.40 Percentage of Homes Sold between Q3 2007 and Q2 2008 That Were in Foreclosure
United States = 18.6%

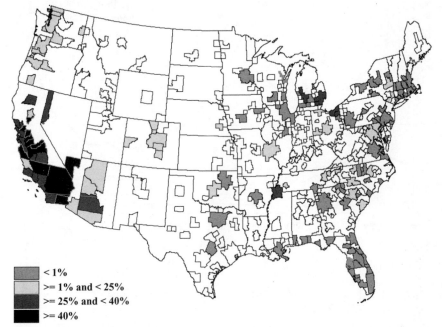

Legend:
- < 1%
- >= 1% and < 25%
- >= 25% and < 40%
- >= 40%

SOURCES: Zillow.com, Milken Institute.

Although the mortgage market has always experienced some level of foreclosures, as Figure 3.44 shows, the average number of foreclosures has more than doubled recently. While 661,362 were recorded over the period covering the second quarter of 1999 to the second quarter of 2006, there were 1.3 million foreclosures over the two-year period from the third quarter of 2006 to the second quarter of 2008.[9]

These are sobering figures, and behind the numbers are countless stories of families in crisis. Homeowners in foreclosure find their credit scores ruined and their lives in upheaval. In many neighborhoods, empty properties sit neglected, driving nearby home values down even further. Municipalities have faced growing fiscal challenges as their tax bases erode.

The subprime share of all home mortgage foreclosures is dramatic, as seen in Figure 3.45 and Appendix Table A.29. Although subprime loans accounted for only 12 percent of all loans in June 2008, they accounted

Figure 3.41   Subprime Delinquencies Skyrocket (Quarterly, 1998–Q2 2008)

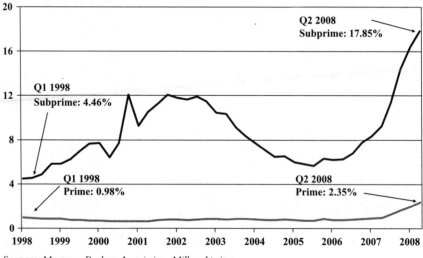

SOURCES: Mortgage Bankers Association, Milken Institute.

Figure 3.42   Subprime Mortgages Entering Foreclosure Take off (Quarterly, 1998–Q2 2008)

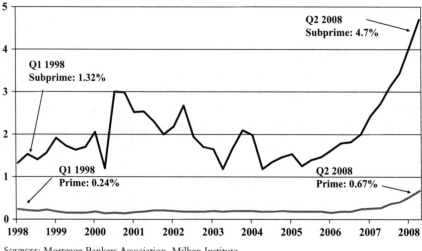

SOURCES: Mortgage Bankers Association, Milken Institute.

Figure 3.43 Subprime ARMs Have the Worst Default Record
(Quarterly, Q2 1998–Q2 2008)

Home mortgage loans delinquent or in foreclosure (percentage of number)

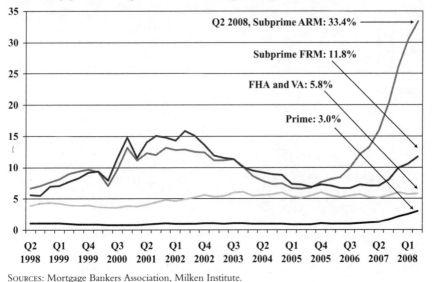

SOURCES: Mortgage Bankers Association, Milken Institute.

Figure 3.44 Foreclosures Are Nothing New But Their Numbers Have
Doubled (Quarterly, Q2 1999–Q2 2008)

Thousands of foreclosures per year

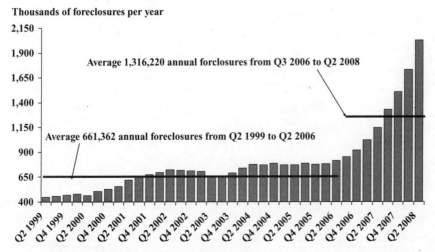

SOURCES: Mortgage Bankers Association, Milken Institute.
NOTE: Data are as of June 2008. Numbers are expanded to reflect 85 percent coverage.

Figure 3.45   Subprime Loans Accounted for Half or More of Foreclosures since 2006

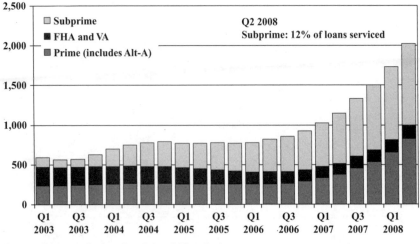

Number of home mortgage loan foreclosures started (annualized rate in thousands)

SOURCES: Mortgage Bankers Association, Milken Institute.
NOTE: Data are as of June 2008. Numbers are expanded to reflect 85 percent coverage.

for half of all foreclosures. Even as far back as December 2003, subprime mortgage loans accounted for a large percentage of all foreclosures and continued to do so thereafter.

Subprime default rates should not be a surprise to anyone, given the characteristics of these instruments, as indicated in Table 3.7 as of September 2008. This table shows the characteristics of subprime mortgage loans for the nation, as well as Arizona, California, Florida, and Nevada, all of which have high foreclosure rates on such loans. In particular, as more new loans were made over the period 2003 to 2006, lenders steadily lowered underwriting standards to maintain their volume of business. This led to more "NINJA" loans—loans made to individuals who had no verified income, job, or assets. In addition, more piggyback loans (loans that combined two mortgages to cover the purchase of a single home) were made. The longer the housing boom continued, the more lax the lending standards became—and sure enough, we can see much earlier and higher foreclosure rates among subprime loans with later vintages from 2004 and earlier through 2006. Furthermore, notice the high percentage of subprime mortgages that involved

Table 3.7 Subprime Loans, Known to Be Risky, Accounted for Many Foreclosures (September 2008)

Characteristics of Subprime Mortgages	United States	Arizona	California	Florida	Nevada
Total housing units	127,901,934	2,667,502	13,308,346	8,718,385	1,102,379
Number of subprime loans	2,886,183	70,982	435,974	300,490	35,367
Percent owner occupied	90.9%	92.0%	93.9%	88.7%	89.8%
Loans per 1000 housing units	20.5	24.5	30.8	30.6	28.8
Average current interest rate	8.4%	8.2%	7.6%	8.3%	8.1%
Average current interest rate for ARMs	8.8%	8.5%	8.0%	8.7%	8.4%
Average outstanding loan balance	$183,537	$175,074	$326,259	$178,333	$216,665
Average loan age (months)	37	30	32	32	31
Average FICO score	618	622	640	617	627
Average combined LTV at origination	84.7	83.8	81.7	83.0	85.1
Percentage with at least one late payment in last 12 months	58.6%	59.6%	61.8%	63.7%	61.0%
Percentage with a payment 60+ days past due	15.5%	15.6%	15.0%	14.5%	16.4%
Percentage in foreclosure	11.0%	10.8%	13.5%	22.5%	12.2%
Percentage originated in 2007	14.9%	19.8%	15.7%	17.8%	14.9%
Percentage originated in 2006	37.0%	50.3%	42.4%	45.5%	44.1%
Percentage originated in 2005	25.6%	20.9%	28.0%	23.4%	31.6%
Percentage originated in or before 2004	22.5%	9.0%	14.0%	13.2%	9.4%
Percentage with no or low documentation	32.8%	36.5%	46.2%	41.7%	37.7%
Percentage of purchases	35.4%	32.3%	37.6%	37.9%	40.5%
Percentage of cash-out refinances	55.4%	61.4%	56.5%	57.1%	53.9%
Percentage resetting in next 24 months	3.3%	2.9%	5.1%	3.3%	3.2%

SOURCES: Federal Reserve Bank of New York, Milken Institute.

cash-out refinances in the table, exceeding 50 percent nationwide and in each of the four states.

It is particularly striking to note that the rate of foreclosures on subprime loans originated increased dramatically in each year beginning in 2003. Some estimates indicate a near doubling of the foreclosure rate over this period, and for loans originated in 2006, the foreclosure rate of 5.5 percent *just six months from origination* actually exceeded the corresponding foreclosure rates for all previous years (see Figure 3.46).

Most of the foreclosures on subprime loans occur in the first few years after the loans have been made (see Appendix Tables A.30 and A.31). Indeed, the national foreclosure rate on subprime mortgage loans originated in 2006 was slightly higher than 10 percent from January 2006 through September 2007 and nearly 20 percent for loans made in California. As of November 2007, there was one foreclosure for every 617 households, according to RealtyTrac.

It was plain to see a clear increase in foreclosure rates associated with subprime mortgage loans over this time period. Given the increasing volume and dollar amount of subprime loans being made, the Federal Reserve, the Federal Deposit Insurance Corporation (FDIC), and other regulatory authorities should have initiated corrective action well before

Figure 3.46 Early Problems: Foreclosure Rates of Subprime Loans by Origination Year (1998–2006)

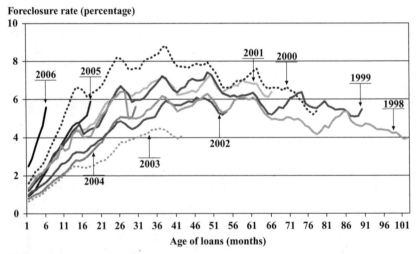

SOURCES: LoanPerformance, Milken Institute.

August 2007—especially because many financial institutions specializing in these types of loans either were already experiencing financial difficulties or had failed by then. Indeed, why do we have numerous and well-staffed regulatory agencies at all if they are asleep at the wheel?

There is no denying that the recent collapse is painful, but it is important to keep a bit of historical perspective (especially because panic can be a self-fulfilling prophecy). Some have likened this financial turmoil to the Great Depression, but any serious comparison reveals that as of November 2008, we have yet to experience anything like the dire situation that prevailed in the 1930s.

As Figure 3.47 shows, the Dow Jones Industrial Average (DJIA) has declined sharply during the recent turmoil. But the decline was far worse during the Great Depression. The DJIA index plunged by 89.1 percent from September 3, 1929, to July 8, 1932, whereas the decline from October 9, 2007, to October 27, 2008, was less than half this level, at 42.3 percent. It is clear, moreover, that volatility in the stock prices has occurred many times over the past century, with both positive and negative swings in the index. This can be seen in Figure 3.48, which shows the yearly percentage changes in the DJIA index. (Table 3.8 provides more detailed information on the movement of the DJIA

Figure 3.47 Dow Jones Industrial Average Index
(Daily, 1910–October 31, 2008)

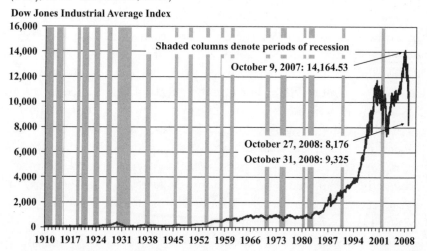

Sources: Datastream, Milken Institute.

Figure 3.48   Dow Jones Industrial Average Index
(Daily, 1910–October 31, 2008)

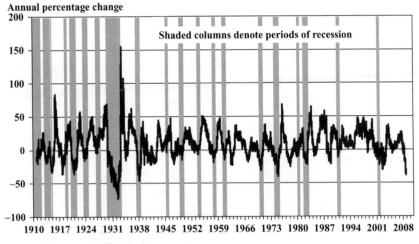

SOURCES: Datastream, Milken Institute.

index from the peak to the trough during the recessions over the past 80 years.)

Although recent bank failures have been alarming, these events are far from reaching Depression-era magnitude. From 1929 to 1933, more than 10,000 banks were shuttered. In contrast, there are currently fewer than 120 banks on the FDIC's problem bank list (although the number is expected to increase). Whereas the money supply declined three years in a row from 1930 to 1932 (and by more than 10 percent in 1932), it has not been declining in recent months (as of this writing in November 2008). Indeed, it increased by more than 6 percent on an annualized basis in September 2008. Furthermore, real GDP declined by nearly 15 percent in 1932, but it declined by just 0.3 percent in the third quarter of 2008 (although bigger declines are soon expected). Last, in the Great Depression about one-half of urban households with an outstanding mortgage were in default. In mid-2008, 9.2 percent of home mortgages were either delinquent or in foreclosure. Clearly, things would have to get much worse then they stord at this writing for the situation to truly be considered as devastating as the Great Depression.

Table 3.8 provides more detailed information on the percentage change in the DJIA index from the peak to the trough during the

Table 3.8 The Fallout from the Subprime Mortgage Market in Historical Perspective

Recession	Recession Starts	Recession Ends	DJIA Index Peak	DJIA Index Trough	DJIA Index Change from Peak through Trough	Unemployment Rate Peak
August 1929–March 1933	August 1929	March 1933	September 1929	July 1932	–89%	24.9%
May 1937–June 1938	May 1937	June 1938	March 1937	March 1938	–49%	19.0%
February 1945–October 1945	February 1945	October 1945	May 1946	n.a.	n.a.	1.9%
November 1948–October 1949	November 1948	October 1949	June 1948	June 1949	–16%	7.0%
July 1953–May 1954	July 1953	May 1954	January 1953	September 1953	–13%	5.9%
August 1957–April 1958	August 1957	April 1958	April 1956	October 1957	–19%	7.4%
April 1960–February 1961	April 1960	February 1961	January 1960	October 1960	–17%	6.9%

(Continued)

Table 3.8 *(Continued)*

Recession	Recession Starts	Recession Ends	DJIA Index Peak	DJIA Index Trough	DJIA Index Change from Peak through Trough	Unemployment Rate Peak
December 1969–November 1970	December 1969	November 1970	December 1968	May 1970	–36%	5.9%
November 1973–March 1975	November 1973	March 1975	January 1973	December 1974	–45%	8.6%
January 1980–July 1980	January 1980	July 1980	September 1978	April 1980	–16%	7.8%
July 1981–November 1982	July 1981	November 1982	April 1981	August 1982	–24%	10.8%
July 1990–March 1991	July 1990	March 1991	July 1990	October 1990	–21%	6.8%
March 2001–November 2001	March 2001	November 2001	January 2000	September 2001	–30%	5.5%
Today's market*	December 2007	?	14,165 as of October 9, 2007	8,176 as of October 27, 2008	–43%	6.5% as of October 2008

SOURCES: *Barron's*, October 13, 2008, U.S. Bureau of Labor Statistics, Milken Institute.

*NOTE: The current situation was not confirmed as a recession until December 1, 2008, when the National Bureau of Economic Research declared that a recession had actually been in effect since December 2007.

recessions over the past 80 years. As may be seen, the biggest decline, almost 90 percent, occurred during the Great Depression. The most recent decline was 40 percent, from the peak on October 9, 2007, to a trough on October 27, 2008—far short of the financial crisis during the 1930s. Furthermore, the unemployment rate of 6.5 percent in October 2008, although generally expected to increase, was far below the 25 percent rate recorded during the Great Depression. It is therefore a far stretch to compare the current situation to the 1930s, unless conditions deteriorate far more severely than most would expect.

Chapter 4

When Will the Crisis End?

...10 to 15 million households will end up in negative equity territory and will be likely to default on their homes and walk away from them. Then, the losses for the financial system from [these] massive defaults will be of the order of $1 trillion to $2 trillion, a multiple of the $200 to $400 billion of losses currently estimated for mortgage related securities.

—"The Forthcoming 'Jingle Mail' Tsunami: 10 to
15 Million Households Likely to Walk Away from Their
Homes/Mortgages Leading to a Systemic Banking Crisis"
Nouriel Roubini's Global EconoMonitor
February 19, 2008

Well, I think we're getting close to the bottom.

—Dick Kovacevich, Chairman of Wells Fargo
BusinessWeek
November 3, 2008

The major disruptions in the mortgage and credit crisis have been accompanied by unexpected and surprising twists—and no one knows for certain when the tumult will end or what the ultimate cost to the nation will be. In this section, we look at a variety of estimates of the losses in the financial sector. Many observers and analysts have attempted to quantify the damages, but their estimates have varied widely, ranging from perhaps undue optimism to downright doom. We will also examine scenarios for when the housing market might hit bottom.

101

The losses in the financial sector are vast, but the damage has not been contained there. Even solid, profitable companies in other industries were affected by the credit squeeze. The uncertainty hanging over the marketplace caused wild volatility in the stock market throughout 2008, but the overall trend was clearly dismal.

While financial giants were calculating the mounting losses on their balance sheets, millions of ordinary Americans watched in dismay as their investment accounts were shrinking by the day. The Congressional Budget Office estimated that U.S. pension funds had lost $1 trillion from the second quarter of 2007 to the second quarter of 2008, and the cumulative decline in pension fund assets in the previous 18 months was likely to reach $2 trillion as of October 2008.[1] The effect on current retirees and those nearing retirement age was devastating, and it remains to be seen how losses in pension funds and retirement accounts, if not reversed, will strain the Social Security system in the years to come.

What Is the Damage Scorecard to Date?

How Big Is the Black Hole? The Estimates Grow...
In a report dated Nov. 15, chief U.S. economist Jan Hatzius [Goldman Sachs] said a 'back-of-the-envelope' estimate of credit losses on outstanding mortgages could reach around $400 billion.
"Mortgage Crisis May Slash Lending Up to $2 Trillion"
CNBC
November 16, 2007

We use several methods to estimate the ultimate losses on these securities. Our best (very uncertain) guess is that the losses will total about $400 billion, with about half being borne by leveraged U.S. financial institutions.
David Greenlaw, Jan Hatzius, Anil K. Kashyap, Hyun Song Shin
"Leveraged Losses: Lessons from the Mortgage Market Meltdown"
U.S. Monetary Policy Forum Conference Draft
February 29, 2008

(Continued)

Financial firms are likely to face at least $600 billion of losses as the crisis triggered by the collapse of subprime mortgages batters banks, brokers and insurers, UBS AG analysts said.

> Abigail Moses and Yalman Onaran
> "Financial Firms Face $600 Billion of Losses, UBS Says"
> Bloomberg
> February 29, 2008

The continuing decline in the U.S. housing market and wider economic slowdown is contributing to new loan deterioration—delinquencies on prime mortgages and commercial real estate as well as corporate and consumer loans are increasing. With default rates yet to peak and the recent heightened market distress, declared losses on U.S. loans and securitized assets are likely to increase further to about $1.4 trillion . . . .

> "Financial Stress and Deleveraging Macrofinancial
> Implications and Policy"
> Global Financial Stability Report
> International Monetary Fund
> October 2008

"There are significant downside risks still to the market and the economy," [Nouriel] Roubini, 50, a New York University professor of economics, said in an interview with Bloomberg Television. "We're going to be surprised by the severity of the recession and the severity of the financial losses." . . . Roubini said total credit losses resulting from the meltdown of the subprime mortgage market will be "closer to $3 trillion," up from his previous estimate of $1 trillion to $2 trillion.

> Bloomberg
> October 14, 2008

Table 4.1 Estimates of Losses from the Crisis in Mortgage and Credit Markets (June 30, 2007–October 7, 2008)

Date	Estimate	Source	Note
6/30/2007	$250 billion	Institutional Risk Analytics	Subprime losses
7/19/2007	$50–$100 billion	Ben Bernanke, Chairman of Federal Reserve Board	Credit losses
10/9/2007	$100–$150 billion	David Wyss, Standard and Poor's	Subprime losses
10/17/2007	$100–$200 billion	William C. Dudley, Federal Reserve Bank of New York	Subprime losses
11/12/2007	$300–$400 billion	Deutsche Bank AG analysts	Subprime losses
11/22/2007	$300 billion	Organization for Economic Cooperation and Development	Subprime losses
1/17/2008	$100–$500 billion	Ben Bernanke, Chairman of Federal Reserve Board	Subprime losses
1/31/2008	$265 billion	Standard & Poor's	Subprime and collateralized debt obligation losses
2/11/2008	$400 billion	Peer Steinbruck, German finance minister at G7 meeting	Subprime losses
2/11/2008	$125–$175 billion	Bear Stearns analyst	Credit losses
2/29/2008	At least $600 billion	UBS AG analysts	Credit losses
3/3/2008	$600 billion	Geraud Charpin, head of European credit strategy at UBS in London	Credit losses

Date	Amount	Source	Type
3/8/2008	$325 billion	JPMorgan Chase & Co	Credit losses
3/10/2008	$215 billion	Head of Japan's Financial Services Agency	Subprime losses
3/13/2008	$285 billion	Standard & Poor's	Subprime losses
3/25/2008	$460 billion	Goldman Sachs	Credit losses
4/8/2008	$945 billion	International Monetary Fund	Credit losses
4/15/2008	$350–$420 billion	Organization for Economic Cooperation and Development	Credit losses
4/29/2008	$800 billion	Barclays Capital	Credit losses
5/14/2008	$400 billion	Krishnan Ramadurai, Fitch's Financial Institutions Group	Subprime losses
5/19/2008	$379 billion	Bloomberg	Credit losses
5/20/2008	$170 billion	Oppenheimer & Co.	Credit losses
8/4/2008	$1–$2 trillion (later revised to $3 trillion on 10/14/2008)	Nouriel Roubini, New York University	Credit losses
10/7/2008	$1.4 trillion	International Monetary Fund	Credit losses

Sources: Various news media, Milken Institute.
Note: For more details about sources of these estimates, see Appendix Table A.32.

Table 4.1 provides estimates from various sources of the likely sub-prime and credit losses; they range from a low of $50 billion to a high of $3 trillion. By comparison, the savings and loan crisis of the 1980s cost $408 billion in 2007 dollars, of which 82 percent was borne by taxpay-ers. About half of the costs, moreover, were associated with problems in Texas, while the current problem is nationwide. The estimates have ballooned quite substantially over time, as observers trying to quantify the costs of the crisis have assessed the snowballing effect of the subprime mortgage market meltdown across the broader financial sector and the real economy.

Worldwide through October 31, 2008, financial institutions have taken cumulative losses/write-downs of $685 billion, according to Bloomberg data and as shown in Figures 4.1 and 4.2. They have raised $688 billion in capital and cut 149,220 jobs. More recently, Citigroup announced it was cutting another 52,000 jobs. The numbers are con-tinuing to grow.

Figure 4.3 shows the sources of the capital raised by firms worldwide from July 2007 to December 2007 and from January 2008 to July 2008. Public investors have been the dominant source of funds for the most recent period, accounting for slightly more than two-thirds of the $300 billion raised. Figure 4.4 shows the types of financial instruments used to

Figure 4.1 Losses/Write-Downs, Capital Raised, and Jobs Cut by Financial Institutions Worldwide through October 31, 2008

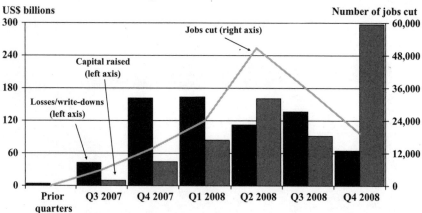

SOURCES: Bloomberg, Milken Institute.
NOTE: Number for Q4 2008 is through October 31, 2008.

raise capital. North American banks have relied most heavily on issuing preferred stock, while European banks have relied most heavily on rights issuance.

Table 4.2 shows that the top 10 financial institutions accounted for 63 percent of the losses/write-downs, 58 percent of the capital raised,

Figure 4.2   Cumulative Losses/Write-Downs, Capital Raised, and Jobs Cut by Financial Institutions Worldwide through October 31, 2008

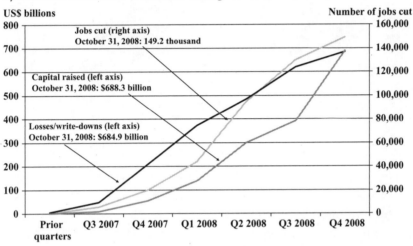

SOURCES: Bloomberg, Milken Institute.
NOTE: Number for Q4 2008 is through October 31, 2008.

Figure 4.3   Worldwide Capital Raised by Source (July 2007–July 2008)

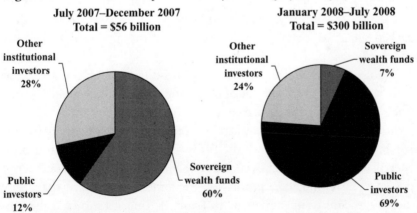

SOURCES: International Monetary Fund, Milken Institute.

Figure 4.4   Worldwide Capital Raised by Type of Instrument
(July 2007–August 2008)

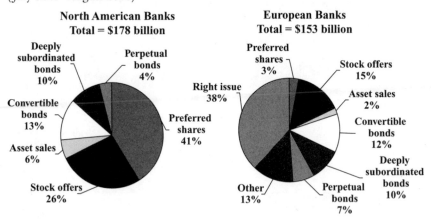

SOURCES: International Monetary Fund, Milken Institute.

and 68 percent of the jobs cut. More detailed information on these issues
is provided in Appendix Table A.33. The table also shows that financial
institutions beyond the United States are struggling.

Figures 4.5 and 4.6 show the percentage change in stock price and
total loss in market value of selected financial firms from December 2006
to October 2008. Of the 15 firms listed in Figure 4.5, 7 have either failed
or been acquired as of that date. Figure 4.6 shows that those firms still
in business have suffered substantial declines in market value. The status
of the top 25 subprime lenders and private-label issuers of mortgage-
backed securities (MBS) in 2006 is detailed in Appendix Tables A.34
and A.35.

Table 4.3 shows the losses and write-downs of selected financial
firms since the second quarter of 2007, and their cumulative net income
from 2004 to the third quarter of 2008. Overall, the total losses and
write-downs exceed the cumulative net income for the firms by roughly
$86 billion. However, four of the firms (Citigroup, Washington Mutual,
Merrill Lynch, and Wachovia) account for all the net losses and write-
downs. The cumulative profits for the other firms more than offset
their losses and write-downs, with Bank of America showing the most
positive result, over this time period.

Table 4.2 Losses/Write-Downs, Capital Raised, and Jobs Cut by the Top 10 Financial Institutions Worldwide through October 31, 2008

	Losses/Write-Downs (US$ Billions)	Percentage of Total
Wachovia, United States	96.5	14.1
Citigroup, United States	68.1	9.9
Merrill Lynch, United States	58.1	8.5
Washington Mutual, United States	45.6	6.7
UBS, Switzerland	44.2	6.5
HSBC, United Kingdom	27.4	4.0
Bank of America, United States	27.4	4.0
National City, United States	26.2	3.8
JPMorgan Chase & Co., United States	20.5	3.0
Wells Fargo, United States	17.7	2.6
Others	253.1	37.0
Grand total	**684.8**	**100.0**
	Capital Raised (US$ Billions)	**Percentage of Total**
Citigroup, United States	74.0	10.8
Bank of America, United States	55.7	8.1
Royal Bank of Scotland, United Kingdom	52.8	7.7
JPMorgan Chase & Co., United States	44.7	6.5
UBS, Switzerland	31.6	4.6
Wells Fargo, United States	30.8	4.5
Merrill Lynch, United States	29.9	4.3
Barclays, United Kingdom	28.2	4.1
HBOS PLC, United Kingdom	24.9	3.6
Morgan Stanley, United States	24.6	3.6
Others	291.1	42.3
Grand total	**688.3**	**100.0**
	Jobs Cut (Number)	**Percentage of Total**
Citigroup, United States	23,660	15.9
Lehman Brothers, United States	13,390	9.0
Bank of America, United States	11,150	7.5
Bear Stearns, United States	9,159	6.1
UBS, Switzerland	9,000	6.0
Commerzbank, Germany	9,000	6.0
Wachovia, United States	8,393	5.6
Royal Bank of Scotland, United Kingdom	7,200	4.8
Merrill Lynch, United States	5,720	3.8
National City, United States	4,900	3.3
Others	47,648	31.9
Grand total	**149,220**	**100.0**

SOURCES: Bloomberg, Milken Institute.

Figure 4.5 Financial Stock Prices Take Big Hits

Percentage change in stock price, December 2006–October 2008

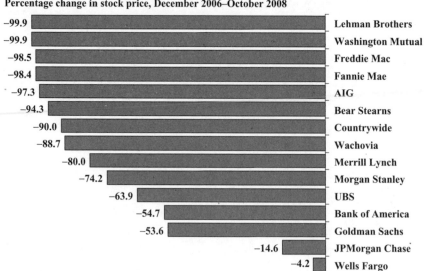

SOURCES: Bloomberg, Milken Institute.

NOTES: The stock price for Bear Stearns is to May 2008. Countrywide's stock price is to June 2008. The stock price for Lehman Brothers is to August 2008.

Figure 4.6 Financial Market Capitalization Takes Big Hit

Total loss in market value: $857 billion, December 2006–October 2008

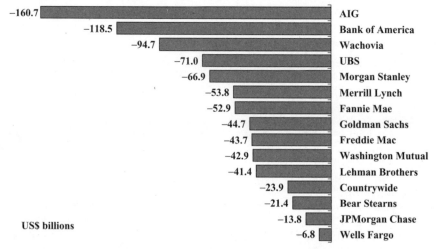

SOURCES: Bloomberg, Milken Institute.

NOTES: The stock price for Bear Stearns is to May 2008. Countrywide's stock price is to June 2008. The stock price for Lehman Brothers is to August 2008.

Table 4.3 Income, Losses, and Write-Downs at Selected Financial Institutions (US$ Billions)

	Net Income						Losses and Write-Downs (Q2 2007–October 31, 2008)	Cumulative Net Income Minus Losses and Write-Downs
	2004	2005	2006	2007	Q1–Q3 2008	Cumulative (2004–Q3 2008)		
Bank of America	13.9	16.5	21.1	15	5.8	72.3	27.4	44.9
Goldman Sachs	4.6	5.6	9.5	11.6	4.4	35.7	4.9	30.8
JPMorgan Chase	4.5	8.5	14.4	15.4	4.9	47.7	20.5	27.2
Wells Fargo	7	7.7	8.4	8.1	5.4	36.6	17.7	18.9
Morgan Stanley	4.5	4.9	7.5	3.2	4	24.1	15.7	8.4
Citigroup Washington	17	24.6	21.5	3.6	−10.4	56.3	68.1	−11.8
Mutual	2.9	3.4	3.6	−0.1	−4.5	5.3	45.6	−40.3
Merrill Lynch	4.4	5.1	7.5	−7.8	−11.8	−2.6	58.1	−60.7
Wachovia	5.2	6.6	7.8	6.3	−33.3	−7.4	96.5	−103.9
Total	**64.1**	**83**	**101.4**	**55.3**	**−35.4**	**268.4**	**354.5**	**−86.1**

Sources: Bloomberg, Milken Institute.

The Pain Spreads throughout the Financial Sector and Beyond

In retrospect, life seemed so much simpler back in the 1980s, when most of the turmoil produced by the savings and loan debacle stayed contained within that industry. There was relatively little securitization of mortgages (as the previous chapter and Figure 3.11 show, securitization—especially of subprime loans—did not really take off until after 1994). The more complex financial instruments associated with the current crisis, such as the collateralized debt obligation (CDO) and the credit default swap (CDS), were not yet on the scene. As a result, the losses did not spread throughout the entire financial sector and beyond.

Conditions today are quite different. The pain has indeed spread far and wide, due chiefly to the issuance of a variety of securities backed by subprime mortgages.

Reckless people have deluded themselves that this was a subprime crisis, but we have problems with credit-card debt, student-loan debt, auto loans, commercial real estate loans, home-equity loans, corporate debt and loans that financed leveraged buyouts. . . . We have a subprime financial system, not a subprime mortgage market.

—Nouriel Roubini
Quoted in the
New York Times Magazine
August 17, 2008

Lenders sold these securities to the capital markets, which then sold them to investors worldwide. Insurers of those securities came into play as well. When the subprime meltdown began in earnest, no one could place an accurate value on many of the securities. That uncertainty resulted in increases in the premiums required on these securities over Treasury securities. As financial institutions took greater and greater losses and write-downs, they were compelled to sell off their own assets. The sector experienced fairly widespread deleveraging and a shortage of liquidity.

The yield spreads of both MBS and high-yield bonds over the 10-year Treasury bond rose considerably after July 2007, as illustrated in Figure 4.7, indicating that the marketplace now viewed these investments with increasing wariness. This is consistent with the problems rippling beyond the mortgage market. Furthermore, the spreads indicate that the

Figure 4.7 Sign of Collapse: Widening Spreads between Mortgage-Backed and High-Yield Bonds (Weekly, 2004–October 31, 2008)

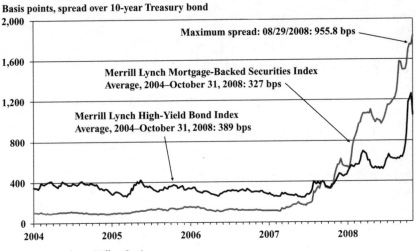

Basis points, spread over 10-year Treasury bond

Maximum spread: 08/29/2008: 955.8 bps

Merrill Lynch Mortgage-Backed Securities Index
Average, 2004–October 31, 2008: 327 bps

Merrill Lynch High-Yield Bond Index
Average, 2004–October 31, 2008: 389 bps

SOURCES: Bloomberg, Milken Institute.

market considered MBS to be riskier than high-yield bonds, which was not the case prior to the summer of 2007.

With financial firms simultaneously deleveraging and seeking outside liquidity to fund their ongoing business operations, it is not surprising that we also see a widening spread in the yields on many financial institution's bonds over Treasury securities. As illustrated in Figure 4.8, bonds on all eight commercial and investment banks depicted saw spreads widening through the second half of 2007, followed by dramatic jumps in the fall of 2008. The spreads widened most for Bear Stearns, Lehman Brothers, and Merrill Lynch, and the least for Citigroup, JPMorgan Chase, and Bank of America. The spread for Goldman Sachs was fairly flat until a spike September 18, 2008, followed by a big decline that was more in line with the last three institutions. These figures also show Fitch's ratings compared to the spreads, with the correlation between the two far from close over the depicted periods.

In addition, as Figure 4.9 shows, even the yield spread between state and local government (municipal) bonds and 10-year Treasury bonds increased to its highest level since 1970, at almost 10 percentage points. This spread is typically negative, because municipal bonds have a tax

Figure 4.8   Yield Spreads: Corporate Bonds vs. Treasury Securities
(2007–October 31, 2008)

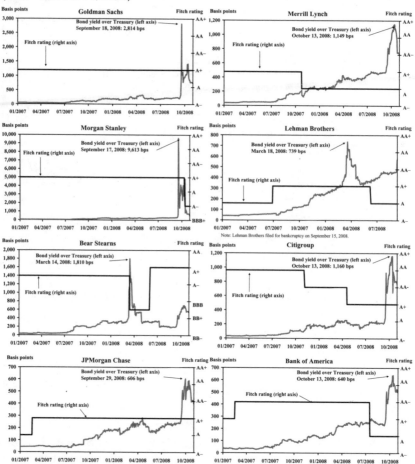

SOURCES: Datastream, Bloomberg, Milken Institute.
NOTE: *Bond yield over Treasury* refers to each firm's bond rate relative to comparable-maturity Treasury
rate.

advantage over Treasury bonds that increases for individuals in higher tax
brackets. But now municipal bonds were being harmed by the exposure
of the monoline insurers that guaranteed them. These monoline insurers
had once limited their coverage only to municipal bonds, but had more
recently ventured into the business of insuring securities backed by
subprime mortgage loans. As they were hit with losses and write-downs
on the MBS they insured, those losses raised questions about the insurers'

Figure 4.9   Widening Spreads between Municipal Bonds and 10-Year Treasury Bonds (Weekly, 1970–October 24, 2008)

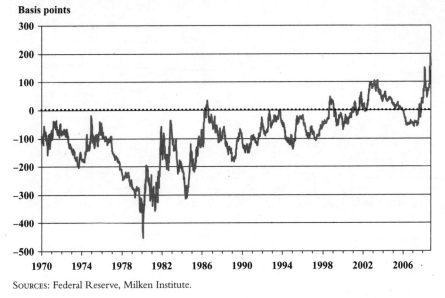

SOURCES: Federal Reserve, Milken Institute.

ability to honor their guarantees on municipal securities, lowering their value. Tightening market conditions also reduced the supply of credit available to state and local governments, when they were increasingly facing shortfalls in revenue and increased expenditures.

An examination of the commercial paper market shows that the credit crunch was also taking a toll on solid companies outside the financial sector. Commercial paper is quite important because it provides firms with a means of obtaining short-term funding to meet payrolls and ongoing expenses. Figure 4.10 and 4.11 show the outstanding amount and the weekly changes in the amount of commercial paper from January 4, 2006, to October 29, 2008. The total amount outstanding, as Figure 4.10 shows, declined by $367 billion from August 8, 2007, to September 26, 2007. It then fell by another $366 billion from September 10 to October 22, 2008, before recovering somewhat, by $101 billion, from October 22 to October 29, 2008.

These steep declines, which reflect a liquidity squeeze in the market, are shown more graphically in Figure 4.11. Asset-backed commercial paper accounted for most of the decline over the entire period, followed

Figure 4.10   Commercial Paper Outstanding Declines Substantially (Weekly, January 4, 2006–October 29, 2008)

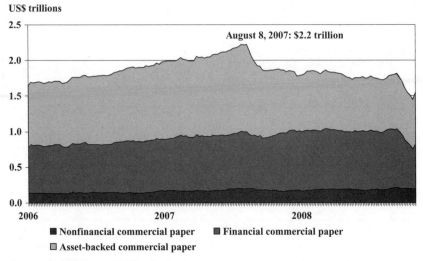

SOURCES: Federal Reserve, Milken Institute.

Figure 4.11   Market for Liquidity Freezes up: Changes in Commercial Paper Outstanding (Weekly, January 4, 2006–October 29, 2008)

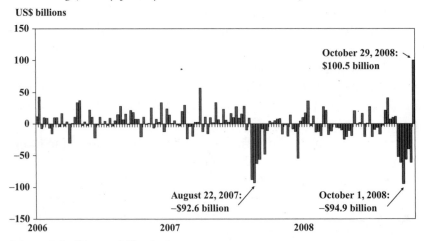

SOURCES: Federal Reserve, Milken Institute.

Figure 4.12   Money Market Funds Suffer Withdrawals

Rank	Fund family (US$ billions)	Total assets as of September 16, 2008	Change since September 12, 2008
1	Fidelity	425.7	−3.5
2	JPMorgan	273.1	2.6
3	BlackRock	268.2	−8.5
4	Federated	234.1	0.7
5	Dreyfus	216.7	9.3
6	Schwab	197.0	1.5
7	Vanguard	190.7	−0.4
8	Goldman Sachs	170.9	−3.8
9	Columbia Management	146.2	0.8
10	Legg Mason	114.3	1.6
11	Morgan Stanley	110.9	−7.5
12	Wells Fargo	108.6	1.5
13	AIM	70.9	−1.6
14	Deutsche	62.9	−1.7
15	UBS	62.3	−0.5
16	Northern	61.4	1.2
17	First American	58.6	−0.3
18	Reserve	57.7	−24.8
19	Evergreen	56.1	−1.0
20	State Street Global Advisors	42.0	−0.1

SOURCE: *The New York Times.*

by financial commercial paper. The slump further demonstrates how the subprime mortgage market meltdown had spread throughout the financial sector.

Some investors grew so shaken by the increasing turmoil in the financial sector that they even began to question the safety of money market funds, except for those funds whose assets consisted mainly of Treasury securities. Figure 4.12 shows that investors took withdrawals from their money market funds from 12 of the top 20 institutions in the four days from September 12 to September 16, 2008; this tumultuous week, shortly after federal regulators seized Fannie Mae and Freddie Mac, also witnessed the failure of Lehman Brothers. During this five-day period, the Reserve Primary Fund suffered massive withdrawals—$24.8 billion, or nearly half of its assets—and on September 16 "broke the buck," which means the value of its shares dropped below a dollar. In the ensuing panic, the company froze its assets and placed a temporary block on withdrawals. Investor confidence was now roiled even in money market funds, which had long been considered a safe haven.

All of the factors discussed above shook confidence, but there was another looming cloud that added to investors' fears: the unregulated market for credit default swaps, which had grown to massive size as investors clamored for yet another way to speculate on mortgage-backed securities. But because these swaps are private contracts between two parties and were not traded via a central clearinghouse, no one could say with certainty just how big each firm's exposure might be when the mortgage market deteriorated. This murkiness added to the market's lack of confidence throughout 2008.

Credit default swaps (CDS) are direct contracts between two parties, allowing an investor to hedge against the risk of defaults on debt payments (such as those on bonds or mortgage-backed securities). One party agrees with a counterparty to swap premiums in exchange for payment if a bond or loan goes into default. These derivative instruments are therefore a form of insurance in which the *spread* is the annual amount a buyer pays over the term of the contract for loss protection. In other words, if the CDS spread is 100 basis points, then a purchaser of $10 million worth of credit default insurance pays the seller of the protection $100,000 per year until the contract expires. The premiums paid are meant to cover the expected losses in the event of a default.

The story does not stop here, however. In the event of a default, there are two forms of settlement, either physical or cash settlement. In the case of physical settlement, the investor delivers or transfers title to the defaulted bond or loan to the seller of the insurance; in the case of cash settlement, the seller pays the investor the difference between the par value (stated or face value) of the defaulted bond or loan and its market price.

This arrangement would seem to be fairly straightforward—except that the amount of CDS outstanding is greater than the amount of the bonds and loans that are protected against losses. How can this happen? CDS buyers are not required to own the underlying bonds or loans being insured.

This means that if the loss to the investors actually holding the bonds or loans is $10 million, or the entire amount insured in our hypothetical scenario above, and there is no recovery, the CDS sellers would be obligated to pay that amount. But the parties who sold protection against the losses (effectively betting that the securities would perform as expected) may be obligated to pay much more—because *other* investors may also have purchased insurance on these same bonds or loans even through they did not own them. As a result, credit default swaps can magnify the ultimate payouts that sellers of the insurance are required to make. They may end up being required to pay out not only the difference between the par value of the bonds or loans and their market value to those who own the bonds or loans, but also exact same amount to many additional investors who purchased the same insurance.

Figure 4.13 provides additional information about market reaction to the spreading financial crisis, using the Credit Derivatives Research (CDR) Counterparty Risk Index, which tracks the credit risk of selected financial institutions that acted as counterparties to most of the contracts traded in the credit default swap market. It clearly shows that the risk, as perceived by the market, of these institutions being able to fulfill their commitments not only trended upward over the past year but also spiked temporarily whenever a bailout action was put in place. For example,

Figure 4.13 Counterparty Risk Increases for Financial Firms (Daily, July 2007–October 31, 2008)

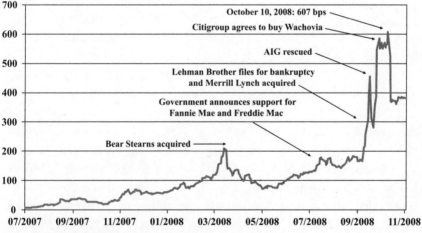

SOURCES: Datastream, Milken Institute.

NOTE: Credit Derivatives Research (CDR) Counterparty Risk Index averages the market spreads of the credit default swaps of 15 major credit derivatives dealers, including ABN Amro, Bank of America, BNP Paribas, Barclays Bank, Citigroup, Credit Suisse, Deutsche Bank, Goldman Sachs Group, HSBC, Lehman Brothers, JPMorgan Chase, Merrill Lynch, Morgan Stanley, UBS, and Wachovia.

Figure 4.14 Jump in GSE Credit Default Swap Spreads over Treasury Securities Finally Initiates Government Support (Daily, January 2008–October 31, 2008)

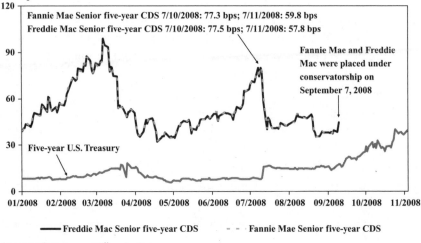

Basis points

Fannie Mae Senior five-year CDS 7/10/2008: 77.3 bps; 7/11/2008: 59.8 bps
Freddie Mac Senior five-year CDS 7/10/2008: 77.5 bps; 7/11/2008: 57.8 bps

Fannie Mae and Freddie Mac were placed under conservatorship on September 7, 2008

Five-year U.S. Treasury

——— Freddie Mac Senior five-year CDS   – – Fannie Mae Senior five-year CDS

SOURCES: Datastream, Milken Institute.

when the Federal Reserve rescued AIG on September 16, 2008, the index shot up 68.1 basis points in a day to reach 456.5 basis points; when Citigroup agreed to buy Wachovia in October 2008, the index reached a record high of 607.1 basis points. The highs over the entire period occurred during the week of October 6, 2008, when the International Monetary Fund issued a bleak global forecast.

Figure 4.14 provides a comparison of the credit default swap spreads for Fannie Mae and Freddie Mac (that is, for Fannie Mae and Freddie Mac bonds) to Treasury securities. The difference between the Treasury securities and the two government-sponsored enterprises (GSEs) widened and narrowed sharply at different times during the first 10 months of 2008. The spread was widest in March, when JPMorgan Chase acquired Bear Stearns, but then fell before rising fairly sharply again until July 11, when Treasury Secretary Henry Paulson announced that the department's "primary focus is supporting Fannie Mae and Freddie Mac in their current form as they carry out their important mission." In response to his statement, the spreads dropped precipitously, by nearly 40 percent in one day.

Tables 4.4 and 4.5 provide more detailed information about the credit default swap premiums for both Fannie Mae and Freddie Mac. These tables show that the premiums were highest for their subordinated debt and increased by well over 100 basis points from June 2007 to March 2008; they increased still further to August 2008 before declining somewhat in October 2008, after the two firms had been put into conservatorship in September 2008 by FHFA. Also, notice that there was a big disconnect between the movements in the CDS spreads and the ratings assigned by Fitch and Moody's for the different time periods. There is, however, a negative correlation between the CDS spreads and the stock prices of the two firms.

The discussion so far has focused on financial institutions and their credit default swap spreads. It is useful, however, to broaden the perspective by looking at the spreads for other types of companies. Table 4.6 shows the average, lowest, and highest spreads for bonds issued by companies in different industries (see Appendix Figure A.17 for more detailed information). As may be seen, the spreads widened considerably for all 18 industries over the period, growing the highest in 2008. Furthermore, the highest spreads were not for banks but for the travel and leisure industry, with automobiles and parts industry a close second. This table demonstrates that the problem that began in the subprime mortgage market contributed to difficulties well beyond the financial sector. Figures 4.15 to 4.17, moreover, show the rolling correlations of daily CDS premiums of the 18 industries over three different time periods. Note that they all jumped from .60 or less to .87 or higher. This is indicative of the widespread liquidity crisis, which limited the ability of firms to fund their ongoing operations and to access the credit market, more generally.

There has been growing concern about the tremendous growth in the credit default swap market, as shown in Figure 4.18. The annualized growth rate from June 2001 to December 2007 was 102 percent. The notional amount—the face amount that is used to calculate payments made on CDS and thus generally does not change hands—increased from less than $1 trillion in 2001 to a record high of slightly more than $62 trillion in 2007 before declining to slightly less than $55 trillion in June 2008 and then still further to $47 trillion on October 31, 2008.

Table 4.4 Senior and Subordinated Credit Default Swap Premiums for Fannie Mae (Selected Years)

Fannie Mae	6/29/2007		3/17/2008		8/20/2008		10/31/2008	
Stock Price ($)	65.33		22.21		4.40		0.93	
Premium (Basis Points)	Senior	Sub	Senior	Sub	Senior	Sub	Senior	Sub
CDS Premium 1Y	1.7	3.6	44.6	171.9	37.6	413.3	40.0	461.9
CDS Premium 2Y	4.1	7.6	51.9	188.5	37.3	367.5	37.5	379.3
CDS Premium 3Y	6.1	10.6	59.1	204.7	37.3	326.5	35.5	311.0
CDS Premium 4Y	8.3	14.1	66.2	222.4	37.1	306.0	36.3	267.1
CDS Premium 5Y	10.0	17.1	73.2	240.8	39.8	294.6	37.5	233.2
CDS Premium 6Y	11.6	19.2	72.9	243.3	42.8	280.4	35.7	241.7
CDS Premium 7Y	13.1	20.4	69.4	242.4	45.0	270.2	34.3	247.6
CDS Premium 8Y	14.2	22.3	68.0	242.4	45.0	266.7	34.4	246.1
CDS Premium 9Y	14.9	23.8	68.1	243.0	45.0	263.9	34.5	245.0
CDS Premium 10Y	15.3	25.2	69.4	243.9	45.0	261.7	34.3	244.0
Rating: Fitch	AAA	AA-	AAA	AA-	AAA	AA-	AAA	AA-
Rating: Moody's	Aaa	Aa2	Aaa	Aa2	Aaa	Aa2	Aaa	Aa2

SOURCES: Datastream, Milken Institute.

Table 4.5 Senior and Subordinated Credit Default Swap Premiums for Freddie Mac (Selected Years)

Freddie Mae	6/29/2007		3/17/2008		8/20/2008		10/31/2008	
Stock Price ($)	60.7		20.62		3.25		1.03	
Premium (Basis Points)	Senior	Sub	Senior	Sub	Senior	Sub	Senior	Sub
CDS Premium 1Y	2.1	4.4	55.8	189.1	37.7	463.4	42.6	369.4
CDS Premium 2Y	3.6	7.5	60.5	203.5	38.2	393.3	42.6	328.7
CDS Premium 3Y	5.3	9.6	65.1	217.7	39.0	340.2	42.6	273.0
CDS Premium 4Y	7.1	12.7	69.6	231.2	39.5	315.9	43.9	237.5
CDS Premium 5Y	9.0	15.3	74.2	244.6	39.8	293.8	44.7	231.7
CDS Premium 6Y	10.1	16.9	79.9	246.2	39.5	275.4	43.6	217.6
CDS Premium 7Y	10.9	17.8	85.5	246.5	39.3	262.1	42.7	207.0
CDS Premium 8Y	11.7	19.3	84.5	246.1	39.1	253.0	42.6	203.0
CDS Premium 9Y	12.6	21.2	82.5	246.4	39.0	245.9	42.6	200.1
CDS Premium 10Y	13.6	23.2	80.0	247.2	38.9	240.2	42.6	197.1
Rating: Fitch	**AAA**	**AA-**	**AAA**	**AA-**	**AAA**	**AA-**	**AAA**	**AA-**
Rating: Moody's	**Aaa**	**Aa2**	**Aaa**	**Aa2**	**Aaa**	**Aa2**	**Aaa**	**Aa2**

SOURCES: Datastream, Milken Institute.

Table 4.6 Average, Lowest, and Highest Credit Default Swap Spreads by Industry (January 2004–October 31, 2008)

Basis Points	Average	Lowest Spread	Date of Lowest Spread	Highest Spread	Date of Highest Spread
Automobiles and parts	447.54	139.70	01/22/04	3,285.32	10/10/08
Banks	58.54	10.20	11/02/06	595.99	09/11/08
Basic resources	117.59	44.14	01/09/04	1,062.20	10/28/08
Chemicals	98.11	44.88	12/28/06	367.55	10/24/08
Construction and materials	110.64	31.72	12/16/04	476.88	10/27/08
Financial services	115.32	21.36	11/09/06	1,176.24	10/10/08
Food and beverage	66.49	29.38	03/11/05	289.80	10/28/08
Health care	77.09	34.20	03/11/05	246.03	10/31/08
Industrial goods and services	88.08	48.55	01/02/04	287.30	10/24/08
Insurance	99.51	17.24	02/19/07	922.57	10/10/08
Media	195.10	56.00	03/09/05	1,429.66	10/16/08
Oil and gas	82.19	42.98	02/23/07	331.66	10/17/08
Personal and household goods	140.87	46.51	03/11/05	556.23	10/28/08
Retail	113.12	41.61	01/01/04	411.12	10/24/08
Technology	150.61	70.95	01/01/04	500.60	10/31/08
Telecommunications	126.16	47.96	05/02/06	707.32	10/24/08
Travel and leisure	361.70	96.32	01/06/04	1,655.59	07/14/08
Utilities	99.33	38.62	02/22/07	357.91	10/10/08

Sources: Datastream, Milken Institute.

Figure 4.15   Average Three-Month Rolling Correlations of Daily Credit Default Swap Premiums of 18 U.S. Industries

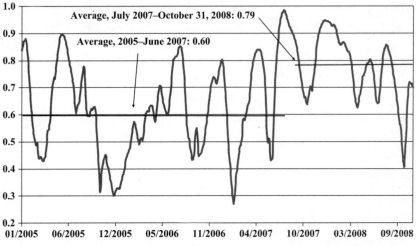

SOURCES: Datastream, Milken Institute.

NOTE: The 18 industries include automobiles and parts, banks, basic resources, chemicals, construction and materials, financial services, food and beverage, health care, industrial goods and services, insurance, media, oil and gas, personal household goods, retail, technology, telecommunications, travel and leisure, and utilities.

Figure 4.16   Average Six-Month Rolling Correlations of Daily Credit Default Swap Premiums of 18 U.S. Industries

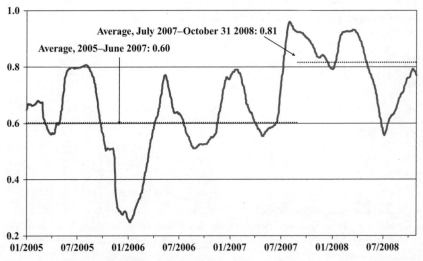

SOURCES: Datastream, Milken Institute.

NOTE: See the figure above for a list of the 18 industries.

Figure 4.17 Average One-Year Rolling Correlations of Daily Credit Default Swap Premiums of 18 U.S. Industries

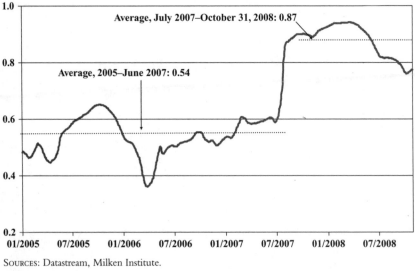

SOURCES: Datastream, Milken Institute.
NOTE: See above for a list of the 18 industries.

Figure 4.18 Rising Risk: The Credit Default Swap Market Nearly Doubled Each Year from June 2001 through October 2008

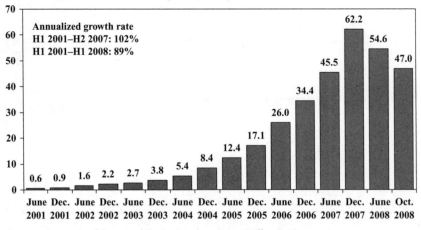

SOURCES: International Swaps and Derivatives Association, Milken Institute.

These reductions were partly due to the industry's own efforts to reduce notional amount of CDS outstanding and partly due to recent auctions and settlements of Fannie Mae, Freddie Mac, and Lehman Brothers CDS contracts.

No one can pinpoint the amount ultimately at risk in the credit default swap market at the present time. Worry about the unknown extent of these losses loomed over the market in 2008. The notional amount is vast (though it has recently declined, as noted above), but the actual exposure to losses is clearly less than this amount. But it remains to be seen exactly how large the true losses will be, which parties will bear those losses, and whether those parties have sufficient capital to absorb them. This is the very reason the regulatory authorities are trying to shift these types of credit derivatives to a central exchange: to better reduce risk so that a failure of a single counterparty does not cause a systemic crisis.

At present, CDS are traded over-the-counter (OTC), which means that they are negotiated one to one between two parties. The failure of Lehman Brothers and the massive Federal Reserve loans to AIG in September 2008 sharpened concern about counterparty risk and heightened interest in establishing a clearinghouse for credit default swaps, especially because many of the swaps insure bonds and loans that are backed by mortgages. A clearinghouse or exchange will enable the netting of offsetting contracts, thereby reducing the notional amount of contracts to a level that actually represents the risk exposure to sellers. This structure, once established, can set up a fund capitalized by participating institutions to help deal with the fallout from a large counterparty failure. The clearinghouse becomes the buyer for every seller and the seller for every buyer of CDS and can therefore use its fund to cover any losses in the event of a member institution default. Furthermore, by employing mark-to-market pricing on a daily basis and liquidating the positions of all member institutions who cannot post additional collateral, a central clearinghouse further reduces the risk of a systemic crisis.

On October 31, 2008, the Depository Trust & Clearing Corporation (DTCC) announced that it will publish aggregate market data from its Trade Information Warehouse (Warehouse), the worldwide central trade registry it maintains on credit derivatives. It began doing so on

Figure 4.19   Estimated Breakdown of Credit Default Swap Buyers and Sellers of Protection (March 2007)

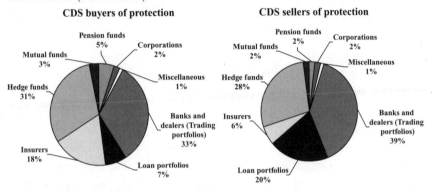

SOURCES: BIS, Milken Institute.

November 4 and plans to continue weekly, with DTCC posting on its web site the outstanding gross and net notional values ("stock" values) of CDS contracts registered in the Warehouse for the top 1,000 underlying single-name reference entities and all indices, as well as certain aggregates of this data on a gross notional basis only. This type of information should prove useful in helping alleviate market concerns about transparency.

Figure 4.19 shows the breakdown of the buyers and sellers of the protection provided by credit default swaps. The biggest buyers and sellers are banks, dealers, and hedge funds, accounting for roughly two-thirds of the market. In the case of U.S. commercial banks, 32 institutions sold $7.6 trillion (notional amount) in credit derivatives in the second quarter of 2008—and 99 percent of all credit derivatives are CDS. The notional amount for the 36 banks that purchased credit derivatives was $7.9 trillion.

Adding these two notional amounts together, one obtains the total notional amount of credit derivatives held by all U.S. banks, which was $15.5 trillion as of June 2008. Figure 4.20 shows the breakdown of this amount by investment grade and maturity. The largest percentage of credit derivatives are investment grade (71 percent) and have a maturity between one to five years (65 percent).

Table 4.7 shows the notional amounts of positions in credit derivatives held by the top 10 bank holding companies in June 2008. These 10 companies account for 99.6 percent of all credit derivatives held by

Figure 4.20 Breakdown of Notional Amount of Credit Derivatives of All U.S. Banks by Investment Grade and Maturity (June 2008)

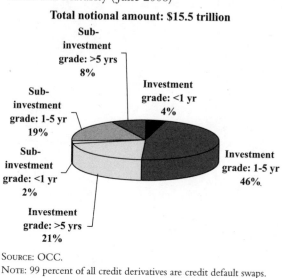

Total notional amount: $15.5 trillion

Sub-investment grade: >5 yrs 8%

Investment grade: <1 yr 4%

Sub-investment grade: 1-5 yr 19%

Sub-investment grade: <1 yr 2%

Investment grade: 1-5 yr 46%

Investment grade: >5 yrs 21%

Source: OCC.
Note: 99 percent of all credit derivatives are credit default swaps.

U.S. banks, with JPMorgan Chase accounting for the largest share at 51 percent. This table shows that the net positions (i.e., beneficiary minus guarantor positions) for all these banks are positive, except for three. The largest negative net position was held by HSBC North America Holdings, at $39 billion. If this institution had to pay out this amount to cover the losses it was insuring, its capital would have been exceeded by $12 billion. In the case of the other two institutions with negative net positions, Bank of America and U.S. Bancorp, these positions are far less than their capital levels.

Table 4.8 shows the gross fair values in credit derivatives held by the top 10 bank holding companies. The gross positive fair value is the total of the fair values of all contracts in which the bank, as both guarantor and beneficiary, would receive payments from its counterparties, without taking into account netting. This value therefore represents the maximum losses to which a bank is exposed if all its counterparties default and no contracts are netted, assuming no collateral is posted by the counterparties. The gross negative fair value is the total of the fair

Table 4.7 Notional Amounts of Positions in Credit Derivatives Held by the Top 10 Bank Holding Companies (June 2008)

	Guarantor Position (US$ Millions)	Beneficiary Position (US$ Millions)	Notional Amount of Credit Derivatives (US$ Millions)	Share of All Credit Derivatives Held by U.S. Banks	Net Position (US$ Millions)	Equity (US$ Millions)
Citigroup	1,537,255	1,672,423	3,209,678	20.7%	135,168	108,871
JPMorgan Chase	3,821,391	4,028,873	7,850,264	50.6%	207,482	132,291
Bank of America	1,369,351	1,344,941	2,714,292	17.5%	(24,411)	176,575
Wachovia	186,699	198,917	385,616	2.5%	12,218	77,871
Taunus Corporation*	5,523	20,155	25,678	0.2%	14,632	1,924
Wells Fargo	827	1,411	2,238	0.0%	584	48,693
HSBC North America Holdings	639,189	600,095	1,239,284	8.0%	(39,095)	27,026
U.S. Bancorp	1,543	627	2,170	0.0%	(917)	22,153
Bank of New York Mellon	2	1,675	1,677	0.0%	1,673	16,755
SunTrust Bank	1,298	1,806	3,104	0.0%	509	19,621

SOURCES: OCC, FDIC, National Information Center, Federal Reserve, Milken Institute.

NOTE: 99 percent of all credit derivatives are credit default swaps.

*Federal holding company, data from National Information Center, Federal Reserve.

Table 4.8 Gross Fair Values of Positions in Credit Derivatives Held by the Top 10 Bank Holding Companies (June 2008; US$ Millions)

	As Guarantor			As Beneficiary			Total Net Fair Value
	Gross Positive Fair Value	Gross Negative Fair Value	Net Fair Value	Gross Positive Fair Value	Gross Negative Fair Value	Net Fair Value	
Citigroup	5,137	123,818	−118,681	138,129	4,885	133,244	14,563
JPMorgan Chase	19,063	252,266	−233,203	277,588	28,796	248,792	15,589
Bank of America	3,917	73,968	−70,051	79,309	3,297	76,012	5,961
Wachovia	353	17,888	−17,535	18,231	315	17,916	381
Taunus Corporation*	86	349	−263	3,013	102	2,911	2,648
Wells Fargo	29	36	−7	76	14	62	55
HSBC North America Holdings	1,978	32,512	−30,534	32,775	3,008	29,767	−767
U.S. Bankcorp	0	1	−1	2	0	2	1
Bank of New York Mellon	0	1	−1	30	0	30	29
SunTrust Bank	48	37	11	50	45	4	15

SOURCES: FDIC, National Information Center, Federal Reserve, Milken Institute.

NOTE: 99 percent of all credit derivatives are credit default swaps.

*Federal holding company, data from National Information Center, Federal Reserve.

values of all contracts in which a bank, as both guarantor and beneficiary, would make payments to its counterparties, without taking into account netting. This value therefore represents the maximum losses to which a bank's counterparties are exposed if a bank defaults and no contracts are netted, assuming no collateral is posted by the bank. Whether a bank on net receives greater payments than what it pays out depends on whether the gross positive fair value of its credit derivative contracts exceeds the gross negative fair value of these contracts. As shown in Table 4.8, to the extent that the fair values are appropriately and accurately calculated, only in the case of one of the institutions, HSBC North America Holdings, is the total net fair value negative at $767 million, which is less than 3 percent of its capital.

The pain that has been plaguing the United States has spread well beyond our borders. Other nations are resolving real estate bubbles of their own, and many foreign investors have absorbed losses in U.S. real estate, mortgage-backed securities, and financial institutions. Reduced spending by the U.S. consumer is also expected to have a worldwide impact. Table 4.9 shows that the market capitalization of the equities that are traded in the world at year-end 2006 and 2007 and October 31, 2008. Total market capitalization rose from 2006 to 2007 by $11 trillion but then declined by $28 trillion (or 47 percent) in the first 10 months of 2008. Similar information is provided for selected individual countries in the same table. Every one of the 20 countries has seen its stock market capitalization decline by at least 29 percent from December 31, 2007, to October 31, 2008. The three countries with the biggest percentage declines are India, Russia, and China, at 67 percent, 66.9 percent, and 63.3 percent, respectively. The United States experienced the biggest absolute decline at $6.2 trillion, which was 35 percent of its 2007 GDP.

Given all the financial problems in so many countries, Figures 4.21 and 4.22 show that credit default swap premiums for selected countries have all risen fairly dramatically in October 2008. Even in the United States, the CDS premium increased by 65 percent from September 26, 2008, to October 31, 2008. It may come as a surprise to many readers, but that does indeed mean that some individuals are betting that the United States may default on some of its Treasury securities.

Table 4.9 Declining Equity Market Capitalizations for Selected Countries

US$ Billions	12/31/2006	12/31/2007	10/31/2008	Year-to-October 2008 Change	Year-to-October Percentage Change	2007 GDP
World total	49,979	60,851	32,500	-28,352	-46.6	54,585
United States	17,467	17,663	11,507	-6,156	-34.9	13,808
Japan	4,873	4,546	3,007	-1,539	-33.8	4,382
United Kingdom	3,808	4,047	2,139	-1,908	-47.1	2,804
China	1,144	4,459	1,638	-2,821	-63.3	3,280
France	2,511	2,737	1,458	-1,279	-46.7	2,594
Hong Kong	1,715	2,654	1,229	-1,425	-53.7	207
Germany	1,758	2,207	1,155	-1,052	-47.6	3,321
Canada	1,506	1,749	1,065	-684	-39.1	1,436
Switzerland	1,202	1,212	863	-349	-28.8	427
Australia	929	1,413	687	-726	-51.4	909
India	816	1,815	599	-1,216	-67.0	1,101
Brazil	708	1,399	651	-748	-53.5	1,314
Spain	951	1,088	574	-515	-47.3	1,440
Italy	1,019	1,106	538	-568	-51.4	2,105
South Korea	815	1,103	445	-658	-59.7	970
Taiwan	650	701	409	-292	-41.7	383
Russia	1,010	996	330	-666	-66.9	1,290
Saudi Arabia	323	507	290	-217	-42.8	382
Argentina	400	565	305	-260	-46.1	260
Sweden	594	577	266	-311	-53.9	455

SOURCES:: WEO, Bloomberg, Milken Institute.

Figure 4.21   CDS Premiums Rise Dramatically for G7 in October 2008
(Weekly, January 4, 2008–October 31, 2008)

CDS premium, basis points

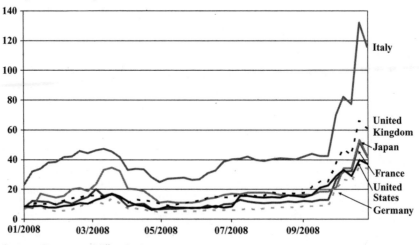

SOURCES: Datastream, Milken Institute.
NOTE: CDS data for Canada is not available.

Figure 4.22   CDS Premiums Rise Dramatically for Emerging Economies in
October 2008 (Weekly, January 4, 2008–October 31, 2008)

CDS premium, basis points

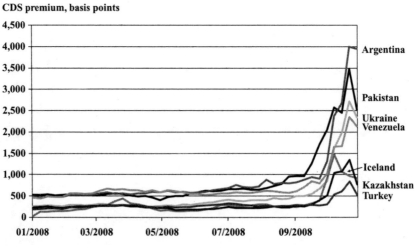

SOURCES: Datastream, Milken Institute.
NOTE: Iceland is included although it is not an emerging economy.

When Will We Hit Bottom?

Everyone is asking: When will we hit bottom? In April 2008, *The Wall Street Journal* posed that question to a group of economists. As shown in Figure 4.23, their answers varied somewhat, but 38 percent expected home prices to bottom out in the first half of 2009, while another 29 percent projected that the decline would extend into the second half of 2009. Only 6 percent thought home prices would not reach bottom until the first half of 2010. Recent events may have changed the minds of many who

Home prices in the U.S. are likely to start to stabilize or touch bottom sometime in the first half of 2009. . . [but] prices could continue to drift lower through 2009 and beyond.

—Alan Greenspan
Quoted in the
The Wall Street Journal
August 14, 2008

responded to the survey. Nevertheless, the question itself is important, and this section attempts to provide some information that may help answer it.

One way to try to answer the question is to look at the rent-to-home price ratio, which is analogous to the reciprocal of the price-to-earnings ratio of stocks. The average ratio of annual rent to price from 1960 to the first quarter of 2008 was 5.04 percent, but it was only 3.48 percent

Figure 4.23 Looking for a Bottom: Survey of Economists
Economists Say the Economy Isn't at Its Low Point Yet and That Home Prices Likely Won't Get There until 2009

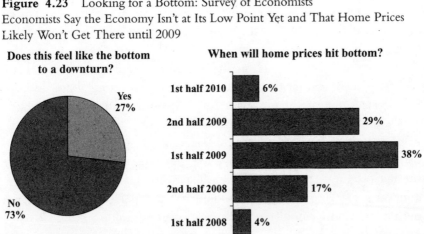

SOURCE: *The Wall Street Journal*, April 11, 2008.

Table 4.10 Declines in Home Prices and the Time It Takes to Get the Rent-to-Price Ratio to a Targeted Value

		Annual Home Price Decline Required				
		−2.0%	**−5.0%**	**−10.0%**	**−15.0%**	**−20.0%**
Rent-to-Price Ratio	3.80%	2010 Q3	2008 Q4	2008 Q2	2008 Q2	2008 Q2
	4.00%	2013 Q1	2009 Q4	2008 Q3	2008 Q2	2008 Q2
	5.00%	2024 Q1	2014 Q1	2010 Q4	2009 Q3	2009 Q1
	5.04% average	2024 Q3	2014 Q2	2010 Q4	2009 Q3	2009 Q1
	6.00%	2026 Q4	2017 Q3	2012 Q3	2010 Q4	2009 Q4

SOURCE: Milken Institute.

NOTE: The average rent-to-price ratio from 1960 to Q1 2008 is 5.04 percent. The starting rent-to-price ratio was 3.93 percent, which was its value in the fourth quarter of 2007. The median sales prices of existing homes are used in these calculations.

in 2006 at the height of the home price bubble. Table 4.10 shows the quarter and year in which different annual home price declines would achieve various rent-to-price ratios. For example, given that the rent-to-price ratio was 3.93 percent in the fourth quarter of 2007, an annual price decline of 10 percent would get that ratio back to the long-run average ratio of 5.04 percent in the fourth quarter of 2010. A 20 percent decline, however, would get the rent-to-price ratio back to the average ratio in the first quarter of 2009.

Table 4.11 shows similar information for different annual rental price growth rates that would get the rent-to-price ratio back to its long-term average value or to a lower or higher ratio. Of course, a simultaneous decline in home prices and increase in rental prices would get that ratio back to 5.04 percent sooner than either trend would if acting alone. Indeed, rental prices increased nationwide in the first three quarters of 2008.

Another way to approach the question is to examine the growth in household income that would be necessary to get the median home price-to-income ratio back to its average value of 3.36 percent over the period 1960 to 2007. As Table 4.12 shows, if household income continues growing at its average rate of 5.02 percent over the same period, the ratio would get back to its average value in 2013. A decline in the median home price, however, would speed up the process considerably given the same growth of median household income.

Table 4.11 Increases in Rental Prices and the Time It Takes to Get the Rent-to-Price Ratio to a Targeted Value

		Rental Price Annual Growth Required				
		3.00%	4.00%	5.00%	5.52% average	6.00%
Rent-to-Price Ratio	**3.80%**	2009 Q3	2009 Q1	2008 Q3	2008 Q3	2008 Q3
	4.00%	2011 Q2	2010 Q2	2009 Q4	2009 Q3	2009 Q2
	5.00%	2019 Q1	2016 Q1	2014 Q2	2013 Q3	2013 Q1
	5.04% average	2019 Q1	2016 Q2	2014 Q3	2013 Q4	2013 Q2
	6.00%	2025 Q1	2020 Q4	2018 Q1	2017 Q1	2016 Q2

Source: Milken Institute.
Note: The average rental price growth rate from 1960 to Q1 2008 is 5.52 percent. The average rent-to-price ratio over the same period is 5.04 percent. The starting rental-price ratio was 3.93 percent, which was its value in the fourth quarter of 2007. The median sales prices of existing homes are used in these calculations.

Table 4.12 Combinations of Household Income Growth Rates and Median Home Price-to-Income Ratio Needed to Get Home Price Back to Its Value in 2006

		Household Income Growth				
		3.00%	4.00%	5.00%	5.02% average	6.00%
Median Home Price-to-Income Ratio	**2.50%**	2027	2022	2019	2019	2017
	3.00%	2020	2017	2015	2015	2014
	3.36% average	2017	2014	2013	2013	2012
	4.00%	2011	2010	2009	2009	2009
	4.50%	2008	2008	2008	2008	2008

Source: Milken Institute.
Note: The average household income growth rate from 1960 to 2007 is 5.02 percent. The average median home price-to-income ratio over the same period is 3.36 percent. The median sales prices of existing homes are used in these calculations.

Figure 4.24 Home Mortgage Debt Share of Household Debt Reaches a New High in 2007 (Quarterly, 1952–Q2 2008)

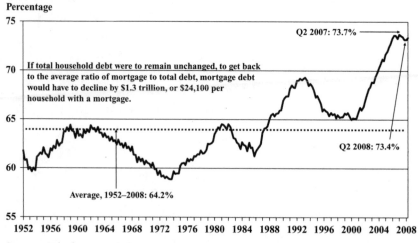

SOURCES: Federal Reserve, Milken Institute.

Continuing these types of scenarios, Figure 4.24 shows that mortgage debt would have to decline by $1.3 trillion, or $24,100 per each household with a mortgage, to lower the average ratio of mortgage debt–to–total household debt to its long-term average ratio of 64.2 percent from 73.4 percent, where it stood in the second quarter of 2008. Figure 4.25 shows that mortgage debt would have to decline by $6.2 trillion to lower the average ratio of mortgage debt–to–disposable personal income to its average ratio of 79.7 percent from 139.5 percent in 2007.

The different scenarios explored above not only indicate various adjustments that may have to occur in some combination to get things back to "normal" but also demonstrate just how far various ratios were deviating from historical norms before the housing bubble burst. These unsustainable deviations should have been a call for action on the part of the regulatory authorities.

Based on market information, Figure 4.26 shows that futures contracts on home prices predict an annualized home price decline of 11 percent from October 2008 to November 2009 and a price decline of 8 percent from October 2008 to November 2010. These price declines are in addition to those that have already occurred, as discussed earlier.

Figure 4.25   Home Mortgage Debt as a Percentage of Disposable Personal Income Reaches a High in 2007 (Quarterly, 1952–2007)

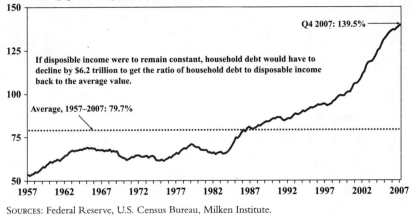

SOURCES: Federal Reserve, U.S. Census Bureau, Milken Institute.

Another perspective on when a bottom will be reached is provided by Table 4.13. This table shows the CDS spreads for different sectors of the economy from January 1, 2004, to October 31, 2008, with the time period broken down into pre– and post–subprime mortgage market meltdown. The low, high, and average CDS spreads as well as the

Figure 4.26   Implied Annualized Price Decline through Expiration Date of Chicago Mercantile Exchange Home Price Futures Contracts

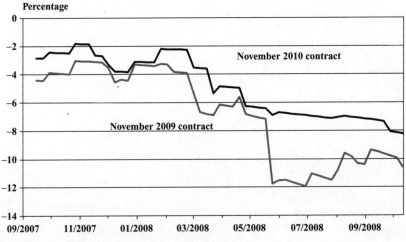

SOURCES: Bloomberg, S&P/Case-Shiller, Milken Institute

Table 4.13 Credit Default Swap Spreads for Different Sectors (January 1, 2004–October 31, 2008)

	Credit Default Swap Spread as of 10/31/2008 (Basis Points)	From July 1, 2007 to October 31, 2008 (Basis Points)				From January 1, 2004 to June 30, 2007 (Basis Points)			
		High	Low	Average	Standard Deviation	High	Low	Average	Standard Deviation
Automobiles and parts	2,012	3,285	294	809	549	637	140	309	122
Banks	150	596	19	157	99	33	10	21	6
Basic resources	885	1,062	91	223	173	122	44	77	15
Chemicals	334	368	76	161	61	109	45	74	15
Construction and materials	460	477	79	197	87	158	32	78	33
Financial services	948	1,176	46	327	247	49	21	34	7
Food and beverage	284	290	50	122	54	61	29	45	6
Health care	246	246	66	131	35	74	34	56	7
Industrial goods and services	275	287	73	129	45	107	49	72	10
Insurance	611	923	31	260	194	79	17	38	13
Media	1,174	1,430	127	452	317	138	56	97	17
Oil and gas	281	332	61	118	50	121	43	68	18
Personal and household goods	442	556	125	291	81	121	47	83	14
Retail	388	411	89	198	77	123	42	80	12
Technology	501	501	118	216	76	205	71	126	29
Telecommunications	520	707	58	197	114	225	48	99	42
Travel and leisure	1,295	1,656	218	645	341	511	96	253	86
Utilities	323	358	67	136	60	149	39	85	27

SOURCES: Datastream, Milken Institute.

140

Figure 4.27 Stock Market Volatility Reaches Record High
(Daily, January 1, 1990–October 31, 2008)

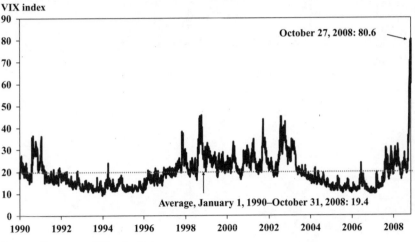

SOURCES: Datastream, Milken Institute.
NOTE: The Chicago Board Options Exchange VIX Index is a measure of the implied stock market volatility of the S&P 500.

standard deviation of the spreads are provided for the two subperiods. For every sector, the average spread was higher post–June 30, 2007, than pre–June 30, 2007, and the standard deviation was also higher in the second subperiod. One would expect that when the financial sector and real economy return to more normal conditions, the CDS spreads shown for October 31, 2008, would decline to much lower levels for the different sectors. Notice in particular that the spread for the financial services sector was 948 basis points on that date, which is far greater than the average of 34 basis points for the first subperiod and even greater than the average of 327 basis points for the crisis period.

Figure 4.27 shows the degree of investor nervousness as reflected in the VIX Index, which is a measure of the expected stock market volatility. It reached a record high of 80.6 on October 27, 2008. Over the past nearly two decades, the average value was only 19.4 and all the previous peaks were less than 50. The near-term outlook based on this index was quite chaotic as of October 27, 2008. A decline in the VIX Index to a value much closer to the average would be consistent with less uncertainty and more stability in the financial sector and the real economy.

Chapter 5

What Went Wrong...?

How did the problems in the subprime mortgage area—with losses that probably will ultimately turn out to be in a range of $100–$200 billion—lead to such broad market distress?
—William C. Dudley, Executive Vice President
Federal Reserve Bank of New York
"May You Live in Interesting Times"
Remarks delivered at the Federal Reserve Bank of Philadelphia
October 17, 2007

The crisis in the housing and credit markets demands a full accounting of what went wrong. It is virtually impossible to prevent a similar disruption in the future (or at least contain its severity) without thoroughly understanding the factors that caused this turmoil. In conducting such an assessment, it is important to keep in mind that there have been previous crises in the United States and elsewhere in the world. Indeed, roughly two-thirds of the more than 180 member countries of the International Monetary Fund have experienced financial crises in the past 40 years. One must be careful, therefore, not to attribute the disruption in the United States to factors that somehow are uniquely American. It may well be that there are several common contributing factors behind these events, which have occurred in all parts of the world and at all levels of income.

Examining the current dilemma also calls for a dose of perspective from the very outset. To be sure, the mortgage markets are currently in distress, with falling home prices and an increasing wave of foreclosures. But these problems should be understood in context, juxtaposed against

Figure 5.1   The Mortgage Problem in Perspective (Mid-2008)

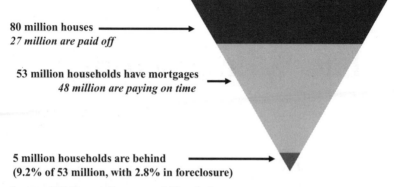

80 million houses
27 million are paid off

53 million households have mortgages
48 million are paying on time

5 million households are behind
(9.2% of 53 million, with 2.8% in foreclosure)

SOURCES: U.S. Treasury Department, Milken Institute.

And do not forget that the vast majority of even subprime borrowers have been making their payments. Indeed, fewer than 15 percent of borrowers in this most risky group have even been delinquent on a payment, much less defaulted.

—Austan Goolsbee
" 'Irresponsible' Mortgages Have Opened Doors to Many of the Excluded"
The New York Times
March 29, 2007

the size of the overall market. Figure 5.1 does just that, illustrating that of the approximately 80 million houses in the United States, 27 million are paid off, while the remaining 53 million have mortgages. Of those households with mortgages, 5 million (or 9 percent) are behind in their payments and roughly 3 percent are in foreclosure. By contrast, in the depths of the Great Depression, about one-half of urban households with outstanding mortgages were in default.[1]

The rising foreclosure rate is a serious economic and societal concern, and it raises thorny and unavoidable issues. As Harvard University's Lawrence Summers, now head of the National Economic Council, stated, "... we need to ask ourselves the question, and I don't think the question has been put in a direct way and people have developed an answer; what is the optimal rate of foreclosures? How much are we prepared to accept?"[2] It is not clear what foreclosure rates are optimal for different groups of borrowers, simply from a social welfare standpoint. One thing we do know for certain, however: In a world full of inherent risk and uncertainty, if we want individuals to be able to purchase homes on credit, the optimal rate of foreclosure cannot be zero.

. . . with Origination Practices and New Financial Products?

Rapidly rising foreclosure rates among subprime home mortgage loans have led some observers to conclude that origination practices and new financial products were the culprits behind the distress in this market. Some have argued that many of the new loan products introduced in recent years and offered to subprime borrowers should never have been made available and should be prohibited going forward.

To argue that the loan "product" is the source of the problem is to ignore a fundamental truth: The ability or willingness of individuals to repay loans depends on their financial situation, not on the products they are offered. The marketplace and a borrower's personal financial circumstances may both deteriorate, leading to serious difficulties, including foreclosure. In some parts of the country, home prices have fallen so dramatically that houses are now worth less than the remaining balances owed on them, leading some borrowers to simply choose to walk away from their commitments. In addition, borrowers may lose their jobs, suffer divorce or serious illness, or otherwise find themselves in dire financial straits. All of these factors contribute to increases in foreclosures, regardless of the mortgage product used to make the initial purchase of a home.

Some individual loan products, however, have become particularly associated with escalating foreclosure rates, especially among subprime borrowers. Appendix Tables A.36 and A.37 show cumulative foreclosure starts for both prime and subprime borrowers from January 1999 through September 2007 (and it is worth noting that not all foreclosure starts actually result in foreclosure). Both groups of borrowers experienced foreclosures using 29 of the different mortgage products, indicating foreclosure is a possible outcome of virtually every mortgage product, prime or subprime.

Of course, foreclosure rates on subprime mortgages are higher than those for prime mortgages, regardless of product type. But that result is generally expected, because subprime borrowers are defined as carrying greater credit risk—and that is especially true of those borrowers with little or no "skin in the game."

One new financial product has been the particular target of criticism by the news media: the hybrid adjustable-rate mortgage. Its notoriety is likely to continue until a bottom is reached through government action, because turmoil in the mortgage market is expected to worsen as interest rates on these loans continue to reset upward in the months and years ahead (see Appendix Table A.38 for reset dates for adjustable-rate first mortgages originated from 2004 to 2006). Loans with this rate-reset feature are known as *hybrids* because their interest rates are fixed, generally at a low rate, for an initial period before becoming variable (often with caps that limit the size of the possible increase over a given year or over the entire term of the loan). These loans have been the object of growing concern in the past year or two, because a relatively large number of borrowers with shaky credit histories took out subprime hybrid mortgage loans and are struggling to afford the higher monthly payments that accompany these rate adjustments.

As long as home prices were rising, hybrids posed few problems. Relying on the newfound equity created by escalating home values, borrowers would simply refinance their loans before the interest rates reset to a higher level. But recent declines in home prices have left many of these borrowers unable to refinance. As a result, many home-owners will be hard-pressed to avoid foreclosure when the resets take place.

Because hybrid loans—especially subprime hybrids—have become so controversial, it is important to assess their longer-term role in home foreclosures against other products in the mortgage market. Figures 5.2 through 5.5 provide that comparison by showing home mortgage orig-inations and cumulative foreclosures for prime and subprime borrowers. The numbers, covering the period January 1999 to July 2007, are based on a sample of 80 million mortgage loans from LoanPerformance. Fig-ure 5.2 shows that of almost 71 million prime mortgage originations, nearly 84 percent were fixed-rate mortgages (mostly 30-year, fixed-rate loans), 10 percent had adjustable rates, and less than 5 percent were hybrid mortgages. By contrast, Figure 5.3 shows that of the 9.5 mil-lion subprime mortgages originated during this period, 44 percent were

Figure 5.2 Prime Mortgage Originations
(January 1999–July 2007)

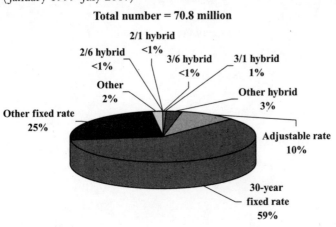

Total number = 70.8 million

2/1 hybrid
<1%

2/6 hybrid
<1%

3/6 hybrid
<1%

3/1 hybrid
1%

Other
2%

Other hybrid
3%

Other fixed rate
25%

Adjustable rate
10%

30-year
fixed rate
59%

SOURCES: LoanPerformance, Milken Institute.

fixed-rate loans, 16 percent had adjustable rates, and 32 percent were hybrid mortgages.

Although both prime and subprime borrowers used all three types of loan products, subprime borrowers relied more heavily on hybrid loans. Most of these are 2/28 and 3/27 mortgages, with short-term fixed interest rates (holding for the first 2 and 3 years, respectively),

Figure 5.3 Subprime Mortgage Originations
(January 1999–July 2007)

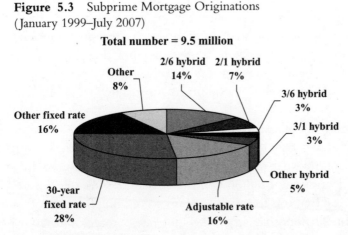

Total number = 9.5 million

2/6 hybrid
14%

2/1 hybrid
7%

Other
8%

3/6 hybrid
3%

3/1 hybrid
3%

Other fixed rate
16%

Other hybrid
5%

30-year
fixed rate
28%

Adjustable rate
16%

SOURCES: LoanPerformance, Milken Institute.

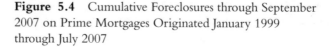

Figure 5.4   Cumulative Foreclosures through September 2007 on Prime Mortgages Originated January 1999 through July 2007

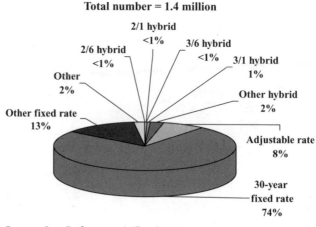

SOURCES: LoanPerformance, Milken Institute.

followed by variable interest rates for the remaining 28 or 27 years of the loan's term. (The 2/28 mortgages include 2/6 and 2/1 mortgages or mortgages that reset after six months and 1 year, respectively, after the initially 2-year fixed rate ends. Similarly, 3/27 mortgages include 3/6 and 3/1 mortgages or mortgages that reset after six months and 1 year, respectively, once the 3-year fixed-rate period is over.)

The cumulative foreclosure starts that accompanied these different mortgage products are presented in Figures 5.4 and 5.5. Even though attention has been focused on high and rising foreclosure rates in the subprime market, the total number (but not the percentage) of foreclosures on prime mortgages is actually slightly higher than the total number of foreclosures on subprime mortgages: 1.4 million versus 1.3 million.

Among all prime mortgage foreclosures, 74 percent occurred with 30-year, fixed-rate loans. Hybrids and adjustable-rate mortgages accounted for less than 12 percent of prime foreclosures. In contrast, hybrid loans comprised 36 percent of all subprime foreclosures during this period (with 2/28 and 3/27 loans accounting for most of these). Yet fixed-rate loans posted almost the same rate of foreclosure, at 31 percent, with adjustable-rate loan foreclosures close behind, at 26 percent.

Figure 5.5 Cumulative Foreclosures through September 2007 on Subprime Mortgages Originated January 1999 through July 2007

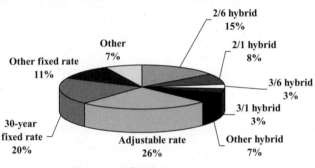

Total number = 1.3 million

2/6 hybrid
15%

Other
7%

2/1 hybrid
8%

Other fixed rate
11%

3/6 hybrid
3%

3/1 hybrid
3%

30-year
fixed rate
20%

Adjustable rate
26%

Other hybrid
7%

SOURCES: LoanPerformance, Milken Institute.

Clearly, differences exist among the types of products most closely associated with foreclosures among prime and subprime borrowers. It is important to note, however, that more than 800,000 homes financed by subprime mortgages *other than* hybrid loans had gone into foreclosure by the end of September 2007, according to data from LoanPerformance. Foreclosures are obviously a problem throughout the subprime market, even without taking into account the effects of hybrid loans and their interest rate resets.

Without home price increases, hybrid loans surely exacerbate the foreclosure problem when interest rates reset upward, but they are not the basic cause of it. Indeed, Table 5.1 shows that of all the 2/28 and 3/27 subprime loans in foreclosure as of July 2007, approximately 57 percent and 83 percent, respectively, had not yet seen their interest rates reset to higher levels.

Table 5.1 Selected Subprime Hybrid Loans in Foreclosure (July 2007)

Product type	Age of Loans (Percent)					Total
	< 1 year	< 2 years	< 3 years	< 5 years	> = 5 years	
2/28 hybrid	13.2	44.2	27.5	12.0	3.1	100
3/27 hybrid	7.1	46.1	29.9	12.9	3.9	100

SOURCES: LoanPerformance, Milken Institute.

In the first part of this decade, foreclosures were mainly a problem of the prime mortgage market, given its dominance. Today they are more heavily concentrated in the subprime mortgage market, given its growth, but the pain has also spread to the Alt-A and prime mortgage markets. So far, in response to the worsening problems associated with subprime loans, lenders have dramatically scaled back their willingness to offer such products, particularly those with reset features. However, the majority of subprime borrowers have benefited enormously from product diversity that offered access to credit and homeownership.

Some observers maintain that origination practices are quite different for prime and subprime mortgage loans. But such a view is mistaken. There has been no shortage of stories about mortgages with danger-ously high loan-to-value ratios and low- or no-documentation loans to subprime borrowers ending up in default. Low- or no-documentation (stated income) loans may be appropriate for some borrowers, such as those receiving significant portions of their income that may not be reflected in past pay stubs or immigrants who frequently rely on relatives and other financial resources not reflected in any standard documenta-tion. The media often gives the impression that these types of mortgage loans go only to subprime borrowers. However, Figures 5.6 and 5.7

Figure 5.6 Mortgage Originations: Loan-to-Value (LTV) Ratio (2006)

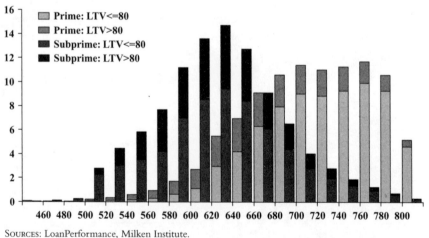

Sources: LoanPerformance, Milken Institute.

Figure 5.7   Mortgage Originations: Documentation (2006)

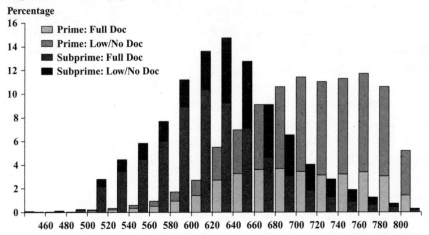

SOURCES: LoanPerformance, Milken Institute.

show that loans with these characteristics were granted to both prime and subprime borrowers. One cannot, therefore, conclude that these particular origination practices were used to target only subprime borrowers. Prime borrowers appeared to find these types of loans desirable as well. For more detailed information on various loan types, products, and characteristics associated with different FICO scores, see Appendix Tables A.39 through A.44.

The bottom line? Product innovation is beneficial, and attempts to curtail such innovation in the mortgage market could mean little or no access to credit for borrowers who would not otherwise qualify for loans, even if those borrowers are in a position to repay. Government actions that are too sweeping and severe could limit the availability of mortgage products, thereby denying borrowers a wider menu of choices for finding the product that best suits their needs.

We must therefore be careful in reacting to the subprime mortgage market turmoil with measures that would curtail credit for those with limited access to traditional mortgage products. A wider range of products can accommodate a wider range of borrowers, better matching risk-and-return combinations.

Part of what went wrong in the mortgage origination process can be attributed to the simple fact that new products create learning curves for both lenders and borrowers. To the extent that problems arise for lenders, they will make adjustments in the products they offer. Borrowers, too, must educate themselves or obtain appropriate assistance to learn which products are most suitable for their current and expected future financial status. The process by which lenders and borrowers decide on specific mortgage products is imperfect and can create difficulties for both parties, ultimately resulting in renegotiations of mortgage terms and even the curtailment or discontinuation of some products, as we have seen amid the current turmoil. Moreover, regulatory authorities should always be vigilant against fraudulent activity in mortgage markets, especially during periods of rapid credit expansion.

More generally, it is clear that origination practices did not always provide adequate information to potential borrowers that would enable them to make informed decisions, especially regarding new products being offered by innovative financial firms. Many borrowers simply did not understand the terms of their loans.

Figure 5.8 indicates that consumers often receive insufficient information—or information that is too complex—regarding home mortgage loans. In addition to documenting this situation, the Federal Trade Commission demonstrates that information can be provided in a modified form so that a significantly higher percentage of individuals can correctly understand the terms of their home mortgage loans.

These findings suggest that instead of trying to limit the products financial institutions can offer, it makes more sense to concentrate efforts on better informing potential customers about the available options and about the specific terms of their loans. On November 12, 2008, the U.S. Department of Housing and Urban Development (HUD) began to require mortgage lenders and brokers to provide borrowers with an easy-to-read standard good faith estimate (GFE) that will clearly answer the key questions they have when applying for a mortgage, including the following: What is the term of the loan? Is the interest rate fixed or can it change? Is there a prepayment penalty should the borrower choose to refinance at a later date? Is there a balloon payment? and What are total closing costs? The new standardized GFE will be required beginning January 1, 2010. This change updates the requirements of the Real Estate Settlement Procedures Act (RESPA), a 1974 law that sets federal rules for home purchase transactions.

Figure 5.8 There Are Better Ways to Disclose Information about Home Mortgage Loans

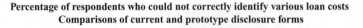

**Percentage of respondents who could not correctly identify various loan costs
Comparisons of current and prototype disclosure forms**

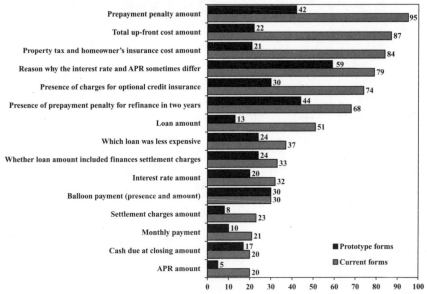

SOURCE: Federal Trade Commission, June 2007.

No matter how much information is disclosed, however, there undoubtedly will always be consumers who do not understand the products they choose. But this does not mean that products should be banned if they cannot be understood by *everyone* in the marketplace.

. . . with Securitization and Rating Agencies?

The broad industry shift from an originate-to-hold model (in which a lender initiates and then keeps loans in its own portfolio) to an originate-to-distribute model relies on the ability to sell mortgage-backed securities (MBS) to investors. Rating agencies play a crucial role in providing information about the quality of such securities—but in the wake of the mortgage market meltdown, their performance has been called into question.

Table 5.2 shows that as of November 5, 2008, AAA-rated securities accounted for 29 to 45 percent of all rated fixed-income securities that

Table 5.2 Distribution of Fixed-Income Securities Rated by S&P, Moody's, and Fitch*

S&P			Moody's			Fitch		
AAA	16,907	45%	Aaa	15,289	42%	AAA	8,273	29%
AA+	240	1%	Aa1	437	1%	AA+	694	2%
AA	2,098	6%	Aa2	3,865	11%	AA	2,319	8%
AA–	3,414	9%	Aa3	3,434	9%	AA–	3,188	11%
A+	2,623	7%	A1	1,520	4%	A+	3,594	13%
A	2,602	7%	A2	2,557	7%	A	3,718	13%
A–	2,027	5%	A3	1,456	4%	A–	939	3%
BBB+	903	2%	Baa1	1801	5%	BBB+	1485	5%
BBB	1,371	4%	Baa2	1,688	5%	BBB	1,626	6%
BBB–	1,359	4%	Baa3	728	2%	BBB–	431	2%
All Investment Grades	**33,544**	**90%**	**All Investment Grades**	**32,775**	**89%**	**All Investment Grades**	**26,267**	**92%**
BB+	238	1%	Ba1	183	0%	BB+	254	1%
BB	313	1%	Ba2	220	1%	BB	534	2%
BB–	331	1%	Ba3	337	1%	BB–	143	1%
B+	339	1%	B1	277	1%	B+	617	2%
B	330	1%	B2	566	2%	B	76	0%
B–	1,189	3%	B3	1,039	3%	B–	315	1%

CCC+	293	1%	Caa1	909	2%	CCC+	78	<1%
CCC	214	1%	Caa2	186	1%	CCC	94	<1%
CCC−	104	<1%	Caa3	89	0%	CCC−	24	<1%
CC	36	<1%	Ca	120	0%	CC+	21	<1%
C	11	<1%	C	36	0%	CC	19	<1%
D	303	1%				CC−	–	–
Total	**37,245**		**Total**	**36,737**		**Total**	**28,479**	

SOURCES: Bloomberg, Milken Institute.

*These securities were U.S. dollar-denominated fixed-income securities issued in the United States between January 1, 2000, and September 30, 2008, that are still outstanding and rated as of November 5, 2008.

were issued between January 1, 2000, and September 30, 2008, and are still outstanding. Of all securities that were rated, Standard & Poor's (S&P) gave AAA ratings most frequently, whereas Fitch Ratings was the least generous with top ratings. All three credit rating agencies (the third major player being Moody's) have been designated as nationally recognized statistical rating organizations (NRSRO) by the Securities and Exchange Commission (SEC).

Investors have long assumed that a security with a AAA rating is of the highest credit quality (therefore it usually offers a relatively low yield). Yet the only direction such a security can go is down, given its top rating. Conversely, lower-rated securities benefit from higher yields and the possibility of an increase in value as well. It is interesting to note, as the table shows, that around 90 percent or more of the securities were rated investment grade by the three agencies. To the extent that investors rely on such ratings as a substitute for their own research or due diligence, they do so at their own risk.

Focusing more narrowly on the ratings of mortgage-backed securities from 2005 to 2007, 56 percent of these securities that were rated as investment grade were eventually downgraded to below investment grade, as Table 5.3 shows. Even among the securities rated AAA, roughly one in six were downgraded within three years. (One might note that it is not clear that ratings across different industries are as comparable as those within the industries.)

Table 5.3   56 Percent of MBS Issued from 2005 to 2007 Were Eventually Downgraded

S&P	Total	Downgraded	Downgraded as a Percentage of Total
AAA	1,032	156	15.1%
AA(+/−)	3,495	1,330	38.1%
A(+/−)	2,983	1,886	63.2%
BBB(+/−)	2,954	2,248	76.1%
BB(+/−)	789	683	86.6%
B(+/−)	8	7	87.5%
Total	**11,261**	**6,310**	**56.0%**

SOURCES: Inside Mortgage Finance, Milken Institute.
NOTE: A bond is considered investment grade if its credit rating is BBB− or higher by S&P.

Figure 5.9 When Is a AAA Not a AAA? Multilayered Mortgage Products Create New and Higher Ratings

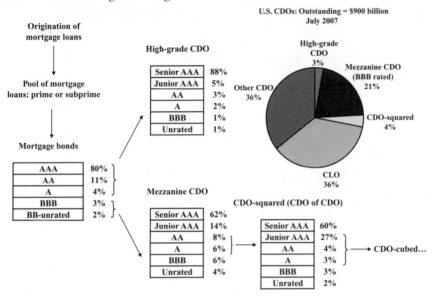

SOURCES: International Monetary Fund, Milken Institute.

NOTE: The equity tranche absorbs approximately the first 3 percent of credit losses in a portfolio. Losses then affect the mezzanine tranches; the first of these commonly covers the next 3 percent of losses up to 6 percent. Additional tranches can also be created to cover losses up to 12 percent, beyond which the losses begin to hit senior, AAA-rated tranches. Both first and second mortgages can be securitized in a similar fashion.

The rating process for subprime mortgage bonds was marked by a fundamental conflict: Agencies received fees from the very issuers who requested the ratings—and almost everything wound up as AAA. Securities were "sliced and diced" precisely to obtain these high ratings, as shown in Figure 5.9, and bank regulatory authorities assign favorable capital treatment to bonds rated AAA. As it turned out, this designation in all too many cases simply implied that the bonds were the best of the worst. Not surprisingly, as Figure 5.10 shows, rating agencies were eventually forced to downgrade many asset-backed securities, both AAA and those with lower ratings, as the crisis unfolded. Of course, AAA securities can only move down the rating scale as time passes, which raises the question of why an investor would ever purchase such a security given the performance of rating agencies over time and knowing that lower-rated securities may possess an upside gain.

Figure 5.10 Downgrades in the Asset-Backed Securities Markets

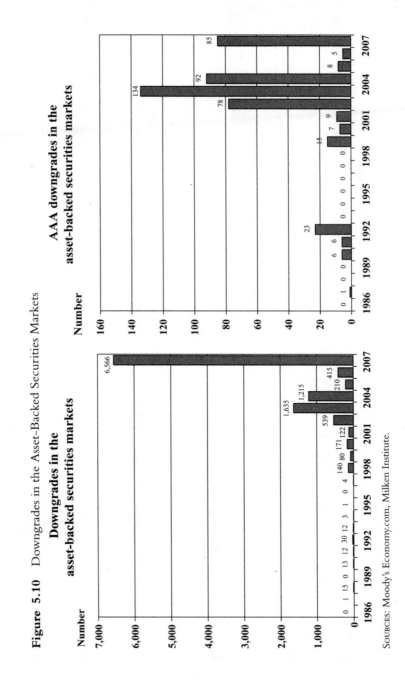

SOURCES: Moody's Economy.com, Milken Institute.

Figure 5.11   Subprime Mortgage-Backed Securities Downgrades
(2005–2007 Issuance)

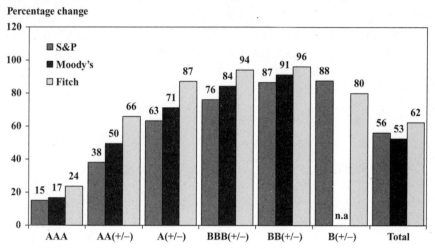

SOURCES: Inside Mortgage Finance, Milken Institute.

Figure 5.11 shows that the deterioration of subprime mortgage-backed securities was especially severe, with more than half of all securities issued between 2005 and 2007 eventually downgraded by the three major rating agencies. It should have been obvious to every investor in subprime MBS that ratings are no substitute for careful research or due diligence before purchases. In the height of the housing boom, there was little appreciation for the risk inherent in CDOs backed by mortgages with loan-to-value ratios exceeding 90 percent but without documentation of the borrower's income. (Mortgage loans based on the borrower's "stated income," with little or no documentation to verify that figure, have been dubbed "liar loans.") Figure 5.12 shows the extent to which the growth in MBS has contributed to the rise of structured finance collateral in collateralized debt obligations.

It is interesting to compare individual companies' S&P credit ratings and the corresponding credit default swap (CDS) spread.[3] These items are listed in Table 5.4 for those companies in the S&P 500 for which both types of information are available. It is apparent that the ratings and the CDS spreads do not track one another very closely; the high, low, and average CDS spreads do not consistently match the ratings of S&P.

For example, a company with a rating of A+ has a spread of 2,999 basis points, whereas another company with a rating of BB+ has a spread of 795 basis points. Companies with the same ratings, moreover, have vastly different spreads. In particular, two companies are rated A+ but the difference in CDS spreads is 2,987 basis points. It is reported that a CDS spread of 600 basis points implies a debt rating of B1, 13 notches below AAA.[4] In summary, ratings cannot substitute for due diligence on the part of investors.

...with Leverage and Accounting Practices?

With respect to capital, the current housing crisis has reinforced two things. First, financial institutions need to have enough capital to weather a downturn, and second, in times like these, it is critical that they have enough capital to continue delivering liquidity to the market.

—Testimony of Daniel H. Mudd, President and CEO, Fannie Mae U.S. Senate Committee on Banking, Housing, and Urban Affairs Hearing on "Reforming the Regulation of the Government Sponsored Enterprises" Washington, D.C. February 7, 2008

One fundamental truth governs all financial institutions: The greater the leverage, the smaller the decline in asset values that can be absorbed before insolvency sets in. This is why regulatory authorities overseeing financial institutions set minimum capital requirements, whether risk-based or simple leverage-based standards.

The capital of a financial institution is analogous to the deductible on a casualty insurance policy. The first hit up to a predetermined amount in the event is borne by the individual (or, in this case, the firm). The greater the deductible (or capital), the larger the share of any losses that must be borne by the insured (or by equity owners of a firm). This type of arrangement is meant to give individuals (or firms) an incentive not to engage in excessively risky activities when protection against losses are provided by casualty insurance (deposit insurance or, more generally, government bailouts).

Figure 5.13 shows the leverage ratios for different types of financial institutions,

Figure 5.12 The Growth in Mortgage-Backed Securities Has Contributed to the Rise of Structured Finance Collateral in Collateralized Debt Obligations (Quarterly CDO Issuance, 2005–Q3 2008)

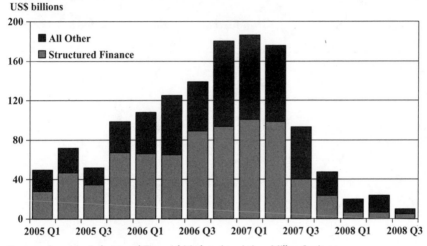

SOURCES: Securities Industry and Financial Markets Association, Milken Institute.

as measured by total assets relative to common equity. It is clear that as of June 2008, depository institutions were far less leveraged than other types of financial firms. The leverage ratio of Freddie Mac is obviously extraordinary as compared to other firms (even Fannie Mae). In this particular case, there were 68 dollars in assets for each dollar in equity, so a decline of as little as 1.5 percent in asset value would render Freddie Mac insolvent. Letting regulated institutions grow too big with inadequate capital cushions is a policy designed to produce disaster.

Figure 5.14 provides more information on the leverage ratios employed by various financial firms in selected years. It is obvious that the leverage ratios vary widely, but they were far lower for commercial and savings banks than for investment banking companies and the two government-sponsored enterprises (GSEs) in June 2008. The most highly leveraged of these institutions have failed, been put into conservatorship, or been acquired. Two of the institutions, Goldman Sachs and Morgan Stanley, are being transformed into financial holding companies and therefore will have to undergo a substantial deleveraging process.

Furthermore, the two big mortgage giants, Fannie Mae and Freddie Mac, were subject to a minimum statutory capital requirement equal to

Table 5.4   Selected S&P 500 Companies' Credit Ratings by S&P and
Associated CDS Spreads as of October 17, 2008

			CDS Spreads (Basis Points)		
	S&P's Ratings	Number of Companies	Highest	Lowest	Average
Investment grade	AAA	3	56	15	41
	AA+	1	95	95	95
	AA	5	86	49	74
	AA−	9	265	54	118
	A+	17	2,999	12	346
	A	36	1,040	38	151
	A−	34	2,557	51	427
	BBB+	43	1,114	38	222
	BBB	41	1,210	61	271
	BBB−	17	1,235	89	359
Speculative grade	BB+	12	795	130	419
	BB	14	938	168	522
	BB−	8	1,352	337	713
	B+	4	3,925	418	1,612
	B	3	2,686	894	1,523
	B−	2	4,718	3,701	4,209

SOURCES: S&P, Bloomberg, Datastream, Milken Institute.
NOTE: Credit ratings of S&P 500 companies and the associated CDS spreads for those firms for which
both ratings and CDS spreads are available.

the sum of 2.5 percent of their on-balance sheet assets plus .45 percent
of their outstanding off-balance sheet guarantees. This low requirement
obviously allowed for both institutions to leverage their capital substantially through both the acquisition of on-balance-sheet assets and
off-balance-sheet guarantees.

The advantage of leverage is that it enables institutions to achieve
higher rates of return on equity more easily. Stock buyback purchases
clearly help to accomplish this goal. But the risk of insolvency is simply
being shifted to debt holders when this occurs. During times when asset
values are declining, it may be difficult to roll over debt and raise capital,
which points out the serious weakness of a business model based on high
leverage.

Figure 5.13 Leverage Ratios of Different Types of Financial Firms (June 2008)

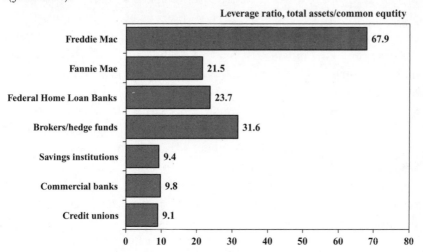

Leverage ratio, total assets/common equity

SOURCES: Federal Deposit Insurance Corporation, Office of Federal Housing Enterprise Oversight, National Credit Union Administration, Bloomberg, Google Finance, Milken Institute.

Figure 5.14 Selected Financial Institutions' Leverage Ratios (Selected Years)

Leverage ratio, total assets/total shareholder equity

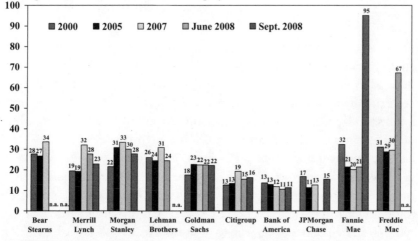

SOURCES: Bloomberg, Milken Institute.
NOTE: Freddie Mac's total shareholder equity as of September 2008 is −$13,795 million.

How could $1.2 trillion in subprime mortgages outstanding cause such a large global financial disaster? Leverage is certainly a part of the problem. If banks maintain a leverage ratio of 10:1, they would allocate only $120 billion of capital to support $1.2 trillion. With such a small amount of capital, a 10 percent decline in the $1.2 trillion underlying assets could wipe out all of the banks' capital. Of course, some of the institutions were more highly leveraged than 10:1, and in some areas, home price have fallen much more than 10 percent. (If the ratio were 30:1, as some institutions had on their balance sheets prior to the crisis, then the supporting capital for $1.2 trillion would be only $40 billion.) These situations can force some institutions into insolvency if capital cannot be raised. In mortgage-backed securities, the equity tranche was designed to absorb the first hit from declines in the underlying assets; the cushion was typically between 2 to 15 percent, so those tranches were the first to be hit when home prices fell and in some cases, they have been wiped out. In addition, the continuing decline of home prices, the widely dispersed nature of mortgage-backed securities, and the complexity of resecuritization (for example, CDOs became CDOs-squared and even CDOs-cubed) led to increased uncertainty in the marketplace about exactly how much and where the losses were. The increased uncertainty, in turn, led to heightened demand for a limited supply of liquid assets, exacerbating the liquidity freeze.

It is useful to compare the leverage ratios of different firms to their credit ratings. Figure 5.15 provides such a comparison for eight institutions at three different points in time: 2000, 2005, and 2007. As may be seen, there is much more variation in leverage ratios than in credit ratings. Indeed, the leverage ratio ranges from a low of 11.2 to a high of 33.5, whereas the ratings range from a high of AA+ to a low of A (all investment-grade ratings). Furthermore, a simple regression between the leverage ratios and ratings over the period 2000 to September 2008 indicates that the leverage ratio would have to increase by 16.5 before the credit rating would decline one level. Credit ratings based on this type of analysis do not appear to be sensitive to substantial swings in leverage ratios.

Figure 5.16 shows the market's assessment of selected financial institutions at several points in time from 2000 to 2008. It is apparent that

Figure 5.15 Increased Leverage Leads to Slight Decrease in Issuer Rating

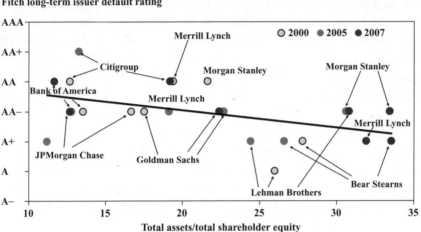

SOURCES: Bloomberg, Milken Institute.

this assessment not only changed but also had sharply deteriorated by September 2008, at which time the market capitalization was greater than the accounting capitalization for only some of the institutions (Goldman Sachs, Citigroup, Bank of America, and JPMorgan Chase).

Figure 5.16 Selected Financial Institutions' Market-to-Book Ratios (Selected Years)

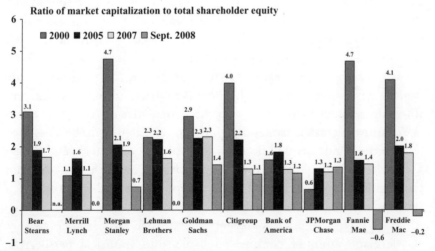

SOURCES: Bloomberg, Milken Institute.

In view of the high leverage ratios of the five biggest investment banks (Goldman Sachs, Morgan Stanley, Merrill Lynch, Lehman Brothers, and Bear Stearns) and what has recently happened to them, it is instructive to consider an action taken by the SEC in April 2004. At that time, the SEC voted unanimously in an open meeting to allow the five big U.S. brokerages to be designated as "consolidated supervised entities" (CSEs). The brokerages with CSE status were able to use in-house, risk-measuring computer models in line with the 1988 Basel Capital Accord (Basel I) to determine how much capital they needed to cushion against unexpected losses. It was reported at the time that under Basel I standards, some institutions could soon be cutting their capital reserves by as much as 50 percent. But the SEC's CSE rule added a $5-billion floor to the Basel I model, reportedly reducing the likely level of reductions to 20 to 30 percent.

SEC Commissioner Paul Atkins predicted that monitoring the sophisticated models used by the brokerages under the CSE rules—and stepping in when capital falls too low—would "present a real management challenge" for the commission. Because the new CSE rules applied to the largest brokerages without bank affiliates, SEC Commissioner Harvey Goldschmid noted, "If anything goes wrong, it's going to be an awfully big mess."[5]

More than four years later, on September 26, 2008, in the midst of the financial crisis, SEC Chairman Christopher Cox announced that the CSE program was ending. He also stated that "...a massive hole remains: the approximately $60 trillion credit default swap market, which is regulated by no agency of government."[6]

It has always been clear that firms that grow too big, with too little capital, are disasters waiting to happen. Regulated firms are no different from unregulated firms, except to the extent that market participants fail to impose greater market discipline on regulated firms because they assume the regulators will do so in their place—or, worse yet, because they believe that regulators will grant forbearance or otherwise bail out the regulated firms with the assistance of the federal government if necessary.

It is useful to put the recent capital–asset ratio, or, conversely, the leverage ratio, of commercial banks into historical perspective. Figures 5.17 and 5.18 show the dramatic decline in the capital–asset

Figure 5.17 Capital–Asset Ratio for Commercial Banks Shows Long-Term Decline (1896–Q2 2008)

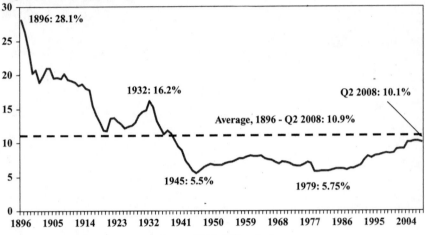

SOURCES: *Historical Statistics of the United States,* FDIC, Milken Institute.

Figure 5.18 Leverage Ratio for Commercial Banks Shows Long-Term Increase (1896–Q2 2008)

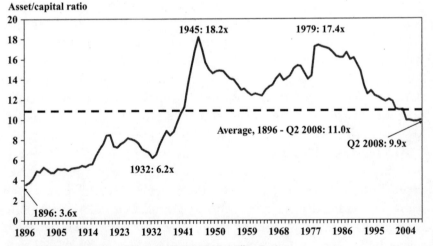

SOURCES: *Historical Statistics of the United States,* FDIC, Milken Institute.
NOTE: The leverage ratio is the reciprocal of the capital–asset ratio.

Figure 5.19   Selected Balance Sheet Items for All Commercial Banks
(Quarterly, 1994–Q2 2008)

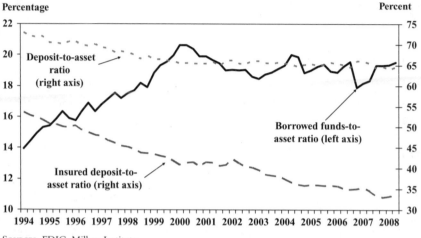

Sources: FDIC, Milken Institute.

ratio and the long-term increase in the leverage of commercial banks,
respectively. Indeed, each dollar of capital supported $3.56 of assets in
1896, whereas the same dollar supported $9.89 of assets in 2007. The
historical average of the capital–asset ratio over this long period is 10.9
percent, and Figure 5.16 shows that in every year since 1939, the capital-
asset ratio exceeded this average. Furthermore, the leverage ratio in 2007
is roughly 60 percent higher than its value during the Great Depression.
The sharp decline in the capital–asset ratio after the Great Depression indicates that Federal Deposit Insurance replaced a substantial portion of capital as depositors' major source of protection against banking
losses.

The leverage issue for financial firms is compounded by the fact
that they also rely on borrowings to fund their assets. In particular,
Figure 5.19 shows selected items from the balance sheet of all commercial
banks. It indicates that banks had increasingly substituted borrowed funds
for deposits, especially over the period from 1994 to 2000. In 1994,
borrowed funds were 14 percent of total assets, but they had increased
to 20 percent in the second quarter of 2008. In contrast, the deposit-
to-asset ratio declined to 64 percent in the second quarter of 2008 from
73 percent in 1994. Most strikingly, the insured deposit–to-asset ratio

declined to 34 from 54 over the same period. This means that insured deposits only fund approximately one-third of total assets at banks. At the same time, banks are relying more heavily on borrowed funds. This means they must be able to roll over those funds to maintain the same total amount of assets, apart from any increases in equity. This puts banks in a more difficult position to the extent that asset values decline and those investors from whom they borrow funds become increasingly reluctant to lend funds. In such a situation, banks are required to raise additional capital or sell assets or a combination of the two.

More detailed information on leverage and borrowings for financial firms is provided in Table 5.5. Many of the firms included in the table not only are highly leveraged but rely heavily on short-term borrowings. When that is the case, firms are more susceptible to serious financial problems when their assets decline in value because they face not only a decline in equity but also increased difficulties in rolling over their short-term borrowings. At the same time, to the extent that they have relied on short-term borrowings to meet payrolls and other ongoing expenses rather than holding cash or other extremely liquid assets, the scramble to obtain cash only exacerbates problems.

The Emergency Economic Stabilization Act of 2008 restates the Securities and Exchange Commission's authority to suspend the application of Statement No. 157 of the Financial Accounting Standards Board (FASB) if the SEC determines that doing so is in the public interest and would protect investors. FASB Statement No. 157 (Fair Value Measurements, or FAS 157), issued in September 2006, and FASB Statement No. 159 (Fair Value Option for Financial Assets and Financial Liabilities, or FAS 159), issued in February 2007, were both effective as of 2008, with early adoption permitted in 2007. FAS 157 clarifies "fair value" and establishes a framework for developing fair value estimates for the fair value measurements that are already required or permitted under other standards. Fair value continues to be used for derivatives, trading securities, and available-for-sale securities. Changes in fair value go through earnings for the derivatives and trading securities. Changes in the fair value of available-for-sale securities are reported in other comprehensive income. Available-for-sale securities and held-to-maturity debt securities are written down to fair value through earnings if impairment is other than temporary and mortgage loans held for sale are reported at

Table 5.5 Dependency on Leverage and Short-Term Borrowings for Selected Financial Firms (November 13, 2008)

	Company	Total Assets (US$ Millions)	Total Equity (US$ Millions)	Total Market Capitalization (US$ Millions)	Leverage Ratio (Percent)	Deposits to Total Liabilities (Percent)	Long-Term Borrowing to Total Liabilities (Percent)	Short-Term Borrowing to Total Liabilities (Percent)
1	JPMorgan Chase	2,251,469	145,843	129,028	15	46	13	21
2	Wells Fargo	622,361	46,957	101,904	13	61	19	15
3	Bank of America	1,831,177	161,039	85,299	11	52	15	26
4	Citigroup	2,050,131	126,062	52,534	16	41	20	28
5	US Bancorp	247,055	21,675	44,163	11	62	18	17
6	Bank of New York Mellon	267,510	27,513	33,497	10	73	11	8
7	Goldman Sachs Group	1,081,773	49,220	29,778	22	3	17	44
8	American Express	127,218	12,519	23,256	10	10	50	12
9	PNC Financial Services Group	145,610	16,288	21,466	9	66	17	8
10	Merrilll Lynch	875,780	38,355	18,812	23	11	20	56
11	Schwab	52,760	4,063	18,541	13	45	2	5
12	State Street	285,564	13,064	17,032	22	55	2	37
13	BB&T	137,041	12,935	15,790	11	71	17	8
14	Morgan Stanley	987,403	35,765	12,680	28	4	18	43
15	Blackrock	21,697	13,056	12,581	2	0	11	2
16	Suntrust Banks	174,777	17,956	12,047	10	74	15	6
17	Capital One	154,803	25,612	11,765	6	77	6	12
18	Wachovia	764,378	52,986	11,172	14	59	26	10

19	Northern Trust	79,244	4,836	10,112	16	84	6	4
20	Hudson City Bancorp	51,775	4,786	8,866	11	37	31	32
21	M & T Bank	65,247	6,417	7,148	10	72	21	5
22	Blackstone	11,949	8,650	6,930	1	0	0	48
23	Regions Financial	144,292	19,705	6,670	7	72	11	14
24	People's United Financial	20,042	5,239	6,239	4	96	1	1
25	Fifth Third Bancorp	116,294	10,696	5,249	11	73	12	11
26	Keycorp	101,290	8,651	4,757	12	70	17	8
27	New York Community Bancorp	32,140	4,263	4,585	8	51	24	24
28	National City	143,691	15,838	4,540	9	75	19	4
29	Marshall & Ilsley	63,501	6,492	3,785	10	70	14	14
30	Ameriprise Financial	99,150	6,717	3,767	15	8	2	0
31	Zions Bancorporation	53,974	5,596	3,707	10	80	6	13
32	SLM	164,991	5,356	3,411	31	0	74	24
33	Comerica	65,153	5,100	3,291	13	66	26	6
34	Capitol Federal Financial	7,892	864	3,201	9	56	40	3
35	Fannie Mae	896,615	9,435	3,105	95	0	62	32

SOURCES: Bloomberg, November 14, 2008; Milken Institute.

171

the lower of cost or fair value. Loans held for investment are also subject to impairment but are written down based on the present value of discounted cash flows. FAS 159 allows banks to elect a fair value option when assets are recognized on the balance sheet and to report certain financial assets and liabilities at fair value with subsequent changes in fair value included in earnings. Existing eligible items could be fair-valued as early as January 2007 under FAS 159, if a bank adopted FAS 157.

Some have argued that fair value accounting is inappropriate during the current crisis because it leads to unreasonably depressed values for assets. More generally, its use tends to be procyclical, so that during economic downturns, asset values are marked down, worsening the situation for firms. Some experts maintain that fair value accounting should be suspended during crises and downturns, if not totally eliminated.

But eliminating this standard may allow deeply troubled firms to avoid disclosing the seriousness of their difficulties, thereby misleading creditors and investors. It is not clear, moreover, that such accounting leads to a worsening of the financial condition of individual firms. Instead, it is more likely that deterioration in the marketplace is simply depressing the asset value of firms and that fair value accounting simply reflects this fact. Market discipline depends heavily on the disclosure of timely and accurate information, and any accounting practices that prevent such disclosure enable firms to avoid the discipline of the marketplace. No one ultimately benefits if the suspension or elimination of fair value accounting results in such a situation. According to Lawrence Summers, "...nothing in the experience of the past year gives confidence in the judgment of those who believe that market prices substantially undervalue their assets."[7]

...with Fannie Mae and Freddie Mac?

The federal government has assumed an ever more important role in providing funding for the housing market over time. It does so through a variety of institutions, including Ginnie Mae, Fannie Mae, Freddie Mac, and the Federal Home Loan Banks. Figure 5.20 shows that these institutions increased their share of home mortgages outstanding, including those held in portfolio and those that have been securitized,

The Special Role of Fannie Mae and Freddie Mac

Let me be clear—both companies have prudent cushions above the OFHEO-directed capital requirements and have increased their reserves. We believe they can play an even more positive role in providing the stability and liquidity the markets need right now.

    James B. Lockhart, Director, Office of Federal Housing
    Enterprise Oversight
    March 19, 2008

We are a stockholder-owned corporation .... The U.S. government does not guarantee, directly or indirectly, our securities or other obligations.

    Federal National Mortgage Association
    Form 10-Q, p. 95
    Filed August 8, 2008

Fannie Mae and Freddie Mac are also working through this challenging period. They play an important role in our housing markets today and need to continue to play an important role in the future. Their regulator has made clear that they are adequately capitalized.

    Henry Paulson, U.S. Treasury Secretary
    Testimony on regulatory reform before the House Committee on
    Financial Services
    July 10, 2008

What's important are facts—and the facts are that Fannie and Freddie are in sound situation .... They have more than adequate capital. They're in good shape.

    Senator Christopher Dodd
    CNN's *Late Edition*
    July 13, 2008

(Continued)

Our proposal was not prompted by any sudden deterioration in conditions at Fannie Mae or Freddie Mac. OFHEO has reaffirmed that both GSEs remain adequately capitalized. .... Let me stress that there are no immediate plans to access either the proposed liquidity or the proposed capital backstop.

Henry Paulson, U.S. Treasury Secretary
Testimony on GSE Initiatives before the Senate Banking Committee
July 15, 2008

We have no plans to insert money into either of those two institutions . . . .

Henry Paulson, U.S. Treasury Secretary
NBC's *Meet the Press*
August 10, 2008

They [the Bush administration] should have wiped out the shareholders, nationalized the institutions with legislation that they are to be reconstituted—with necessary taxpayer support to make them financially viable as five or ten individual privately held units, and auctioned off.

Alan Greenspan
Interview with David Wessel
The Wall Street Journal
August 14, 2008

from zero in 1952 to more than 40 percent after 1990, with Fannie Mae and Freddie Mac being the biggest institutions. (For information on the characteristics of their mortgage loans, see Appendix Tables A.45 through A.49.)

Fannie Mae was established in 1938 as a response to the Great Depression. Freddie Mac was established many years later (in 1970) to further expand the secondary market for home mortgages. These two government-sponsored enterprises (GSEs) do not write individual loans; instead, they buy and sell mortgages in the secondary market, providing a flow of liquidity to the nation's lenders. Figure 5.21 shows that these

Figure 5.20 The Growing Role of Agencies and Government-Sponsored
Enterprises (GSEs) in Funding Home Mortgages (Selected Years)

Percentage, GSE share of home mortgages outstanding

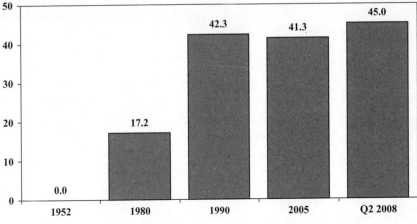

SOURCES: Federal Reserve, Milken Institute.
NOTE: Agencies and GSEs include Ginnie Mae, Fannie Mae, Freddie Mac, and the Federal Home
Loan Banks.

two institutions had more than $1.7 trillion in assets and had securitized
another $3.9 trillion in the second quarter of 2008. In comparison,
all the commercial banks and saving institutions in the country were
holding $3 trillion in residential real estate assets. Fannie and Freddie,
therefore, became the dominant players in the home mortgage market,
holding or guaranteeing more than $5.5 trillion in home mortgages.
Appendix Tables A.50 and A.51 compare the evolving roles of Fannie
Mae and Freddie Mac versus commercial banks and savings institutions
in the residential real estate market.

Both Fannie Mae and Freddie Mac grew substantially from 1990
through the second quarter of 2008. From $133 billion in total assets
and $288 billion in securitized mortgages outstanding in 1990, Fannie
Mae grew to hold $1 trillion in total assets and $1.3 trillion in outstanding mortgage backed securities by 2003 (see Figure 5.22). Issues
surrounding its accounting practices led to a decline in its total assets
by 2008 but not its securitized mortgages outstanding; by the third
quarter of 2008, Fannie's assets had declined to $897 billion while its

securitized mortgages outstanding had climbed to over $2.3 trillion. At the same time, Freddie Mac's total assets increased continuously, from $41 billion in 1990 to $804 billion in the third quarter of 2008, while its off-balance-sheet securitized home mortgages also grew steadily from $316 billion to $1.5 trillion.

Figure 5.21   The Importance of Fannie Mae and Freddie Mac vs. Commercial Banks and Savings Institutions in the Residential Real Estate Market (Q2 2008)

US$ billions

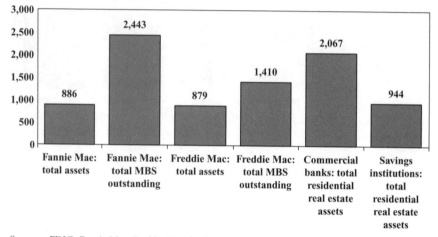

SOURCES: FDIC, Fannie Mae, Freddie Mac, Milken Institute.

Figure 5.22   Fannie Mae and Freddie Mac's Growth since 1990

US$ billions

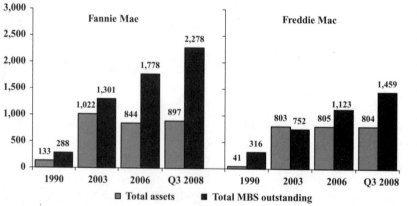

SOURCES: Fannie Mae, Freddie Mac, Milken Institute.

Figures 5.23 and 5.24 offer two alternative ways of looking at how these two institutions grew so large with so little capital over the three and a half years leading up to the summer of 2008. More specifically, they

Figure 5.23 Capital Ratios for Fannie Mae and Freddie Mac (2005–Q3 2008)

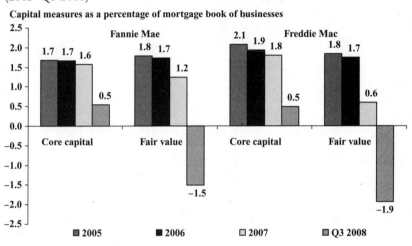

SOURCES: Fannie Mae, Freddie Mac, Milken Institute.

Figure 5.24 Fannie Mae and Freddie Mac Are Highly Leveraged (2005–Q3 2008)

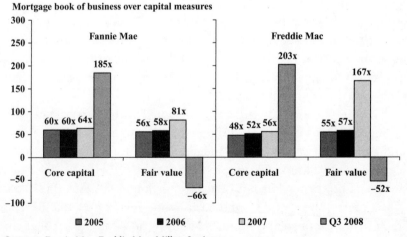

SOURCES: Fannie Mae, Freddie Mac, Milken Institute.

Figure 5.25 Reported Earnings of Fannie Mae and Freddie Mac
(Quarterly, 2006–Q3 2008)

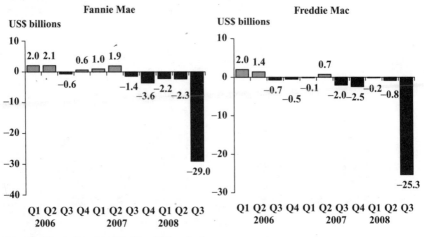

SOURCES: Fannie Mae, Freddie Mac, Milken Institute.

show the ratio of the mortgage book of business (that is, the mortgage portfolio, mortgage-backed securities held by third parties, and other guarantees) relative to both book and fair value measures of capital as well as the corresponding reciprocal ratios. Both of these institutions were enormously highly leveraged. Such thin capital ratios meant that any significant decline in the value of their assets would wipe out their capital. Unfortunately, both institutions did indeed suffer catastrophic losses when housing prices began to decline, as shown in Figure 5.25. On a fair value basis, Fannie Mae reported it was near insolvency in the second quarter of 2008, while Freddie Mac reported it was actually insolvent. One quarter later, however, both institutions were reporting insolvency on a fair value basis.

This dire situation can largely be explained by the fact that both institutions have had a mandate not simply to focus on profits but to provide funding for affordable housing. Indeed, in addition to creating the Office of Federal Housing Enterprise Oversight (OFHEO), the Federal Housing Enterprises Financial Safety and Soundness Act (FHEFSSA) of 1992 established HUD-imposed housing goals on Fannie Mae and Freddie Mac for financing affordable housing and housing in inner cities and other rural and underserved markets.[8]

Table 5.6 Housing Goals Set by HUD for Fannie Mae and Freddie Mac

	1997–2000 Housing Goals (%)	2001–2004 Housing Goals (%)	2005–2008 Housing Goals (%)			
			2005	2006	2007	2008
Low and moderate income	42	50	52	53	55	56
Underserved areas	24	31	37	38	38	39
Special affordable housing	14	20	22	23	25	27

SOURCES: Federal Register, Milken Institute.

In 1996, HUD increased the affordable housing goal from 40 percent to 42 percent of their financing to go to borrowers with low and moderate incomes for each year from 1997 through 1999. This goal was increased to 50 percent for the years 2001 to 2004 and increased still further in subsequent years as shown in Table 5.6. There are also goals for underserved areas (i.e., low-income and/or high-minority census tracts and rural counties) and special affordable housing (i.e., very-low-income families and low-income families living in low-income areas).

Also, as shown in Figures 5.26 and 5.27, both institutions recently were holding relatively large amounts of securities backed by subprime and Alt-A mortgages. The subprime-backed securities alone accounted for 71 percent of the core capital of Fannie Mae and 116 percent of the core capital of Freddie Mac. Furthermore, Figure 5.28 shows that the interest-only conventional mortgages securitized by Freddie Mac increased from $25 billion in 2005 to $159 billion, or more than 500 percent, in 2007. But, more generally, the real problem that caused their downfall was that the two institutions were highly leveraged, as shown by Figure 5.24, particularly given the riskiness of the types of mortgage loans just discussed.

It is important to briefly discuss the capital requirements imposed on Fannie Mae and Freddie Mac to better understand the degree to which they were leveraged. Both companies were subject to two types of capital requirements: (1) a minimum level of capital equal to the sum of 2.5 percent of their on-balance-sheet assets plus 0.45 percent

Figure 5.26   Characteristics of Mortgage Loans and Mortgage-Related Securities in Freddie Mac's and Fannie Mae's Retained Portfolios (Selected Years)

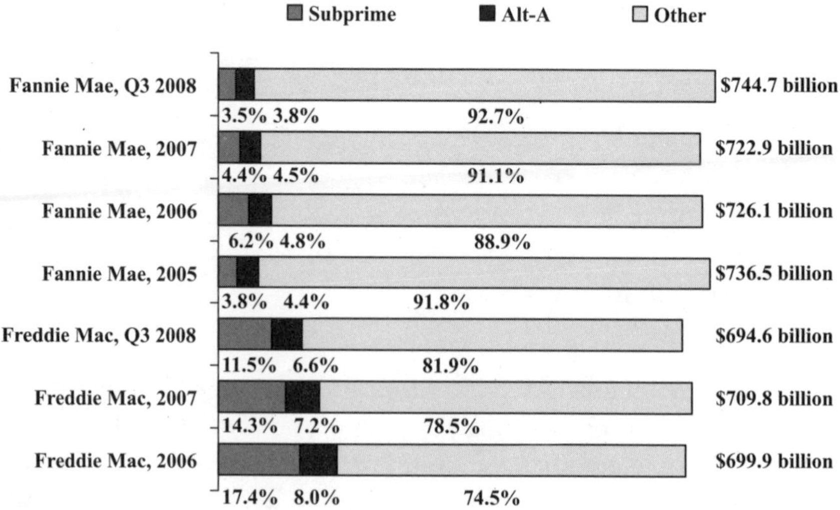

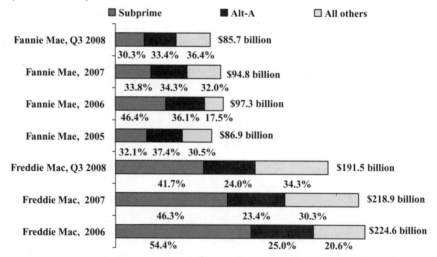

SOURCES: Fannie Mae, Freddie Mac, Milken Institute.

Figure 5.27   Characteristics of Mortgage Loans and Mortgage-Related Securities in Freddie Mac's and Fannie Mae's Retained Private–Label Portfolios (Selected Years)

SOURCES: Office of Federal Housing Enterprise Oversight, Fannie Mae, Freddie Mac, Milken Institute.

Figure 5.28 Freddie Mac's Guaranteed PCs and Structured Securities by Single-Family Conventional Mortgage Products (2005–2007)

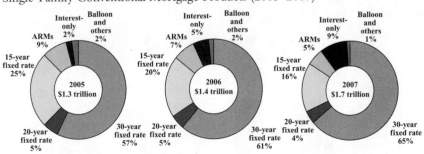

Sources: Freddie Mac, Milken Institute.

of their outstanding off-balance-sheet guarantees and (2) critical capital levels for the two items at 1.25 percent and 0.25 percent, respectively. These capital requirements were specified in FHEFSSA. However, in early 2004, OFHEO directed that each of the two companies maintain a capital level at least 30 percent above the statutory minimum. This additional capital requirement was reduced to 20 percent on March 19, 2008. Despite these additional capital requirements, the minimum level of capital required still allowed for substantial leverage.

A related issue that speaks to Fannie Mae and Freddie Mac's involvement in subprime mortgages is that in May and July of 2006, temporary investment caps on their mortgage portfolios were established. But on September 19, 2007, OFHEO provided Fannie Mae and Freddie Mac with more flexibility in managing their mortgage portfolios to comply with the investment caps of 2006. The reason for doing so was stated by OFHEO as follows:

> With the ongoing concerns about the subprime mortgage market, both Fannie Mae and Freddie Mac have announced commitments to purchase tens of billions of dollars of subprime mortgages over the next several years. The portfolio cap flexibility plus their ongoing ability to securitize mortgages, sell assets, and replace maturing assets, will enhance each Enterprise's ability to purchase or securitize, over the next six months up to $20 billion or more of subprime mortgages, refinanced mortgages for borrowers with lower credit scores, and affordable multi-family housing mortgages. These efforts should assist lenders in helping some subprime borrowers avoid foreclosure.[9]

Figure 5.29   Foreign Share of Purchases of Newly Issued GSE Debt Declines Abruptly in August 2008

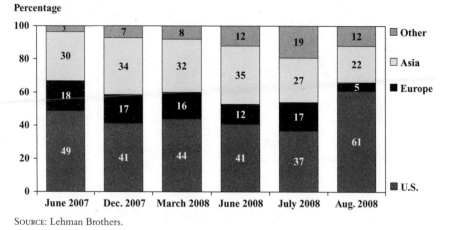

SOURCE: Lehman Brothers.

OFHEO finally removed the portfolio growth caps for both companies on March 1, 2008.

The serious stress in the U.S. financial sector has raised concerns that foreign investors might diversify away from many U.S. dollar-denominated financial assets. As Figure 5.29 shows, the foreign share of purchases of newly issued GSE debt did indeed decline abruptly, from 63 percent in July 2008 to 39 percent in August 2008. These types of actions by foreign investors have contributed to the federal government's sense of urgency regarding the need to stabilize the financial system. The government did reassure the creditors of Fannie Mae and Freddie Mac when the two companies were placed into conservatorship in early September 2008 and their solvency was guaranteed.

...with Tax Benefits for Homeownership?

The federal government has always promoted homeownership as a social good and, to that end, has devised tax incentives to encourage it. Owner-occupants of homes may deduct mortgage interest on their primary and secondary residences as itemized nonbusiness deductions. In general, the mortgage interest deduction is limited to interest on debt no greater than the owner's basis in the residence, and is also limited to no more than $1 million. Interest on up to $100,000 of other debt secured by a lien on a principal or second residence is also deductible, irrespective of the purpose of borrowing, provided the debt does not exceed the fair market value of the residence. Owner-occupants of homes may also deduct property taxes on both primary and secondary residences.

Furthermore, interest earned on state and local bonds used to finance homes purchased by first-time, low- to moderate-income buyers is tax exempt. The amount of state and local tax-exempt bonds that can be issued to finance these and other private activity is limited. The combined volume cap for private activity bonds, including mortgage housing bonds, rental housing bonds, student loan bonds, and industrial development bonds, was $62.50 per capita ($187.5 million minimum) per state in 2001 and $75 per capita ($225 million minimum) in 2002. The Community Renewal Tax Relief Act of 2000 accelerated the scheduled increase in the state volume cap and indexed the cap for inflation, beginning in 2003. States may issue mortgage credit certificates (MCCs) in lieu of mortgage revenue bonds. MCCs entitle home buyers to income tax credits for a specified percentage of interest on qualified mortgages. The total amount of MCCs issued by a state cannot exceed 25 percent of its annual ceiling for mortgage-revenue bonds.

These types of benefits to home buyers clearly contribute to increased demand for homes. To this extent, the existing tax code promotes homeownership. In the process, it contributes to the origination of mortgages, higher home prices, and increased home building.

An individual in the maximum income tax bracket who itemizes and takes out a mortgage at a 6 percent interest rate to purchase a home would effectively be paying roughly a 4 percent interest rate. This provides an incentive to many individuals to become homeowners.

As shown in Figure 5.30, the estimated tax savings due to mortgage interest deductions on owner-occupied homes was $85 billion in 2007 and is projected to steadily climb to $130 billion by 2013. But it is fair to question whether these tax benefits should be continued, even though they have existed for many years and did not cause the recent bubble in housing prices.

...with Regulation and Supervision?

Market events over the past year have reiterated some of the risks associated with the growing business of subprime lending.... Institutions considering or engaging in this type of lending should recognize the additional risks inherent in this activity and determine if these risks are acceptable and controllable, given the institution's staff, financial condition, size, and level of capital support.

—Richard Spillenkothen,
Director
Division of Banking
Supervision and
Regulation,
Federal Reserve
FRB: Supervisory Letter
SR 99-6 (GEN) on
subprime lending
Washington, D.C.
March 5, 1999

Financial institutions do not answer solely to the marketplace; they are heavily regulated and supervised by numerous federal and state authorities. Indeed, the current crisis cannot be chalked up to a lack of regulators. It is not even clear that the existing regulators need more powers. It is worth considering whether there are simply too many regulators with overlapping responsibilities—who did not adequately use the powers already granted to them to contain the emerging problems in the subprime mortgage market before they spread throughout the financial sector. In addition to regulatory authorities, there are at least 10 U.S. congressional committees that have some jurisdiction over the financial services sector.

There were undeniable signs that a housing price bubble was growing, fueled by the excessive credit being provided to consumers, especially to subprime borrowers. Table 5.7 provides ample evidence that the Federal Reserve (and presumably other regulatory authorities) were aware of the warning signals for a relatively long time before the bubble actually burst. Indeed, even if the top officials from these regulatory agencies did not appreciate or wish to act earlier on the information they had, their subordinates apparently fully understood and appreciated the growing magnitude of the problem. Going forward, much more effort should be devoted to preemptive actions that can prevent assets bubbles rather than to reactive actions designed to clean up the mess once the bubbles have burst.

As we try to understand what went wrong with regulation and supervision, it worth noting that after the FDIC seized IndyMac, the agency issued the following statement:

> Under the IndyMac program, eligible mortgages will be modified into sustainable mortgages permanently capped at the current Freddie Mac survey rate for conforming mortgages, which is currently about 6.5 percent. Modifications are designed to achieve sustainable payments at a 38 percent debt-to-income (DTI) ratio of principal, interest, taxes, and insurance. To reach this metric for affordable payments, modifications could adopt a combination of interest rate reductions, extended amortization, and principal forbearance.[10]

It is possible to construct alternative scenarios using the FDIC's debt-to-income ratio of 38 percent as a ceiling to assess whether mortgage payments are affordable and sustainable.[11] This is done based on assumptions regarding mortgage payments for a home purchased at the median price, with a 30-year conforming, fixed-rate loan with alternative loan-to-value (LTV) ratios. Figures 5.31 and 5.32 show the results of this exercise for the nation and for California, respectively, examining historical affordability trends for a household with the median income purchasing a home at the median price. These figures show that, given the increase in the median price of homes nationwide and in California, any mortgage payments with an LTV ratio of

The United States has experienced an unprecedented housing boom in recent years. As of 2005, we estimated that there were a record 89 cities with 'boom' real estate conditions, in which home prices, after inflation, had appreciated by at least 30 percent during the prior three years. . . . Banks have benefited from the boom through rapid loan growth and servicing fees associated with mortgage underwriting, equity liquidation, and new construction lending. . . . However, buyers are facing increasing budget pressure as home prices continue to escalate. . . . Weakening home sales volumes and rising inventories of unsold homes further attest to the slowdown in housing that has begun to emerge.

—Economic Conditions and Emerging Risks in Banking
A Report to the FDIC, Board of Directors
Federal Deposit Insurance Corporation
May 9, 2006

Figure 5.30 Estimated Tax Savings by Individuals Due to Mortgage Interest
Deduction on Owner-Occupied Homes

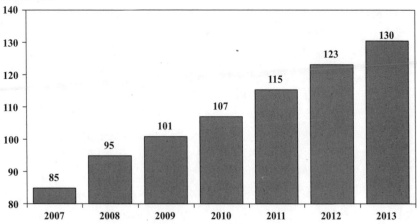

SOURCES: Office of Management and Budget, Milken Institute.

80 percent or higher would not have been affordable and sustainable after
2005, based on the FDIC's figure. The triggering year for this situation
would have occurred in 2001 in the case for California.

If indeed the 38 percent debt-to-income ratio is deemed by the
FDIC to be the dividing line between prudent and imprudent loans,
then there was ample opportunity for regulatory authorities to take
action against institutions making such loans that exceeded this cutoff,
especially in California.

Before concluding this section, it is important to discuss some of
the problems faced by FDIC-insured institutions in recent years. These
institutions, particularly commercial banks, were not only funding the
subprime mortgage loans on their own balance sheets but were also
providing both on- and off-balance-sheet funding to other financial
firms involved in subprime loans. In addition, they were directly involved
in securitizing such loans through special-purpose entities (SPEs). As a
result of these and other activities, many depository institutions became
overextended, with some failing or being acquired by stronger banks
when the housing price bubble burst.

Table 5.7 Major Events and Supervisory Responses Related to Real Estate and Nontraditional and Subprime Lending

Date	Events and Supervisory Responses
1990 and 1994	Poor real estate appraisal practices are identified as contributing to real estate lending problems at failed institutions in the late 1980s and early 1990s. Pursuant to the Financial Institutions Reform, Recovery and Enforcement Act of 1989, the Federal Reserve and other federal banking agencies (the agencies) adopt real estate appraisal regulations to establish appropriate standards for regulated institutions' real estate appraisal practices. In 1994, the agencies amend their appraisal regulations and issue the "Interagency Appraisal and Evaluation Guidelines" to further promote sound appraisal practices.
1993	In response to poor real estate lending practices in the late 1980s and early 1990s that led to thrift and bank failures, and the FDIC Improvement Act of 1991, the agencies adopt regulations and guidelines on real estate lending standards for commercial and residential lending. These guidelines impose supervisory loan-to-value (LTV) limits and capital limitations on high-LTV loans.
1998 through 2002	Five institutions close because of problems related to subprime lending, including poor underwriting, fraud, and valuation of securitization and residual interests. • July 1998: BestBank • September 1999: First National Bank of Keystone • November 1999: Pacific Thrift and Loan • July 2001: Superior Bank • February 2002: NextBank
1999	The agencies identify problems related to the risk management practices and valuation of securitization and residual interests at federally regulated subprime lenders. In December 1999, the agencies issue the "Interagency Guidance on Asset Securitization Activities," describing the proper valuation of residual interests and highlighting situations in which such interest should be assigned no value.

(Continued)

Table 5.7   (*Continued*)

Date	Events and Supervisory Responses
March 1999	Problems are observed at both regulated and nonregulated subprime lenders, resulting in the bankruptcy of several nonregulated lenders. In March 1999, the agencies issue the "Interagency Guidance on Subprime Lending" to address concerns with monoline subprime lending institutions.
October 1999	"Interagency Guidance on High Loan-to-Value (LTV) Residential Real Estate Lending" is issued to remind institutions that risks are higher in residential mortgages when the LTV ratio exceeds 90 percent and to encourage institutions to take this into account in their own risk management practices.
January 2001	"Expanded Guidance for Subprime Lending Programs" is issued in response to the increasing number of monoline subprime lending institutions, particularly those focused on credit card and residential mortgage lending. The guidance addresses a number of concerns related to the subprime lending business model and inappropriate risk management practices and underwriting standards.
2001	As a result of concerns with predatory lending in the subprime mortgage market, the Federal Reserve revises the rules implementing the Home Ownership and Equity Protection Act (HOEPA) to extend HOEPA's protections to higher-cost loans and to strengthen HOEPA's prohibitions and restrictions, including a requirement that lenders generally document and verify a consumer's ability to repay a high-cost mortgage loan.
2002	The Federal Reserve expands the data collection and disclosure rules under the Home Mortgage Disclosure Act (HMDA) to increase transparency in the subprime mortgage market. New data elements are added on loan pricing for certain higher-priced loans, which helps to facilitate the federal banking and thrift agencies' ability to identify potential problems in the subprime market. The Federal Reserve also expands the share of nondepository state-regulated mortgage companies that must report HMDA data, which has provided a more complete picture of the mortgage market, including the subprime area.

Table 5.7 (*Continued*)

Date	Events and Supervisory Responses
2003	The agencies observe weaknesses in regulated institutions' appraisal practices, and in October, they issue the "Interagency Guidance on Independent Appraisal and Evaluation Functions." The statement reinforces the importance of appraiser independence from the loan origination and credit decision process to ensure that valuations are fairly and appropriately determined.
2003 to 2006	The Federal Reserve issues three formal enforcement actions and three informal actions, which involve mortgage lending issues, including subprime mortgage lending. Formal enforcement actions include: • Citigroup Inc. and CitiFinancial Credit Company: cease-and-desist order, 5/27/04 • Doral Financial Corporation: cease-and-desist order, 3/16/06 • R&G Financial Corporation: cease-and-desist order, 3/16/06
March 2004	The Federal Reserve and the FDIC issue "Interagency Guidance on Unfair or Deceptive Acts or Practices by State-Chartered Banks." This guidance describes standards that the agencies will apply to determine when acts or practices by state-chartered banks are unfair or deceptive. Such practices are illegal under section five of the Federal Trade Commission Act.
2004 to 2005	The agencies observe a rapid growth of mortgage products that allow for the deferral of principal and sometimes interest (interest-only loans and payment option ARMs) that contain the potential for substantial payment shock when the loans begin to fully amortize. In 2004 and 2005, the Federal Reserve and the other agencies review the nontraditional mortgage lending activity and risk management practices at selected major regulated institutions. During this time, Federal Reserve staff meet with various industry and consumer groups to discuss the trends and practices in the nontraditional mortgage markets. In December 2005, the agencies issue the proposed "Interagency Guidance on Nontraditional Mortgage Products."

(*Continued*)

Table 5.7   (*Continued*)

Date	Events and Supervisory Responses
February 2005	The agencies, under the auspices of the Federal Financial Institutions Examination Council, issue "Interagency Guidance on the Detection, Investigation, and Deterrence of Mortgage Loan Fraud Involving Third Parties" to assist the banking industry in detecting, investigating, and deterring third-party mortgage fraud. The term *third-party* refers to the parties necessary to execute a residential mortgage other than a financial institution or a legitimate borrower (including mortgage brokers, real estate appraisers, and settlement agents).
2005	As a result of the 2003 interagency guidance on appraisal independence, many institutions start to review their appraisal procedures and ask for additional guidance on appropriate practices. In March the agencies issue a follow-up document, including questions and answers to promote sound appraisal and collateral valuation practices.
May 2005	In response to supervisory concerns that regulated institutions' risk management practices are not keeping pace with the rapid growth and changing risk profile of their home equity loan portfolios, the agencies issue the "Interagency Credit Risk Management Guidance for Home Equity Lending."
2005 to 2006	The Federal Reserve conducts supervisory reviews of mortgage lending, including subprime lending activity, at large banking institutions with significant mortgage programs. The focus of these reviews is an assessment of the adequacy of the institutions' credit risk management practices, including lending policies, underwriting standards, appraisal practices, portfolio limits and performance, economic capital, credit stress testing, management information systems, and controls over third-party originations.
October 2006	The agencies issue the "Interagency Guidance on Nontraditional Mortgage Product Risks," addressing the need for institutions to have appropriate risk management practices and underwriting standards, including an assessment of a borrower's ability to repay the loan at the fully indexed rate, assuming a fully amortizing repayment schedule, including any balances added through negative amortization. The guidance details recommended practices for lenders' consumer disclosures so that a borrower receives clear, balanced, and timely information.

Table 5.7 (*Continued*)

Date	Events and Supervisory Responses
October 2006	The agencies issue two additional documents related to the nontraditional mortgage guidance: (1) "Proposed Illustrations of Consumer Information for Nontraditional Mortgage Products" and (2) an addendum to the May 2005 "Interagency Credit Risk Management Guidance for Home Equity Lending."
March 2007	The agencies call for public comment on the "Proposed Statement on Subprime Mortgage Lending," which addresses risk management, underwriting standards, and consumer disclosure practices for a regulated institution's subprime mortgage lending activity.
April 2007	The agencies issue a formal document encouraging financial institutions to work with homeowners who are unable to make mortgage payments. In this document, the agencies stress that prudent workout arrangements that are consistent with safe and sound lending practices are generally in the long-term best interest of both the financial institution and the borrower and that institutions will not face regulatory penalties if they pursue reasonable workout arrangements with borrowers.
May 2007	The agencies issue final illustrations of consumer information intended to help institutions implement the consumer protection portion of the "Interagency Guidance on Nontraditional Mortgage Product Risks" that the agencies adopted October 4, 2006. The illustrations consist of (1) a narrative explanation of nontraditional mortgage products, (2) a chart comparing interest-only and payment option adjustable-rate mortgages (ARMs) to a traditional fixed-rate loan, and (3) a table that could be included with monthly statements for a payment option ARM showing the impact of various payment options on the loan balance.
June 2007	The agencies issue a final "Statement on Subprime Mortgage Lending" to address issues relating to certain ARM products that can cause payment shock. The statement describes the prudent safety and soundness and consumer protection standards that institutions should follow to ensure borrowers obtain loans they can afford to repay.

(*Continued*)

Table 5.7   (*Continued*)

Date	Events and Supervisory Responses
July 2007	Three federal agencies and two associations of state regulators announce that they will cooperate in an innovative pilot project to conduct targeted consumer-protection compliance reviews of selected nondepository lenders with significant subprime mortgage operations.
August 2007	The agencies issue proposed illustrations of consumer information for certain ARM products. The illustration consists of (1) an explanation of some key features and risks that the Subprime Statement identifies, including payment shock, and (2) a chart that shows the potential consequences of payment shock in a concrete, readily understandable manner.
September 2007	The agencies issue the "Statement on Loss-Mitigation Strategies for Servicers of Residential Mortgages" to encourage federally regulated financial institutions and state-supervised entities that service securitized residential mortgages to determine the full extent of their authority under pooling and servicing agreements to identify borrowers at risk of default and pursue appropriate loss mitigation strategies designed to preserve homeownership.
December 2007	The agencies propose and ask for public comment on changes to Regulation Z (Truth in Lending) to protect consumers from unfair or deceptive home mortgage lending and advertising practices.
July 2008	The Federal Reserve Board grants the Federal Reserve Bank of New York the authority to lend to Fannie Mae and Freddie Mac if necessary. In July, the Board approves a final rule for home mortgage loans to better protect consumers and facilitate responsible lending. The rule prohibits unfair, abusive, or deceptive home mortgage lending practices and restricts certain other mortgage practices. The final rule also establishes advertising standards and requires certain mortgage disclosures to be given to consumers earlier in the transaction.

Table 5.7 (*Continued*)

Date	Events and Supervisory Responses
September 2008	Fannie Mae and Freddie Mac are placed into conservatorship. The agencies issue joint release on Fannie Mae and Freddie Mac. In this release, the agencies state that they have been assessing the exposures of banks and thrifts to Fannie Mae and Freddie Mac and are prepared to work with institutions that hold common or preferred shares of the two GSEs to develop capital-restoration plans pursuant to the capital regulations and the prompt corrective action provisions of the Federal Deposit Insurance Corporation Improvement Act.
October 2008	The Federal Reserve Board approves final amendments to Regulation C that revise the rules for reporting price information on higher-priced mortgage loans. The changes are intended to improve the accuracy and usefulness of data reported under the Home Mortgage Disclosure Act.

SOURCES: Federal Reserve, Milken Institute.

The problems that grew in depository institutions are reflected in Figure 5.33, which shows the increase in noncurrent loans beginning in June 2006 and the acceleration that took place after September 2007. Delinquent loans climbed from $49 billion in June 2006 to $83 billion

Figure 5.31 Alternative Measures of the Affordability of Mortgage Debt Nationwide (Quarterly, Q2 1972–Q4 2007)

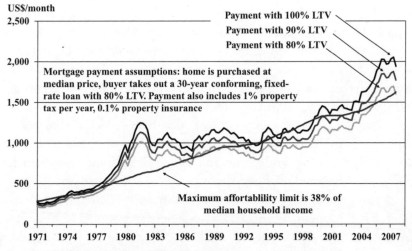

SOURCES: Moody's Economy.com, Milken Institute.

Figure 5.32 Alternative Measures of the Affordability of Mortgage Debt for California (Quarterly, Q2 1979–Q1 2008)

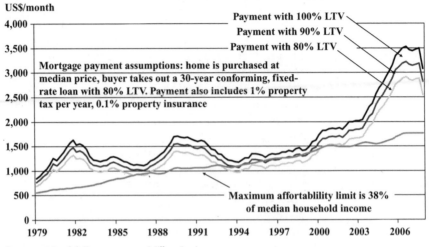

SOURCES: Moody's Economy.com, Milken Institute.

in September 2007 and then to $163 billion in June 2008. Also shown is the coverage ratio (i.e., the ratio of loan-loss reserve to noncurrent loans). Clearly, the value of troubled loans has been growing faster than the reserves set aside to cover losses. To maintain the same coverage ratio as in the mid-2000s, much larger loan-loss reserves would have been needed, thereby contributing to still further reductions in income and capital. The average coverage ratio over the period was 135 percent, so an additional $75 billion in loan-loss reserves would have been needed in June 2008 to restore the average coverage ratio. To get back to the same ratio that existed in March 2005, loan-loss reserves would have had to increase by $136 billion.

Table 5.8 shows the major factors that have recently impacted the earnings of FDIC-insured institutions. It is clear that deterioration in asset quality at these institutions and the resulting increase in loan-loss provisions have produced negative earnings over the past year.

During periods of severe financial distress, it is interesting to consider what happens to the CD rates offered by troubled depository institutions. During the savings and loan crisis of the 1980s, the shakiest institutions typically offered the highest rates on their deposits, thereby

Table 5.8 Major Factors Affecting FDIC-Insured Institutions' Earnings Contributions to Pretax Earnings Growth, as Compared to Previous Year, in US$ Billions

	Q1 2008 vs. Q1 2007	Q2 2008 vs. Q2 2007
Positive factor		
Increase in net interest income	8.3	8.2
Negative factors		
Decrease in noninterest income	1.7	7.4
Increase in loan-loss provision	27.9	38.8
Decrease in gains on securities sales	0.4	2.8
Increase in noninterest expense	3.2	6.6
Net effect of the above factors	**−24.9**	**−47.4**

SOURCES: *Quarterly Banking Profile*, FDIC; Milken Institute.

hoping to grow their way out of their problems. However, to pay the higher rates on deposits and still earn a profit, they had to invest any newly acquired funds in riskier assets. These institutions were effectively gambling for resurrection: offering higher rates in an attempt to obtain more funds. Depository institutions typically do not pay out more cash when they pay higher deposit rates but instead merely allow the increased

Figure 5.33 Reserve Coverage Ratio of All FDIC-Insured Institutions

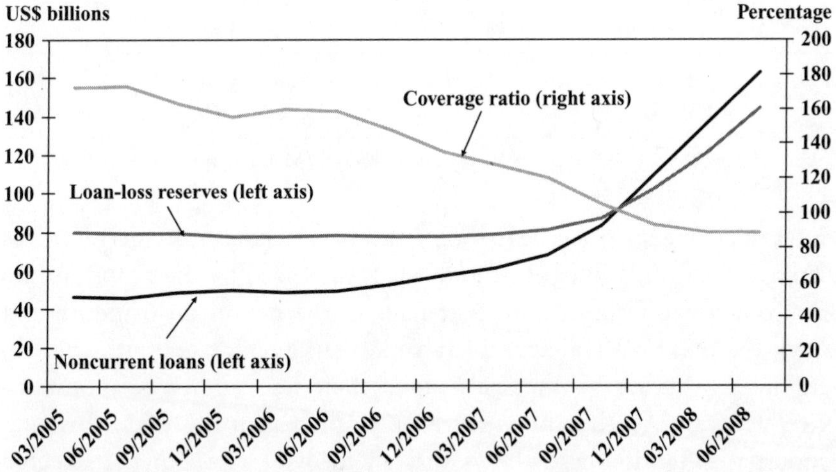

SOURCES: *Quarterly Banking Profile*, FDIC; Milken Institute.

Table 5.9   IndyMac Offers the Highest CD Rates in the Nation One Week
before Its Seizure by the FDIC on July 11, 2008

	Bank	6-Month CD Rate (July 5, 2008)		Bank	12-Month CD Rate (July 5, 2008)
1	IndyMac Bank	4.10	1	IndyMac Bank	4.40
2	Crestmark Bank	4.00	2	Wachovia	4.25
3	Wachovia	4.00	3	Crestmark Bank	4.20
4	Christian Community CU	4.00	4	Century Bank Direct	4.11
5	ISN Bank	3.82	5	State Bank of India	4.06
6	Century Bank Direct	3.76	6	Ascencia Bank	4.01
7	GMAC Bank	3.70	7	Washington Mutual	4.00
8	Ascencia Bank	3.66	8	UmbrellaBank	4.00
9	Corus Bank	3.62	9	Tennessee Commerce Bank	4.00
10	E-Loan	3.61	10	Digital Credit Union	4.00
	National average	**3.14**		**National average**	**n.a.**
	6-month LIBOR	**3.11**		**12-month LIBOR**	**3.29**

SOURCES: Bank Deals, Federal Reserve, Moody's Economy.com, Milken Institute.

interest payments to accrue in their customers' accounts. In this regard, as
Table 5.9 shows, right before IndyMac was seized by the FDIC in July
2008, it was offering the highest rates in the nation on 6-month and
12-month CDs. When a troubled bank offers a high rate on its deposits,
it forces healthier banks to also raise their rates to remain competitive. However, such actions serve only to weaken the entire banking
industry. The table also shows that all the CD rates for the selected
institutions are higher than the LIBOR rates. This is unusual because

Figure 5.34   Outstanding Federal Home Loan Bank Advances Held by
FDIC-Insured Institutions (1991–Q2 2008)

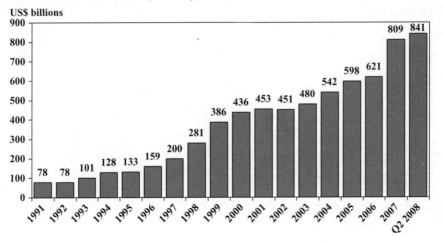

SOURCES: *Quarterly Banking Profile,* FDIC; Milken Institute.

the LIBOR rates are paid for wholesale funds, while CD rates are paid
for retail funds and are therefore typically lower to cover the significant costs of operating a retail branch network. Higher CD rates offered
by financial institutions may indicate that they are in need of capital
and should be a signal that merits closer examination by regulatory
agencies.

It is also interesting to note the growing importance of advances to
FDIC-insured institutions from 1991 to the second quarter of 2008, as
shown in Figures 5.34 and 5.35. The Federal Home Loan Banks are able
to issue securities at relatively low spreads over Treasury securities and
then lend funds to depository institutions. Their advances are heavily
collateralized and therefore analogous to the issuance of covered bonds
that are sold to the Federal Home Loan Banks. As the figures show, the
advances funded less than 2 percent of the assets at depository institutions
in 1991 but more than 6 percent by the second quarter of 2008. (To
date, the Federal Home Loan Banks have never lost any money due to
the failure of institutions to which they extended advances, even in cases
in which losses were imposed on the FDIC.)

Brokered deposits have also assumed greater importance to FDIC-
insured institutions from 1992 to the second quarter of 2008, as shown

Figure 5.35 Ratio of Outstanding Federal Home Loan Bank Advances to FDIC-Insured Institution Assets (1991–Q2 2008)

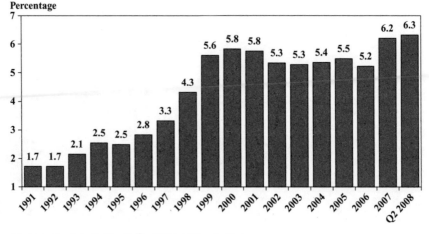

SOURCES: *Quarterly Banking Profile*, FDIC; Milken Institute.

in Figures 5.36 and 5.37. They grew from $58 billion in 1992 to $644 billion in the second quarter of 2008, and the percentage of total assets funded by them increased from 1.3 percent to nearly 5 percent. Brokered deposits are so named because a broker arranges for individuals who want to deposit more than the amount covered by FDIC

Figure 5.36 Outstanding Brokered Deposits (1992–June 2008)

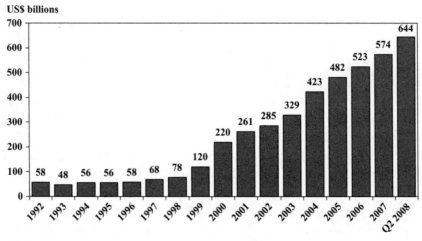

SOURCES: FDIC, Milken Institute.

Figure 5.37 Outstanding Brokered Deposits to FDIC-Insured Institution Assets (1992–June 2008)

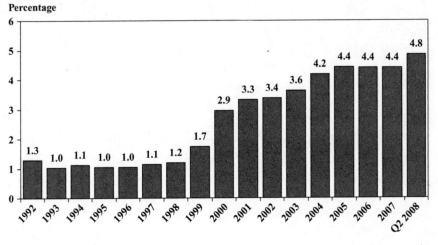

SOURCES: FDIC, Milken Institute.

insurance to have their money divided up into smaller amounts and deposited in a number of different banks. Promontory Financial Group is a company with a system called CDARS (certificate of deposit account registry service), which provides such a service. It has more than 2,500 member institutions and provides FDIC insurance coverage up to $50 million. Promontory charges about 12.5 basis points on a one-year CD to get access to federally insured funds. In contrast, the FDIC charges insurance premiums of 5 to 43 basis points. Given the increases in deposit insurance coverage in 2008, such companies apparently received some premiums for coverage that is now provided by the FDIC itself.

IndyMac Bank, which had $32 billion in assets, funded about one-third ($10 billion) of them with advances from the Federal Home Loan Bank of San Francisco before its failure and roughly another one-sixth ($5.5 billion) from brokered deposits. This situation raises serious issues about the extent to which such advances and brokered deposits help an institution avoid failure or simply enable it to postpone the inevitable while gambling for resurrection. If so, these particular sources of funds are merely shifting additional risk to the FDIC, which in the case of IndyMac Bank is estimated to cost $8.9 billion.

Table 5.10 provides information on the extent to which selected banks and all FDIC-insured institutions rely on brokered deposits and Federal Home Loan Banks advances as compared to total deposits and insured deposits for December 2000 and June 2008. It shows that brokered deposits and Federal Home Loan Banks have become more important in funding assets—even more important than equity—over this time period. Also, it may be noted that total deposits, and especially insured deposits, are relatively less important at these institutions than one might expect.

To put the current problem for depository institutions into historical perspective, Table 5.11 shows that between 1980 and October 2008, 5,468 commercial and savings banks, savings and loans, and credit unions failed. These institutions held $1.3 trillion in assets and imposed losses on the three relevant federal insurance funds and U.S. taxpayers of $204 billion. These losses do not include losses to stockholders or uninsured creditors. Most of the problems occurred during the 1980 to 1995 period, which saw 95 percent of the failures, 72 percent of the assets, and 94 percent of the losses, respectively. The worst problems were in the savings and loans industry, which accounted for 80 percent of the total cost of resolution. Most notably, the cost per dollar of assets of failed institutions in some years was alarmingly high for all three types of depository institutions. The current outlook is for an increase in the number of failures in the near future.

Another issue involves the Community Reinvestment Act (CRA), which was originally passed into law in 1977 to help ensure that all banking institutions insured by the FDIC would make credit available to the lower-income communities in which they are chartered. Federal bank regulatory authorities, including the Federal Reserve, conduct examinations of the institutions for CRA compliance. The original statute was amended in 1989 to require public disclosure of each institution's rating and performance evaluation. This information has enabled various advocacy groups to better position themselves in exercising their right under CRA to comment on a bank's noncompliance with the law.

Although there are no specific penalties imposed on institutions for noncompliance with CRA, their records are taken into account by the regulatory authorities when considering any applications for expansion

Table 5.10 Decreasing Reliance on Uninsured Deposits for Selected Financial Institutions (Selected Years)

	Date	Total Assets (US$ Billions)	Liabilities Share of Total Assets	Deposits Share of Total Assets	Insured Deposits Share of Total Assets	Brokered Deposits Share of Total Assets	FHLB Advances Share of Total Assets
All FDIC-Insured Institutions	June 2008	13,300	89.8	64.5	40.9	4.8	6.3
	Dec. 2000	7,463	91.5	65.9	47.8	3.0	3.0
JPMorgan Chase	June 2008	1,454	90.9	57.4	17.4	0.2	0.0
	Dec. 2000	603	93.9	48.8	20.3	0.0	0.0
Bank of America	June 2008	1,670	89.4	52.9	32.5	0.2	3.1
	Dec. 2000	610	91.5	63.3	44.3	0.0	1.4*
Citigroup	June 2008	1,325	91.8	61.9	29.4	5.6	6.9
	Dec. 2000	488	92.2	61.3	30.5	1.2	0.8
Wachovia	June 2008	782	90.0	60.8	38.6	9.0	7.1
	Dec. 2000	241	93.0	62.2	40.8	2.8	2.3*
Wells Fargo	June 2008	558	91.3	64.7	42.3	1.1	2.2
	Dec. 2000	284	90.3	62.8	44.7	0.5	0.0
U.S. Bank	June 2008	242	91.1	59.1	31.4	0.3	7.1
	Dec. 2000	73	92.5	73.5	53.4	1.8	4.3*
Washington Mutual Bank FSB	June 2008	46	36.5	10.4	10.2	9.1	23.3
	Dec. 2000	1	93.0	42.4	29.3	0.0	46.9
Washington Mutual Bank	June 2008	307	92.1	61.3	46.6	11.1	19.0
	Dec. 2000	155	93.9	42.4	36.1	9.1	32.0
IndyMac Bank	June 2008	31	96.3	61.7	53.2	17.9	32.8
	Dec. 2000	6	90.9	14.4	12.0	1.6	22.1

SOURCES: FDIC, Milken Institute.
*Data are as of December 2001.

Table 5.11 Failed Federally Insured Depository Institutions: Number, Assets, and Resolution Costs (1980–October 2008)

	Failed Commercial and Savings Banks				Failed Savings and Loans				Failed Credit Unions			
Year	Number	Assets (US$ Millions)	Cost (US$ Millions)	Cost/ Assets (%)	Number	Assets (US$ Millions)	Cost (US$ Millions)	Cost/ Assets (%)	Number	Shares (US$ Millions)	Cost (US$ Millions)	Cost/ Shares (%)
1980	10	236	31	13.1	11	1,458	167	11.5	239	n.a.	33	n.a.
1981	10	4,859	782	16.1	28	13,908	1,018	7.3	349	136	44	32.4
1982	42	11,632	1,169	10	76	27,748	1,213	4.4	327	156	79	50.6
1983	48	7,207	1,425	19.8	54	19,655	1,024	5.2	253	102	55	53.9
1984	80	3,276	1,635	49.9	27	5,783	833	14.4	130	208	20	9.6
1985	120	8,735	1,044	12	36	7,066	1,025	14.5	94	47	12	25.5
1986	145	7,638	1,728	22.6	51	24,182	3,605	14.9	94	116	29	25
1987	203	9,231	2,028	22	47	10,921	4,509	41.3	88	327	52	15.9
1988	221	52,683	6,866	13	222	113,965	52,203	45.8	85	297	33	11.1
1989	207	29,402	6,215	21.1	327	146,811	51,140	34.8	114	285	74	26
1990	169	15,729	2,889	18.4	213	134,766	21,473	15.9	164	339	49	14.5
1991	127	62,524	6,037	9.7	144	82,626	10,823	13.1	130	267	77	28.8
1992	122	45,485	3,707	8.1	59	45,980	4,741	10.3	114	223	107	48

1993	41	3,527	655	18.6	9	6,339	532	8.4	71	265	20	7.5
1994	13	1,402	208	14.8	2	142	14	9.9	33	255	36	14.1
1995	6	753	104	13.8	2	456	66	14.5	26	545	13	2.4
1996	5	190	39	20.4	1	33	22	67.3	19	19	2	10.5
1997	1	28	5	18	0	0	0	0	16	n.a.	1	n.a.
1998	3	290	226	77.9	0	0	0	0	18	n.a.	4	n.a.
1999	7	1,523	614	40.3	1	69	1	1.7	23	n.a.	8	n.a.
2000	6	383	31	8	1	31	1	4.2	29	n.a.	15	n.a.
2001	3	56	6	10.3	1	1,765	266	15	22	n.a.	6	n.a.
2002	10	2,821	376	13.3	1	52	n.a.	n.a.	15	n.a.	16	n.a.
2003	3	947.	66	7	0	0	0	0	13	n.a.	10	n.a.
2004	3	157	4	2.5	1	13	n.a.	n.a.	21	n.a.	13	n.a.
2005	0	0	0	0	0	0	0	0	15	n.a.	17	n.a.
2006	0	0	0	0	0	0	0	0	16	n.a.	6	n.a.
2007	2	141	12	8.4	1	2,474	108	4.4	12	n.a.	43	n.a.
2008												
Oct.	13	10,285.	2,328	23	3	337,824	8,042 ·	2.4	n.a.	n.a.	n.a.	n.a.

SOURCES: FDIC, National Credit Union Administration, Barth and Brumbaugh (1997), Milken Institute.
NOTE: The three savings and loan failures in 2008 were IndyMac Bank, Washington Mutual Bank, and Ameribank.

through merger, acquisition, or branching. This provides the advocacy groups an opportunity to support or oppose any bank's application for expansion. In response to this situation, many institutions have made efforts to provide the type of lending that would be viewed favorably in their CRA examinations. It has been argued by some that in meeting their CRA obligations, institutions may have been pushed into making unprofitable or excessively risky loans.[12] This is despite CRA's mandate that institutions fulfill their obligations in a way that is consistent with safe and sound operations.

In summary, the CRA undoubtedly opened the door for some federally insured depository institutions to be pressured into making some loans that would have not otherwise been made, worsening their risk exposure. However, it is too big a stretch to lay the entire blame for the crisis on the CRA.

...with the Greed Factor?

There is a portion of subprime credit seekers who are manipulating, or "gaming," the traditional credit risk model methodologies for access to credit otherwise unavailable to them. Traditional credit risk models do not suppress authorized user tradelines (i.e., a consumer added to the account of a cardholder as a user). A subset of low-score or no-score

(Continued)

It was inevitable that the problems in the financial sector would lead to finger-pointing—and there is no shortage of blame to go around. There is no doubt that pure, old-fashioned greed played a major role in the events that transpired. As Figure 5.38 shows, investors were increasingly making second home purchases from 2003 to 2007. That share continued to rise as the housing bubble emerged and then dropped once the bubble burst. This undoubtedly reflects the fact that many people purchased second homes simply to flip them for higher prices. Some individuals successfully made a profit, but many others may have walked away or ended up in default.

In addition to investors and speculators who helped to drive up home prices to dangerous levels, other individuals engaged in fraud (from property flipping with falsely inflated appraisals to lying on loan applications) to the detriment of lending institutions. Table 5.12 shows a growing number of cases of mortgage fraud documented in suspicious activity reports from 2002 to 2007 by the Federal Bureau of Investigation. It also shows that dollar losses accelerated over this period, totaling $3.7 billion.

The Financial Crimes Enforcement Network (a part of the U.S. Treasury Department) reported that many of the fraudulent activities involved financial professionals in the mortgage industry, including mortgage brokers, loan officers, and lenders who are familiar with the mortgage loan process and therefore know how to exploit vulnerabilities in the system. Some recent developments, such as NINJA loans, made it easier for brokers or originators to simply falsify income and assets on mortgage applications. When mortgage transactions are affected by fraudulent activity, demand is artificially inflated and eventual home price declines may thus be steeper.

Even in the absence of fraud, the housing bubble seemed to promise such quick, outsized profits that many market participants simply threw caution to the wind. Both domestic and foreign investors in securities backed by subprime

consumers are using this loophole to artificially present themselves to credit grantors as prime prospects. This group of consumers is gaining access to increased credit extension amounts and favorable rates when, in fact, their risk score without these authorized user trades would suggest a higher-risk profile. This aspect of traditional credit risk scores is creating a cottage industry on the Internet and an opportunity for "would-be" credit gamers, increasing the risk in the lending portfolios of financial institutions. While this practice is not illegal, its manipulative and exploitive undertones are concerning and may be best categorized as abuse that borderlines fraudulent behavior.

—"Vantage Score Addresses Deficiencies in Traditional Scores in the Subprime Consumer Sector" White Paper Experian May 7, 2007

Figure 5.38   Investor Share of Second Home Purchases (Selected Years)

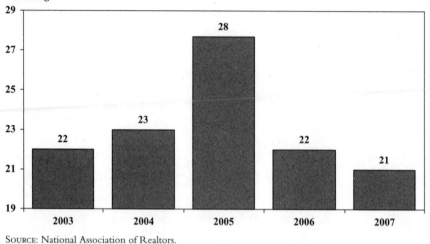

SOURCE: National Association of Realtors.

loans—particularly in the more exotic types—must now more fully appreciate the fact that the marketplace is sometimes quite harsh in punishing those who seek out ever-higher returns without properly taking into account the correspondingly greater risk.

There's an old Wall Street adage that there's a nexus between fear and greed. If you diminish fear, you get more greed. People got braver issuing this stuff. All the participants felt they could act merely as agents and collect fees. Nobody was prepared to say "I have liability."

—Lewis S. Ranieri
BusinessWeek
June 26, 2008

Table 5.12   Mortgage Fraud Reported in Suspicious
Activity Reports (2002–2007)

Year	Number	Dollar Losses (US$ millions)
2002	5,623	293
2003	6,936	225
2004	17,127	429
2005	21,994	1,014
2006	35,617	946
2007	46,717	813

SOURCE: Federal Bureau of Investigation, 2007 Mortgage Fraud Report.

Assessing the Role of Various Factors to Explain Foreclosures

Most individuals enter foreclosure not because of the loan product they received but rather because of the financial circumstances they find themselves in *after* they obtain those mortgage loans. These factors include unemployment (an increasingly important issue as the economy weakens), divorce, health problems, and especially declines in housing prices that leave homes worth less than their outstanding mortgage balances. By recognizing the key role these factors play, it becomes clear that legislation and regulations cannot and should not try to prevent subprime lending altogether (or innovation in the mortgage markets more generally), because that will shut off credit completely to millions who want to become homeowners. Although higher standards are needed, it would be a mistake to react to an era of easy credit by forcing the pendulum to swing too dramatically in the opposite direction.

The traditional causes of foreclosure, even before there was subprime lending, were job loss, divorce and major medical expenses. And the national foreclosure data seem to suggest that these issues remain paramount.

—Austan Goolsbee
"'Irresponsible' Mortgages
Have Opened Doors to
Many of the Excluded"
The New York Times
March 29, 2007

Instead, actions should focus on better educating consumers on complex loan products and simplifying the documents necessary for informed decision-making. After all, consumers must be allowed to choose mortgage products, even if some expose borrowers to interest-rate risk. The marketplace itself will eliminate the most toxic products.

More thought must also be given to what foreclosure rate is acceptable on subprime mortgage loans in the absence of fraud on the part of either the lender or borrower. Surely it would be unreasonable to enact legislation or implement regulations based on the premise that the only socially desirable foreclosure rate is zero. If that were the case, hardly anyone would qualify for a home mortgage loan in a world full of risk.

Let's begin by taking a broad view of foreclosures in selected metropolitan areas. Figure 5.39 plots five-year housing price gains against foreclosure rates, showing that foreclosures were fairly high in metropolitan areas whether or not they had housing bubbles. Some of these areas simply suffered from relatively weak economies—after all, other economic factors beyond collapsing housing bubbles can cause residents to lose their homes. Figure 5.40 shows similar information after

Figure 5.39 Drivers of Foreclosures: Strong Appreciation or Weak Economies?

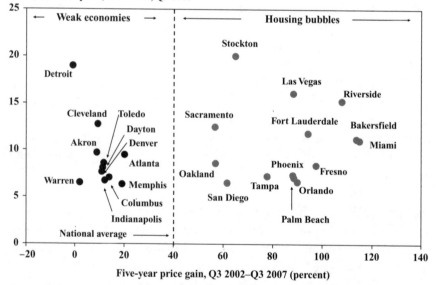

SOURCES: U.S. Treasury Department, RealtyTrac, Office of Federal Housing Enterprise Oversight, Milken Institute.

Figure 5.40   After the Housing Bubble Burst in 2007: Foreclosures Highest for Areas with Biggest Price Declines

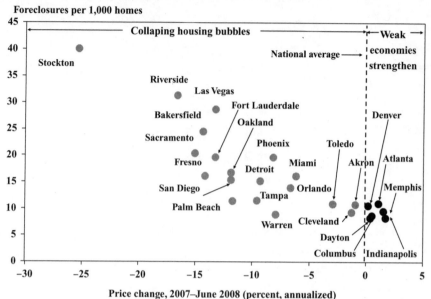

Foreclosures per 1,000 homes

SOURCES: RealtyTrac, Office of Federal Housing Enterprise Oversight, Milken Institute.

the housing bubble burst. This time, the highest foreclosure rates were in those areas that had experienced the biggest run-up in home prices.

A number of foreclosure and default models have been used in economic and finance literature to understand the foreclosure phenomenon. Although the independent variables differ from study to study, the usual suspects, such as FICO scores, are included in most models, as are loan and borrower characteristics and macroeconomic conditions.

Based on the specifications in the literature and data availability, we have examined the determinants of foreclosure start rates, using state-level panel data with time-period and product-type fixed effects.[13] The independent variables can be separated into four groups. The first group includes dummies for product types, dummies for origination years, and a dummy for prime/subprime loans to capture the fixed effects. The second group includes the age of loans, as well as its interaction with product type. The third group includes state-specific macro variables, such as household income, home prices, and unemployment rates. The last group includes loan characteristic variables at the time of loan origination, such as average FICO score, initial interest rates, and loan-to-value ratio. Specifically, the model takes the following form:

$$
\begin{aligned}
FS_{itop} = {} & \alpha_1 + \alpha_2^* dumprime \\
& + \alpha_3 y + \alpha_4 p + \beta_1 p^* age_0 \\
& + \beta_2^* chhhinc_{it} \\
& + \beta_3^* chhprice_{it} \\
& + \beta_4^* chunem_{it} \\
& + \beta_5^* own_{itop} + \beta_6^* wfico_{itop} \\
& + \beta_7^* wiir_{itop} + \beta_8^* wltv_{itop} \\
& + \varepsilon
\end{aligned}
$$

where

FS_{itop} is foreclosure start rate of product type p, originated in year o, for state i at year t;

Dumprime is a dummy that takes value of 1 if the type is prime and 0 otherwise.

y is the year of origination dummies;

p is product type dummies;

age_0 is age of loans originated in year o;

$chhhinc_{it}$ is annual percentage change in household income of state i at time t;

$chhprice_{it}$ is annual percentage change of home price of state i at time t;

$chunem_{it}$ is change in unemployment rate (percentage point);

own_{itop} is the share of owner-occupied loans of state i at year t of product type p that were originated in year o;

$wfico_{itop}$ is the average FICO score of loans originated in year o in state i at year t that are product type p;

$wiir_{itop}$ is the average initial interest rate;

$wltv_{itop}$ is the average initial loan-to-value ratio; and

ε is the error term.

The last two groups of factors—macroeconomic environment and loan characteristics—are often cited in the economic literature. (Note that full details on all of the sources referred to in this section can be found in the References list.) Rose (2006), Elliehausen, Staten, and Steinbuks (2006), Li and Ernst (2006), Ho and Pennington-Cross (2007), and

Figure 5.41   Default Rates of Subprime Home Mortgage Loans and
Year-over-Year Change in Employment (January 1998–September 2008)

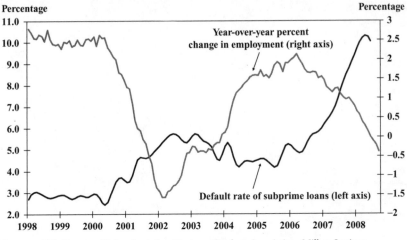

SOURCES: U.S. Bureau of Labor Statistics, Mortgage Bankers Association, Milken Institute.
NOTE: Data for default rate of subprime loans only updated to June 2008.

Gerardi, Rosen, and Willen (2007) include household income as a part
of their assessments of mortgage market. Variations of the home price
variable are also used by several mortgage studies, including Gerardi,
Rosen, and Willen (2007), Li and Ernst (2006), and Bocian, Ernst, and
Li (2006).

Unemployment was found to have a positive and significant relationship with mortgage default rates by Danis and Pennington-Cross
(2005) and was found to have a negative and significant relationship with
subprime loan volume by Li and Ernst (2006). Figure 5.41 shows that
slower growth in employment has been associated with higher default
rates on subprime home mortgages over the past decade.

Owner occupancy status and FICO scores are also important loan
characteristics that can affect default and foreclosure rates. Borrowers
with lower FICO scores tend to have higher foreclosure rates (Rose,
2006a) and default rates (Danis and Pennington-Cross, 2005a, 2005b).

Previous studies generally suggested that the loan-to-value (LTV)
ratio is a primary determinant of default. Focusing on subprime mortgage delinquency, Capozza and Thomson (2006) find that LTV ratio has
a positive and significant relationship with the likelihood of foreclosure
when a loan is already in default. Danis and Pennington-Cross (2005a,
2005b) suggest that for subprime loans, LTV ratio at origination is

Figure 5.42   Median Percentage Down Payment on Home Purchases
(Selected MSAs, 2006)
United States = 10%

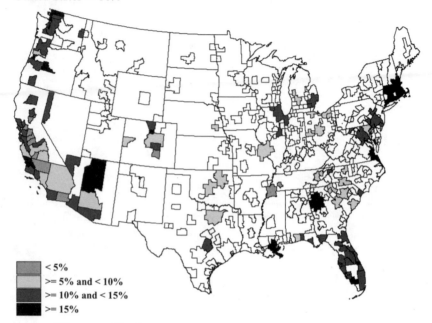

< 5%

>= 5% and < 10%

>= 10% and < 15%

>= 15%

SOURCES: Zillow.com, Milken Institute.

positively correlated with delinquency. Pennington-Cross and Ho (2006)
find that higher LTV ratio is associated with higher default and prepayment probability. Figure 5.42 and Appendix Table A.52 show the median
percentage of down payment for home purchases in 2006. In the vast
majority of metropolitan areas, the down payment was less than 15
percent—and in several areas, the median down payment was even less
than 5 percent.

   The impact of interest rates on the subprime default rate is less clear.
Chomsisengphet and Pennington-Cross (2006) note that "the subprime
market has provided a substantial amount of risk-based pricing in the
mortgage market by varying the interest rate of a loan based on the borrower's credit history and down payment." Danis and Pennington-Cross
(2005a, 2005b) find that the interest rate has a negative and significant
impact on delinquency and default rates.

   The LoanPerformance database, the Home Mortgage Disclosure
Act (HMDA) database, and the American Financial Services Association

(AFSA) database are among the common data sources used in empirical studies on mortgage markets, especially the subprime mortgage market. However, each database covers only a part of the mortgage market. In other words, they provide a partial rather than a comprehensive picture of the entire universe of all mortgage loans. (For a more detailed comparison of mortgage databases, see Appendix Table A.53.)

Table 5.13 shows the list of variables, definitions, and sources. Our assessment relied on aggregate loan-level data from the LoanPerformance database and state-level macroeconomic and financial data from various sources, including the U.S. Census Bureau, the National Association of Realtors, and the U.S. Bureau of Labor Statistics.

Table 5.14 shows the regression results for all loans, for prime loans, and for subprime loans. The loan sample includes loans made from 2000 through 2006. Foreclosures are reported monthly; the last period for reported foreclosures in the sample was December 2006.

The benchmark period for origination year dummies was 2006. In the three regressions, the coefficients of time dummies show that the foreclosure rate for loans originated in all years prior to 2006 are significantly lower than those loans originated in 2006. This period is the point in time when the share of subprime loans peaked and underwriting standards deteriorated substantially.

Product-type fixed-effect coefficients for all regressions suggest that the all products have statistically significantly higher foreclosure rates when benchmarked against fixed-rate products, with the exception of other hybrid prime mortgage products.

The coefficients of the product-type fixed-effect also show that adjustable-rate mortgages in general have the highest foreclosure start rates (higher than those of hybrid 2/28 and 3/27). When we separate loan types into prime loans and subprime loans, however, the 2/28 hybrid mortgage has the highest foreclosure start rate among prime loans (1.30 percentage points higher than that of fixed-rate mortgage), while the adjustable-rate mortgage has the highest foreclosure rate among subprime loans (1.75 percentage points higher than that of fixed-rate mortgages).

The loan age of a fixed-rate mortgage is negative and significant for all subprime loans in the sample, regardless of product type. It is, however, not significant for prime loans. As compared to fixed-rate

Table 5.13 Variable Definitions and Sources

Code	Definition	Source
FORS	Foreclosure start rate by state by product type by time period	LoanPerformance
AGE	Age of the loan since year of origination	LoanPerformance
DUMPRIME	Dummy of prime loan. It takes value 1 if the loan group is a prime group and 0 otherwise.	LoanPerformance
DUM2000	Dummy for the year 2000 origination. It takes value 1 if the year of origination is 2000 and 0 otherwise.	LoanPerformance
DUM2001	Dummy for the year 2001 origination. It takes value 1 if the year of origination is 2001 and 0 otherwise.	LoanPerformance
DUM2002	Dummy for the year 2002 origination. It takes value 1 if the year of origination is 2002 and 0 otherwise.	LoanPerformance
DUM2003	Dummy for the year 2003 origination. It takes value 1 if the year of origination is 2003 and 0 otherwise.	LoanPerformance
DUM2004	Dummy for the year 2004 origination. It takes value 1 if the year of origination is 2004 and 0 otherwise.	LoanPerformance
DUM2005	Dummy for the year 2005 origination. It takes value 1 if the year of origination is 2005 and 0 otherwise.	LoanPerformance
DUMT228	Dummy for 2–28 product type. It takes value 1 if the loan group is 2–28 type and 0 otherwise.	LoanPerformance

Variable	Description	Source
DUMT327	Dummy for 2–27 product type. It takes value 1 if the loan group is 2–27 type and 0 otherwise.	LoanPerformance
DUMTARM	Dummy for ARM product type. It takes value 1 if the loan group is ARM type and 0 otherwise.	LoanPerformance
DUMTOHY	Dummy for other hybrid product type. It takes value 1 if the loan group is other hybrid type and 0 otherwise.	LoanPerformance
DUMTOTH	Dummy for all other product types. It takes value 1 if the loan group is all other types and 0 otherwise.	LoanPerformance
CHHHINC	Change in household income	U.S. Census
CHHPRICE	Change in home price	National Association of Realtors and Moody's Economy.com estimates
CHUNEM	Change in unemployment	Bureau of Labor statistics
OWN	Share of mortgage loan with owner-occupied status	LoanPerformance
WFICO	Average FICO score at origination	LoanPerformance
WIIR	Average interest rate at origination	LoanPerformance
WLTV	Average LTV at origination	LoanPerformance

SOURCE: Milken Institute.

Table 5.14   Regression Results: Dependent Variable: Foreclosure Start Rate

	All Observations	Prime	Subprime
C	1.0307***	−0.5045***	5.7596***
AGE	−0.0355***	0.0036	−0.0727***
DUMPRIME	−0.5605***		
DUM2000	−0.2655***	−0.3141***	−0.1919***
DUM2001	−0.3366***	−0.2732***	−0.2999***
DUM2002	−0.4304***	−0.2107***	−0.5087***
DUM2003	−0.3903***	−0.1974***	−0.5209***
DUM2004	−0.2247***	−0.0938***	−0.3692***
DUM2005	−0.1016***	−0.0339	−0.1409***
DUMT228	0.8605***	1.3095***	0.5506***
DUMT327	0.2544***	0.1537***	0.257***
DUMTARM	0.9344***	0.055**	1.7564***
DUMTOHY	0.3986***	0.0363	0.7341***
DUMTOTH	0.3062***	0.2233***	0.4422***
DUMT228*AGE	−0.1315***	0.0425***	−0.1096***
DUMT327*AGE	−0.0427***	0.0013	−0.0793***
DUMTARM*AGE	−0.0851***	−0.0009	−0.1842***
DUMTOHY*AGE	−0.0285***	−0.006	−0.0681***
DUMTOTH*AGE	−0.0262***	−0.0207***	−0.0454***
CHHHINC	−0.002*	−0.0004	−0.0027
CHHPRICE	−0.0164***	−0.0077***	−0.0251***
CHUNEM	0.0794***	0.0087	0.0874***
OWN	−0.0037***	−0.0005	−0.0076***
WFICO	−0.0007***	0.0004***	−0.007***
WIIR	0.0294***	0.0655***	−0.0314***
WLTV	0.0082***	0.0029***	0.0107***
Adjusted R^2	0.2954	0.3496	0.2911
Number of observations	22,662	10,767	11,895

SOURCE: Milken Institute.

***, **, and * indicate level of significant at 1 percent, 5 percent, and 10 percent, respectively.

mortgages, all other types of subprime mortgages show foreclosure rates decreasing with the loans' age.

Among subprime loans, there is strong evidence, regardless of loan type, that as loans age, the number of foreclosure starts declines. Among ARM subprime mortgages, aging of loans leads to more dramatic declines in foreclosure start rates, as compared with other types of mortgages. For each year that loans age, the foreclosure rates of ARM subprime mortgages fall by 0.25 percentage points.

For prime loans, however, the effect of age on foreclosure starts is more ambiguous. As prime loans age, 2/28 and 3/27 hybrid loans tend to have higher foreclosure rates than fixed-rate loans. However, this is significant only for 2/28 mortgages.

State-specific macroeconomic climate also has a significant impact on foreclosure rates. State-level growth in household income has a negative impact on foreclosure start rates at the 10 percent significance level for all loans. Growth in home prices has a negative and significant impact on foreclosure start rates across all loans and each of the two subcategories (prime loans and subprime loans). Higher unemployment rates are associated with increased foreclosure start rates for all loans, prime loans, and subprime loans but are not significant for prime loans.

Loan characteristics are also important determinants of foreclosure start rates. A pool of loans with a higher share of owner-occupied properties, regardless of where they are originated or product type, tends to have lower foreclosure start rates. This is statistically significant for all loans and subprime loans. Higher average FICO scores are associated with lower foreclosure rates for all loans and subprime loans but with higher foreclosure rates for prime loans. Higher initial interest rates are associated with higher foreclosure start rates for all loans and prime loans but with lower foreclosure start rates for subprime loans. Loan-to-value ratios have negative and significant impacts on all loans, prime loans, and subprime loans.

Chapter 6

So Far, Only Piecemeal Fixes

I n the wake of such a multifaceted and sweeping crisis, how have the private sector and the government responded?

History tells us that in any period of financial crisis, the federal government will enact new laws and regulations—and the current situation is no different. The government has taken a number of dramatic steps to try to contain the turmoil spreading throughout the financial sector and prevent it from bleeding into the real economy.

In many respects, however, the government has engaged in a series of flip-flops that have exacerbated the uncertainty gripping the marketplace. In March 2008, Bear Stearns was bailed out—but six months later, Lehman Brothers was allowed to fail. Within weeks, the government shifted gears yet again, as American International Group (AIG) was rescued. No convincing rationale for this differential treatment of institutions has ever been provided.

On another front, when the U.S. Treasury Department received authorization to spend up to $700 billion to shore up the financial system, officials initially indicated that the money would be used to purchasing troubled assets. But shortly thereafter, the first $125 billion was used instead for injecting capital into nine of the biggest institutions. Again, the public received no clear explanation for this sudden switch in strategy.

Even as billions—and likely trillions—of taxpayer dollars are deployed, the public has found the response to be confusing and patchwork at best. This chapter documents and provides context for the various actions taken by the Treasury, the Federal Reserve, the Federal Depository Insurance Corporation (FDIC), Congress, and the White House, as well as the private sector.

The Landscape Shifts for Lenders

After the freewheeling era of the housing boom, the mortgage meltdown dramatically altered the behavior of market participants. Faced with losses and write-downs, financial institutions tightened their lending standards for commercial and residential real estate loans, as shown in Figures 6.1 and 6.2. Indeed, examining trends since 1990, the net percentage of surveyed loan officers who reported stricter standards for commercial real estate loans reached an all-time high of roughly 80 percent in the third quarter of 2008. Figure 6.2 shows that lending standards for prime, nontraditional, and subprime mortgages all also tightened sharply after 2006.

Figures 6.3 shows demand for all types of residential mortgages plummeted after 2006, mirroring the falloff in demand for commercial mortgages. This indicates that lenders and investors reacted to the

Figure 6.1   Tightened Standards and Weaker Demand for Commercial Real Estate Loans (Quarterly, 1990–Q3 2008)

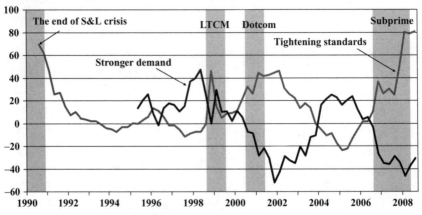

Net percentage of domestic respondents reporting tightening standards and stronger demand for commercial real estate loans

SOURCES: Federal Reserve, Milken Institute.

Figure 6.2   Tightened Standards for Residential Mortgage Loans
(Quarterly, 1990–Q3 2008)

Net percentage of domestic respondents reporting tightening standards for residential real
estate loans

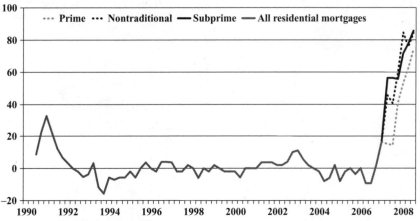

SOURCES: Federal Reserve, Milken Institute.
NOTE: The breakdown into the three subcomponents only became available in the first quarter of
2007.

Figure 6.3   Weaker Demand for Residential Mortgage Loans
(Quarterly, 1990–Q3 2008)

Net percentage of domestic respondents reporting stronger demand for residential real
estate loans

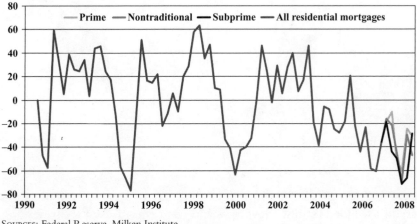

SOURCES: Federal Reserve, Milken Institute.
NOTE: The breakdown into the three subcomponents only became available in the first quarter of
2007.

Figure 6.4   Washington Mutual Reverses Its Mortgage Origination Strategy

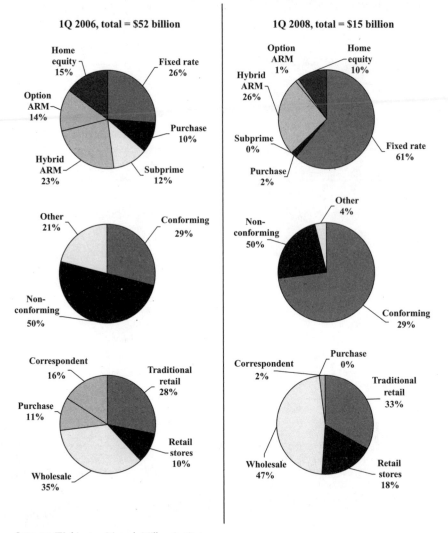

SOURCES: Washington Mutual, Milken Institute.

deterioration in the housing and mortgage markets by curtailing the credit extended to new mortgages and mortgage-backed securities.

Many financial institutions abandoned their previous mortgage origination strategies. Washington Mutual, for example, as shown in Figure 6.4, not only reduced its originations but also stopped originating subprime mortgages altogether, shifted away from nonconforming to conforming loans, and relied less on correspondents and more on retail outlets for originations in the first quarter of 2008. But its efforts were clearly too little, too late for the bank to survive the turmoil as an independent entity. Other financial institutions responded by scaling back their mortgage lending operations in a similar manner. As a matter of fact, in the third quarter of 2008, subprime loan originations came to a virtual standstill. Certain mortgage products, like the 2/28 and 3/27 loans, have almost disappeared.

Other institutions are taking steps to modify the terms on their mortgages for borrowers who are behind on their payments or are likely to be in the near future. JPMorgan Chase, for example, on October 31, 2008, announced a loan modification plan that covered $70 billion mortgages, or 4.7 percent of the total mortgages it holds or services. More than 400,000 borrowers may qualify for modifications on their mortgages.

Citigroup also launched a loan modification program on November 11, 2008. This program reaches out to a select group of 500,000 homeowners, particularly those in areas that are likely to face extreme economic distress, who are not currently behind on their mortgage payments but may require assistance to remain current. Moreover, Citigroup is systematically implementing its practice of not initiating a foreclosure or completing a foreclosure sale on any eligible borrower in cases where it owns the mortgage, the home in question is the principal residence of the borrower is seeking to stay in it, and the borrower is working in good faith with Citigroup and has sufficient income for affordable mortgage payments. Citigroup has also streamlined its existing loan modification program to rework delinquent loans. It is based on a simplified formula to determine an affordable payment as a percentage of the borrower's gross income and will reduce the monthly payment to that amount by applying one or more of the following: interest rate reduction, extension of term, or forgiveness of principal.

On October 10, 2007, HOPE NOW was unveiled by Treasury Secretary Henry Paulson and Housing Secretary Alphonso Jackson. HOPE NOW is a national alliance of HUD-approved counselors, lenders, servicers, investors, and other mortgage market participants. Its goal is to maximize outreach efforts to homeowners in distress, enabling them to stay in their homes and to create a unified, coordinated plan to assist as many homeowners as possible. The group launched a national direct mail campaign to contact at-risk borrowers, encouraging them to either call their lender or a credit counselor. This alliance agreed to adopt a standard process model that streamlines work flow, productivity, and communications between servicers and counselors. It also works to expand the capacity of an existing national network to counsel borrowers and connect them with servicers, developing common communications guidelines that will be used to respond to at-risk borrowers to offer them the best possible solutions, customized for each borrower.

A member of the alliance, the American Securitization Forum (which represents servicers, investors, and other secondary market participants) announced in October 2007 that counseling fees can be reimbursed from securitization transactions in appropriate circumstances. Moreover, under HOPE NOW, the servicers agreed to develop cross-industry technology solutions to more effectively connect servicers and counselors to better serve the homeowner. The initiative's progress is to be measured by a common set of metrics to be developed by the alliance.

HOPE NOW has had to overcome some resistance on the part of servicers to the concept of modifying the terms of mortgage loans, because it is costly for them to do so and clearly reduces their profits. There may also be conflicts between the first- and second-lien holders on the mortgages that impede modifications. At the same time, the servicers may have concerns about legal liability to the investors in mortgage-backed securities when the underlying mortgages change terms.

In October 2008, HOPE NOW announced that it has so far helped 2.5 million homeowners avoid foreclosure; roughly two-thirds of these were subprime borrowers. Figure 6.5 tracks the program's progress, showing the total accumulated number of loans (broken out by prime and subprime loans) that have been addressed through new accumulated loan repayment plans. Figure 6.6 shows similar information for new accumulated loan modifications, and Figure 6.7 illustrates new accumulated workout plans, which includes both new loan repayment plans and new loan modifications.

Even as HOPE NOW has attempted to help homeowners, the number of foreclosure sales has been rising steadily. Figure 6.8 shows that 1 million foreclosure sales were completed between the third quarter of

Figure 6.5 HOPE NOW Alliance Program: Accumulated Borrower Repayment Plans (Q3 2007–Q3 2008)

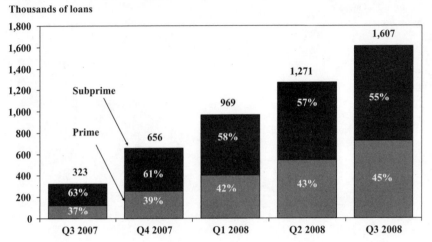

SOURCES: HOPE NOW, Milken Institute.

NOTE: Repayment plans allow borrower to become current and catch up on missed payments that are appropriate to the borrower's circumstances, which involves deferring or rescheduling payments. In these cases, the full amount of the loan is ultimately expected to be paid within the original contractual maturity of the loan.

Figure 6.6 HOPE NOW Alliance Program: Accumulated Borrower Modifications (Q3 2007–Q3 2008)

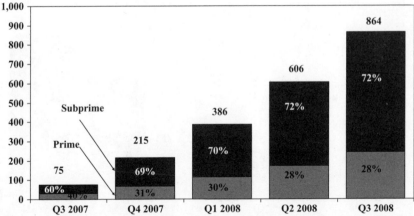

SOURCES: HOPE NOW, Milken Institute.

NOTE: Modifications permanently alter terms of the original loan contract. They can involve reducing the interest rate, forgiving a portion of the principal, or extending the maturity date of the loan.

Figure 6.7   HOPE NOW Alliance Program: Accumulated Borrower Workouts (Q3 2007–Q3 2008)

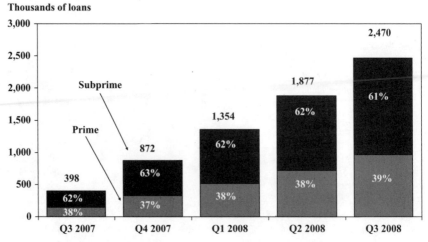

Sources: HOPE NOW, Milken Institute.
Note: Workout plans include both repayment plans and modifications.

Figure 6.8   HOPE NOW Alliance Program: Accumulated Foreclosure Sales (Q3 2007–Q3 2008)

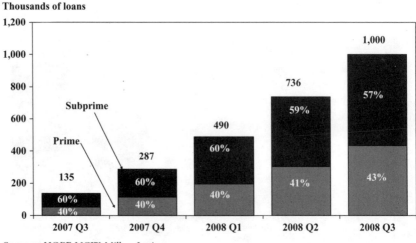

Sources: HOPE NOW, Milken Institute.

Figure 6.9 Commercial Bank Lending Increases over Time
(Weekly, January 3, 1973–October 25, 2008)

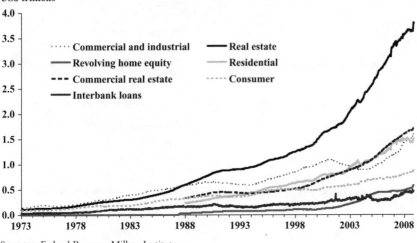

SOURCES: Federal Reserve, Milken Institute

2007 and the third quarter of 2008. For more details on the number of
loans addressed by HOPE NOW from July 2007 to September 2008, see
Appendix Tables A.54 and A.55. Of course, over time more information
should become available to track how many of the loans modified by
HOPE NOW will prove to be sustainable over the long term.

Although there has been serious concern about a recent lack of
credit and liquidity within the commercial banking industry, the news
media may have given the misleading impression that credit is no longer
available and liquidity does not exist. To correct these misperceptions,
Figure 6.9 shows that various types of loans have generally shown no
sharp declines over the long period from January 3, 1973, to October
25, 2008, with the exception of commercial and industrial loans. These
loans decreased during the period from April 2001 to May 2004, at the
same time that real estate loans were rapidly increasing.

Indeed, Figure 6.10 shows the weekly percentage changes in bank
credit, commercial and industrial loans, all real estate loans, residential
real estate loans, revolving home equity loans, commercial real estate
loans, consumer loans, and interbank loans. There is no clear pattern
in these changes for different types of loans from 1973 to October 25,

Figure 6.10 Percentage Changes in Commercial Bank Loans of Different Types over Time (Weekly, January 3, 1973–October 25, 2008)

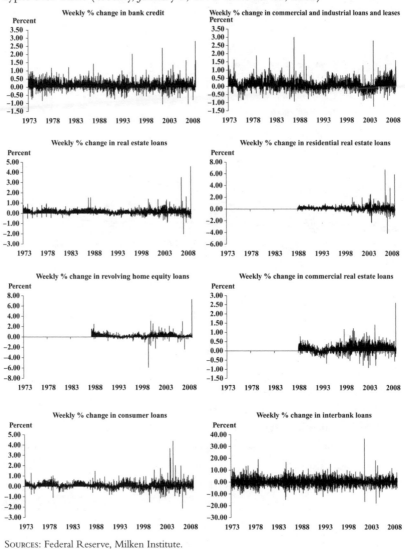

SOURCES: Federal Reserve, Milken Institute.

2008; some are negative and others positive. The important point is that since 2007 or so the changes have not all been negative, which would indicate a complete drying up of credit.

Figure 6.11 shows the same type of information but for a shorter time period and with absolute changes rather than percentage changes. Once

Figure 6.11 Changes in Commercial Bank Loans of Different Types over Time (Weekly, January 3, 2007–October 25, 2008)

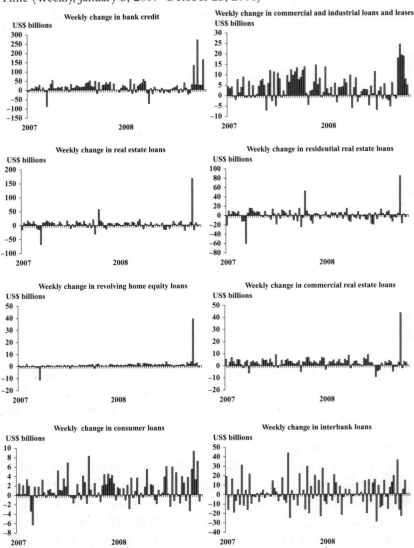

Sources: Federal Reserve, Milken Institute

again, the data show that there is no steady and persistent decrease in loans outstanding by commercial banks since January 3, 2007. Indeed, bank credit outstanding for all commercial banks increased by $482 billion, or 5 percent, in October. This means that credit is still being made available

Figure 6.12   Net Borrowing by Households and Nonfinancial Businesses (Quarterly, Q1 1990–Q2 2008)

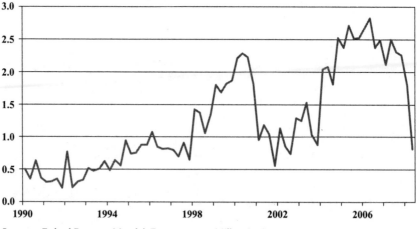

Seasonally adjusted annualized figure, US$ trillions

SOURCES: Federal Reserve, Moody's Economy.com, Milken Institute.

but on more stringent terms to more creditworthy borrowers. Some banks, however, have experienced an increase in their loans when loans they had planned to keep off their balance sheets were forced back on and existing lines of credit were drawn on.

Despite the availability of these different types of credit, Figure 6.12 shows that net borrowing by households and nonfinancial businesses rose to a record high of $2.8 trillion in the second quarter of 2006 and then declined sharply by $2 trillion or 71 percent to $811 billion in the second quarter of 2008.

Commercial banks have also increased their liquidity but only recently by substantial amounts. As Figure 6.13 shows, banks held relatively small amounts of excess reserves (between $800 million and $4.6 billion) from October 17, 2007, to September 17, 2008. However, during the week of September 17, 2008, excess reserves jumped to $68.8 billion, then to $136 billion during the week of October 8, 2008, and then still further to $363.6 billion during the week of November 5, 2008. This indicates that banks began to accumulate excess reserves at a time when "cash was king." Liquidity became a matter of survival, as some banks had significant short-term, nondeposit liabilities that required interest

Figure 6.13   Excess Reserves Take Off
(Weekly, January 3, 2007–November 5, 2008)

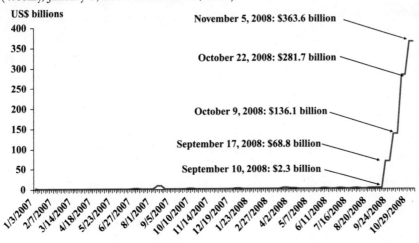

SOURCES: Federal Reserve, Milken Institute

and principal payments—and it was becoming ever more difficult to roll them over except at relatively high rates.[1] Such funds were needed to meet payrolls and to cover other ongoing operating expenses. This situation underscores the problem with borrowing short and lending long (not to mention having too many assets with too little capital) when a crisis occurs. Financial institutions that are highly leveraged and illiquid are choosing a business model destined for disaster.

The Federal Reserve Intervenes to Provide Liquidity and Higher-Quality Collateral

As the earlier quotes indicate, the Federal Reserve has not won universally rave reviews for its response to the crisis. It is therefore important to examine some of the actions taken by the Fed to stem the bleeding in the financial sector and to soften the decline in real economic activity.

Beginning on August 17, 2007, the Fed cut the discount rate 10 times, from 6.25 percent to 1.25 percent on October 29, 2008. Similarly, beginning on September 18, 2007, the Fed lowered its target federal

Its (the Federal Reserve's) mistake was to cut interest rates so dramatically at the same time that it extended its credit facilities. It would have been better to lend freely at a penalty rate. Higher interest rates would have made its emergency credit more costly and led to better-targeted lending and less inflation.

—Barry Eichengreen
"What the Fed Can Learn
from History's Blunders"
Financial Times
August 19, 2008

I don't see that they've achieved what they should have been trying to achieve. So my verdict on this present Fed leadership is that they have not really done their job.

—Anna Schwartz
"Bernanke Is Fighting the
Last War"
Interview with
Brian M. Carney
The Wall Street Journal
October 18, 2008

funds rate nine times, from 5.25 percent to 1.0 percent on October 29, 2008.[2] Another steep cut followed in December 2008.

However, as Figure 6.14 shows, although the federal funds rate declined over this period, the 30-year fixed mortgage rate remained relatively flat from mid-2006 to December 2008, and the gap between the two rates widened significantly. A portion of the widening was due to a slight increase in mortgage rates, which did not help improve the affordability of fixed-rate mortgages during 2008 as a workout option for troubled adjustable-rate mortgages.

Figure 6.15 compares trends in the target federal funds rate, AAA corporate bond yield, high-yield corporate bond yield, and Freddie Mac's 30-year fixed mortgage rate over the same period as the previous figure. It basically tells the same story but shows that reductions in the target federal funds rate have failed to lower high yield corporate yields or AAA corporate bond yields. In fact, the AAA corporate bond yield increased somewhat at the end of the period, while high-yield corporate bond yields increased sharply. This move reflects the greater perceived risk associated with these securities.

In addition to cutting the discount rate and target federal funds rate, the Federal Reserve established a number of new and historic programs between August 2007 and October 2008.

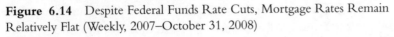

Figure 6.14   Despite Federal Funds Rate Cuts, Mortgage Rates Remain Relatively Flat (Weekly, 2007–October 31, 2008)

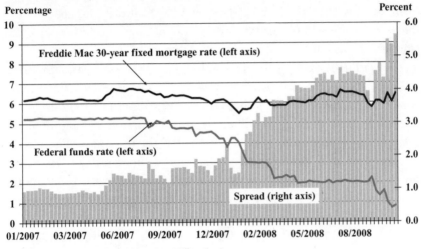

SOURCES: Federal Reserve, Freddie Mac, Milken Institute.

Figure 6.15   Increasing Spreads between Corporate Bonds, Mortgage Securities, and Target Federal Funds Rate (Weekly, 2007–October 31, 2008)

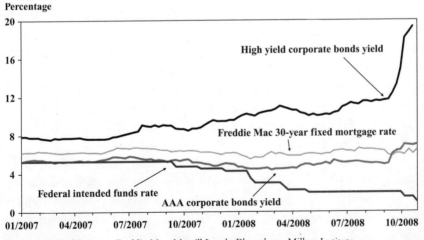

SOURCES: Federal Reserve, Freddie Mac, Merrill Lynch, Bloomberg, Milken Institute.

First, the Term Discount Window Program (TDWP), announced on August 17, 2007, essentially extends the term of discount window loans from overnight to up to 90 days. Depository institutions that borrow under either the TDWP or the conventional discount window pay the primary credit rate.

Several months later, on December 12, 2007, came an announcement of the Term Auction Facility (TAF), under which the Federal Reserve auctions off loans to depository institutions every other Thursday for a term of 28 days. The size of the auction is set (initially at $75 billion), and depository institutions bid for the funds. The interest rate paid is the lowest rate that exhausts the funds (or the lowest rate proposed by any bidder if the total requests are smaller than the amount to be auctioned). Consequently, the rate can be higher or lower than the primary credit rate.

The Federal Reserve took further action by establishing the Term Securities Lending Facility (TSLF) on March 11, 2008. The TSLF establishes term swaps of securities between the Federal Reserve and primary dealers, who are permitted to exchange various securities for U.S. Treasuries for a term of 28 days. The securities are auctioned weekly, with the amount of the auction and the Treasuries available determined in advance of the auction. The rate is essentially the spread between the rate on Treasuries being auctioned and the rate on the pledged collateral presented by the primary dealers. On May 2, 2008, agency securities, agency mortgage-backed securities (MBS), AAA/Aaa-rated private-label real estate MBS, collateralized MBS, agency-collateralized mortgage obligations, and other asset-backed securities were added to the list. The Treasury securities so borrowed could then be repo-ed overnight and used to liquefy what might otherwise be illiquid assets in a period of market turmoil.

The Primary Dealer Credit Facility (PDCF) was announced on March 16, 2008, extending overnight borrowing from the Federal Reserve to primary dealers. (Currently, there are 20 dealers with whom the Federal Reserve trades government securities, including both banks and investment banks.) The loans are overnight but may be renewed daily for a period of six months or longer if conditions warrant. The interest rate charged is the primary credit rate. The collateral requirements under the PDCF differ somewhat from those used for regular discount borrowing.

U.S. Treasuries, agency securities, agency MBS, and investment-grade debt facilities can be used for borrowing.[3]

In addition to setting up these programs, on March 14, 2008, the Federal Reserve Bank of New York, in conjunction with JPMorgan Chase, provided a 28-day emergency loan to Bear Stearns. Two days later, Bear Stearns signed a merger agreement with JPMorgan Chase in a stock swap worth $2 a share. In addition, the Federal Reserve agreed to issue a nonrecourse loan of $29 billion to JPMorgan Chase, thereby assuming the risk of the less liquid assets of Bear Stearns.

As the financial problems continued, the Federal Reserve made a dramatic move on September 16, 2008: stepping in to prevent the financial collapse of AIG, which suffered a liquidity crisis following the downgrading of its credit rating. This action was taken under section 13(3) of the Federal Reserve Act, which was added in 1932 and allows the Fed to make loans under "unusual and exigent circumstances." Federal Reserve officials announced the creation of a credit facility with a 24-month term (with a 2 percent fee upfront and at an interest rate of 8.50 percent on the portion it has not yet borrowed and 8.50 percent over the three-month London Inter-Bank Offered Rate [LIBOR] on the borrowed amount), under which AIG is allowed to draw up to $85 billion, in exchange for warrants for a 79.9 percent equity stake in AIG and the right to suspend dividends to previously issued common and preferred stock. AIG announced the same day that its board accepted the terms of the Federal Reserve's rescue package.

On October 8, 2008, the Federal Reserve Board authorized the Federal Reserve Bank of New York to borrow securities from certain regulated U.S. insurance subsidiaries of the AIG. Under this program, the New York Fed may borrow up to $37.8 billion in investment-grade, fixed-income securities from AIG in return for cash collateral. These securities were previously lent by AIG's insurance company subsidiaries to third parties. Drawdowns to that date under the existing $85 billion New York Fed loan facility have been used, in part, to settle transactions with counterparties returning these third-party securities to AIG. This new program allows AIG to replenish liquidity used in settling those transactions, while providing enhanced credit protection to the New York Fed and U.S. taxpayers in the form of an interest in these securities. On October 30, 2008, AIG said it would be able to borrow up to

$20.9 billion from the Commercial Paper Funding Facility (CPFF) program. This brings AIG's maximum total borrowing from the Fed to $143.7 billion.[4]

The Federal Reserve's actions to shore up AIG did not end there. On November 10, 2008, the interest rate on the new credit facility was reduced to match the three-month LIBOR plus 300 basis points, and the fee on undrawn funds was reduced to 75 basis points. The life of the credit facility was extended from two years to five years. The Treasury Department also announced its intention to purchase $40 billion of newly issued AIG preferred shares under the Troubled Asset Relief Program (TARP). This purchase allows the Federal Reserve to reduce from $85 billion to $60 billion the total amount available under the original credit facility created on September 16, 2008. The Federal Reserve Board also authorized the Federal Reserve Bank of New York to establish two new lending facilities relating to AIG under section 13(3) of the Federal Reserve Act.

In one new program, the Residential Mortgage-Backed Securities Facility (RMBSF), the New York Federal Reserve Bank will lend up to $22.5 billion to a newly formed limited liability company (LLC) to fund the LLC's purchase of residential mortgage-backed securities from AIG's U.S. securities lending collateral portfolio. AIG will make a $1 billion subordinated loan to the LLC and bear the risk for the first $1 billion of any losses on the portfolio. The loans will be secured by all of the assets of the LLC and will be repaid from the cash flows produced by these assets as well as proceeds from any sales of these assets. The New York Fed and AIG will share any residual cash flows after the loans are repaid. Proceeds from this facility, together with other AIG internal resources, will be used to return all cash collateral posted for securities loans outstanding under AIG's U.S. securities lending program. As a result, the $37.8 billion securities lending facility established by the New York Fed on October 8, 2008, is expected to be repaid and terminated.

The other new facility, the Collateralized Debt Obligations Facility (CDOF), allows the New York Federal Reserve Bank to lend up to $30 billion to a newly formed LLC to fund the LLC's purchase of multisector collateralized debt obligations (CDOs) on which AIG Financial Products has written credit default swap (CDS) contracts. AIG will make a $5 billion subordinated loan to the LLC and bear the risk for the first

$5 billion of any losses on the portfolio. In connection with the purchase of the CDOs, the CDS counterparties will concurrently unwind the related CDS transactions. The loans will be secured by all of the LLC's assets and will be repaid from cash flows produced by these assets as well as the proceeds from any sales of these assets. The New York Fed and AIG will share any residual cash flows after the loans are repaid.

The Treasury purchase of $40 billion of newly issued AIG preferred shares is not part of the $250 billion that was set aside for purchase of preferred shares of banks. Instead, the money will come from the $100 billion in second-round funding that President Bush requested from the $700 bailout package, leaving $350 billion still to be allocated as of late 2008.[5]

Efforts have also been undertaken to address liquidity issues on a broader global scale. On September 18, 2008, the Bank of Canada, the Bank of England (BoE), the European Central Bank (ECB), the Federal Reserve, the Bank of Japan, and the Swiss National Bank (SNB) announced measures designed to ease pressures in the U.S. dollar short-term funding markets. The Federal Open Market Committee (FOMC) authorized a $180 billion expansion of its temporary reciprocal currency arrangements (swap lines) to provide dollar funding for both term and overnight liquidity operations by the other central banks. Furthermore, to assist in the expansion of other central banks' operations, the FOMC on October 13, 2008, authorized increases in the sizes of its temporary swap facilities with the BoE, the ECB, and the SNB so that these central banks can meet demand for U.S. dollar funding. These arrangements have been authorized through April 30, 2009.

Things did not stop here. On September 22, 2008, the Federal Reserve allowed Goldman Sachs and Morgan Stanley to become bank holding companies. Also, on November 10, 2008, the Federal Reserve approved the application of American Express to become a bank holding company. To provide increased liquidity support to these firms as they transition to bank holding company structures, the Federal Reserve Bank of New York was authorized to extend credit to the U.S. broker-dealer subsidiaries of Goldman Sachs and Morgan Stanley against all types of collateral that may be pledged at the Federal Reserve's primary credit facility for depository institutions or at the existing PDCF. The Federal Reserve has also made these collateral arrangements available to the broker-dealer subsidiary of Merrill Lynch. In addition, the Federal Reserve Bank of New York was also authorized to extend credit to the London-based broker-dealer subsidiaries of Goldman Sachs, Morgan Stanley, and Merrill Lynch against collateral that would be eligible to be pledged at the PDCF.

Allowing these two investment banking firms to become bank holding companies raises interesting issues regarding the Gramm-Leach-Bliley Act, which allowed the creation of financial holding companies encompassing commercial banking, investment banking, and insurance activities within a single entity. Some have blamed Gramm-Leach-Bliley for the financial crisis, but this conclusion is totally wrong. Of the big five investment banks, the three (Merrill Lynch, Lehman Brothers, and Bear Stearns) that got into the deepest trouble were all unaffiliated with banks. Furthermore, because banks eventually acquired two (Merrill Lynch and Bear Stearns) of these three firms, it can be said that the Act therefore helped the government find a satisfactory resolution for dealing with them.

Under the $700 billion Emergency Economic Stabilization Act (see full details in the next section of this chapter), the Federal Reserve was authorized to pay interest on required and excess reserves of depository institutions. On November 5, 2008, the Fed announced that the rate on required reserves would be set equal to the average target federal funds rate over the reserve maintenance period and the rate on excess balances would be set equal to the lowest FOMC target rate in effect during the reserve maintenance period. These changes became effective for the maintenance periods beginning November 6, 2008.

On October 14, 2008, the Federal Reserve announced further details of its Commercial Paper Funding Facility (CPFF) program, created a week earlier to provide a broad liquidity backstop for the commercial paper market (in which corporations sell short-term debt), thus increasing the availability of credit for businesses and households. Under the CPFF, the Federal Reserve Bank of New York will finance the purchase both unsecured and asset-backed commercial paper from eligible issuers through its primary dealers (limited only to highly rated, U.S. dollar-denominated, three-month commercial paper). Federal Reserve pricing will be based on the then-current three-month overnight index swap (OIS) rate plus fixed spreads. For unsecured commercial paper, the lending rate is the three-month OIS + 100 basis points, plus 100 basis points as an unsecured credit surcharge. For asset-backed commercial paper, the lending rate is the three-month OIS + 300 basis points. On the first day of the program, General Electric borrowed just under $5 billion.[6] The CPFF began on October 27, 2008, and will cease purchasing commercial paper on April 30, 2009, unless the program is extended.

On October 21, 2008, in a move designed to restore faith in the safety of money market accounts, the Federal Reserve announced the creation of the Money Market Investor Funding Facility (MMIFF) to provide liquidity to U.S. money market investors. Under the MMIFF, authorized under Section 13(3) of the Federal Reserve Act, the New York Fed provides senior secured funding to special purpose vehicles (PSPVs) as part of an industry-supported private-sector initiative to finance the purchase of eligible assets from eligible investors. Eligible assets include U.S. dollar-denominated certificates of deposit and commercial paper issued by highly rated financial institutions and having remaining maturities of 90 days or less. Eligible investors include U.S. money market mutual funds and over time may include other U.S. money market investors. The MMIFF provides assurance that money market mutual funds can liquidate their investments if cash is needed to cover withdrawals from customers. The New York Fed will lend to each PSPV, on a senior secured basis, 90 percent of the purchase price of each eligible asset; the PSPVs will hold the eligible assets until they mature, and proceeds from the assets will be used to repay the Federal Reserve loans and asset-backed commercial paper. The PSPVs will be authorized to purchase up to $600 billion in eligible assets, and because the New York Fed will provide 90 percent of the financing, Federal Reserve lending for this program could total $540 billion. The PSPVs will cease purchasing assets on April 30, 2009, unless the facility's mandate is extended, and the New York Fed will continue to fund the PSPVs until their underlying assets mature.

The MMIFF complements the Commercial Paper Funding Facility (discussed above) and the Asset Backed Commercial Paper Money Market Mutual Fund Liquidity Facility (AMLF, which will be discussed later in this section), announced on September 19, 2008, which extends loans to banking organizations to purchase asset-backed commercial paper from money market mutual funds. The AMLF, CPFF, and MMIFF are all intended to improve liquidity in short-term debt markets and thereby increase the availability of credit.

On November 25, 2008, the Fed created the Term Asset-Backed Securities Loan Facility (TALF), under which the New York Fed will make up to $200 billion of loans. TALF loans will have a one-year term, will be nonrecourse to the borrower and will be fully secured by eligible asset-backed securities (ABS). Treasury will provide $20 billion of credit protection to the Fed in connection with the TALF. Eligible collateral will include U.S. dollar-denominated cash (that is, not synthetic) ABS that have a long-term credit rating in the highest investment-grade rating category (for example, AAA) from two or more major nationally recognized statistical rating organizations (NRSROs) and do not have a long-term credit rating of below the highest investment-grade rating category from a major NRSRO. The underlying credit exposures of eligible ABS initially must be auto loans, student loans, credit card loans, or small business loans guaranteed by the U.S. Small Business Administration. All U.S. persons that own eligible collateral may participate in the TALF. Collateral haircuts will be established by the FRBNY for each class of eligible collateral. Haircuts will be determined based on the price volatility of each class of eligible collateral.

On the same day, the Fed announced initiation of a program to purchase the direct obligations of housing-related government-sponsored enterprises (GSEs)—Fannie Mae, Freddie Mac, and the Federal Home Loan Banks—and MBS backed by Fannie Mae, Freddie Mac, and Ginnie Mae. Purchases of up to $100 billion in GSE direct obligations under the program will be conducted with the Fed's primary dealers through a series of competitive auctions. Purchases of up to $500 billion in MBS will be conducted by asset managers selected via a competitive process. Purchases of both direct obligations and MBS are expected to take place over several quarters, with a start date at the end of 2008.

As a result of all these sweeping actions, the composition of the Fed's balance sheet changed dramatically, as shown in Table 6.1 and Figure 6.16. Its total assets grew from $880 billion in July 2007 to $885 billion in April 2008, finally hitting $996 billion in mid-September 2008. The increase over the entire period was 13 percent or $115 billion.

Table 6.1 Consolidated Statement of Condition of All Federal Reserve Banks

US$ Millions	11/26/2008	10/29/2008	10/8/2008	9/18/2008	4/2/2008	7/4/2007
Assets						
Gold certificate account	11,037	11,037	11,037	11,037	11,037	11,037
Special drawing rights certificate account	2,200	2,200	2,200	2,200	2,200	2,200
Coin	1,642	1,645	1,522	1,468	1,340	924
Securities, repurchase agreements, term auction credit, and other loans	1,234,185	1,241,215	1,170,550	849,133	802,036	820,989
Securities held outright	488,628	490,089	490,684	479,839	581,240	790,553
U.S. Treasury	476,407	476,469	476,579	479,839	581,240	790,553
Bills	18,423	18,423	18,423	21,740	92,985	277,019
Notes and bonds, nominal	410,491	410,757	411,731	411,731	445,050	474,672
Notes and bonds, inflation-indexed	41,071	40,806	39,832	39,832	38,437	34,459
Inflation compensation	6,422	6,484	6,593	6,536	4,769	4,403
Federal agency	12,221	13,620	14,105	0	0	0
Repurchase agreements	80,000	80,000	100,000	98,000	76,000	30,250
Term auction credit	406,508	301,363	149,000	150,000	100,000	
Other loans	259,048	369,763	430,866	121,294	44,796	186
Net portfolio holdings of Commercial Paper Funding Facility LLC	294,094	144,808	–	–	–	–
Net portfolio holdings of LLCs funded through the Money Market Investor Funding Facility	0	–	–	–	–	–
Net portfolio holdings of Maiden Lane LLC	26,979	26,848	29,487	29,367	–	–
Net portfolio holdings of Maiden Lane III LLC	21,148	–	–	–	–	–

(Continued)

241

Table 6.1 (*Continued*)

US$ Millions	11/26/2008	10/29/2008	10/8/2008	9/18/2008	4/2/2008	7/4/2007
Items in process of collection	1,096	1,083	1,191	908	4,733	4,916
Bank premises	2,180	2,174	2,170	2,168	2,145	2,045
Other assets	514,523	539,670	374,943	99,289	61,911	38,288
Total assets	2,109,083	1,970,680	1,593,099	995,570	885,401	880,399
Liabilities						
Federal Reserve notes, net of F.R. Bank holdings	835,083	823,713	811,692	796,094	779,560	781,376
Reverse repurchase agreements	99,761	94,655	77,349	46,633	41,061	32,209
Deposits	1,117,260	1,005,698	655,226	106,045	17,840	21,238
Depository institutions	611,195	425,972	183,314	89,102	11,417	16,755
U.S. Treasury, general account	17,355	19,484	5,544	5,512	6,013	4,117
U.S. Treasury, supplementary financing account	479,054	558,864	459,246	–	–	–
Foreign official	187	187	101	102	98	96
Other	9,470	1,192	7,021	11,330	312	269
Deferred availability cash items	2,611	2,317	2,736	2,614	3,260	5,822
Other liabilities and accrued dividends	11,482	3,879	4,109	2,849	3,734	5,665
Total liabilities	2,066,197	1,930,261	1,551,112	954,235	845,455	846,311
Capital accounts						
Capital paid in	20,871	20,314	20,312	20,211	19,548	16,163
Surplus	17,170	18,335	18,523	18,516	18,471	15,399
Other capital accounts	4,844	1,769	3,153	2,608	1,927	2,527
Total capital	42,886	40,418	41,988	41,335	39,946	34,088

SOURCES: Federal Reserve, Milken Institute.

Figure 6.16 Federal Reserve Assets Increased But Asset Quality Deteriorated (Weekly, January 5, 2000–November 26, 2008)

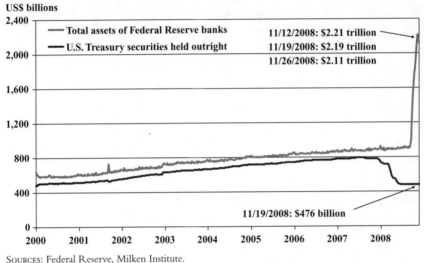

SOURCES: Federal Reserve, Milken Institute.

In the next two months, however, total assets more than doubled, climbing by $1 trillion to $2.1 trillion by November 26, 2008. For the most part, the Fed's initial response involved simply swapping troubled private-sector securities for government-sector securities or making loans to the private sector. It was not adding to the supply of credit until late in 2008. Apparently not until relatively late in the game did the Fed's concerns about inflationary pressures give way to concerns about slowing real economic activity.

As Table 6.1 shows, the new Supplementary Financing Program that began on September 17, 2008, led to an increase of Treasury deposits of $459 billion in exchange for an equivalent amount of Treasury securities. Although the Fed could have acquired such securities through open market operations, this would have led to an expansion in the money supply. Because this created the danger of inflation, the Fed chose the other course of action. But despite its worries about inflation, the actual federal funds rate has declined below the target federal funds rate, which means the Fed has allowed an expansion in credit and thus an increase in its total assets. Moreover, the Fed lowered the target federal funds rate by 50 basis points to 1.5 percent on October 8, 2008, and then again to 1 percent on October 29, rather than maintaining it by selling government securities through open market operations. Furthermore, the Fed has seen its holdings of Treasury securities held outright decline to $477 billion as of October 8, 2008. Given the increased risk exposure of asset value declines now on the Fed's balance sheet, its $40 billion in capital seems shakier than it did just a short time ago. Indeed, on October 23, 2008, the Federal Reserve reported an (unrealized) loss of $2.7 billion on the $29 billion in troubled assets it took over from Bear Stearns.

The overall impacts of the recent and largely unprecedented actions by the Fed are summarized in Table 6.2. It is apparent that the balance sheet ballooned tremendously in a relatively short period of time, as detailed above. But the Fed's total assets back in mid-2007, before the crisis, were mainly constrained by the public's holdings of cash and depository institutions' holdings of reserves. Since then, the Treasury's deposits have provided leeway for sufficient growth in the balance sheet. As a result, the Federal Reserve's assets now exceed $2.1 trillion and its assumed responsibilities beyond targeting prices have grown enormously.[7]

One concern about the Fed's recent actions is that they may exacerbate inflation if the current recession follows a V-shaped recovery. The housing price bubble came about because interest rates were capped too low for too long. Figure 6.17 shows that from October 2002 through April 2005, real short-term interest rates were negative. After remaining positive for 25 months, real interest rates became negative once again in January 2008. Indeed, they grew substantially more negative in recent months than in the earlier part of the decade. The cuts in the target federal funds rate under Chairman Bernanke have been far more aggressive then those under his predecessor, Chairman Greenspan. As Figure 6.18 shows, the effective federal funds rate was close to zero in November 2008 and was actually below the target federal fund rate for two months or so. This situation leaves little room for the Fed to lower rates still further. Depending on how low they remain and how long they stay low, the possibility remains that other asset bubbles may form.

Table 6.2 Impact of Recent Actions on the Fed's Balance Sheet (US$ Billions)

	7/5/2007	11/26/2008	Date of Announcement of Action	Notes
Treasury securities held outright	790.6	476.4	—	Before the crisis, these securities accounted for nearly 90 percent of the Federal Reserve's assets. This figure had declined to 22.5 percent on November 26, 2008.
Miscellaneous	51.6	87.5	—	Including $11 billion in gold certificate account
Foreign currencies and other assets	38.3	514.5	—	U.S. dollars were swapped for foreign currencies so that foreign central banks could satisfy local demand for U.S. dollars.
Term Discount Window Program (TDWP)	—	91.7	10/17/07	The program extends the term of discount window loans from overnight to up to 90 days.
Term Auction Facility (TAF)	—	406.5	12/12/07	The Federal Reserve auctions off loans under the TAF every Thursday for a term of 28 days. It may expand TAF lending to $900 billion by the end of 2008.
Primary Dealer Credit Facility (PDCF)	—	57.9	3/16/08	The PDCF extends overnight borrowing from the Federal Reserve to primary dealers.

(Continued)

Table 6.2 (*Continued*)

	7/5/2007	11/26/2008	Date of Announcement of Action	Notes
Asset Backed Commercial Paper Money Market Mutual Fund Liquidity Facility (AMLF)	—	53.3	9/19/08	Loans to banks so that they can buy asset-backed commercial paper from money market funds.
Commercial Paper Funding Facility (CPFF)	—	294.1	10/7/08	Under the CPFF, a special-purpose vehicle (SPV) will purchase from eligible issuers three-month U.S. dollar-denominated commercial paper through the New York Fed's primary dealers.
Money Market Investor Funding Facility (MMIFF)	—	0.0	11/24/08	The MMIFF provides assurance that money market mutual funds can liquidate their investments if cash is needed to cover withdrawals from customers.
Bear Stearns	—	27.0	3/14/08	Market value of the initial $29 billion mortgage-backed securities, acquired by the Federal Reserve from JPMorgan Chase to fund its purchase of Bear Stearns and now held by Maiden Lane LLC.

AIG	—	100.7	9/16/08	This includes: a $85 billion two-year secured loan to AIG on September 16, 2008; an additional $20.9 billion credit line under CPFF on October 30, 2008; and a $22.5 billion lending facility to purchase MBS from AIG and another $30 billion facility to purchase CDOs on which AIG has written CDS contracts (both of these facilities were created on November 10, 2008). As of November 25, 2008, $79.6 billion of credit was extended to AIG and $21.1 billion was extended for purchasing CDOs.
Total assets	880.4	2,109.6		
Memo:				
Term Securities Lending Facility (TSLF)	—	193.2	3/11/08	The TSLF establishes term swaps between the Federal Reserve and primary dealers. Collateral can be Treasury securities, federal agency securities, and other highly rated debt securities.

Sources: Federal Reserve, Milken Institute.

Figure 6.17   Negative Real Short-Term Interest Rates
(Monthly, January 2000–September 2008)

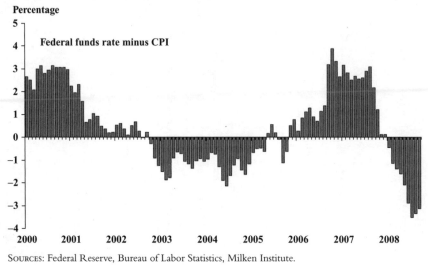

SOURCES: Federal Reserve, Bureau of Labor Statistics, Milken Institute.

Figure 6.18   The Federal Reserve Has Little Maneuvering Room
(Daily, June 1, 2008–November 14, 2008)

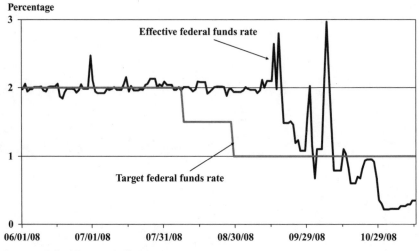

SOURCES: Federal Reserve, Milken Institute.

Congress and the White House Take Steps to Contain the Damage

Congress and the White House have made their own attempts to rein in the housing and credit crises.[8] On August 31, 2007, a month after the failure of two Bear Stearns hedge funds that were heavily invested in securities backed by subprime mortgages, President Bush announced a new initiative to help an estimated 240,000 families avoid foreclosure. The Federal Housing Administration (FHA) launched the FHASecure plan, which allows borrowers in default to qualify for refinancing if they have strong credit histories and had been making timely mortgage payments before their interest rates reset.

Shortly thereafter, in October 2007, the formation of HOPE NOW was announced. This national alliance (described in greater detail earlier in this chapter) was created to reach out to distressed homeowners and prevent foreclosures. It is a collaboration of credit and homeowners' counselors, mortgage servicers, and mortgage market participants that will explore a variety of methods to reach out to at-risk homeowners, including a direct-mail campaign to encourage at-risk borrowers to call their mortgage servicer or credit counselors. The alliance aims to improve communications between servicers and nonprofit counselors to speed outreach and to develop and explain options for at-risk borrowers and develop standards with investors to enable counseling sessions for homeowners to be funded by servicing contracts.

Two months later, President Bush further announced that HOPE NOW had developed a plan to assist up to 1.2 million homeowners by refinancing existing loans into new private mortgages, moving them into an FHASecure plan or freezing their current interest rates for five years.

Then, in February 2008, President Bush signed into law the Economic Stimulus Act. While tax rebates for low- and middle-income taxpayers and tax incentives to stimulate business investment were the centerpiece, the package also increased the maximum size of loans eligible for purchase by Fannie Mae and Freddie Mac.

Five months later, in July 2008, the Housing and Economic Recovery Act (HERA) authorized the FHA to guarantee up to $300 billion in new 30-year fixed-rate mortgages for subprime borrowers if lenders voluntarily write down principal loan balances to 90 percent of current appraisal value. It also established a single regulator—the Federal Housing Finance Agency (FHFA)—for Fannie Mae, Freddie Mac, and the Federal Home Loan Banks (all GSEs). FHFA represents a merger of the Office of Federal Housing Enterprise Oversight (OFHEO) and the Federal Housing Finance Board (FHFB), to be finalized by July 30, 2009. The Act also provides temporary authority to the Treasury secretary to purchase any obligations and other securities in any amounts issued by the GSEs involved in the mortgage market.

As the financial crisis escalated in the autumn of 2008, the federal government made several increasingly dramatic moves. On September 7, the FHFA placed Fannie Mae and Freddie Mac into conservatorship, while Treasury announced a temporary program to purchase GSE mortgage-backed securities to help make loan financing available to home buyers.

Less than two weeks later, in an effort to head off a massive and destructive run on assets, Treasury announced a temporary guaranty program for money market mutual funds. On the same day, the Securities and Exchange Commission (SEC) temporarily banned short selling, which some believe was unduly contributing to plunging stock prices.

The most sweeping action of all came on October 3, 2008, when the Emergency Economic Stabilization Act (EESA) was signed into law. The Act empowers Treasury to use up to $700 billion to inject capital into financial institutions, purchase or insure mortgage assets, and purchase any other troubled assets that Treasury deems necessary for market stability. In a follow-up move, Treasury unveiled the Troubled Assets Relief Program (TARP); its initial strategy was purchasing $250 billion of senior preferred shares, with half of this amount going to nine big financial institutions.

Each of these historic government actions is explained in greater detail in the pages that follow.

The Economic Stimulus Act of 2008

In February 2008, this act was signed into law with the goal of boosting the U.S. economy and averting or lessening a recession. It provided tax rebates to low- and middle-income taxpayers, tax incentives to stimulate business investment, and an increase in the limits imposed on mortgages eligible for purchase by government-sponsored enterprises. The total cost of this bill was projected by the Congressional Budget Office at $124 billion over 2008 to 2018.

The tax rebates were paid via checks issued to individual taxpayers during 2008. Most taxpayers below the income limit received a rebate of at least $300 and up to $600 per person (at least $600 and up to $1,200 for married couples filing jointly). Businesses received a one-time depreciation tax deduction equal to 50 percent of the cost of specified kinds of new investment during 2008. The law also raised the limits on the value of new productive capital that businesses may exclude from their income as business expenses during 2008. Previously, the limit on expensable productive capital investments had been $128,000, reduced (but not below zero) by the amount by which the value of those investments exceeded $510,000. The law raised those limits to $250,000 and $800,000, respectively.

Housing and Economic Recovery Act of 2008

On July 30, President Bush signed the Housing and Economic Recovery Act of 2008.[9] This legislation covers FHA modernization and an FHA-backed rescue plan, GSE oversight reform and backstop, tax incentives, low-income and affordable housing, Truth in Lending Act (TILA) reform, empowering states, and licensing.

The Act authorizes a $25 million appropriation to FHA to improve technology, processes, and program performance; eliminate fraud; and provide appropriate staffing. Effective January 1, 2009, it also alters the requirements for loans that can guaranteed by the FHA: The loan limit was increased to the lesser of 115 percent of the local median home price or $625,500, with a floor for lower priced markets of $271,000. It also created a 12-month stay on FHA's proposal for risk-based premiums, set down payment requirements at 3.5 percent, and prohibited seller-funded down payment assistance (either direct or through a third party).

Regarding GSE oversight, the Act created a new regulator (five-year term, appointed by the president and confirmed by the Senate) with oversight authority similar to that of bank regulators. It established a new affordable housing fund and capital magnet fund to be funded by a 4.2-basis-point fee on all new loans, significantly changed the affordable housing goals, and raised the conforming loan limit (to the higher of $417,000 or 115 percent of the local median home price, not to exceed

$625,500; changes became effective January 1, 2009). In addition, the Act authorized the Treasury secretary to temporarily increase the GSEs' lines of credit and, if necessary, to buy equity in the GSEs to restore confidence to credit markets. It also provided a role for Treasury and the Fed in GSE oversight to ensure safety and soundness.

The law also created a voluntary program, HOPE for Homeowners (H4H), which encourages lenders to write down the loan balance of a borrower in distress in exchange for an FHA-guaranteed loan not to exceed 90 percent of the newly appraised value of the home. Borrowers would be required to pay an upfront mortgage insurance premium of 3 percent and an annual mortgage insurance premium of 1.5 percent. To qualify, the borrower must have a debt-to-income ratio above 31 percent on the original loan. The loan amount may not exceed a maximum of $550,440, and the program is capped at $300 billion. This program began on October 1, 2008, and ends September 30, 2011. Media reports indicate, however, that it has gotten off to a rocky start.[10]

Under the Act, a $7,500 refundable tax credit is created for first-time home buyers. Moreover, the Act expands the volume cap for the low-income housing tax credit, allows for tax-exempt treatment of bonds guaranteed by the Federal Home Loan Banks, and exempts the low-income housing tax credit from the alternative minimum tax. The Act also encourages the development of low-income and affordable housing by harmonizing multifamily FHA mortgage insurance programs with the low-income housing tax credit.

The Act requires that TILA disclosures be delivered to borrowers seven days prior to loan closing. It requires that borrowers receive examples of how payments would change based on rate adjustments and information on the maximum possible payment under the loan terms. Consumers are also to receive early disclosures before paying anything more than a nominal fee that covers the cost of a credit report.

Furthermore, the Act raises the cap by $11 billion on tax-free bonds that state housing finance agencies may use to help at-risk homeowners by refinancing troubled loans. It also appropriates $4 billion for states to purchase and renovate abandoned and foreclosed properties, reducing the blight and neglect in communities with high foreclosure rates. In addition, it encourages state officials to create a national licensing system for residential loan originators, allows HUD to create its own national licensing system if the states fail, establishes minimum qualifications for all loan originators, and requires federal regulators to create a registry for banks and thrift employees who originate loans.

Conservatorship of Fannie Mae and Freddie Mac

On September 7, 2008, the federal government seized control of Fannie Mae and Freddie Mac, with FHFA appointed as conservator and charged with overseeing their affairs and bringing them back to financial health. To promote stability in the secondary mortgage market and lower the cost of funding, the GSEs were charged with modestly increasing their mortgage-backed security (MBS) portfolios through the end of 2009. Then, to address systemic risk, their portfolios will be gradually reduced by 10 percent per year, largely through natural runoff, eventually stabilizing at a lower, less risky size.

The move was structured so that each company would maintain a positive net worth. Treasury receives senior preferred stock with a liquidation preference, an upfront $1 billion issuance of senior preferred stock with a 10% coupon from each GSE, quarterly dividend payments, warrants representing an ownership stake of 79.9% in each GSE going forward, and receives a quarterly fee starting in 2010. The agreements are spelled out in contracts between Treasury and each GSE; they are indefinite in duration and have a capacity of $100 billion each. If the FHFA determines that a GSE's liabilities have exceeded its assets under generally accepted accounting principles, Treasury will contribute cash capital to the GSE equal to the difference between liabilities and assets. An amount equal to each such contribution will be added to the senior preferred stock held by Treasury, which will be senior to all other preferred stock, common stock, or other capital stock to be issued by the GSE.

The agreements also specify many other terms and conditions. Without the prior consent of Treasury, each GSE shall not make any payment to purchase or redeem its capital stock or pay any dividends (other than dividends on the senior preferred stock); issue capital stock of any kind; enter into any new or adjust any existing compensation agreements with "named executive officers"; terminate conservatorship other than in connection with receivership; sell, convey, or transfer any of its assets outside the ordinary course of business except as necessary to meet their obligation under the agreements to reduce their portfolio of retained mortgages and MBS; increase its debt to more than 110 percent of its debt as of June 30, 2008; and acquire or merge with another entity. Also, each GSE's retained mortgage and mortgage-backed securities portfolio shall not exceed $850 billion as of December 31, 2009, and shall decline by 10 percent per year until it reaches $250 billion.

In the meantime, Treasury established a new secured lending credit facility that will be available to Fannie Mae, Freddie Mac, and the Federal Home Loan Banks. The GSE Credit Facility (GSECF) will provide secured funding on an as-needed basis under terms established by the Treasury secretary. Funding is provided directly by Treasury from its general fund held at the Federal Reserve Bank of New York in exchange for guaranteed MBS issued by Freddie Mac and Fannie Mae or advances made by the Federal Home Loan Banks. All such assets pledged against loans are acceptable with appropriate collateral margins as determined by Treasury.

To further support the availability of mortgage financing for millions of Americans, Treasury launched a temporary program to purchase GSE MBS. Treasury is committed to investing in agency MBS, with the size and timing subject to the discretion of the Treasury secretary. The scale of the program will be based on developments in the capital markets and housing markets. Treasury can hold this portfolio of MBS to maturity and, based on mortgage market conditions, may make adjustments to the portfolio. This program will expire on December 31, 2009, with Treasury's temporary authorities granted by the Congress in the Housing and Economic Recovery Act of 2008.

Because the GSEs are in conservatorship, it has been decided that they will no longer be managed with a strategy to maximize common shareholder returns, a strategy that historically has encouraged risk-taking. It is not clear exactly what the new strategy is going to be. It should also be noted that holders of the subordinated debt of these two GSEs were not wiped out. This is important because some have argued that by putting such debt holders at risk of loss, the yield on a firm's debt relative to the yield on U.S. Treasury securities will then serve as a market-based indicator of the risks being taken by the firm. Government bailouts, however, reduce the value of such an indicator.

Figure 6.19   Spreads of Fannie Mae and Freddie Mac Debt Yields over Treasury Rates Reaches All-Time High (Daily, January 1, 2008–November 19, 2008)

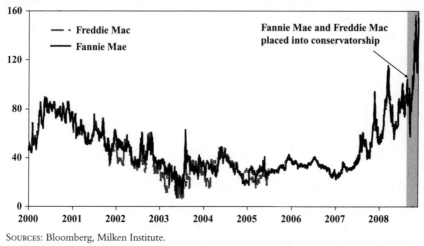

SOURCES: Bloomberg, Milken Institute.

It is interesting that after Fannie Mae and Freddie Mac were placed in the conservatorship, the yields on three-year debt issued by the two institutions compared to the yield on comparable-maturity Treasury securities rose to an all-time high, as shown in Figure 6.19. This indicates that there is still some concern on the part of investors about what will eventually happen to the two companies because the government has not provided an explicit guarantee on the debt issued by them.

Guaranty Program for Money Market Funds

On September 19, 2008, Treasury announced the establishment of a temporary guaranty program for the U.S. money market mutual fund industry, under authority of the Gold Reserve Act of 1934. This Act, which was amended in 1976, allows Treasury's Exchange Stabilization Fund to "... deal in gold, foreign exchange, and other instruments of credit and securities the secretary considers necessary" subject to approval of the president.[11] For the next year, Treasury pledged to insure the holdings of any publicly offered eligible money market mutual fund—both retail and institutional—that pays a fee to participate in the program. It was established due to concerns about the net asset value of money market funds falling below $1, which Treasury believed would exacerbate global financial market turmoil and cause severe liquidity strains in world markets.

This action followed as the report on September 16, 2008, that Reserve's Primary Fund broke the buck, with its shares worth only 97 cents on the dollar, largely because of its investments in the short-term debt of Lehman Brothers. Many money market mutual funds are a key source of funding for corporations to pay for payroll and other key short-term operating expenses.

Temporary Ban on Short Selling in Financial Companies

In June 2007, the SEC had abolished the uptick rule, which stated that a stock could not be shorted unless it had gone up in price.[12] But as the financial crisis gained momentum, the SEC took temporary emergency action on September 19, 2008, to prohibit short selling—and not just naked short selling (in which investors can short a stock without first borrowing the shares). The SEC's action initially applied to the securities of 799 companies and was scheduled to terminate on October 2. However, the ban was subsequently extended to October 8 and expanded to nearly 1,000 stocks. The prohibition covered not just financial companies but also companies like GM, GE, and IBM, which have significant revenue derived from financial activities. Shortly after the ban expired, selected traders were once again allowed to take short positions in even the companies on the list.

The purpose of the ban was to protect companies from a collapse in their stocks prices due to short sellers betting against the companies. Some argue, however, that a firm's financial condition, not short sellers, causes its stock price to decline. Studies will undoubtedly examine this tumultuous period to determine whether the ban had the desired effect. It is also interesting to note that there are hedge funds whose business strategy is based on short sales, and they were adversely affected, demonstrating that changes in government regulations can have unintended consequences.

The Emergency Economic Stabilization Act (EESA)

After a swift but bitter debate on Capitol Hill came to a close, the EESA was signed into law on October 3, 2008. (When Congress initially rejected an earlier version of this legislation on September 29, 2008, the Dow Jones Industrial Average fell by 778 points.) The Act empowered Treasury to use up to $700 billion to inject capital into financial institutions, to purchase or insure mortgage assets, and to purchase any other troubled assets that Treasury and the Federal Reserve deem necessary to promote financial market stability.

The TARP portion of the legislation gave Treasury $250 billion immediately, then required the president to certify that additional funds were needed ($100 billion, then $350 billion subject to Congressional disapproval). Treasury must report on the use of the funds and the progress in addressing the crisis. EESA also establishes an oversight board so that—in theory—Treasury cannot act in an arbitrary manner. It also calls for a special inspector general to protect against waste, fraud, and abuse.

The new law also gives the Federal Reserve the authority to pay interest on reserves and temporarily increases FDIC and National Credit Union Administration (NCUA) deposit insurance from $100,000 up to $250,000 until December 31, 2009. The Act temporarily raises the borrowing limits at Treasury for the FDIC and the National Credit Union Share Insurance Fund. It also restates the SEC's authority to suspend the application of Financial Accounting Standards Board Statement No. 157 (Fair Value Measurements, or FAS 157) if the SEC determines that it is in the public interest and protects investors.

It should be noted that in setting up TARP, discussions revolved around exactly how Treasury would spend the authorized funds. Some of this discussion revolved around whether to follow the models set by three earlier government operations set up to deal with similar problems in past crises:

- **Reconstruction Finance Corporation (RFC; 1932):** The RFC was created during the Hoover administration in 1932 and retained by President Roosevelt. It provided aid to state and local governments and made loans to banks, railroads, farm mortgage associations, and other businesses, with most repaid. It eventually ended operation in 1957.

- **Home Owner's Loan Corporation (HOLC; 1933):** The HOLC was established by the Home Owners Loan (or Refinancing) Act under President Franklin D. Roosevelt. Under the Act, Treasury was authorized to invest in HOLC stock. It could also issue bonds. The HOLC was used to extend shorter-term loans to fully amortized, longer-term loans, helping to refinance troubled mortgages and prevent foreclosure. The HOLC ended its operation in 1951, reportedly having earned a small profit.

- **Resolution Trust Corporation (RTC; 1989):** The RTC was created by the Financial Institutions Reform Recovery and Enforcement Act (FIRREA) of 1989. It was a government-owned asset management company that would manage and resolve all formerly FSLIC-insured institutions that were placed under conservatorship or receivership from January 1, 1989, through August 9, 1992. The assets liquidated by the RTC were primarily real estate-related assets, including mortgage loans, that had been assets of savings and loan associations (S&Ls) declared insolvent by the Office of Thrift Supervision during the S&L crisis of the 1980s. The RTC ended operations in 1995.

Troubled Assets Relief Program (TARP)

Shortly after the EESA was passed, on October 14, 2008, Treasury announced the TARP Capital Purchase Program (CPP) to purchase up to $250 billion of senior preferred shares in financial institutions (following the British approach of boosting bank capital in exchange for equity stakes). The program was available to qualifying U.S. controlled banks, savings associations, and certain bank and savings and loan holding companies engaged only in financial activities that elect to participate by November 14, 2008.

The program called for Treasury to determine eligibility and allocations for interested parties after consulting with the appropriate federal banking agency. The minimum subscription amount available to a participating institution is 1 percent of risk-weighted assets. The maximum subscription amount is the lesser of $25 billion or 3 percent of

risk-weighted assets. Treasury funded the senior preferred shares purchased under the program by year-end 2008. The senior preferred shares
qualify as Tier 1 capital and rank senior to common stock and *pari passu*
(which is at an equal level in the capital structure) with existing preferred
shares, other than preferred shares, which by their terms rank junior to
any other existing preferred shares.

The senior preferred shares pay a cumulative dividend rate of 5 percent annually for the first five years and reset to a rate of 9 percent
annually after year five. The senior preferred shares are nonvoting, other
than class voting rights on matters that could adversely affect the shares.
The senior preferred shares are callable at par after three years. Prior to
the end of three years, the senior preferred may be redeemed with the
proceeds from a qualifying equity offering of any Tier 1 perpetual preferred or common stock. Treasury may also transfer the senior preferred
shares to a third party at any time. In conjunction with the purchase
of senior preferred shares, Treasury receives warrants to purchase common stock with an aggregate market price equal to 15 percent of the
senior preferred investment. The exercise price on the warrants is the
market price of the participating institution's common stock at the time
of issuance, calculated on a 20-trading-day trailing average.

Companies participating in the program must adopt Treasury's standards for executive compensation and corporate governance for the
period during which Treasury holds equity issued under this program.
These standards generally apply to the chief executive officer, the chief
financial officer, and the three other most highly compensated executive
officers. The financial institution must meet certain standards, including (1) ensuring that incentive compensation for senior executives does
not encourage unnecessary and excessive risks that threaten the value of
the financial institution; (2) required clawback of any bonus or incentive
compensation paid to a senior executive based on statements of earnings,
gains, or other criteria that are later proven to be materially inaccurate;
(3) prohibition on the financial institution from making any golden
parachute payment to a senior executive based on the Internal Revenue Code provision; and (4) agreement not to deduct for tax purposes
executive compensation in excess of $500,000 for each senior executive.

On October 28, 2008, the first round of $125 billion disbursed un-
der the TARP Capital Purchase Program was allocated to nine of the

nation's largest financial institutions. On November 14, $33.6 billion was allocated to 21 institutions as part of the $125 billion second round. Another 23 institutions received an additional $2.9 billion on November 21, brining the total funds allocated under the TARP Capital Purchase Program to $161 billion. The amounts injected into each of these institutions are provided in Table 6.3, and the relative importance of these amounts to some of these institutions is shown in Table 6.4. Treasury officials originally said the department would release a list of institutions at the time they were selected to receive capital injections from TARP but later decided to let the recipient institutions make the announcements at that time, with Treasury later posting a list when payments are actually made.

It may be that some of the selected institutions were being rewarded for having already acquired, or perhaps being prompted to acquire, troubled financial institutions. Indeed, it was reported that National City, after being told it should not expect to receive a capital injection from Treasury, announced its acquisition by PNC Financial Services Group, which indicated that it did receive an injection of $7.7 billion.[13]

The use of TARP funds in this way puts Treasury, which does not disclose the criteria it relies on, in a position of picking winners and losers, especially in cases where weaker financial institutions are denied capital and thereby forced into being acquired by those institutions that *are* allowed access to the available funds. The benefit of this procedure, however, is that it potentially relieves the FDIC from having to seize weaker institutions that might otherwise fail. (Interestingly enough, the Federal Deposit Insurance Corporation Improvement Act of 1991 was designed to require bank supervisors to take prespecified actions, including requiring banks to recapitalize themselves, when bank capital starts to decline below certain "prompt corrective action" threshold levels. Apparently, this act did not have the desired effect insofar as government capital has been injected into banks.)

On November 12, 2008, Treasury announced that it was evaluating programs that would further leverage the impact of a TARP investment by attracting private capital, potentially through matching investments. In this regard, Table 6.5 shows that sovereign wealth funds had already made investments in selected U.S. financial institutions (Citigroup, Merrill Lynch, and Morgan Stanley) before the Treasury injected capital in these firms under CPP. The table also shows the initial investment

Table 6.3 Institutions and Capital Injections under TARP Capital Purchase Program (as of November 25, 2008)

Date of Payment Authorization	Name of Institution	Transaction Type (Purchase or Sale)	Description	Price Paid (US$ Millions)
10/28/2008	Bank of America	Purchase	Preferred stock with warrants	15,000
10/28/2008	Bank of New York Mellon	Purchase	Preferred stock with warrants	3,000
10/28/2008	Citigroup	Purchase	Preferred stock with warrants	25,000
10/28/2008	Goldman Sachs	Purchase	Preferred stock with warrants	10,000
10/28/2008	JPMorgan Chase	Purchase	Preferred stock with warrants	25,000
10/28/2008	Morgan Stanley	Purchase	Preferred stock with warrants	10,000
10/28/2008	State Street	Purchase	Preferred stock with warrants	2,000
10/28/2008	Wells Fargo	Purchase	Preferred stock with warrants	25,000
10/28/2008*	Merrill Lynch	Purchase	Preferred stock with warrants	10,000
11/14/2008	Bank of Commerce	Purchase	Preferred stock with warrants	17
11/14/2008	1st FS Corporation	Purchase	Preferred stock with warrants	16
11/14/2008	UCBH Holdings	Purchase	Preferred stock with warrants	299
11/14/2008	Northern Trust Corporation	Purchase	Preferred stock with warrants	1,576
11/14/2008	SunTrust Banks	Purchase	Preferred stock with warrants	3,500
11/14/2008	Broadway Financial	Purchase	Preferred stock with warrants	9
11/14/2008	Washington Federal	Purchase	Preferred stock with warrants	200
11/14/2008	BB&T	Purchase	Preferred stock with warrants	3,134
11/14/2008	Provident Bancshares	Purchase	Preferred stock with warrants	152
11/14/2008	Umpqua Holdings	Purchase	Preferred stock with warrants	214
11/14/2008	Comerica	Purchase	Preferred stock with warrants	2,250
11/14/2008	Regions Financial	Purchase	Preferred stock with warrants	3,500

(Continued)

Table 6.3 (*Continued*)

Date of Payment Authorization	Name of Institution	Transaction Type (Purchase or Sale)	Description	Price Paid (US$ Millions)
11/14/2008	Capital One Financial	Purchase	Preferred stock with warrants	3,555
11/14/2008	First Horizon National	Purchase	Preferred stock with warrants	867
11/14/2008	Huntington Bancshares	Purchase	Preferred stock with warrants	1,398
11/14/2008	KeyCorp	Purchase	Preferred stock with warrants	2,500
11/14/2008	Valley National Bancorp	Purchase	Preferred stock with warrants	300
11/14/2008	Zions Bancorporation	Purchase	Preferred stock with warrants	1,400
11/14/2008	Marshall & Ilsley	Purchase	Preferred stock with warrants	1,715
11/14/2008	U.S. Bancorp	Purchase	Preferred stock with warrants	6,599
11/14/2008	TCF Financial	Purchase	Preferred stock with warrants	361
11/21/2008	First Niagara Financial Group	Purchase	Preferred stock with warrants	184
11/21/2008	HF Financial Corp.	Purchase	Preferred stock with warrants	25
11/21/2008	Centerstate Banks of Florida Inc.	Purchase	Preferred stock with warrants	28
11/21/2008	City National Corporation	Purchase	Preferred stock with warrants	400
11/21/2008	First Community Bankshares Inc.	Purchase	Preferred stock with warrants	42
11/21/2008	Western Alliance Bancorporation	Purchase	Preferred stock with warrants	140
11/21/2008	Webster Financial Corporation	Purchase	Preferred stock with warrants	400

11/21/2008	Pacific Capital Bancorp	Purchase	Preferred stock with warrants	181
11/21/2008	Heritage Commerce Corp.	Purchase	Preferred stock with warrants	40
11/21/2008	Ameris Bancorp	Purchase	Preferred stock with warrants	52
11/21/2008	Porter Bancorp Inc.	Purchase	Preferred stock with warrants	35
11/21/2008	Banner Corporation	Purchase	Preferred stock with warrants	124
11/21/2008	Cascade Financial Corporation	Purchase	Preferred stock with warrants	39
11/21/2008	Columbia Banking System, Inc.	Purchase	Preferred stock with warrants	77
11/21/2008	Heritage Financial Corporation	Purchase	Preferred stock with warrants	24
11/21/2008	First PacTrust Bancorp, Inc.	Purchase	Preferred stock with warrants	19
11/21/2008	Severn Bancorp, Inc.	Purchase	Preferred stock with warrants	23
11/21/2008	Boston Private Financial Holdings, Inc.	Purchase	Preferred stock with warrants	154
11/21/2008	Associated Banc–Corp	Purchase	Preferred stock with warrants	525
11/21/2008	Trustmark Corporation	Purchase	Preferred stock with warrants	215
11/21/2008	First Community Corporation	Purchase	Preferred stock with warrants	11
11/21/2008	Taylor Capital Group	Purchase	Preferred stock with warrants	105
11/21/2008	Nara Bancorp, Inc.	Purchase	Preferred stock with warrants	67
			Total	161,472

SOURCE: U.S. Treasury Department.
*Settlement deferred pending merger.

Table 6.4 Relative Importance of Capital Injections under TARP for Selected Institutions

Name of Bank Holding Company	Capital Injection Oct. 28, 2008, US$ Billions	Equity Capital	Tier 1 Capital June 30, 2008, US$ Billions	Total Deposits	Risk-Weighted Assets	Total Assets	Injection Relative to	
							Common Stock	Tier 1 Capital
Bank of America	15	177	110	883	1,218	1,670	8	14
Bank of New York Mellon	3	17	10	99	116	186	18	29
Citigroup	25	109	88	820	978	1,325	23	28
Goldman Sachs	10	46*	n.a.	n.a.	n.a.	1,082*	22	n.a.
JPMorgan Chase	25	132	92	834	1,073	1,454	19	27
Morgan Stanley	10	36*	n.a.	n.a.	n.a.	987*	28	n.a.
State Street	2	13	9	101	66	139	16	22
Wells Fargo	25	49	37	361	460	558	51	68
Merrill Lynch	10	35	n.a.	n.a.	n.a.	931	29	n.a.

SOURCES: FDIC, U.S. Treasury Department, Milken Institute.
*As of Aug. 31, 2008.

Table 6.5 Sovereign Wealth Funds' Investments in Selected Institutions

Institution	Investor	Stake (Percentage)	Investment Amount (US$ Billions)	Instrument Type	Current Value, November 4, 2008 (US$ Billions)	Total Assets of Investor (US$ Billions)	Investment Share of Total Assets (Percentage)
Citigroup	Abu Dhabi Investment Authority	4.9	7.5	New convertible preferred stock	3.9	875	0.9
Citigroup	Government of Singapore Investment Corporation	3.7	6.9	New convertible preferred stock	3.0	330	2.1
Citigroup	Kuwait Investment Authority	1.6	3.0	New convertible preferred stock	1.3	264	1.1
Merrill Lynch	Kuwait Investment Authority	3.0	2.0	New convertible preferred stock	1.0	264	0.8
Merrill Lynch	Korea Investment Corporation	3.0	2.0	New convertible preferred stock	1.0	30	6.7
Merrill Lynch	Temasek Holdings	9.4	4.4	New common stock	3.0	134	3.3

(*Continued*)

Table 6.5 *(Continued)*

Institution	Investor	Stake (Percentage)	Investment Amount (US$ Billions)	Instrument Type	Current Value, November 4, 2008 (US$ Billions)	Total Assets of Investor (US$ Billions)	Investment Share of Total Assets (Percentage)
Morgan Stanley	China Investment Corporation	9.9	5.0	New convertible preferred stock	2.0	200	2.5
Barclays PLC	Temasek Holdings	1.8	2.0	Common stock	0.5	134	1.5
Credit Suisse	Qatar Investment Authority	1.0	0.6	Common stock	0.4	60	1.0
UBS	Government of Singapore Investment Corporation	9.8	9.8	New convertible preferred stock	4.8	330	3.0
UBS	Saudi Arabia Monetary Authority Foreign Holdings	2.0	1.8	New convertible preferred stock	1.0	365	0.5

SOURCES: Sovereign Wealth Fund Institute, institutions' financial statements.

amounts and the current value of those investments as of November 4, 2008. Furthermore, Treasury was also considering broadening access to nonbank financial institutions not eligible for the current capital program.

On November 21, 2008, the Office of the Comptroller of the Currency (OCC) announced that it had granted its first conditional preliminary approval of a new type of national bank "shelf-charter," designed to facilitate new equity investments in troubled depository institutions. The new mechanism involves the granting of preliminary approval to investors for a national bank charter. The charter remains inactive, or "on the shelf," until such time as the investor group is in a position to acquire a troubled institution. By granting the preliminary approval, the OCC expands the pool of potential buyers available to buy troubled institutions and in particular the new equity capital available to bid on troubled institutions through the FDIC's bid process. The first such approval was granted on November 24, 2008, to establish the Ford Group Bank.

An additional or alternative approach is to ask or require debt holders to swap their debt for an equity share in a troubled institution. This particular approach to help recapitalize institutions, however, has not received much attention. Although it is not clear why it was apparently left off the menu of options, it should receive more serious consideration. Rather than protecting all debt holders from sizable losses to maintain confidence in at least the biggest financial institutions, debt/equity swaps have the benefit of relieving at least a portion of the stability-enhancing obligation of the government to inject capital into institutions and/or guarantee their debts.

As of November 21, 2008, 53 "winning" publicly traded institutions had received capital injections. The capital injections amounted to $161.5 billion. Privately held institutions have until December 8, 2008, to apply for funds. This means that $88.5 billion remains to be allocated. The names of the "losing" institutions have not been publicly revealed. The intent of the capital injections is to encourage lending on a larger scale and improve investor confidence in banks.

The Treasury, FDIC, and the Fed issued the "Interagency Statement on Meeting the Needs of Creditworthy Borrowers" on November 12, 2008. It stated that the agencies expect all banking organizations to fulfill their fundamental role in the economy as intermediaries of credit to businesses, consumers, and other creditworthy borrowers. They expressed the concern that if banking organizations tighten their underwriting standards excessively or retreat from making sound credit decisions, current market conditions may be exacerbated, leading to slower growth and potential damage to the economy as well as the long-term interests and profitability of individual banking organizations.

On November 24, 2008, up to $306 billion of Citigroup's assets (an asset pool of loans and securities backed by residential and commercial real estate and other such assets on Citigroup's balance sheet) were guaranteed by the government. Under this plan, Citigroup takes the first loss up to $29 billion, and any loss in excess of that amount is shared by the government (90 percent) and Citigroup (10 percent). Treasury (via TARP) takes the second loss up to $5 billion, while FDIC takes the third loss up to $10 billion. The Federal Reserve funds the remaining pool of assets with a nonrecourse loan, subject to Citigroup's 10 percent loss sharing, at a floating rate of overnight interest swap plus 300 basis points.

A New Tax Break for Banks

Attracting little notice at the time, Treasury issued a new regulation (Notice 2008-83) on September 30, 2008, allowing banks—and only banks—that acquire another bank to offset their profits with losses from the loan portfolio of the acquired bank. Because the corporate tax rate is 35 percent, this means acquiring banks can avoid paying $35,000 in taxes for every $100,000 in losses they can use to offset profits. This created tremendous incentive for healthier institutions to acquire troubled institutions. (For example, Wells Fargo is acquiring Wachovia. Some media reports estimated that Wells Fargo may be able to use losses of more than $70 billion to obtain tax savings of $19.4 billion—exceeding the $15.1 billion it paid for Wachovia. It was also reported by news media that PNC was set to receive large tax breaks.[14]) It is interesting to note that the tax law being changed was designed precisely to prevent tax-motivated acquisitions of corporations losing money.

In addition, Treasury also implemented a tax break that allows community banks suffering losses on preferred stocks in Fannie Mae and Freddie Mac to treat those losses as ordinary losses rather than capital losses. These tax benefits to banks are in addition to the $700 billion available under the TARP and will further increase the federal budget deficit.

The FDIC Takes Steps to Instill Greater Confidence in Depository Institutions

Before discussing the steps taken by FDIC to deal with the financial crisis, it is important to discuss trends in depository institutions in recent years. Figure 6.20 shows that the number of FDIC-insured "problem" institutions (those in weak condition, which are placed under greater regulatory scrutiny) rose to a high of 136 in 2002 as a result of the 2001 recession and then declined to a low of 50 in 2006 before rising once again to 117 institutions in June 2008.

The situation looks somewhat different when examined in terms of the total assets held by problem institutions. Although these assets followed a path similar to the number of problem institutions, Figure 6.21 shows that total assets reached a high of $78.3 billion, which was roughly double the figure following the recession at the beginning of the decade.

Both of these tallies conspicuously omit Washington Mutual (the largest banking failure in U.S. history), which was acquired by JPMorgan Chase in September 2008, and Wachovia, which was later acquired by Wells Fargo. These two troubled institutions were presumably not included in the problem bank list because of their size. Officials no doubt feared that if the public learned more than $1 trillion in assets were held in problem institutions, that announcement might trigger a catastrophic run on all banks.

FDIC analysis suggests that a 5 percent reduction in uninsured deposits would reduce Gross Domestic Product growth by 1.2 percent per year in a normal economy and 2.0 percent per year in a stressed economy. With U.S. economic growth currently stressed, a run of this magnitude could result in, or deepen and prolong, recession. FDIC data indicate rapid and substantial outflows of uninsured deposits from institutions that are perceived to be stressed. The systemic nature of this threat is further evidenced by the increasing number of bank failures.

—Federal Deposit
Insurance Corporation
12 CFR Part 370
October 23, 2008
[6714-01-P]

Figure 6.20   Number of FDIC-Insured "Problem" Institutions

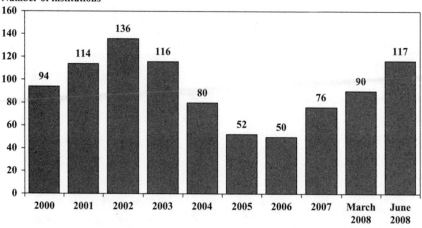

SOURCES: *Quarterly Banking Profile,* FDIC; Milken Institute.

The determination that an institution should be placed in the FDIC's problem list is based on the CAMELS rating system, with C representing capital adequacy, A asset quality, M management, E earnings, L liquidity, and S sensitivity to market risk. The scores range between 1 and 5, with

Figure 6.21   Assets of FDIC-Insured "Problem" Institutions

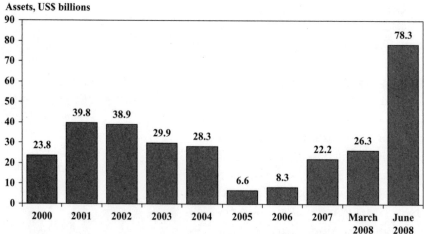

SOURCES: *Quarterly Banking Profile,* FDIC; Milken Institute.

the best banks rated a 1 and the worst banks rated a 5. Banks with 4 and 5 overall ratings are put on the problem list. However, the problem bank list is not made public and neither are examination reports of banking institutions prepared by the regulatory authorities. The agency periodically releases only the number of institutions on the list and their total assets.

In response to the growing number of weakened institutions and several high-profile bank failures, the FDIC took steps to instill greater confidence in all federally insured depository institutions. On October 3, 2008, the EESA temporarily raised the basic limit on federal deposit insurance coverage from $100,000 to $250,000 per depositor.[15] The increased deposit insurance limit means that an individual with $250,000 to deposit can now put it all in one bank rather than splitting it into deposits at least three banks to be guaranteed coverage. The legislation provides that the basic deposit insurance limit will return to $100,000 after December 31, 2009.

"The FDIC is taking this unprecedented action because we have faith in our economy, our country, and our banking system," said FDIC Chairman Sheila C. Bair. "The overwhelming majority of banks are strong, safe, and sound. A lack of confidence is driving the current turmoil, and it is this lack of confidence that these guarantees are designed to address."[16] There are two questions that arise with respect to this comment. First, if "the overwhelming majority of banks are strong, safe, and sound," why do they require capital injections? Second, what is the "lack of confidence" that is "driving the current turmoil?"

The FDIC's reserves had fallen to $45.2 billion as of June 30, 2008, representing 1.01 percent of insured domestic deposits—well below the statutory ratio of 1.15 percent. To rectify the situation, on October 7, 2008, the FDIC adopted a plan to replenish reserves. It also proposed new rules to increase the rates banks pay for deposit insurance and adjusted the process by which those rates are set. Currently, banks pay anywhere from five basis points to 43 basis points for deposit insurance. Under the proposal, the assessment rate schedule would be raised uniformly by 7 basis points (annualized) beginning on January 1, 2009. Beginning with the second quarter of 2009, changes would be made to the deposit insurance assessment system to make the increase in assessments fairer by requiring riskier institutions to pay a larger share. Together, the proposed changes would help ensure that the reserve ratio returns to at least 1.15 percent by the end of 2013.[17]

Proposed changes to the assessment system include assigning higher premiums to institutions with a significant reliance on secured liabilities, which generally raise the FDIC's loss in the event of failure. The proposal also would assess higher rates for institutions with a significant reliance on brokered deposits but, for well-managed and well-capitalized institutions, only when accompanied by rapid asset growth. (Brokered deposits combined with rapid asset growth have played a role in a number of costly failures, including some recent ones.)' The proposal also would provide incentives by reducing rates for institutions to hold long-term unsecured debt and, for smaller institutions, high levels of Tier 1 capital. The FDIC also voted to maintain the Designated Reserve Ratio at 1.25 percent as a signal of its long-term target for the fund.

On October 14, 2008, Secretary Paulson signed the systemic risk exception to the FDIC Act after receiving a recommendation from the boards of the FDIC and the Federal Reserve and consulting with the president. This move enabled the FDIC to temporarily guarantee the senior debt of all FDIC-insured institutions and their holding companies, as well as deposits in non–interest-bearing deposit transaction accounts. Regulators were to implement an enhanced supervisory framework to assure appropriate use of this new Temporary Liquidity Guarantee Program (TLGP). The ability to issue guaranteed debt under the program was scheduled to expire on June 30, 2009, and the full protection for deposits in non–interest-bearing transaction deposit accounts would revert back to the statutory limits on December 31, 2009. Under the plan, certain newly issued senior unsecured debt (the Debt Guarantee Program) issued on or before June 30, 2009, would be fully protected in the event the issuing institution subsequently fails or its holding company files for bankruptcy. This includes promissory notes, commercial paper, interbank funding, and any unsecured portion of secured debt. Coverage would be limited to June 30, 2012, even if the maturity exceeds that date. This guarantee will enable banks to use other shorter-term guaranty programs until they are able to issue the longer-term debt with the government guarantee.

Participants were to be charged a 75-basis-point fee to protect their new debt issues, and a 10-basis-point surcharge was to be added to a participating institution's current insurance assessment to fully cover the non-interest-bearing deposit transaction accounts. The other part of the program provides for a temporary unlimited guarantee of funds in non-interest-bearing transactions accounts (the Transaction Account Guarantee Program or TAG).[18]

On November 21, 2008, FDIC strengthened TLGP. Chief among the changes is that the debt guarantee will be triggered by payment default rather than bankruptcy or receivership. Another change is that short-term debt issued for one month or less will not be included in the TLGP. Eligible entities will have until December 5, 2008, to opt out of TLGP. The fee structure was changed to a sliding scale, depending on length of maturity. Shorter-term debt will have a lower fee structure and longer-term debt will have a higher fee. The range will be 50 basis points on debt of 180 days or less, and a maximum of 100 basis points for debt with maturities of one year or longer on an annualized basis. It is not yet clear how all these types of guarantees affect the allocation of investor funds among institutions and financial instruments and across countries.

The FDIC also adopted a mortgage modification program in August 2008 to address foreclosures after it took over IndyMac Bank (which became IndyMac Federal Bank). Under the program, eligible mortgages would be modified into mortgages permanently capped at the current Freddie Mac survey rate for conforming mortgages. Modifications are designed to achieve sustainable payments at a 38 percent debt-to-income (DTI) ratio of principal, interest, taxes, and insurance. To reach this metric for affordable payments, modifications could adopt a combination of interest rate reductions, extended amortization, and principal forbearance. Interest rate reductions below the current Freddie Mac survey rate may be made for a period of five years where such reductions are necessary to achieve a 38 percent DTI, and the reduced rate is consistent with maximizing net present value. For these loans, after five years, the interest rate would increase by no more than 1 percent per year until it is capped at the Freddie Mac survey rate where it would remain for the balance of the loan term. Other modification features could be combined with an interest rate reduction, as necessary and consistent with maximizing the value of the mortgage, to achieve sustainable payments. Modifications are offered to borrowers only where doing so will achieve an improved value for IndyMac Federal Bank or for investors in securitized or whole loans.

The Government's Actions Drive up the Deficit

The federal government's actions have been piecemeal—and largely reactive rather than proactive—responses to the mortgage market meltdown and the spreading financial crisis, which have now depressed the real economy. They have not so far addressed the bigger and more long-term issue of how to reform the structure of regulation and supervision to prevent a similar crisis from happening again.

The crisis and the onset of recession have contributed to a significant increase in the federal budget deficit, as shown in Figure 6.22, and a rise in the federal public debt–to-GDP ratio, as shown in Figure 6.23. Some of the steps taken to deal with trouble financial institutions, moreover, are not recorded in the federal budget totals. The outlook for the deficit and the national debt given all these developments is anything but bright and may constrict the government's future ability to invest in infrastructure, health care, education, alternative energy, and other areas.

Figure 6.22 Federal Budget Surplus (Deficit)–to-GDP Ratio (1976–September 2008)

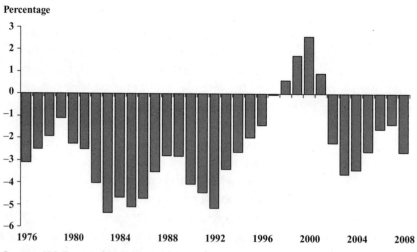

SOURCES: U.S. Bureau of the Public Debt, Milken Institute.

Figure 6.23   Federal Public Debt–to–GDP Ratio (1976–September 2008)

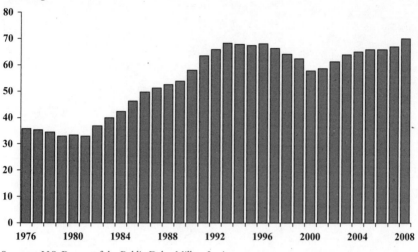

SOURCES: U.S. Bureau of the Public Debt, Milken Institute.

In addition, on October 20, 2008, Fed Chairman Ben Bernanke said a new fiscal stimulus package "seems appropriate" in view of the continuing weak economy.[19] Any additional spending attached to a new stimulus will only worsen the deficit.

Table 6.6 provides a summary of all the different federal government programs—including those of the Federal Reserve, Treasury, the FDIC, and other agencies—that have been announced in response to the turmoil as of November 25, 2008. A tally indicates that the loans, guarantees, and investments committed under these programs total at least $7.5 trillion.

In summary, only piecemeal fixes have been implemented so far, frequently saving only one financial institution at a time or zigzagging from one approach to another.

Other countries have also taken similar fixes to deal financial problems. Table 6.7 shows that the United States has committed to the largest financial rescue package, not surprisingly given the size of its financial sector. Several of the countries have also expanded their deposit guarantees. But eventually, longer-term proposals will have to be considered for overhauling regulation and forming strategies to prevent this type of chaos from ever happening again.

Table 6.6 A Growing Tab for Taxpayers

Program	Loans, Guarantees, and Investments	Date Announced	How the Programs Work
Federal Reserve Programs			
Term Discount Window Program (TDWP)	$92 billion as of 11/26/2008	10/17/2007	Extends the term of discount window loans from overnight to up to 90 days.
Term Auction Facility (TAF)	$407 billion as of 11/26/2008	12/12/2007	The Fed auctions off loans under the TAF every Thursday for a term of 28 days. It may expand TAF lending so that $900 billion of TAF credit will potentially be outstanding over year end 2008.
Term Securities Lending Facility (TSLF)	$193 billion as of 11/26/2008	3/11/2008	Establishes term swaps between the Fed and primary dealers. Collateral can be Treasury securities, federal agency securities, and other highly rated debt securities.
Bear Stearns	Up to $29 billion	3/14/2008	The Fed acquired $29 billion in mortgage backed securities from JPMorgan Chase to fund its purchase of Bear Stearns. As of November 26, 2008, the market value of these mortgage-backed securities is $27.0 billion.
Primary Dealer Credit Facility (PDCF)	$58 billion as of 11/26/2008	3/16/2008	Extends overnight borrowing from the Federal Reserve to primary dealers.

Program	Amount	Date	Description
AIG	Up to $173 billion	9/16/2008	AIG received an $85 billion, two-year secured loan on September 16, 2008, in exchange for warrants for a 79.9 percent equity stake in the firm. It was given an additional $37.8 billion on October 8 and another $20.9 billion credit line under CPFF on October 30, 2008. On November 10, Treasury purchased $40 billion of newly issued AIG preferred stock under the TARP (potentially reducing the original loan from $85 billion to $60 billion), terminated the $37.8 billion lending facility previously established, created a new lending facility to purchase up to $22.5 billion MBS from AIG and another facility to lend up to $30 billion to purchase CDOs on which AIG had written CDSs. As of November 26, 2008, $79.6 billion of credit was extended to AIG and $21.1 billion was extended to purchase CDOs.
Asset Backed Commercial Paper Money Market Mutual Fund Liquidity Facility (AMLF)	$53 billion as of 11/26/2008	9/19/2008	Loans to banks so that they can buy asset-backed commercial paper from money market funds.

(Continued)

Table 6.6 (*Continued*)

Program	Loans, Guarantees, and Investments	Date Announced	How the Programs Work
Expansion of the Federal Open Market's temporary reciprocal currency arrangements (swap lines)	Up to $620 billion	9/29/2008	The Federal Open Market Committee authorized a $330 billion expansion of its swap lines for U.S. dollar liquidity operations by other central banks, raising the total cap to $620 billion (up to $30 billion by the Bank of Canada, $80 billion by the Bank of England, $120 billion by the Bank of Japan, $15 billion by Danmarks Nationalbank, $240 billion by the ECB, $15 billion by the Norges Bank, $30 billion by the Reserve Bank of Australia, $30 billion by the Sveriges Riksbank, and $60 billion by the Swiss National Bank).
Commercial Paper Funding Facility (CPFF)	Up to $1.8 trillion	10/7/2008	The CPFF will be structured as a credit facility to a special purpose vehicle (SPV). The SPV will purchase from eligible issuers three-month U.S. dollar-denominated commercial paper through the New York Fed's primary dealers. Eligible issuers are U.S. issuers of commercial paper, including U.S. issuers with a foreign parent company. The SPV will only purchase U.S. dollar-denominated commercial paper [including asset-backed commercial paper (ABCP)] that is rated at least A-1/P-1/F1 by a major nationally recognized statistical rating organization (NRSRO) and, if rated by multiple major NRSROs, is rated at least A-1/P-1/F1 by two or more major NRSROs.

The maximum amount of a single issuer's commercial paper the SPV may own at any time will be the greatest amount of U.S. dollar-denominated commercial paper the issuer had outstanding on any day between January 1 and August 31, 2008. The SPV will not purchase additional commercial paper from an issuer whose total commercial paper outstanding to all investors (including the SPV) equals or exceeds the issuer's limit. As of 11/26/2008, $294 billion was outstanding.

Money Market Investor Funding Facility (MMIFF) — Up to $540 billion — 10/21/2008

The MMIFF provides assurance that money market mutual funds can liquidate their investments if cash is needed to cover withdrawals from customers. As of 11/26/2008, outstanding amount was zero.

Term Asset-Backed Securities Loan Facility (TALF) — Up to $200 billion — 11/25/2008

TALF loans will have a one-year term, will be nonrecourse to the borrower, and will be fully secured by eligible ABS. Treasury will provide $20 billion of credit protection to the Fed in connection with the TALF. Eligible collateral will include U.S. dollar-denominated cash (that is, not synthetic) ABS that have a long-term credit rating in the highest investment-grade rating category (for example, AAA) from two or more major nationally recognized statistical rating organizations (NRSROs) and do not have a long-term credit rating of below the highest investment-grade rating category from a major NRSRO. The underlying credit exposures of eligible ABS initially must be auto loans, student loans, credit card loans, or small business loans guaranteed by the U.S. Small Business Administration. All U.S. persons that own eligible collateral may participate in the TALF. Collateral haircuts will be established by the FRBNY for each class of eligible collateral. Haircuts will be determined based on the price volatility of each class of eligible collateral.

(Continued)

279

Table 6.6 (*Continued*)

Program	Loans, Guarantees, and Investments	Date Announced	How the Programs Work
Purchase of GSE direct obligations and MBS	Up to $600 billion	11/25/2008	The Fed will purchase the direct obligations of housing-related government-sponsored enterprises (GSEs)–Fannie Mae, Freddie Mac, and the Federal Home Loan Banks–and mortgage-backed securities (MBS) backed by Fannie Mae, Freddie Mac, and Ginnie Mae.
			Purchases of up to $100 billion in GSE direct obligations under the program will be conducted with the Fed's primary dealers through a series of competitive auctions and will begin in the first week of December. Purchases of up to $500 billion in MBS will be conducted by asset managers selected via a competitive process with a goal of beginning these purchases before year-end 2008. Purchases of both direct obligations and MBS are expected to take place over several quarters.
Congress and the Bush Administration			
FHA Secure	$50 billion	8/31/2007	Guarantees $50 billion in mortgages.
Economic Stimulus Act	$124 billion	2/13/2008	Provided tax rebates in 2008. Most taxpayers below the income limit received rebates of $300–$600. Also gave businesses a one-time depreciation tax deduction on specific new investment and raised the limits on the value of new productive capital that may be classified as business expenses during 2008. The Congressional Budget Office (CBO) estimates the net cost of the stimulus to be $124 billion.

Housing and Economic Recovery Act of 2008	$24.9 billion	7/30/2008	The CBO estimates that the Act will increase budget deficits by about $24.9 billion over the 2008 to 2018 period.
Purchase of GSE Debt and Equity	$25 billion	7/30/2008	Designed to shore up Fannie Mae and Freddie Mac.
HOPE for Homeowners	Up to $300 billion	7/30/2008	This voluntary program encourages lenders to write down the loan balances of borrowers in exchange for FHA-guaranteed loans up to 90 percent of the newly appraised home value. Program runs through September 2011.
Conservatorship of Fannie Mae and Freddie Mac	Up to $200 billion	9/7/2008	Treasury and FHFA established contractual agreements to ensure that each company maintains a positive net worth. They are indefinite in duration and have a capacity of $100 billion each. Treasury also established a new secured lending credit facility, available to Fannie Mae, Freddie Mac, and the Federal Home Loan Banks. Funding is provided directly by Treasury in exchange for eligible collateral from the GSEs (guaranteed mortgage backed securities issued by Freddie Mac and Fannie Mae, as well as advances made by the Federal Home Loan Banks). To further support the availability of mortgage financing, Treasury is initiating a temporary program to purchase GSE MBS, with the size and timing subject to the discretion of the Treasury Secretary.

(Continued)

Table 6.6 *(Continued)*

Program	Loans, Guarantees, and Investments	Date Announced	How the Programs Work
Guaranty Program for Money Market Funds	Up to $50 billion	9/19/2008	To restore confidence in money market funds, Treasury made available up to $50 billion from the Exchange Stabilization Fund.
IRS Notice 2008-83	?	9/30/2008	Allows banks to offset their profits with losses from the loan portfolio of banks they acquire. Initial media reports indicate that Wells Fargo alone may be able to claim more than $70 billion in losses from its acquisition of Wachovia, obtaining tax savings that exceed the market value of Wachovia as of November 7, 2008.
Emergency Economic Stabilization Act	Up to $700 billion	10/3/2008	Empowers Treasury to use up to $700 billion to inject capital into financial institutions, to purchase or insure mortgage assets, and to purchase any other troubled assets necessary to promote financial market stability.
Troubled Assets Relief Program (TARP)	*$179 billion as of November 7, 2008*	10/14/2008	Part of the EESA, TARP allows Treasury to purchase up to $250 billion of senior preferred shares in selected banks. The first $125 billion was allocated to nine of the nation's largest financial institutions on October 28, 2008. An additional $34 billion was allocated to 21 banks as of October 29, 2008. On November 23, 2008, Treasury purchased an additional $20 billion of preferred shares from Citigroup.

Federal Deposit Insurance Corporation		
Increase FDIC insurance coverage	10/3/2008	A provision of EESA temporarily raised the basic limit on federal deposit insurance coverage from $100,000 to $250,000 per depositor. Limits are scheduled to return to $100,000 after December 31, 2009.
Temporary Liquidity Guarantee Program (TLGP)	$1.5 trillion 10/14/2008	Temporarily guarantees the senior debt of all FDIC-insured institutions and their holding companies, as well as deposits in non-interest-bearing deposit transaction accounts. Certain newly issued senior unsecured debt issued on or before June 30, 2009, would be fully protected in the event the issuing institution subsequently fails, or its holding company files for bankruptcy. This includes promissory notes, commercial paper, interbank funding, and any unsecured portion of secured debt. Coverage would be limited to June 30, 2012.
		The other part of the program provides for a temporary unlimited guarantee of funds in noninterest-bearing transactions accounts (the Transaction Account Guarantee Program, or TAG)
		On November 21, 2008, FDIC strengthened TLGP. Chief among the changes is that the debt guarantee will be triggered by payment default rather than bankruptcy or receivership.
		Another change is that short-term debt issued for one month or less will not be included in the TLGP. Eligible entities will have until December 5, 2008, to opt out of TLGP.

(Continued)

Table 6.6 (*Continued*)

Program	Loans, Guarantees, and Investments	Date Announced	How the Programs Work
Treasury, Federal Deposit Insurance Corporation, and Federal Reserve			
Guarantee a portion of an asset pool of loans and securities backed by residential and commercial real estate and other such assets on Citigroup's balance sheet	$249 billion (with $5 billion via TARP)	11/23/2008	Up to $306 billion of Citigroup's assets are guaranteed. Citigroup takes the first loss up to $29 billion, and any loss in excess of that amount is shared by the government (90%) and Citigroup (10%). Treasury (via TARP) takes the second loss up to $5 billion, while FDIC takes the third loss up to $10 billion. The Federal Reserve funds the remaining pool of assets with a nonrecourse loan, subject to Citigroup's 10 percent loss sharing, at a floating rate of overnight interest swap plus 300 basis points.
Total of loans, guarantees and investments committed	**$7.5 trillion plus ?**	**As of 11/26/08**	**The final tab for taxpayers will only become known once the crisis is over.**

Table 6.7   Size of Financial Rescue Packages and Expanded Deposit Guarantees

	GDP (US$ Billions, 2007)	Total Bailout and Stimulus Package (US$ Billions, as of November 25)	Expanded Deposit Guarantees
Austria	323	100	n/a
France	2,271	50–450	n/a
Germany	2,915	151–645	Yes
India	878	41	n/a
Japan	4,377	68	n/a
Netherlands	678	44–250	Yes
Russia	'989	209–210	n/a
Singapore	137	100	n/a
South Korea	888	80–130	Yes
Spain	1,233	111	n/a
Sweden	394	190	Yes
Switzerland	389	66	n/a
United Kingdom	2,436	450–590	Yes
United States	13,808	7,510	Yes

SOURCES: *BusinessWeek*, December 1, 2008; *Financial Times*, November 14, 2008; Milken Institute.

Most important of all, the government must perform extensive counterfactual analyses to provide information as to what would have happened under scenarios involving different federal responses. Such analyses would be invaluable in designing strategies for heading off future crises. In the next chapter, various proposals are discussed with this goal in mind.

Chapter 7

Where Should We Go from Here?

But whether incipient bubbles can be detected in real time and whether, once detected, they can be defused without inadvertently precipitating still greater adverse consequences for the economy remain in doubt ... [F]inding a way to identify bubbles and to contain their progress would be desirable, though history cautions that prospects for success appear slim.

> —Alan Greenspan, Former Chairman of the Federal Reserve
> Remarks before the Economic Club of New York
> New York City
> December 19, 2002

Executives at U.S. mortgage giant Fannie Mae like to tell their critics that the American method of financing home loans is the "envy of the world."

> —James R. Hagerty

Fannie Says U.S. Housing Finance Is Program Envied By the World; Italy, Among Others, Sees Flaws

> —*The Wall Street Journal*
> July 12, 2004

Providing assistance to developing countries in strengthening their financial institutions—for example, by improving bank regulation and supervision and by increasing financial transparency—could lessen the risk of financial crises and thus increase both the willingness of those countries to accept capital inflows and the willingness of foreigners to invest there.

—Ben S. Bernanke, Governor of the Federal Reserve
"The Global Saving Glut and the U.S. Current Account Deficit"
Virginia Association of Economics, Richmond, Virginia
March 10, 2005

Congress is contemplating a serious tightening of regulations to make the new forms of lending more difficult. New research from some of the leading housing economists in the country, however, examines the long history of mortgage market innovations and suggests that regulators should be mindful of the potential downside in tightening too much.

—Austan Goolsbee
" 'Irresponsible' Mortgages Have Opened Doors to Many of
the Excluded"
The New York Times
March 29, 2007

We have a lot of specialists and high-powered organizations. But they don't warn us of the array of potential problems in advance, and nobody seems to have a well-tuned plan to handle them. Given the threats posed by the financial crisis, a better framework for dealing with systemic crises is urgently needed. The policies recently instituted by the Treasury and the Federal Reserve to deal with financial crises seem improvised, rather than part of a consistent, well-articulated policy. There is still a risk that financial dominoes will begin to fall. . . . If the Bear Stearns crisis had such a potential for disaster, what will we do if a major hedge fund fails or if several crises happen at once? The government has already felt it necessary to take measures to bail out Fannie Mae and Freddie Mac. What if the next case is worse? No one in government seems to feel a responsibility for warning about such possibilities and formulating a detailed policy for dealing with them.

—Robert J. Shiller
"Crisis Averted. What of the Next One?"
Economic View, *The New York Times*
August 9, 2008

Key Factors That Should Drive Reform

Through the end of 2008, the response to the mortgage meltdown consisted of temporary fixes, as discussed in Chapter 6. Reacting to events rather than anticipating them, the government largely improvised serial bailouts to contain the damage, which spread throughout the financial sector and into the real economy. The damage has also spread to other countries around the world.

So where should we go from here? The answer must be based on a careful consideration of how the initial problems arose and how they evolved over time into a full-blown crisis.

There are essentially three interrelated factors that together gave rise to the housing bubble and its subsequent collapse: liquidity, credit, and leverage. Liquidity and credit are two sides of the same coin. In the low-interest-rate environment of 2001 to 2004, liquidity was plentiful, and as investors searched for higher yields, they fueled a credit boom in the housing sector. Home mortgage originations skyrocketed to an all-time high, while housing starts and sales also set new records. The outpouring of credit that financed all this activity was provided by highly leveraged financial institutions. The loans they did not keep on their own balance sheets were securitized and sold to investors around the world.

The brakes were suddenly slammed when the home price bubble burst and the excess inventory of homes swelled. These two factors—coupled with an alarming rise in home foreclosures—signaled that this was the beginning of an actual crisis rather than a temporary retrenchment. The initial government responses sometimes reversed course, and officials failed to clearly convey their intended purposes; these moves proved ineffective at halting the spreading carnage. The government's flip-flops did not help calm the public and instill confidence that our financial institutions were safe and sound, nor did they offer real hope that progress was quickly being made to stabilize the financial sector.

Once home prices collapsed and an increasing number of homes fell into foreclosure, certain long-overdue lessons became crystal clear to everyone. Financial institutions rapidly reversed course from the days of easy credit and rushed to deleverage. There was a sectorwide move to quickly repair balance sheets by raising more capital and selling off assets before values fell still further. But while this behavior makes sense on the individual firm level, the ramifications can be serious when many firms attempt to deleverage all at once.

The immediate results produced a credit crunch and liquidity freeze. Financial institutions sharply raised lending standards and curtailed credit lines, as they themselves were attempting to roll over credit that had been extended to them. The rush was on to obtain and hold onto cash to meet payrolls and cover other ongoing operating expenses.

Hanging over everything was growing uncertainty about the value of various assets backed with home mortgages, especially subprime home mortgages; as home prices fell further and foreclosures mounted, those worries only intensified. No one knew for sure exactly where the most troubled assets were held and how much their values would fall—because those assets were scattered on the balance sheets of multiple financial institutions and embedded in many different pools of loans that were serving as collateral for complex mortgage-backed securities or collateralized debt obligations. Uncertainty, heightened by a lack of transparency, is the biggest enemy of capital markets.

It perhaps came as a rude awakening to financial institutions and investors that holding many individual mortgages on the balance sheet or combining them in a large pool did not necessarily offer the kind of diversification that lowers risk. Indeed, the values of many of the mortgages, especially subprime loans, turned out to be positively correlated with one another. Because they were dispersed among investors far and wide, the mortgages created negative ripple effects throughout the entire financial sector when their values plummeted. This turmoil caused a flight to safety, pushing down rates on Treasury securities and thereby widening credit spreads across all classes of securities. This development was in sharp contrast to the period from 2001 to 2004, when the Federal Reserve repeatedly cut rates due to concerns about deflation. In 2008, it has not been a case of the Fed pushing rates down but rather an instance of investors doing so by putting ever larger portions of their funds in Treasury securities.

The bottom line is that greater efforts must be undertaken to ensure that financial institutions are never excessively leveraged, never operate with insufficient liquidity, and never let themselves get into a position from which they are unable to provide credit to the marketplace.

A well-functioning financial system is one in which this situation simply does not occur.

Excessive leverage is a key factor that explains how $1.2 trillion in subprime mortgages outstanding caused such widespread financial distress. If banks maintain a leverage ratio of 10:1, they would allocate only $120 billion of capital to support $1.2 trillion—and a 10 percent decline in the underlying assets could wipe them out. Of course, some institutions were even more highly leveraged than 10:1, and in some areas, home price have fallen much more than 10 percent. (In fact, some institutions were leveraged at 30:1 prior to the crisis.) These situations can force some institutions into insolvency if capital cannot be raised.

Financial institutions must prepare themselves during good times so that they do not find themselves excessively leveraged, lacking liquidity, or unable to supply credit when the inevitable storm clouds roll in. Risk-based capital requirements are procyclical, for example, so that in good times, greater leverage is allowed based on the risk-weighting of assets, while in bad times, the risk-weighting works in the opposite direction. The challenge for policymakers in designing a national financial regulatory regime is to correct these types of these narrowly focused requirements, which are counterproductive for the broader economy. More generally, they must develop the most appropriate mix of private and governmental reactions to the inherent market failures that can affect financial systems. It is important to take into account that market discipline becomes virtually nonexistent if there is a general perception that the government can always be counted on to make sure financial institutions operate safely and soundly—and that if they do not, the government will nevertheless be there to cover losses when they are large and widely spread.

The U.S. credit market is by far the most highly evolved in the world. The United States, relative to anywhere else, has a larger number and wider variety of nonfinancial firms about which there is increasingly widespread and publicly available information. In addition, there are multiple ways for a greater variety of financial service firms to efficiently invest in nonfinancial firms. But the financial crisis has called into question the reliability of available information, the complexity of some of the financial products in the marketplace, and the adequacy of our existing regulatory structure. Most importantly, it demonstrates that the foremost goal of regulation should be to prevent a systemic financial crisis that spills over to adversely affect economic growth.

Regulation should not be designed to ensure the solvency of individual financial firms but instead to prevent broad crises from taking hold in the financial sector. In fact, regulation should facilitate prompt resolution (that is, corrective action to resolve the deteriorating performance of a firm before things get even worse). Prompt resolution at minimum cost reallocates more resources more efficiently than a drawn-out process, minimizing losses to stockholders, bondholders, and other creditors. In the case of banking firms with deposit insurance, prompt resolution means that the deposit insurance agency suffers fewer losses and the taxpayer, who is a contingent creditor if there are insufficient deposit insurance fund reserves, faces a lower risk of sharing in those losses. To the extent that this is not or cannot be done, the government may be forced to take steps that would not be considered during ordinary times.

The current financial crisis is no ordinary time. However, as we detailed with overwhelming evidence in Chapter 3, it was quite obvious that a housing bubble was forming and that insufficient regulatory actions were taken to limit its growth and magnitude while there was still time to take preventive containment measures. Because it did not take a proactive stance early, the government (specifically the Fed, along with other bank, securities, and insurance regulatory authorities) was left with applying a piecemeal approach to deal with the ever-widening problems after the fact.

Another goal of regulation is to allocate credit fairly, widely, and productively. Governments can make loans directly, thus becoming an intermediator between taxpayers and selected borrowers. By making loan guarantees available to selected borrowers (such as veterans, for example), governments can also affect lending by financial firms. More generally, governments can provide broad subsidies by insuring deposits for banks on selected products or services. In general, direct loans, loan guarantees, and broad subsidies reduce the cost of borrowing below what the private financial system would otherwise charge, with the goal of supporting selected products. These products, called *merit goods,* are selected because in some fashion, the government decides to reduce their cost and thereby make them more generally available. The most conspicuous merit good in the United States is housing finance; the government (i.e., Congress and the White House) has long supported the existence of a separate savings and loan industry and offered tax advantages to home buyers. It also developed a secondary market in home mortgages by creating government-sponsored enterprises. With this support, the enterprises and banking institutions received explicit mandates to provide affordable housing finance to lower-income families and to distressed areas. This housing-finance system clearly broke down and is now in dire need of repair.

A regulatory structure that encourages a competitive financial system is another desirable goal; the result is a more efficient financial marketplace and a more efficient allocation of scarce resources, thereby promoting economic growth, supporting entrepreneurship, and reducing income inequality. Thus, a goal of regulation is to promote and to maintain competitive markets and to intervene only when it is cost-effective to do so to offset market failures. This is particularly important given the ongoing integration of global financial markets and the increasing competition among various international financial sectors. This particular goal may merit the establishment of a separate competition regulatory authority, given that current financial services regulatory authorities do not primarily focus in this area.

The next section will explore several important issues that policymakers must address in any future reshaping of financial market regulations.

Issues for Policymakers

There is a wide variety of views about how to reform regulation of the financial sector. Rather than comparing and contrasting various opinions, we have identified several primary issues for policymakers to carefully consider as they move forward. This discussion will necessarily venture beyond housing finance or foreclosure reforms. As IMF Managing Director Dominique Strauss-Khan stated, "The world was going through the most dangerous financial crisis since the Great Depression of the 1930s and it is the result of three failures: a regulatory and supervisory failure in advanced economies, a failure in risk management in the private financial institutions, and a failure in market discipline mechanisms."[1]

What Type of Regulatory Reform Will Minimize, If Not Entirely Eliminate, Asset Price Booms and Busts, Which Are So Destructive to Wealth Accumulation and Economic Activity?

It is a disappointing fact, but throughout U.S. history, almost all of the major banking laws have been drafted in response to various financial crises. The few that were not were essentially ratifications of developments that were already occurring due to market forces as our economy modernized over the past three decades. The timelines in Figures 7.1, 7.2, and 7.3 show all the major banking laws, noting those that were responses to crises and those that were not.

Every time a new set of laws is enacted, it seems that the accompanying statement is "never again." Clearly, more of the effort to reform the regulation of financial institutions and markets must be channeled toward *preventing* crises rather than implementing reforms after they occur. Steps need to be taken not to deflate asset price bubbles but to prevent them from forming. As already discussed, there were early and ample signals—acknowledged by the regulatory authorities—that a housing price bubble was emerging. These signals should have triggered regulatory actions to tighten overly loose credit policies and to curtail the excessive use of leverage that was becoming common throughout the financial system.

A greater emphasis on liquidity, credit, and capital leverage is needed—paying greater attention to both on- and off-balance-sheet assets. Regulators should also focus on the degree to which both on- and off-balance-sheet assets, or subsets of important assets, are positively correlated with one another, regardless of where they are located in the financial system. In other words, if one financial institution is experiencing difficulties that stem from one particular type of asset, it is important to determine whether other institutions have similar holdings and address that risk proactively throughout all of the institutions.

The regulatory challenge is to design a regulatory regime to address the broad issues of systemic risks.

Figure 7.1 Origin of U.S. Banking Institutions and Expanding Regulatory Role of Government

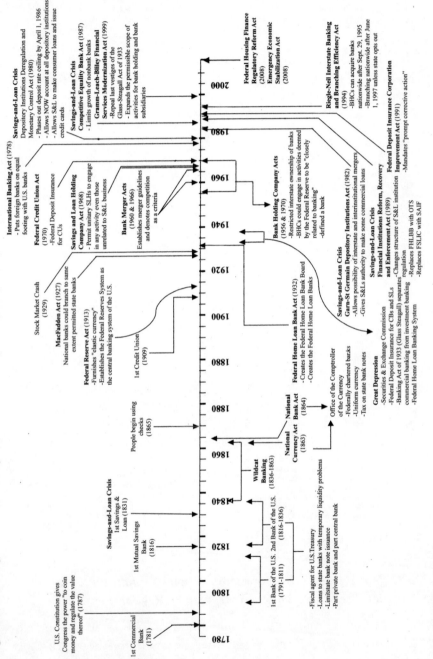

SOURCE: Milken Institute.

295

Figure 7.2   Most U.S. Banking Laws Are Responses to Crises

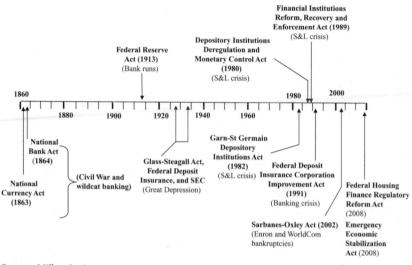

SOURCE: Milken Institute.

Figure 7.3   Some U.S. Banking Laws Not Instituted as Crisis Responses

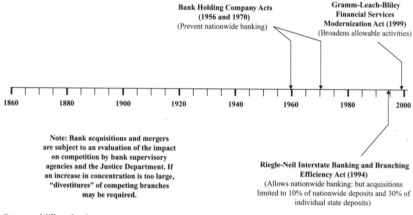

SOURCE: Milken Institute.

Do Differences in the Size or Composition of Financial Sectors in Countries Necessitate Different Regulatory Regimes?

Table 7.1 shows the size and composition of each G-20 country's financial system. These nations collectively account for about two-thirds of both the world's population and its GDP. They also account for

Table 7.1 Comparative Information on Population, GDP, Size, and Composition of the Financial Systems for G–20 Countries (2007)

	Share of World Total (%)					Ratios				
	Population	GDP	Bank Assets (BA)	Equity Market Capitalization (MC)	Bonds Outstanding (BO)	(BA+MC+BO)/ GDP	BA/ GDP	MC/ GDP	BO/ GDP	BA/(MC + BO)
Argentina	0.6	0.4	0.1	0.9	0.2	3.0	0.3	2.2	0.5	0.1
Australia	0.3	1.4	1.5	2.3	1.5	4.2	1.5	1.5	1.2	0.5
Brazil	2.9	2.2	1.6	2.3	1.3	2.7	1.0	1.0	0.7	0.6
Canada	0.5	2.3	2.5	2.9	2.0	3.7	1.5	1.1	1.0	0.7
China	20.2	5.0	6.1	7.3	2.2	3.5	1.7	1.3	0.5	0.9
France	0.9	4.1	6.0	4.5	5.5	4.6	2.1	1.0	1.6	0.8
Germany	1.3	5.3	7.7	3.6	7.1	4.2	2.0	0.6	1.6	0.9
India	17.8	1.8	0.9	3.0	0.6	2.6	0.7	1.5	0.4	0.4
Indonesia	3.5	0.6	0.2	0.3	0.1	1.2	0.4	0.5	0.2	0.6
Italy	0.9	3.4	3.4	1.8	5.3	3.8	1.4	0.5	1.9	0.6
Japan	1.9	6.7	11.3	7.5	11.6	5.4	2.3	1.0	2.0	0.8
Mexico	1.6	1.5	0.8	0.7	0.6	1.6	0.7	0.4	0.4	0.9
Russia	2.2	1.9	0.8	1.6	0.2	1.4	0.6	0.8	0.1	0.6
Saudi Arabia	0.4	0.6	0.3	0.8	0.01	2.1	0.7	1.3	0.02	0.5
South Africa	0.7	0.4	0.4	0.7	0.2	3.4	1.2	1.6	0.6	0.5
South Korea	0.7	1.4	1.3	1.8	1.5	3.6	1.2	1.1	1.2	0.5
Turkey	1.1	1.1	0.5	0.5	0.3	1.4	0.6	0.4	0.4	0.8
United Kingdom	0.9	4.1	13.0	6.7	4.8	7.2	4.4	1.5	1.4	1.5
United States	4.6	20.5	16.5	29.0	37.9	4.6	1.1	1.5	2.2	0.3
Total	63.1	64.8	74.9	78.3	82.9	3.5	1.4	0.9	1.2	0.7

SOURCES: International Monetary Fund, Bloomberg, Bank for International Settlements, Milken Institute.

three-fourths or more of the world's bank assets, bonds outstanding, and equity market capitalization. The most recent financial crisis has underscored the fact that financial systems in different countries are interconnected. The turmoil that swept through the U.S. financial sector quickly ensnared other countries around the world. It is therefore important that these key countries, in particular, work together to better coordinate regulatory policies that can prevent emerging crises from deepening and spreading across national borders.

Table 7.1 also shows that the G-20 countries have different types of financial systems. Countries like China, Germany, Japan, and the United Kingdom have bank-oriented financial systems, while the United States has a capital markets–oriented system. These differences undoubtedly call for regulatory regimes that will differ in some respects even though the overriding goals may be the same.

For example, a financial system in which banks are dominant is also one in which bank loans are the main source of funding for businesses. The regulatory focus will therefore be on banks. In contrast, a financial system in which capital markets are dominant is one in which stocks and bonds are the main source of funding for businesses. Nonbank financial institutions assume more importance in these cases, especially when banks are prohibited or restricted from engaging directly in securities activities.

However, banks may be able to work around some constraints through off-balance-sheet activities, such as setting up special investment vehicles through which assets of the banks can be securitized. They may also choose to fund a significant portion of their assets by issuing securities themselves. The focus of regulation in this kind of environment must be on the extent to which the connections between banks and the capital markets pose potential liquidity, credit, and leverage problems if there is an abrupt and sharp decline in the value of an important subset of assets that is spread throughout the financial sector, especially if there is little knowledge about where these deteriorating assets are located.

The regulatory challenge is to design a regulatory regime that promotes greater cross-country cooperation but that also allows for national differences in financial systems. This also requires a reassessment of whether there should be a supranational regulator or whether bigger roles should instead be assigned to international organizations such as the Basel Committee on Banking Supervision and the International Monetary Fund.

What Is the Appropriate Structure of Regulation?

The United States is currently burdened with multilayered, overlapping, inconsistent, and costly regulation, as shown in Figure 7.4. The regulatory structure is in dire need of reform. The issue, of course, is which regulatory structure is most appropriate for the United States.

Table 7.2 shows that there is a single supervisor in more than 90 percent of all countries, so the United States is clearly out of step with almost all of the rest of the world. Furthermore, the table shows that the central bank is a bank supervisor in two-thirds of all countries, including the United States. But in approximately one-third of all the nations, there is a consolidated supervisor for banking, securities, and insurance; the United States has a single supervisor for each of these industries and an umbrella regulator, namely the Federal Reserve, which comes into play when all these activities are conducted within

Figure 7.4 The Convoluted U.S. Financial Regulatory Regime

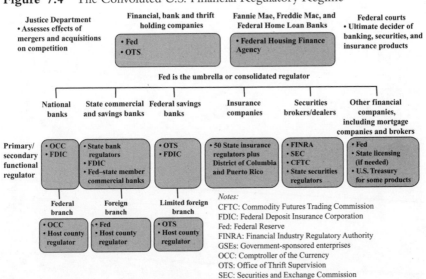

SOURCES: The Financial Services Roundtable (2007), Milken Institute.

Table 7.2 Who Supervises Banks and How Many Licenses Are Required?

	What Body/Agency Supervises Banks?			Is There a Single Financial Supervisory Agency for all of the Main Financial Institutions (Insurance Companies, Contractual Savings Institutions, and Savings Banks)?	Is There a Single Financial Supervisory Agency for all of the Activities in which Commercial Banks are Allowed to Do Business?	Is There More Than One Body/Agency That Grants Licenses to Banks?	Is More Than One License Required (e.g., One for Each Banking Activity, Such As Commercial Banking, Securities Operations, Insurance, etc.)?
	Central Bank	A Single Bank Supervisory Agency/Super Intendancy	Multiple Bank Supervisory Agencies/Super Intendancies				
Argentina	Yes	Yes	No	No	Yes	No	No
Australia	No	Yes	No	Yes	No	No	Yes
Brazil	Yes	No	No	No	No	No	No
Canada	No	Yes	No	No	No	No	Yes
China	No	Yes	No	No	Yes	No	Yes
France	No	Yes	No	No	Yes	No	Yes
Germany	Yes	Yes	No	Yes	Yes	No	No
India	Yes	No	No	No	No	No	Yes
Indonesia	Yes	No	No	No	No	No	Yes
Italy	Yes	Yes	No	No	No	No	Yes
Japan	No	Yes	No	Yes	Yes	No	No
Mexico	No	Yes	No	No	Yes	Yes	No
Russia	Yes	No	Yes	No	No	Yes	Yes
Saudi Arabia	Yes	No	No	No	No	No	No
South Africa	Yes	No	No	No	Yes	No	No
South Korea	Yes	No	Yes	No	n/a	No	Yes
Turkey	No	Yes	No	No	No	No	No
United Kingdom	No	Yes	No	Yes	Yes	No	No
United States	Yes	No	Yes	No	No	Yes	No
All countries	82 Yes, 58 No	68 Yes, 72 No	9 Yes, 131 No	44 Yes, 96 No	84 Yes, 52 No	9 Yes, 134 No	67 Yes, 76 No

Sources: World Bank, Milken Institute.

a financial services holding company. The table also provides information on whether dual banking (i.e., more than one bank chartering authority) exists and whether multiple licenses are required for banks that are allowed to engage in a variety of financial activities. Also, see Appendix Tables A.56, A.57, and A.58 for information on the structure and scope of supervisory regimes in individual countries. It is fair to wonder whether the sheer size of the bureaucracy depicted in Figure 7.4 prevented an effective and timely response as events were unfolding.

The United States should seriously consider more dramatic consolidation and streamlining to reduce the number of financial regulatory agencies and separate licenses required by financial institutions to provide their services nationwide. Creating a greater regulatory focus on preventing a systemic crisis requires such consolidation to achieve a more uniform and broader degree of regulatory oversight.

Every Country Regulates Banks, But What Is a Bank?

It might be strange to say it, but most people probably do not actually know the distinction between banks and other financial firms. A bank is defined legally as a firm that makes commercial and industrial (i.e., business) loans, accepts demand deposits, and offers deposits insured by the FDIC. But today, in the United States, if you examine the balance sheet of all banks, you would find that the legally defined bank is a relatively small component of the larger entity. Bank activities now extend far beyond these three services. They provide many different types of loans, offer uninsured deposits, issue different types of securities, invest in different types of securities, and engage in different types of off-balance-sheet activities.

Today banks must understand and manage more complex risks—and bank examiners and supervisory authorities must similarly be adequately skilled to fulfill their oversight responsibilities.

In the wake of the recent financial crisis, many more banks and even nonbank financial institutions have come to better appreciate that deposits are a relatively reliable and low-cost source of funds. Because they had been relying heavily on short-term borrowings or security issuance to fund short-term cash needs, some banks found themselves scrambling to acquire and then hoard cash to cover their required ongoing operating expenses. Even some investment banks that are transforming themselves into banks have come to appreciate the advantages of deposits over repurchase agreements to obtain funds for the very same short-term purposes, especially during periods of financial turmoil.

There is a new appreciation that banks need not only to be adequately capitalized to curtail excessive leverage but also to have sufficient liquidity and longer-term liabilities in the event of a widespread flight to safety, which would include cash. It has also become clear that off-balance-sheet activities need to be more carefully monitored and controlled, because they can have important implications for both the balance sheets and income statements of the banks themselves—not to mention others—when financial turmoil occurs.

Beyond these specific issues, there is the question of what activities are allowable for banks. Table 7.3 shows that the G-20 countries (and nations beyond this group) differ with respect to whether a bank is a financial institution that can engage in a wide range of activities. Some countries say yes; others say no. It will be important to explore whether greater uniformity can provide for a more level and competitive international playing field for banks, and where the line should be drawn to achieve a safer, sounder, and more stable banking system.

Still another issue is which organizational form (i.e., a holding company, with separately capitalized subsidiaries, or directly in a bank or the subsidiary of a bank) is most appropriate if the widest range of activities is allowed. Recent work by Barth, Caprio, and Levine (2006) thoroughly explores these and other related issues and finds that greater leeway into these activities is beneficial to both bank performance and stability.

The regulatory challenge is to decide on the appropriate composition of the on- and off-balance-sheet activities allowed by banks to ensure adequate liquidity, capital, and duration match of assets and liabilities. The right balance must be struck to allow banks to be competitive while ensuring they operate prudently.

How Concentrated Is the Banking Industry, How Big and Complex Are Banks, and How Globalized Are Banks?

Competition in banking differs across countries—and banks in countries like the United States are becoming bigger, more globalized, and more

Table 7.3   What Activities Are Allowed for Banks in G–20 Countries and in All Countries?

	What Kinds of Securities Activities Can Banks Engage In?			What Kinds of Insurance Activities Can Banks Engage In?		What Kinds of Real Estate Activities Can Banks Engage In (Other Than Real Estate Banking Operations are Conducted or Resulting from Foreclosure on Loans)?		
	Underwriting?	Dealing and Brokering?	Mutual Funds?	Underwriting?	Selling?	Investment?	Development?	Management?
Argentina	Yes	Yes	No	No	Yes	No	No	No
Australia	Yes	Yes	No	No	Yes	Yes	No	No
Brazil	Yes	Yes	Yes	Yes	Yes	Yes	No	No
Canada	Yes	Yes	Yes	Yes	Yes	Yes	Yes	Yes
China	No	No	No	No	Yes	No	No	No
France	Yes	Yes	No	No	Yes	Yes	No	Yes
Germany	Yes	Yes	Yes	No	Yes	Yes	Yes	Yes
India	Yes	Yes	Yes	Yes	Yes	No	No	No
Indonesia	No	No	No	No	No	No	No	No
Italy	Yes	Yes	Yes	No	Yes	No	No	No
Japan	Yes	Yes	Yes	Yes	Yes	No	No	No
Mexico	Yes	Yes	Yes	No	Yes	Yes	Yes	Yes
Russia	Yes	Yes	No	No	No	Yes	No	Yes
Saudi Arabia	Yes	Yes	Yes	No	Yes	No	No	No
South Africa	Yes	Yes	No	No	Yes	Yes	No	No
South Korea	Yes	No	No	No	Yes	Yes	No	No
Turkey	Yes	Yes	Yes	Yes	Yes	Yes	Yes	Yes
United Kingdom	Yes	Yes	Yes	Yes	Yes	Yes	Yes	Yes
United States	Yes	Yes	Yes	Yes	Yes	No	No	No
All countries	96 Yes, 22 No	94 Yes, 23 No	69 Yes, 46 No	21 Yes, 96 No	73 Yes, 44 No	52 Yes, 66 No	30 Yes, 88 No	38 Yes, 79 No

Sources: World Bank, Milken Institute.

Note: Information is based on a survey for which 118 countries responded to the questions in the table.

Figure 7.5   Percentage of Deposits and Assets Held by Five Largest Banks

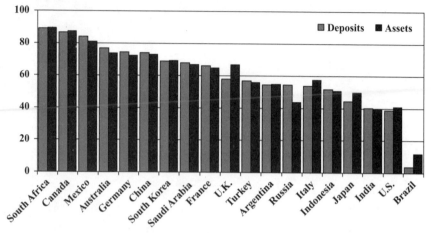

SOURCES: World Bank, Milken Institute.

complex in terms of their organization form and the mix of products they offer.

Figure 7.5 shows the share of total deposits held by the five largest banks in the G-20 countries. It is clear that there is substantial diversity in concentration ratios among these countries, with several countries having quite high concentration ratios. Figure 7.6, moreover, shows that in the United States there has been a fairly dramatic shift in the total asset share accounted for by banks with more than $10 billion in assets. These 84 banks represent only slightly more than 1 percent of the 7,203 commercial banks, but their asset share increased from 42 percent in 1984 to 80 percent in the second quarter of 2008. The biggest banks have gotten bigger. However, what is important for pricing decisions and economic efficiency is not the degree of concentration per se but rather competition, including potential competition from both domestic and foreign firms that may enter a market.

Perhaps even more important for U.S. financial stability than the increasing concentration of assets and deposits among a few dominant banks is the size and complexity of those banks.

Figures 7.7 and 7.8 show the size, organizational maze, and product complexity of Citigroup. This type of banking organization poses severe

Figure 7.6 Big Banks Increasingly Dominate U.S. Banking Industry: Asset Shares by Bank Size

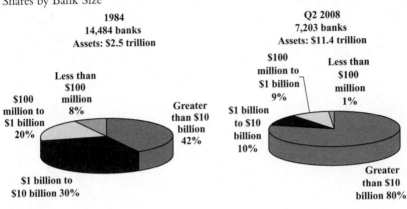

SOURCES: World Bank, Milken Institute.

challenges for both internal risk managers and the regulators of such institutions. Indeed, Citigroup has emerged as a particularly problematic institution as the financial crisis has evolved. Citigroup has 200 million customer accounts and its credit commitments totaled $1,631 billion in

Figure 7.7 Citigroup's Organizational Structure Is Extremely Complex

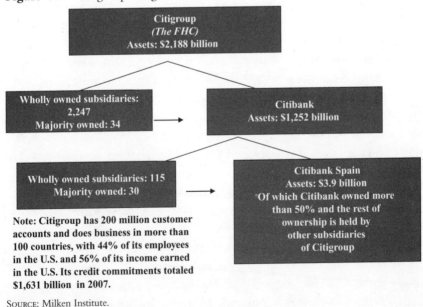

Note: Citigroup has 200 million customer accounts and does business in more than 100 countries, with 44% of its employees in the U.S. and 56% of its income earned in the U.S. Its credit commitments totaled $1,631 billion in 2007.

SOURCE: Milken Institute.

Figure 7.8   Citigroup's Product Complexity Challenges Regulators and Its Internal Risk Managers

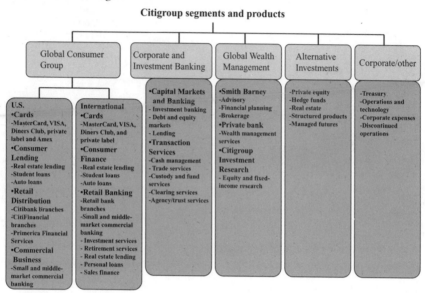

Citigroup segments and products

SOURCE: Milken Institute.

2007. From a high of $286 billion in February 2001, its stock market capitalization plunged to just $20 billion in November 2008. This perilous drop reflected enormous losses and potential losses related to the firm's involvement in subprime mortgages and CDOs, among other factors.

Because Citigroup has apparently been deemed too big, too interconnected, or too important to be allowed to fail, the government took action, providing a $306 billion package of guarantees, liquidity access, and capital on November 23, 2008 (on top of $25 billion in a capital injection provided just weeks earlier). But did rating agencies provide adequate ratings, and did regulatory authorities take appropriate steps in a timely manner to curtail imprudent activities by the bank?

An even more important issue is what regulatory reforms are necessary to reduce any systemic risk that such institutions collectively pose. Should these behemoths be broken up once things die down?

In addition to those issues, banking institutions have become increasingly global in scope. Table 7.4 shows the top 10 international banks by market capitalization as of November 14, 2008. Citigroup does business

Figure 7.9 Foreign Ownership of Banks

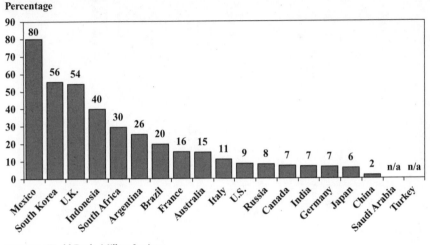

Percentage

SOURCES: World Bank, Milken Institute.

in more than 100 countries, has roughly 40 percent of its assets and more than half of its employees outside the United States, and earns nearly half of its income from abroad. The status of Citigroup, as well as that of several other banks listed in Table 7.4, must necessarily involve the cooperation of the bank regulatory authorities in all the countries in which these banks operate, particularly when problems arise or preferably even earlier to prevent serious problems from escalating. This is all the more vital for countries that have a high degree of their total banking industry assets in the hands of foreign-owned banks. Figure 7.9 shows that this is the case for several of the G-20 countries.

A related issue is the extent to which countries allow their banking industries to be open to foreign banks and, if so, the extent to which they treat foreign banks like domestic banks. For the slightly more than 150 countries that are members of the World Trade Organization (WTO), this becomes a matter of comparing international commitments to actual practices and then, if necessary, adjudicating and serious discrepancies that create disagreements.

In addition, some regulatory exceptions must be resolved. For example, the mixing of banking and commerce is prohibited, but state-chartered industrial loan companies (ILCs) may be owned and operated by firms that engage in commercial activities. Indeed, parent companies

Table 7.4 Globalization of Big Banks

	Nov. 14, 2008 Market Capitalization (US$ Billions)	Total Assets (US$ Billions)	Assets Outside Home Country (%)	Income Outside Home Country (%)	Staff Outside Home Country (%)
Industrial and Commercial Bank of China, China	191	1,190	3	3	0.6
HSBC Holdings, United Kingdom	129	2,354	55	70	65
JPMorgan Chase, United States	129	1,562	62	25	n/a
China Construction Bank Corporation, China	126	904	2	1	n/a
Bank of China, China	109	821	4	3	9
Wells Fargo, United States	109	575	n/a	n/a	n/a
Bank of America, United States	82	1,716	n/a	n/a	n/a
Mitsubishi UFJ Financial, Japan	67	1,933	23	19	27
Banco Santander, Spain	66	1,331	64	75	77
Citigroup, United States	52	2,188	38	43	54

SOURCES: Bank statements, Milken Institute.

that operate ILCs include Merrill Lynch, American Express, Morgan Stanley, BMW Group, Goldman Sachs, General Electric, Toyota, Target, and Volkswagen. These ILCs have more than $200 billion in assets. It remains to be seen what will ultimately be decided with respect to companies like Wal-Mart that sought to acquire an existing ILC.

The regulatory challenge is to decide on an appropriate measure of concentration that does not stifle competition (possibly even creating a new regulatory authority to specifically address competition) while taking into account contestability. Officials must also decide on the most efficient organizational form and product mix, both on- and off-balance sheet, for banking institutions. This should be based on a cost–benefit analysis of various choices. Concerns about prudence should guide these decisions and any necessary restrictions imposed on foreign and domestic entry for banks.

Should Supervision Be on the Basis of Separate Industries or Products/Services?

There is a wide variety of financial service firms, offering a diversity of products. Some are equivalent, while others are hybrid products. But the regulatory treatment of both firms and products is uneven, although regulatory authorities that differ with respect to what they allow financial service firms to do contribute to competition and innovation.

Table 7.5 shows not only that there are different types of financial firms in the United States but also that their individual shares of the total assets have changed substantially over time. The traditional rationale for focusing on banks is that they offer demand deposits and therefore are susceptible to widespread runs that disrupt the entire payments and credit system. The recent financial crisis now clearly indicates the importance of the other, currently less heavily regulated financial firms (at least the biggest ones) to overall financial sector stability.

Furthermore, financial securities firms compete by offering equivalent products. Consider the following: Banks offer time deposits and letters of credit, while insurance companies offer fixed annuities and surety bonds. Securities firms offer money market funds and commercial paper, while banks offer demand deposit and commercial loans. Insurance companies offer variable annuities and reinsurance, while securities

Table 7.5   Changing Importance of U.S. Financial Institutions (1860–Q2 2008)

	1860	1900	1929	1960	1980	2000	Q2 2008
Banking institutions							
Commercial banking	71.4	62.9	53.7	36.0	32.7	18.0	18.8
Savings institutions	17.8	18.2	14	17.6	17.5	3.4	2.9
Credit unions	n.a.	n.a.	n.a.	1.0	1.5	1.2	1.3
Contractual intermediaries							
Property-casualty insurance companies	n.a.	n.a.	n.a.	4.1	4.0	2.4	2.2
Life insurance companies	10.7	13.8	18.6	18.2	10.2	8.7	7.9
Private pension funds	n.a.	0	0.7	6.4	11.3	12.4	9.1
State and local government retirement funds	n.a.	n.a.	n.a.	3.1	4.3	6.4	4.6
Federal government retirement funds	n.a.	n.a.	n.a.	2.2	1.7	2.2	1.9
Others							
GSEs, agency- and GSE-backed mortgage pools	n.a.	n.a.	n.a.	1.9	6.8	12.4	13.1
Mortgage companies	n.a.	1.3	0.6	0.3	0.7	0.7	0.8
Finance companies	n.a.	0	2	4.6	4.7	3.4	3.1
Funding corporations	n.a.	n.a.	n.a.	0.0	0.4	3.3	3.6
Money market mutual funds	n.a.	n.a.	n.a.	0.0	1.7	5.0	5.4
Mutual funds, closed end funds, and exchange traded funds	n.a.	n.a.	2.4	3.7	1.5	12.9	13.3
Security brokers and dealers	n.a.	3.8	8.1	1.1	1.0	3.4	4.6
Issuers of asset-backed securities	n.a.	n.a.	n.a.	0.0	0.0	4.2	7.0
Real estate investment trusts	n.a.	n.a.	n.a.	0.0	0.1	0.2	0.5
Total assets held by financial institutions (US$ billions)	**1**	**16**	**123**	**637**	**4,537**	**36,001**	**62,299**

SOURCES: Federal Reserve, Milken Institute.

firms offer equity mutual funds and catastrophe bonds. In addition, there are such hybrid products as variable-rate CDs for which the interest rate is tied to a specified market index (e.g., the S&P 500), security futures, home mortgages with debt cancellation, and synthetic collateralized loan obligations.

The regulatory challenge is to provide more equal treatment of both firms and products to promote a level playing field as well as overall financial sector stability, taking into account the appropriate balance between self-regulation and state versus federal government regulation.

How Much and What Kind of Financial Activity Is Unregulated or Lightly Regulated?

In some countries like the United States, as Figure 7.10 shows, intermediation (the process of channeling funds from savers to borrowers) has been increasingly done over time through the capital markets rather than banking institutions. Until the recent financial crisis, this was viewed as a positive development. It was thought that the capital markets served as a "spare tire"—that is, if banks got into financial difficulties and cut

Figure 7.10   Increasing Reliance on U.S. Securities Markets for Capital Funding and Portfolio Investment (1900–2008)

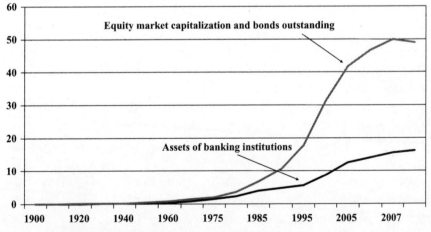

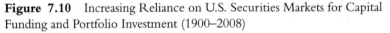

Sources: New York Stock Exchange, Bloomberg, FDIC, Milken Institute.

Figure 7.11   Surge in Amount and Diversity of U.S. Asset-Backed Securities Outstanding

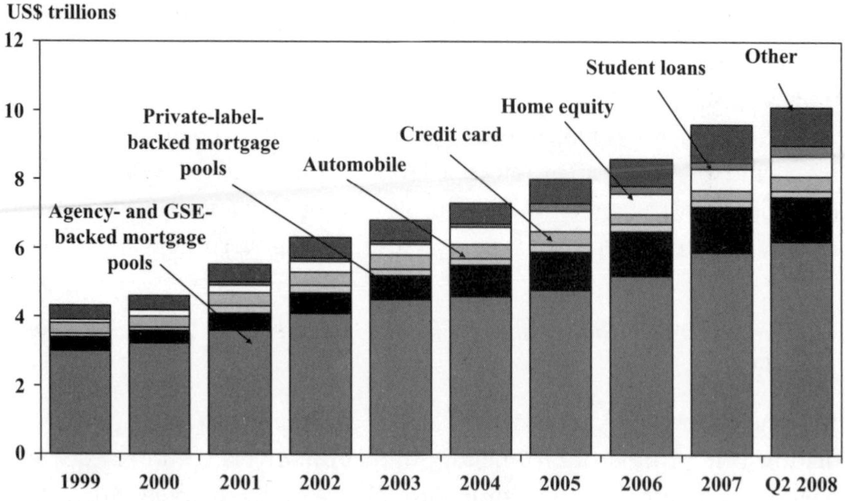

US$ trillions

SOURCES: Securities Industry and Financial Markets Association, Milken Institute.
NOTE: *Agency* refers to Ginnie Mae. *GSE* refers to Fannie Mae and Freddie Mac.

back on lending, businesses could still obtain any needed funds in the capital markets by issuing stocks and bonds. Unfortunately, that spare tire effectively turned out to be a flat tire during the recent financial meltdown.

In addition, many types of bank loans are becoming securitized and involving a wider range of financial players, as Figures 7.11, 7.12, and 7.13 show. This, as discussed earlier, reflects a movement toward an originate-to-distribute rather than an originate-to-hold business model. As a result, there has been substantial growth in mortgage-backed securities, contributing in turn to the rise in structured financial collateral (which includes RMBS, CMBS, CMOs, ABS, CDOs, CDS, and other securitized/structured products). Margin requirements and collateral calls have become far more important in financial markets and can therefore significantly affect the liquidity and overall performance of financial institutions. Greater regulatory attention must be given to these products and the various financial players involved in them, including lightly regulated private equity funds and hedge funds.

Figure 7.12 U.S. Asset-Backed Securities Outstanding

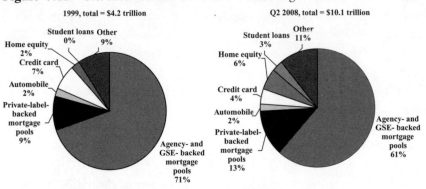

SOURCES: Securities Industry and Financial Markets Association, Milken Institute.
NOTE: *Agency* refers to Ginnie Mae. *GSE* refers to Fannie Mae and Freddie Mac.

The securitization of mortgages, in particular, has raised questions about the extent to which this trend was a major culprit in the recent financial crisis. Some have suggested that an alternative to securitizing mortgages (or other loans for that matter) is issuing covered bonds. These bonds would be issued by banks and collateralized by specific pools of

Figure 7.13 Shares of Consumer Credit: Banks Compared to Pools of Securitized Consumer Assets

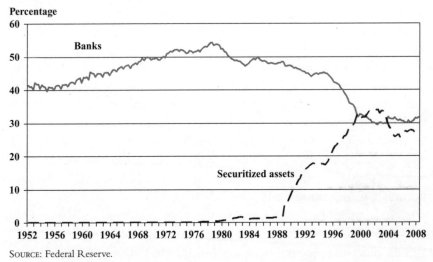

SOURCE: Federal Reserve.

assets, such as mortgages. If the bank issuing the covered bonds should default, the holders of the bonds would have priority claims against the collateral assets, ahead of other creditors and even the FDIC. The holders of the covered bonds would also have recourse to the bank issuing them.

These bonds are used in several European countries, most notably Germany. Currently, because the risk of issuing such bonds by banks is shifted to other liability holders, including the FDIC, they are limited by the FDIC to 4 percent of liabilities.

Covered bonds should be viewed as a complement to, not a substitute for, securitization. Improvements, however, should be made so that there is greater leeway to modify mortgage loans that have been securitized in the event of defaults and to provide greater recourse to the various financial players (such as originators who had little of their own money at risk) involved in selecting the mortgage loans that are securitized. With both covered bonds and securitization available to banks and managed prudently by them, banks can choose between keeping mortgage loans on their balance sheets with required capital backing or securitizing them to eliminate a required capital charge. However, banks must take precautions when attempting to securitize assets off their balance sheets so they do not get caught short of capital in the event they must be brought back onto the balance sheet, as happened during the recent crisis. This, of course, requires greater scrutiny of off-balance-sheet activities of banks by the regulatory authorities than apparently has been the case in the past.

Another issue that merits special attention is the use of various derivatives instruments, especially credit default swaps. Creating a formal exchange for derivatives is important (and, indeed, such an effort is underway as of this writing), because exchange-traded contracts are centralized, with continuously adjusted margin requirements. Further, if a trader defaults, the clearinghouse absorbs the losses with the capital contributed by the member firms. Looking only at banks, five institutions dominate in derivatives, as Figure 7.14 shows.

The regulatory challenge is to devote more attention to financial activity that is unregulated or lightly regulated, including off-balance-sheet activity of regulated financial institutions, without excessive costly and intrusive regulation that unduly hampers innovation.

Figure 7.14   Five Big Banks Dominate in Derivatives (Q2 2008)

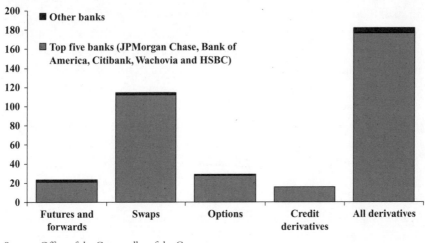

US$ trillions

■ Other banks

■ Top five banks (JPMorgan Chase, Bank of America, Citibank, Wachovia and HSBC)

SOURCE: Office of the Comptroller of the Currency.
NOTE: Notional amounts for all commercial banks.

What Will Promote Effective Market Discipline, Including Adequate Disclosure, Transparency, Reliable Outside Rating Agencies, and Better Information for Consumers about Complex Products and Services They Are Being Offered?

It is asking too much, and is perhaps inappropriate, to rely solely on regulators to monitor and safeguard the activities of financial institutions and financial market participants. Certainly, there is an important role to be played by market discipline. This, however, requires timely and adequate disclosure of financial information, greater transparency regarding financial risks, and more reliable ratings from the rating agencies. It is also essential to provide consumers with better and clearer information, as well as counseling, about complex products and services. This includes the need to simplify and improve mortgage documentation and the need to focus on increasing financial literacy among the broader public. Regulators should redouble their efforts to promote market discipline as a way to supplement, if not lessen, their own authority over the major players in the financial sector.

Market discipline is weakened to the extent there is a widespread belief that the government will always come to the rescue of individuals and firms whenever there are serious and extensive disruptions in the financial sector. Such a belief promotes complacency and, worse yet, an increased culture of risk-taking by individuals and firms.

Clearly, many are crying out for something to be done about the moral hazard issues that have already been raised by the government's actions to date. What can policymakers do to prevent financial institutions from becoming so big and so important that regardless of any reckless behavior on their part the government feels compelled to bail them out? Also, how can policymakers wind down the extensive intervention into the private marketplace that has already taken place and shift consequences back to financial firms in an orderly manner?

As a start, regulatory authorities must be more careful about endorsing, or seeming to endorse, the ratings conferred on firms and products by the major rating agencies. More effort should be devoted to requiring that better and more comprehensive information be provided to market participants so they can perform their own due diligence to a greater extent when making financial decisions.

The regulatory challenge is to strike a better balance between regulations and market discipline by promoting better disclosure and not simply expanding and strengthening the power of regulators whenever there is turmoil in the financial sector—especially without supporting evidence on the efficiency of such steps based on cost–benefit analyses of those powers.

What Can Be Done to More Safely Facilitate Homeownership?

At the outset, it is time to admit that there is nothing wrong with being a renter. But, more importantly, if homeownership is to be promoted by the government, the process needs to be improved, as the mortgage market meltdown so vividly demonstrates. It makes no sense to create financial institutions like Fannie Mae and Freddie Mac that have a dual mandate: earning profits for their shareholders while simultaneously satisfying regulated quotas on the amount of funding that must be provided to low-income families. It is clear by now that this is not a viable business model over time. It is therefore essential to make a clear decision about what to do with Fannie Mae and Freddie Mac, postconser-vatorship.

Beyond dealing with the two mortgage giants, not to mention the Federal Home Loan Banks, there are currently several alternative and not necessarily competing approaches to assisting first-time home buyers:

- **Shared equity programs:** These programs enable households to purchase homes either by offering equity loans or offering the opportunity to buy a share of a home. They support the outright purchase of a home with assistance from an equity loan provided by the government or a private lender. When repaying the equity loan, the homeowner shares in any increase in the property's value with the lender. These programs may be structured to allow individuals to buy a share in a home and pay a rent based on the outstanding equity. Purchasers have the option to buy further shares in the property and, ultimately, achieve full ownership. If the property is sold, the purchaser benefits from any equity that has built up on the share that is owned. These arrangements may also be structured as shared appreciation mortgages, in which the lender agrees to an interest rate lower than the prevailing market rate in exchange for a share of the appreciated value of the collateral property. The share of the appreciated value is determined and due at the sale of the property or at the termination of the mortgage. In addition to promoting homeownership, shared equity programs may be a useful tool in preventing foreclosures. However, currently U.S. banks are prohibited from engaging in real estate activities. This poses a barrier to the implementation of such programs.
- **Down-payment assistance:** Down-payment assistance and community redevelopment programs offer affordable housing opportunities to first-time home buyers, low-income and moderate-income individuals, and families who wish to achieve homeownership. Grant types include seller-funded programs and others, as well as programs that are funded by the federal government, or local governments, often using mortgage-revenue bond funds.
- **Community land trust:** A private, nonprofit corporation created to provide secure, affordable access to land and housing. Ownership of the house is split from ownership of the land underneath, which rests with the community land trust. This arrangement allows the cost of land to be removed from calculations of building price, thereby

lowering costs. This land is conveyed to individual homeowners through a ground lease.

- **Lease-to-purchase options:** An organization develops and leases a home to a household that cannot obtain a mortgage for income or credit reasons and then works with the household to overcome its barriers to a final purchase. In general, the length of time that the home is leased depends on the time an individual or family needs to save down-payment funds or to resolve particular credit issues.

How Can We Limit Foreclosures?

In addition to promoting homeownership, greater thought must be given to keeping families in their homes. This is a particular problem when home prices are falling and there is a growing inventory of unsold homes. Here are a few of possible approaches to limiting foreclosures and better dealing with them:

- **Bankruptcy modification:** Debtors may modify the terms of all debts in bankruptcy, including those secured by mortgages on their principal residences.
- **Possible new legislation for mortgage restructuring that would support Treasury restructuring programs:** Real Estate Mortgage Investment Conduits (REMICs) are special-purpose vehicles for pooling mortgages and issuing mortgage-backed securities. In many cases, loan modification efforts have been hampered by the complexity of these ownership structures. Modifying the REMIC statute and other laws would give servicers the authority and flexibility to modify loan terms without legal liability to investors. Rules can also be changed to provide servicers with further legal comfort in modifying and selling mortgage loans under any government mortgage restructuring programs.
- **Land bank:** A land bank is a public authority created to efficiently acquire, hold, manage, and develop tax-foreclosed property, as well as other vacant and abandoned properties.

The regulatory challenge is to put into place a strategy for better promoting homeownership and for avoiding, to the extent possible, any abnormal increase in home foreclosures if ever again there is another home price bubble.

Concluding Thoughts

What really drove the growth of such dangerous bubbles in the U.S. housing and credit markets? On multiple levels, we have abused credit, which is essential for economic growth and development, by allowing it to grow at unsustainable rates through excessive leverage.

If our nation is to break this cycle, the government must devote much greater effort to identifying and containing emerging crises before they grow to dangerous proportions. If this cannot be done for whatever reason, the government should have a game plan in place before the next financial crisis strikes. Federal, state, and local governments must also be much better prepared to address any surges in budget deficits that result from the inevitable bailouts that occur. Taxpayers deserve no less.

Appendix

Figure A.1 Origin of U.S. Banking Institutions and Expanding Regulatory Role of Government

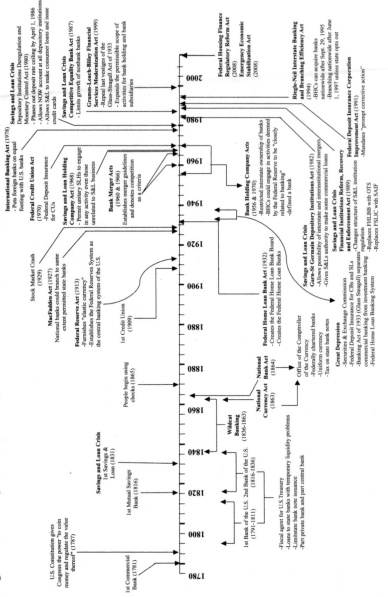

Source: Milken Institute.

Table A.1 Major Depository Financial Institution Legislation

Date of Enactment	Legislation	Key Provisions
September 17, 1787	U.S. Constitution	Grants the federal government the exclusive right to coin money and to regulate its value.
February 25, 1791	Charter for the First Bank of the United States	The first federally chartered bank; chartered for 20 years.
March 10, 1816	Charter for the Second Bank of the United States	The second federally chartered bank; chartered for 20 years.
February 25, 1863	National Currency Act	Provides for the federal chartering of national banks under the supervision of the comptroller of the currency.
June 3, 1864	National Banking Act	Supersedes the National Currency Act of February 25, 1863 (under neither act could national banks make real estate loans).
March 3, 1865	Act of 1865	Legislates state bank notes out of existence by imposing a tax of 10 percent (effective August 1, 1866) per year on their circulating notes.
June 20, 1874	Act of 1874	Changes the name of the Currency Act to the National Bank Act as a matter of law.
December 23, 1913	Federal Reserve Act	Provides for the establishment of the Federal Reserve System to furnish an "elastic currency" by advancing funds to illiquid but solvent member banks. Increases supervision and regulation of banks. Gives national banks the power to make real estate loans but only with respect to farmland.
February 25, 1927	McFadden Act	Enlarges the power of national banks to make real estate loans and permits national banks to branch within the state in which they are located, to the same extent permitted state banks. Prior to this act, national banks had no power to branch.

(Continued)

Table A.1 (*Continued*)

Date of Enactment	Legislation	Key Provisions
July 22, 1932	Federal Home Loan Bank Act	Establishes 12 Federal Home Loan Banks under the supervision of the Federal Home Loan Bank Board to advance funds to savings and loan associations to promote homeownership.
May 27, 1933 June 6, 1934	Securities Act Securities and Exchange Act	Provide for the regulation of securities exchanges, and brokers and dealers in securities, to prevent manipulative and unfair practices in the securities markets. Establishes the Securities and Exchange Commission.
June 13, 1933	Home Owners' Loan Act	Creates federal savings and loan associations. Also creates the Home Owners' Loan Corporation to purchase delinquent home mortgages from financial institutions and refinance the mortgages over longer terms and at lower interest rates.
June 16, 1933	Banking Act of 1933 (and Glass-Steagall Act)	Creates the Federal Deposit Insurance Corporation (FDIC), prohibits the payment of interest-on-demand deposits, establishes Regulation Q (which limited the interest rates that U.S. banks and savings and loans could pay on deposits), and forces a separation between banking and the securities businesses.
June 26, 1934	Federal Credit Union Act	Authorizes federal credit unions in all states. The initial maximum maturity of loans was two years.
June 27, 1934	National Housing Act	Creates the Federal Savings and Loan Insurance Corporation and authorizes the FSLIC to regulate savings and loan holding companies.
August 23, 1935	Banking Act of 1935	Amends the Banking Act of 1933 and the Federal Reserve Act to restructure the Federal Open Market Committee and the Federal Reserve Board. Also permits national banks to make five-year real estate loans.

August 22, 1940	Investment Company Act of 1940	Seeks to prevent abuses through mandating disclosure regarding the investment company's structure, operations, financial condition, and investment policies when shares of the investment company are initially offered to the public and, thereafter, on a regular periodic basis. Investment companies register with the SEC under the 1940 act and typically register their securities under the 1933 act. The provisions in the 1940 act govern, among other things: registration of investment companies, transactions between the investment company and an affiliate (e.g., the investment adviser to the investment company), purchases and sales of investment company shares, and responsibilities of the investment company's directors or trustees. Congress, the SEC, the self-regulatory organizations (SROs), and state regulators are responding to allegations of recent wrongdoing within the mutual fund industry.
August 22, 1940	Investment Adviser Act of 1940	Requires the registration of certain investment advisers with the SEC. The act has rules covering such matters as record-keeping, substantive content of advisory contracts, advertising, custody of client funds and assets, and proxy voting. In addition, the act imposes certain antifraud provisions on individuals who meet the statute's definition of "investment adviser," even if the act does not require those persons to register with the SEC.
May 9, 1956	Bank Holding Company Act (and Douglas amendment)	Prohibits interstate ownership of banks by companies owning more than one bank, unless the law of the state of the bank to be acquired authorized it. Restricts the range of permissible nonbanking activities to those approved by the Federal Reserve Board.

(Continued)

Table A.1 (*Continued*)

Date of Enactment	Legislation	Key Provisions
		Permits the Federal Reserve Board to allow a bank holding company to engage directly in, or acquire, shares of, any company whose activities are found to be so "closely related to banking as to be a proper incident thereto," and which, if engaged in by a bank holding company, will result in a net public benefit.
September 23, 1959	S&L Holding Company Act (Spence Act)	The original legislation for savings and loan association holding companies. It provides for regulation of savings and loan holding companies by the FSLIC. Prohibits savings and loan holding companies from acquiring additional S&Ls but does not prohibit the acquisition of a single S&L by a company that owns no other S&L.
October 23, 1962	Bank Service Corporation Act	Authorizes banks to invest in service corporations that would provide clerical and related financial services to them.
September 2, 1964	Savings and Loan Service Corporation Act	Authorizes federal savings and loan associations to acquire and operate service corporations that would engage (up to 1 percent of their assets) in businesses not otherwise considered permissible for a savings and loan institution to engage in directly, including stock brokerage, insurance brokerage, and agency activities.
July 23, 1965	Coinage Act	Declares that all coins and currencies of the United States, including Federal Reserve notes, are legal tender.
October 16, 1966	Financial Institutions Supervisory Act	Grants authority to the comptroller of the currency, the Federal Reserve Board, the FDIC, and the FSLIC to issue cease-and-desist, and suspension and removal orders that are effective immediately.
September 21, 1966	Interest Rate Control Act	Extends deposit rate ceilings to the thrift institutions.

326

February 14, 1968	Savings and Loan Holding Company Act	Defines a savings and loan holding company as any company that directly or indirectly controls an insured institution (FSLIC–insured savings and loan or FDIC–insured federal savings bank) or other savings and loan holding company.
		Prohibits a multiple savings and loan holding company from controlling insured institutions in more than one state. Later, under the Garn–St Germain Act of 1982, temporary authority is granted to the FSLIC to approve emergency acquisitions of insured institutions, including interstate and interindustry acquisitions.
		Permits unitary savings and loan holding companies (those that control a single savings association and that meet the IRS thriftness test, i.e., 60 percent of their assets must be obligations of the United States or states, residential real estate loans, or urban–renewal loans, included as part of the Garn–St Germain Act of 1982) to engage, through non-FSLIC insured subsidiaries, in any activity, even those unrelated to the savings and loan business (for example, Sears, Roebuck and Company).
		Multiple savings and loan holding companies are allowed to engage only in those activities approved by the FSLIC.
July 24, 1970	Emergency Home Finance Act	Establishes the Federal Home Loan Mortgage Corporation to strengthen the secondary market for conventional mortgages, as well as for federally insured or guaranteed mortgages, through the purchase of residential mortgages from federally insured institutions.
October 19, 1970	Federal Credit Union Act	Establishes the National Credit Union Administration to charter federal credit unions and provide federal insurance of credit union member accounts.

(Continued)

Table A.1 (*Continued*)

Date of Enactment	Legislation	Key Provisions
December 31, 1970	Bank Holding Company Act Amendments of 1970	Subject one-bank holding companies to the same regulations as multiple-bank holding companies and restrict the definition of "bank" to institutions that accept demand deposits and make commercial loans.
October 12, 1977	Community Reinvestment Act	Is intended to encourage depository institutions to help meet the credit needs of the communities in which they operate, including low- and moderate-income neighborhoods, consistent with safe and sound banking operations. Requires that each insured depository institution's record in helping meet the credit needs of its entire community be evaluated periodically. That record is taken into account in considering an institution's application for deposit facilities, including mergers and acquisitions. CRA examinations (see Exam Schedules) are conducted by the federal agencies that are responsible for supervising depository institutions: the Board of Governors of the Federal Reserve System (FRB), the Federal Deposit Insurance Corporation (FDIC), the Office of the Comptroller of the Currency (OCC), and the Office of Thrift Supervision (OTS).
November 10, 1978	Financial Institutions Regulatory and Interest Rate Control Act	Provides for FHLBB chartering of federal savings banks by permitting existing state-chartered mutual savings banks to convert to federal charters.
September 17, 1978	International Banking Act	Subjects foreign banks and foreign holding companies with branches or agencies in the United States to portions of the Bank Holding Company Acts of 1956 and 1970 to place them on an equal footing with U.S. institutions.

328

March 31, 1980	Depository Institutions Deregulation and Monetary Control Act	Authorizes NOW (negotiable order of withdrawal) accounts for individuals and not-for-profit organizations at all federally insured depository institutions, as of December 31, 1980; phases out Regulation Q over a six-year period ending March 31, 1986. Imposes mandatory reserve requirements set by the Federal Reserve Board on all depository institutions and permits these institutions to utilize Federal Reserve services, including discount and borrowing privileges. Increases federal insurance of accounts from $40,000 to $100,000.
		Permanently authorizes automatic transfer services and remote-service units. Preempts state usury ceilings. Authorizes federal savings and loan associations to issue credit cards; to act as trustees; to operate trust departments; to make loans on the basis of commercial real estate; to invest up to 20 percent of their assets in a combination of consumer loans, commercial paper, and corporate debt securities; and to invest up to 3 percent of their assets in service corporations.
October 15, 1982	Garn–St Germain Depository Institutions Act	Expands the authority of the FDIC and the FSLIC to provide direct aid to, and facilitate mergers of, insured depository institutions. Also, for the first time, permits interstate and interindustry acquisitions of troubled financial institutions.
		More specifically, authorizes the FDIC and FSLIC to increase or maintain capital of insured banks and savings and loan associations eligible for assistance through the purchase of capital instruments known as net worth certificates. Authorizes commercial banks and thrifts to offer money market deposit accounts and preempts state restrictions on the enforcement by lenders of due-on-sale clauses.

(Continued)

329

Table A.1 (*Continued*)

Date of Enactment	Legislation	Key Provisions
		Authorizes the FHLBB to charter and regulate federal savings and loan associations and federal savings banks and grants them essentially similar powers (the savings banks could be organized in either stock or mutual form).
		Permits federal associations to make commercial, corporate, business, or agricultural loans, which after January 1984 could constitute up to 10 percent of an association's assets; to invest as much as 30 percent of assets (up from 20 percent) in consumer loans; to offer individual or corporate demand deposit accounts (although corporate checking accounts would be opened only by companies having other business with the association); to increase from 20 percent to 40 percent the investment of assets in loans secured by nonresidential real estate; to invest up to 10 percent of assets in personal property for rent or sale (thereby gaining access to the leasing business); to make educational loans for any educational purpose (rather than just for college or vocational training); to invest up to 100 percent of assets in state or local government obligations; and, for the first time, to invest in other savings and loan associations' time and saving deposits and use such investments to help meet liquidity requirements.
		Abolishes on all counts on January 1, 1984, the slightly higher interest rate that savings and loan associations could pay relative to commercial banks.

Date		Description
August 10, 1987	Competitive Equality Banking Act	Establishes new standards for expedited funds availability. Recapitalizes the Federal Savings & Loan Insurance Company (FSLIC). Expands FDIC authority for open bank assistance transactions, including bridge banks.
August 9, 1989	Financial Institutions Reform, Recovery, and Enforcement Act of 1989	Enacted to restore the public's confidence in the savings and loan industry. FIRREA abolishes the Federal Savings & Loan Insurance Corporation (FSLIC), with responsibility of insuring the deposits of thrift institutions transferred to the FDIC. The FDIC insurance fund created to cover thrifts is named the Savings Association Insurance Fund (SAIF), while the fund covering banks is called the Bank Insurance Fund (BIF).
		FIRREA also abolishes the Federal Home Loan Bank Board. Two new agencies, the Federal Housing Finance Board (FHFB) and the Office of Thrift Supervision (OTS), are created to replace it.
		Finally, FIRREA creates the Resolution Trust Corporation (RTC) as a temporary agency of the government. The RTC is given the responsibility of managing and disposing of the assets of failed institutions. An Oversight Board is created to provide supervisory authority over the policies of the RTC, and the Resolution Funding Corporation (RFC) is created to provide funding for RTC operations.
December 19, 1991	Federal Deposit Insurance Corporation Improvement Act of 1991	The FDICIA greatly increases the powers and authority of the FDIC. Major provisions recapitalize the Bank Insurance Fund and allow the FDIC to strengthen the fund by borrowing from the Treasury.

(Continued)

Table A.1 (*Continued*)

Date of Enactment	Legislation	Key Provisions
		The act mandates a least-cost resolution method and prompt resolution approach to problem and failing banks and orders the creation of a risk-based deposit insurance assessment scheme. Brokered deposits and the solicitation of deposits are restricted, as are the nonbank activities of insured state banks.
		The FDICIA creates new supervisory and regulatory examination standards and puts forth new capital requirements for banks. It also expands prohibitions against insider activities and creates new Truth in Savings provisions.
September 29, 1994	Riegle–Neal Interstate Banking and Branching Efficiency Act of 1994	Permits adequately capitalized and managed bank holding companies to acquire banks in any state one year after enactment. Concentration limits apply, and CRA evaluations by the Federal Reserve are required before acquisitions are approved. Beginning June 1, 1997, allows interstate mergers between adequately capitalized and managed banks, subject to concentration limits, state laws, and CRA evaluations. Extends the statute of limitations to permit the FDIC and RTC to revive lawsuits that had expired under state statutes of limitations.
October 11, 1996	National Securities Markets Improvement Act	Makes substantial changes to the dual system of federal–state regulation while preserving state antifraud authority. For the first time since the New Deal, Congress modernizes the relationship between federal and state securities regulators.

Congress seeks to make the SEC the regulator of nationally based activities, while preserving the role of states over activities that are truly local in nature. At the same time, NSMIA preserves the right of state regulators to prosecute fraud. Among other things, NSMIA preempts state registration and related requirements in the case of offerings of nationally traded securities and securities of registered investment companies.

NSMIA amends Section 18 of the 1933 Securities Act to provide that no state law "requiring or, with respect to, registration or qualification of securities, or registration or qualification of securities transactions, shall directly or indirectly," apply to a "covered security." Covered securities include nationally traded securities (e.g., securities listed or authorized for listing on the NYSE or included or qualified for inclusion in the NASDAQ; securities of a registered investment company (i.e., mutual funds); and offers and sales of certain exempt securities broker–dealers.

NSMIA also preempts to a limited extent state laws that address broker–dealer licensing, capital, custody, financial responsibility, and record-keeping requirements to the extent that such conflicts differ from SEC requirements. This provision, for example, avoids the nightmare that would have occurred if every state securities authority had imposed its own book and records requirement on brokerage firms operating in all 50 states.

| November 3, 1998 | Securities Litigation Uniform Standards Act | Provides that large securities class actions must proceed in federal court, where they will be governed by the PSLRA (Private Securities Litigation Reform Act). |

(Continued)

Table A.1 (*Continued*)

Date of Enactment	Legislation	Key Provisions
November 12, 1999	Gramm–Leach–Bliley Act	Repeals the last vestiges of the Glass-Steagall Act of 1933. Modifies portions of the Bank Holding Company Act to allow affiliations between banks and insurance underwriters. While preserving authority of states to regulate insurance, the act prohibits state actions that have the effect of preventing bank-affiliated firms from selling insurance on an equal basis with other insurance agents. Creates a new financial holding company under Section 4 of the Bank Holding Company Act, authorized to engage in underwriting and selling insurance and securities; conducting both commercial and merchant banking; and investing in and developing real estate and other complementary activities. There are limits on the kinds of nonfinancial activities in which these new entities may engage. Allows national banks to underwrite municipal bonds. Restricts the disclosure of nonpublic customer information by financial institutions. All financial institutions must provide customers the opportunity to "opt out" of the sharing of the customers' nonpublic information with unaffiliated third parties. Imposes criminal penalties on anyone who obtains customer information from a financial institution under false pretenses. Amends the Community Reinvestment Act (1977) to require that financial holding companies cannot be formed before their insured depository institutions receive and maintain a satisfactory CRA rating. Also requires public disclosure of bank community CRA-related agreements. Grants some regulatory relief to small institutions in the shape of reducing the frequency of their CRA examinations if they have received outstanding or satisfactory ratings.

Date	Act	Description
		Prohibits affiliations and acquisitions between commercial firms and unitary thrift institutions. Makes significant changes in the operation of the Federal Home Loan Bank System, easing membership requirements and loosening restrictions on the use of FHLB funds.
July 30, 2002	Sarbanes–Oxley Act	Establishes the Public Company Oversight Board to regulate public accounting firms that audit publicly traded companies. Prohibits such firms from providing other services to client companies along with the audit. Requires that CEOs and CFOs certify the annual and quarterly reports of publicly traded companies. Authorizes, and in some cases requires, the Securities and Exchange Commission to issue rules governing audits. Forbids insiders from trading their companies' securities during pension fund blackout periods. Mandates various studies, including a study of the involvement of investment banks and financial advisors in the scandals preceding the legislation. Also included are whistleblower protections and new federal criminal laws, including a ban on alteration of documents.
July 30, 2008	Federal Housing Finance Regulatory Reform Act of 2008	Establish a single regulator, the Federal Housing Finance Agency (FHFA), for government-sponsored enterprises (GSEs) involved in the home mortgage market. GSEs are privately owned, congressionally chartered financial institutions created to enhance the availability of mortgage credit. The GSEs that would be regulated by FHFA include the Federal National Mortgage Association (Fannie Mae), the Federal Home Loan Mortgage Corporation (Freddie Mac), and the Federal Home Loan Banks (FHLBs).

(Continued)

Table A.1 (*Continued*)

Date of Enactment	Legislation	Key Provisions
		Requires Fannie Mae and Freddie Mac to annually pay amounts equal to 4.2 basis points on each dollar of unpaid principal balance of each enterprise's total new business purchases (that is, 4.2 cents per $100 of the value of the new mortgages purchased or securitized in that year). These assessments would begin during fiscal year 2009 and be deposited into new federal funds.
		Authorizes, from October 1, 2008, through September 30, 2010, a new mortgage guarantee program under the Federal Housing Administration (FHA) that would allow certain at-risk borrowers to refinance their mortgages after the mortgage holder (lender or servicer) agrees to a write-down of the existing loan (that is, a reduction in the amount of loan principal). A portion of the GSEs' assessments would be used to pay the cost of this new program.
		Requires loan originators to participate in a Nationwide Mortgage Licensing System and Registry (NMLSR) that would be administered by either a nonfederal entity or the Department of Housing and Urban Development (HUD) in coordination with the federal banking regulatory agencies.
		Authorizes the appropriation of such sums as are necessary for the Treasury Department's Office of Financial Education to provide grants to state and local governments, Indian tribes, and other entities to support financial education and counseling services.
October 3, 2008	Emergency Economic Stabilization Act of 2008	Provides up to $700 billion to the Secretary of the Treasury to buy mortgages and other assets that are clogging the balance sheets of financial institutions and making it difficult for working families, small businesses, and other companies to access credit, which is vital to a strong and stable economy. EESA also establishes a program that would allow companies to insure their troubled assets.

Requires the Treasury to modify troubled loans—many the result of predatory lending practices—wherever possible to help American families keep their homes. It also directs other federal agencies to modify loans that they own or control. Finally, it improves the HOPE for Homeowners program by expanding eligibility and increasing the tools available to the Department of Housing and Urban Development to help more families keep their homes.

Taxpayers should not be expected to pay for Wall Street's mistakes. The legislation requires companies that sell some of their bad assets to the government to provide warrants so that taxpayers will benefit from any future growth these companies may experience as a result of participation in this program. The legislation also requires the president to submit legislation that would cover any losses to taxpayers resulting from this program from financial institutions.

Executives who made bad decisions should not be allowed to dump their bad assets on the government and then walk away with millions of dollars in bonuses. To participate in this program, companies will lose certain tax benefits and, in some cases, must limit executive pay. In addition, the bill limits "golden parachutes" and requires that unearned bonuses be returned.

Rather than giving the Treasury all the funds at once, the legislation gives the Treasury $250 billion immediately and then requires the president to certify that additional funds are needed ($100 billion and then $350 billion subject to congressional disapproval). The Treasury must report on the use of the funds and the progress in addressing the crisis. EESA also establishes an Oversight Board so that the Treasury cannot act in an arbitrary manner. It also establishes a special inspector general to protect against waste, fraud, and abuse.

Sources: Barth and Regalia (1987); FDIC; Securities Industry and Financial Markets Association; U.S. Senate Committee on Banking, Housing, and Urban Affairs; Milken Institute.

Table A.2 Composition of Housing Units (1980—Q3 2008)

	1980	1985	1990	1995	2000	2002	2003	2004	2005	2006	2007	Q3 2008
All housing units (thousands)	87,739	97,333	106,283	112,655	119,628	119,297	120,834	122,187	123,925	126,012	127,958	130,357
Percentage of Total Housing Units												
Occupied	90.8	90.3	88.7	88.8	88.4	88.0	87.4	87.2	87.3	87.0	86.2	85.7
Owner occupied	59.5	57.7	56.7	57.5	59.6	59.7	59.6	60.2	60.2	59.8	58.7	58.2
Rent occupied	31.2	32.6	32.0	31.3	28.8	28.2	27.7	27.0	27.2	27.1	27.5	27.5
Vacant	9.2	9.7	11.3	11.2	11.6	12.0	12.6	12.8	12.7	13.0	13.8	14.3
Year-round	6.8	7.6	8.6	8.5	8.7	9.0	9.6	9.7	9.6	9.9	10.4	10.6
For rent	1.8	2.3	2.5	2.6	2.5	2.8	3.0	3.1	3.0	3.0	3.0	3.1
For sale only	0.8	1.0	1.0	0.9	1.0	1.0	1.1	1.1	1.2	1.5	1.7	1.7
Other	4.2	4.3	5.1	5.0	5.2	5.2	5.5	5.5	5.4	5.5	5.7	5.8
Seasonal	2.4	2.1	2.8	2.8	2.9	3.0	3.0	3.0	3.0	3.2	3.4	3.7

SOURCES: U.S. Census Bureau, Milken Institute.

NOTES:

1. These estimates are based on the monthly samples of the Housing Vacancy Survey. Size of sample is 72,000.

2. Homeownership is calculated as the ratio of owner-occupied housing units divided by all occupied housing units.

3. Foreclosed properties can be counted as owner occupied, renter occupied, vacant for rent, vacant for sale, and vacant other.

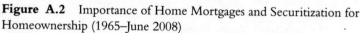

Figure A.2 Importance of Home Mortgages and Securitization for Homeownership (1965–June 2008)

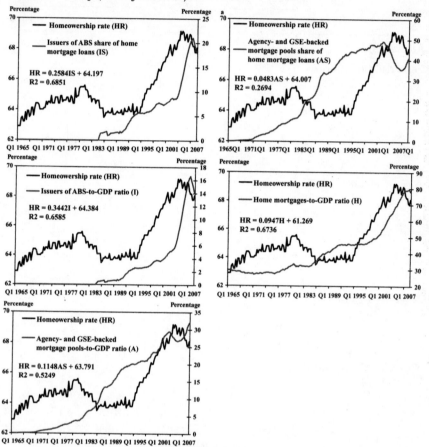

SOURCES: Federal Reserve, U.S. Census Bureau, Milken Institute.

Table A.3   Percentage of Families with a Primary Residence as an Asset, Selected Household Characteristics and Years

		1998	2001	2004
All Families		66.2	67.7	69.1
Percentile of Income				
	Less than 20	38.8	40.6	40.3
	20–39.9	55.3	57.3	57.0
	40–59.9	67.3	66.0	71.5
	60–79.9	79.1	81.8	83.1
	80–89.9	88.2	90.9	91.8
	90–100	93.1	94.4	94.7
Age of Head (Years)				
	Less than 35	38.9	39.9	41.6
	35–44	67.1	67.8	68.3
	45–54	74.4	76.2	77.3
	55–64	80.3	83.2	79.1
	65–74	81.5	82.5	81.3
	75 or more	77.0	76.2	85.2
Race or Ethnicity of Respondent				
	White non-Hispanic	71.8	74.3	76.1
	Non-white or Hispanic	46.8	47.3	50.8
Current Work Status of Head				
	Working for someone else	63.5	64.7	66.5
	Self-employed	81.3	80.3	79.1
	Retired	72.4	73.8	75.8
	Other not working	35.8	43.6	40.0
Housing Status				
	Owner	100.0	100.0	100.0
	Renter or other	0.0	0.0	0.0
Percentile of Net Worth				
	Less than 25	14.0	14.3	15.2
	25–49.9	67.3	69.6	71.2
	50–74.9	89.3	91.4	93.4
	75–89.9	94.0	95.1	96.2
	90–100	95.1	95.8	96.9

SOURCES: Federal Reserve Board, Survey of Consumer Finances; Milken Institute.

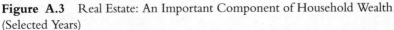

Figure A.3 Real Estate: An Important Component of Household Wealth (Selected Years)

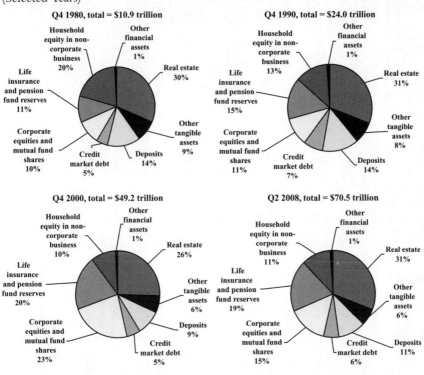

SOURCES: Federal Reserve, Milken Institute.

Table A.4 Originations of Single-Family Mortgages: Conventional and Government-Backed Mortgages by Loan Type (1990–Q2 2008; US$ Millions)

	Single-Family Mortgages	Single-Family ARMs	Single-Family FRMs	Conventional	Conventional ARMs	Conventional FRMs	Government-Backed	Government-Backed ARMs	Government-Backed FRMs
1990	458,440	127,640	330,800	380,513	127,031	253,482	77,927	609	77,318
1991	562,074	135,015	427,059	498,482	132,210	366,272	63,592	2,805	60,787
1992	893,666	204,722	688,944	828,767	195,818	632,949	64,899	8,904	55,995
1993	1,019,861	236,207	783,654	925,009	222,191	702,818	94,852	14,016	80,836
1994	773,121	308,212	464,909	630,767	281,279	349,488	142,354	26,933	115,421
1995	639,430	231,807	407,623	568,394	213,162	355,231	71,036	18,645	52,391
1996	785,329	238,517	546,812	678,414	217,436	460,978	106,915	21,081	85,834
1997	859,120	223,547	635,573	755,478	196,255	559,223	103,642	27,292	76,351
1998	1,450,000	236,231	1,213,769	1,301,470	224,595	1,076,876	148,530	11,636	136,894
1999	1,310,000	317,788	992,212	1,134,304	309,330	824,973	175,696	8,458	167,239
2000	1,048,000	311,349	736,651	929,094	301,852	627,243	118,906	9,497	109,408
2001	2,215,000	367,959	1,847,041	2,044,186	363,673	1,680,513	170,814	4,286	166,528
2002	2,885,000	613,885	2,271,115	2,696,939	600,096	2,096,843	188,061	13,789	174,272
2003	3,945,000	838,689	3,106,311	3,710,699	823,961	2,886,738	234,301	14,729	219,572
2004	2,920,000	1,136,216	1,783,784	2,787,437	1,115,660	1,671,776	132,563	20,556	112,007
2005	3,120,000	1,101,952	2,018,048	3,032,879	1,094,345	1,938,535	87,121	7,607	79,514
2006	2,980,000	922,728	2,057,272	2,895,378	920,723	1,974,655	84,622	2,005	82,617
2007	2,430,000	406,224	2,023,776	2,330,972	404,892	1,926,080	99,028	1,332	97,696
Q1 2008	490,000	63,886	426,113	448,143	63,573	384,570	41,856	313	41,543
Q2 2008	445,000	42,741	402,259	377,659	41,917	335,742	67,341	824	66,517

SOURCE: Office of Federal Housing Enterprise Oversight.

NOTE: FHHA based on data from the Department of Housing and Urban Development, the Federal Housing Administration (FHA), the Department of Veterans Affairs (VA), the Rural Housing Service (RHS), and Inside Mortgage Finance Publications. For an explanation of the methodology used to develop the estimates, see: Pafenberg, F. (2005) Single-Family Mortgages Originated and Outstanding: 1990–2004. For an update of certain of the assumptions made in that article, see http://www.ofheo.gov/media/marketdata/updatedassumptions 2008q2103108.pdf.

Table A.5 Single-Family Mortgages Outstanding: Government-Backed and Conventional Mortgages by Loan Type (1990–Q2 2008; US$ Millions)

	Single-Family Mortgages	Single-Family ARMs	Single-Family FRMs	Conventional Mortgages	Conventional ARMs	Conventional FRMs	Government-Backed	Government-Backed ARMs	Government-Backed FRMs
1990	2,621,286	222,955	2,398,331	2,181,747	218,116	1,963,631	439,539	4,839	434,700
1991	2,788,763	239,473	2,549,290	2,324,176	232,494	2,091,682	464,587	6,979	457,608
1992	2,954,396	264,675	2,689,721	2,494,664	250,144	2,244,520	459,732	14,531	445,201
1993	3,113,834	425,388	2,688,446	2,664,272	396,547	2,267,725	449,562	28,841	420,721
1994	3,291,540	470,132	2,821,408	2,806,591	419,153	2,387,438	484,949	50,979	433,970
1995	3,459,184	527,585	2,931,599	2,946,185	463,232	2,482,953	512,999	64,353	448,646
1996	3,682,790	566,470	3,116,310	3,129,990	491,584	2,638,396	552,800	74,886	477,914
1997	3,917,569	519,066	3,398,503	3,310,724	430,392	2,880,332	606,845	88,674	518,171
1998	4,274,301	561,562	3,712,739	3,639,934	490,299	3,149,635	634,367	71,263	563,104
1999	4,699,578	588,885	4,110,693	4,007,817	527,429	3,480,388	691,761	61,456	630,305
2000	5,126,531	571,650	4,554,881	4,383,182	511,956	3,871,227	743,349	59,694	683,655
2001	5,677,996	625,454	5,052,542	4,922,596	574,959	4,347,636	755,400	50,495	704,905
2002	6,437,356	741,396	5,695,960	5,697,578	697,383	5,000,194	739,778	44,013	695,765
2003	7,227,809	972,418	6,255,391	6,556,929	929,117	5,627,812	670,880	43,301	627,579
2004	8,270,527	1,428,493	6,842,034	7,641,539	1,377,005	6,264,534	628,988	51,488	577,500
2005	9,374,269	1,995,254	7,379,015	8,798,385	1,951,482	6,846,903	575,884	43,772	532,112
2006	10,443,992	2,324,431	8,119,561	9,882,199	2,290,694	7,591,505	561,793	33,737	528,056
2007	11,135,792	2,592,136	8,543,656	10,544,714	2,565,529	7,979,185	591,078	26,607	564,471
Q1 2008	11,239,047	2,455,002	8,784,045	10,629,322	2,429,863	8,199,459	609,725	25,139	584,586
Q2 2008	11,254,223	2,352,635	8,901,587	10,596,329	2,328,013	8,268,315	657,894	24,622	633,272

Source: Office of Federal Housing Enterprise Oversight.

Note: FHFA based on data from the Department of Housing and Urban Development, the Federal Housing Administration (FHA), the Department of Veterans Affairs (VA), the Rural Housing Service (RHS), and the Board of Governors of the Federal Reserve System. For an explanation of the methodology used to develop the estimates, see: Pafenberg, F. (2005) Single-Family Mortgages Originated and Outstanding: 1990–2004. For an update of certain of the assumptions made in that article, see http://www.ofheo.gov/media/marketdata/updatedassumptions2008q2103108.pdf.

Table A.6 Originations of Conventional Single-Family Mortgages: Jumbo and Nonjumbo Mortgages by Loan Type (1990–Q2 2008; US$ Millions)

	Conventional Mortgages	Conventional ARMs	Conventional FRMs	Nonjumbo	Nonjumbo ARMs	Nonjumbo FRMs	Jumbo	Jumbo ARMs	Jumbo FRMs
1990	380,513	127,031	253,482	289,875	75,367	214,507	90,638	51,664	38,974
1991	498,482	132,210	366,272	388,367	81,557	306,810	110,115	50,653	59,462
1992	828,767	195,818	632,949	662,019	125,784	536,235	166,748	70,034	96,714
1993	925,009	222,191	702,818	732,977	131,936	601,041	192,032	90,255	101,777
1994	630,767	281,279	349,488	480,203	172,873	307,330	150,564	108,406	42,158
1995	568,394	213,162	355,231	437,777	126,955	310,822	130,617	86,207	44,410
1996	678,414	217,436	460,978	516,070	113,535	402,534	162,344	103,900	58,444
1997	755,478	196,255	559,223	567,213	107,770	459,442	188,265	88,485	99,780
1998	1,301,470	224,595	1,076,876	986,645	98,664	887,980	314,826	125,930	188,895
1999	1,134,304	309,330	824,973	850,161	144,527	705,633	284,143	164,803	119,340
2000	929,094	301,852	627,243	688,087	130,737	557,351	241,007	171,115	69,892
2001	2,044,186	363,673	1,680,513	1,616,338	145,470	1,470,867	427,848	218,203	209,646
2002	2,696,939	600,096	2,096,843	2,095,522	293,373	1,802,149	601,417	306,723	294,695
2003	3,710,699	823,961	2,886,738	3,033,497	485,359	2,548,137	677,203	338,601	338,601
2004	2,787,437	1,115,660	1,671,776	2,142,424	664,151	1,478,272	645,013	451,509	193,504
2005	3,032,879	1,094,345	1,938,535	2,244,937	597,153	1,647,784	787,942	497,191	290,751
2006	2,895,378	920,723	1,974,655	2,210,332	555,456	1,654,875	685,046	365,267	319,780
2007	2,330,972	401,904	1,929,068	1,874,101	211,024	1,663,078	456,871	190,880	265,990
Q1 2008	448,144	63,573	384,571	391,812	36,517	355,295	56,332	27,056	29,276
Q2 2008	377,659	41,917	335,742	331,282	29,915	301,368	46,377	12,002	34,374

SOURCE: Office of Federal Housing Enterprise Oversight.

NOTE: FHFA based on data from the Department of Housing and Urban Development, the Federal Housing Administration (FHA), the Department of Veterans Affairs (VA), the Rural Housing Service (RHS), and Inside Mortgage Finance Publications. For an explanation of the methodology used to develop the estimates, see: Pafenberg, F. (2005) Single-Family Mortgages Originated and Outstanding: 1990–2004. For an update of certain of the assumptions made in that article, see http://www.ofheo.gov/media/marketdata/updatedassumptions2008q2103108.pdf.

Table A.7 Originations of Government-Backed Single-Family Mortgages: FHA-Insured and VA- and RHS-Guaranteed By Loan Type (1990–Q2 2008; US$ Millions)

	Government-Backed Single-Family Mortgages	Government-Backed ARMs	Government-Backed FRMs	FHA-Insured Single-Family Mortgages	FHA-Insured ARMs	FHA-Insured FRMs	VA-Guaranteed Single-Family Mortgages	VA-Guaranteed ARMs	VA-Guaranteed FRMs	RHS-Guaranteed FRMs
1990	77,927	609	77,318	51,665	609	51,056	24,984	0	24,984	1,278
1991	63,592	2,805	60,787	46,468	2,805	43,663	15,814	0	15,814	1,310
1992	64,899	8,904	55,995	47,859	8,904	38,955	15,692	0	15,692	1,348
1993	94,852	14,016	80,836	78,964	12,248	66,716	14,329	1,768	12,561	1,559
1994	142,354	26,933	115,421	91,133	19,282	71,851	49,252	7,651	41,601	1,969
1995	71,036	18,645	52,391	45,078	13,176	31,902	23,676	5,469	18,207	2,282
1996	106,915	21,081	85,834	71,646	20,224	51,422	33,105	857	32,248	2,164
1997	103,642	27,292	76,351	74,246	27,263	46,983	26,683	29	26,654	2,714
1998	148,530	11,636	136,894	103,087	11,622	91,465	42,455	14	42,441	2,987
1999	175,696	8,458	167,239	122,373	8,451	113,922	49,465	7	49,458	3,859
2000	118,906	9,497	109,408	93,109	9,490	83,618	22,016	7	22,009	3,781
2001	170,814	4,286	166,528	132,377	4,278	128,099	35,114	8	35,107	3,323
2002	188,061	13,789	174,272	142,926	13,776	129,150	41,698	13	41,685	3,437
2003	234,301	14,729	219,572	164,643	13,837	150,806	66,002	892	65,110	3,656
2004	132,563	20,556	112,007	93,865	13,273	80,591	35,160	7,283	27,877	3,539
2005	87,121	7,607	79,514	58,138	5,689	52,448	24,378	1,918	22,460	4,605
2006	84,622	2,005	82,617	55,278	1,400	53,877	24,461	605	23,856	4,884
2007	99,028	1,333	97,695	68,426	845	67,581	25,157	488	24,669	5,445
Q1 2008	41,856	313	41,543	32,551	197	32,354	7,782	116	7,666	1,523
Q2 2008	67,341	824	66,517	54,277	554	53,723	10,706	270	10,436	2,358

SOURCE: Office of Federal Housing Enterprise Oversight.
NOTE: FHFA based on data from the Federal Housing Administration (FHA), the Department of Veterans Affairs (VA), and the Rural Housing Service (RHS). For an explanation of the methodology used to develop the estimates, see: Pafenberg, F. (2005) Single–Family Mortgages Originated and Outstanding; 1990–2004.

Table A.8 Conventional Single-Family Mortgages Outstanding; Jumbo and Nonjumbo Mortgages by Loan Type (1990–Q2 2008; US$ Millions)

	Conventional Mortgages	Conventional ARMs	Conventional FRMs	Nonjumbo	Nonjumbo ARMs	Nonjumbo FRMs	Jumbo	Jumbo ARMs	Jumbo FRMs
1990	2,181,747	218,116	1,963,631	1,854,485	142,835	1,711,650	327,262	75,281	251,982
1991	2,324,176	232,494	2,091,682	1,975,550	151,827	1,823,723	348,626	80,667	267,959
1992	2,494,664	250,144	2,244,520	2,120,464	160,569	1,959,896	374,200	89,575	284,624
1993	2,664,272	396,547	2,267,725	2,264,631	246,836	2,017,795	399,641	149,711	249,930
1994	2,806,591	419,153	2,387,438	2,385,602	256,598	2,129,003	420,989	162,555	258,434
1995	2,946,185	463,232	2,482,953	2,504,258	283,794	2,220,463	441,928	179,438	262,490
1996	3,129,990	491,584	2,638,396	2,660,491	291,851	2,368,631	469,498	199,733	269,766
1997	3,310,724	430,392	2,880,332	2,814,115	247,498	2,566,617	496,609	182,894	313,714
1998	3,639,934	490,299	3,149,635	3,093,944	266,798	2,827,146	545,990	223,501	322,489
1999	4,007,817	527,429	3,480,388	3,406,644	271,457	3,135,188	601,173	255,972	345,200
2000	4,383,182	511,956	3,871,227	3,725,705	246,858	3,478,847	657,477	265,098	392,380
2001	4,922,596	574,959	4,347,636	4,184,206	263,191	3,921,015	738,389	311,768	426,621
2002	5,697,578	697,383	5,000,194	4,842,941	310,827	4,532,114	854,637	386,557	468,080
2003	6,556,929	929,117	5,627,812	5,573,390	441,940	5,131,450	983,539	487,177	496,362
2004	7,641,539	1,377,005	6,264,534	6,495,308	690,252	5,805,056	1,146,231	686,754	459,477
2005	8,798,385	1,951,482	6,846,903	7,478,627	1,022,150	6,456,477	1,319,758	929,332	390,426
2006	9,882,199	2,290,694	7,591,505	8,399,869	1,292,953	7,106,916	1,482,330	997,740	484,589
2007	10,544,714	2,565,529	7,983,406	8,963,007	1,463,261	7,499,746	1,581,707	1,098,046	483,661
Q1 2008	10,629,322	2,429,863	8,199,459	9,034,924	1,382,592	7,652,332	1,594,398	1,047,271	547,127
Q2 2008	10,596,329	2,328,013	8,268,316	9,006,880	1,380,512	7,626,368	1,589,449	947,501	641,948

SOURCE: Office of Federal Housing Enterprise Oversight.

NOTE: FHFA based on data from the Department of Housing and Urban Development, the Federal Housing Administration (FHA) the Department of Veterans Affairs (VA), the Rural Housing Service (RHS), and the Board of Governors of the Federal Reserve System. For an explanation of the methodology used to develop the estimates, see: Pafenberg, F. (2005) Single-Family Mortgages Originated and Outstanding: 1990–2004. For an update of certain of the assumptions made in that article, see http://www.ofheo.gov/media/marketdata/updatedassumptions2008q2103108.pdf.

Table A.9 Government-Backed Single-Family Mortgages Outstanding: FHA-Insured and VA- and RHS-Guaranteed by Loan Type (1990–Q2 2008; US$ Millions)

	Government-Backed Single-Family Mortgages	Government-Backed ARMs	Government-Backed FRMs	FHA-Insured Single-Family Mortgages	FHA-Insured ARMs	FHA-Insured FRMs	VA-Guaranteed Single-Family Mortgages	VA-Guaranteed ARMs	VA-Guaranteed FRMs	RHS-Guaranteed FRMs
1990	439,539	4,839	434,700	278,371	3,995	274,376	161,132	844	160,288	36
1991	464,587	6,979	457,608	298,400	6,177	292,386	165,893	802	165,091	131
1992	459,732	14,531	445,201	286,743	13,662	273,265	172,289	869	171,420	516
1993	449,562	28,841	420,721	263,315	23,487	240,065	184,852	5,354	179,498	1,158
1994	484,949	50,979	433,970	313,108	39,667	263,118	180,222	11,312	168,910	1,942
1995	512,999	64,353	448,646	329,394	48,761	269,597	191,345	15,592	175,753	3,296
1996	552,800	74,886	477,914	361,319	61,510	287,437	199,119	13,376	185,743	4,734
1997	606,845	88,674	518,171	393,887	77,591	302,346	210,043	11,083	198,960	16,865
1998	634,367	71,263	563,104	412,798	63,368	328,180	226,484	7,895	218,589	16,335
1999	691,761	61,456	630,305	462,262	55,395	390,818	219,356	6,061	213,295	26,192
2000	743,349	59,694	683,655	499,899	54,302	438,871	222,862	5,392	217,470	27,314
2001	755,400	50,495	704,905	497,131	45,973	452,165	229,106	4,522	224,584	28,156
2002	739,778	44,013	695,765	486,221	40,249	445,972	225,560	3,764	221,796	27,997
2003	670,880	43,301	627,579	424,592	38,602	385,990	219,513	4,699	214,814	26,775
2004	628,988	51,488	577,500	392,875	40,529	352,346	208,084	10,959	197,125	28,029
2005	575,884	43,772	532,112	345,289	32,721	312,567	202,970	11,051	191,919	27,626
2006	561,793	33,737	528,056	327,340	23,650	303,690	205,798	10,087	195,711	28,655
2007	591,078	26,607	564,471	350,760	17,803	332,957	209,259	8,804	200,455	31,059
Q1 2008	609,725	25,139	584,586	366,772	16,648	350,124	210,821	8,491	202,330	32,132
Q2 2008	657,894	24,622	633,272	409,578	16,275	393,303	215,445	8,347	207,098	32,871

SOURCE: Office of Federal Housing Enterprise Oversight.

NOTE: FHFA based on data from the Federal Housing Administration (FHA), the Department of Veterans Affairs (VA), and the Rural Housing Service (RHS). For an explanation of the methodology used to develop the estimates, see: Pafenberg, F. (2005) Single-Family Mortgages Originated and Outstanding; 1990–2004.

Table A.10 Home Mortgage Security Issuance (1952–Q3 2008)

	Mortgage-Backed Securities (Percent of Total)				
	GNMA	FHLMC	FNMA	Private Label	Total US$ Millions
1985	41.6	35.2	21.4	1.8	110,414
1986	37.7	37.2	22.5	2.6	269,189
1987	39.0	30.8	25.6	4.6	243,236
1988	33.4	24.1	33.2	9.3	165,257
1989	26.6	34.3	32.5	6.6	214,587
1990	24.8	28.5	37.3	9.4	259,285
1991	19.7	29.1	35.6	15.5	317,361
1992	15.0	32.9	35.6	16.4	544,629
1993	20.7	31.3	33.2	14.8	666,646
1994	26.3	27.7	30.9	15.0	422,099
1995	22.9	27.0	34.7	15.4	318,022
1996	22.9	27.2	34.0	15.9	440,324
1997	21.3	23.5	30.7	24.5	486,832
1998	16.0	27.0	35.1	21.9	929,234
1999	18.2	28.0	36.1	17.8	833,029
2000	16.8	26.9	34.2	22.1	615,038
2001	12.7	28.8	38.8	19.7	1,354,960
2002	9.3	29.5	39.0	22.3	1,856,893
2003	8.0	26.3	44.1	21.6	2,716,336
2004	6.6	19.4	28.0	45.9	1,882,836
2005	4.0	18.5	22.3	55.3	2,155,987
2006	4.0	17.6	22.3	56.0	2,045,420
2007	5.1	23.8	33.1	37.9	1,864,544
Q1 2008	11.4	33.6	48.8	6.2	345,326
Q2 2008	16.9	32.7	44.1	6.2	403,514
Q3 2008	32.2	25.5	41.4	0.9	256,832

SOURCES: Inside Mortgage Finance, Milken Institute.

Table A.11   Outstanding Home Mortgage Securities (1980–Q2 2008)

	Mortgage-Backed Securities (Percent of Total)				
	Ginnie Mae	Freddie Mac	Fannie Mae	Private Label	Total US$ Millions
1980	84.5	15.5	NA	NA	111,086
1981	83.8	16.2	0.6	NA	126,187
1982	67.1	24.8	8.1	NA	177,342
1983	65.5	24.2	10.3	NA	244,322
1984	60.7	24.3	11.3	3.7	296,622
1985	54.4	26.3	13.2	6.2	389,841
1986	48.3	31.7	17.0	3.1	543,858
1987	45.5	31.1	19.3	4.0	693,727
1988	43.8	29.6	22.0	4.5	776,683
1989	40.6	30.5	24.2	4.8	909,789
1990	37.6	30.1	27.2	5.2	1,066,920
1991	34.1	29.2	28.9	7.8	1,246,653
1992	29.8	29.3	30.8	10.1	1,407,977
1993	27.3	29.8	31.8	11.1	1,518,908
1994	27.5	29.8	31.5	11.2	1,640,226
1995	27.1	29.4	32.4	11.1	1,744,026
1996	26.6	29.0	33.1	11.3	1,901,567
1997	26.2	28.1	33.3	12.4	2,049,099
1998	23.4	27.9	34.8	14.0	2,301,123
1999	22.4	28.6	35.4	13.6	2,601,940
2000	21.7	29.0	36.0	13.4	2,819,656
2001	18.2	29.3	38.2	14.2	3,251,325
2002	15.3	30.3	38.9	15.5	3,509,783
2003	12.1	28.9	42.0	17.0	3,910,529
2004	10.1	27.2	38.7	24.1	4,383,765
2005	7.9	25.8	34.8	31.5	5,119,719
2006	6.9	24.7	32.5	35.9	5,945,131
2007	6.8	26.2	34.2	32.8	6,598,936
Q1 2008	6.8	26.1	36.2	30.8	6,777,427
Q2 2008	7.1	26.5	36.8	29.6	6,835,875

SOURCES: Inside Mortgage Finance, Milken Institute.

Table A.12   Funding Sources for Home Mortgages (1952–Q2 2008)

Percent of Total	1952	1980	1990	2005	Q2 2008
Commercial banks	19.3	16.6	16.5	19.1	19.2
Savings institutions	40.2	50.0	22.9	10.2	7.9
Credit unions, life insurance, and private pension funds	20.9	2.5	2.7	2.7	3.1
GSE home mortgages	0.0	6.0	4.6	4.8	4.1
Agency- and GSE-backed mortgage pools	0.0	11.2	37.8	36.4	41.0
Private-label backed mortgage pools	0.0	0.0	2.1	17.2	18.0
Other	19.6	13.7	13.5	9.5	6.9
Total (US$ billions)	58.4	957.9	2,623.3	9,383.8	11,254.2

SOURCES: Federal Reserve, Milken Institute.
NOTE: "Agency" refers to Ginnie Mae. GSE refers to Fannie Mae and Freddie Mac.

Table A.13   Originate-to-Hold vs. Originate-to-Distribute Models (1952–Q2 2008)

Percent of Total	1952	1980	1990	2005	Q2 2008
Held in portfolio	100.0	88.8	60.1	46.4	41.0
Securitized	0.0	11.2	39.9	53.6	59.0
Total (US$ billions)	58.4	957.9	2,623.3	9,383.8	11,254.2

SOURCES: Federal Reserve, Milken Institute.

Figure A.4 Mortgage Brokerages Become Major Players in Originating Home Mortgages (1987–2006)

Thousands

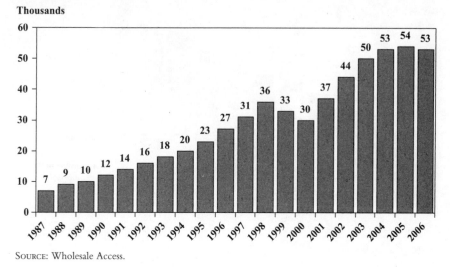

SOURCE: Wholesale Access.

Figure A.5 Mortgage Brokers Account for Majority of Recent Home Mortgage Originations (1987–2006)

Percentage

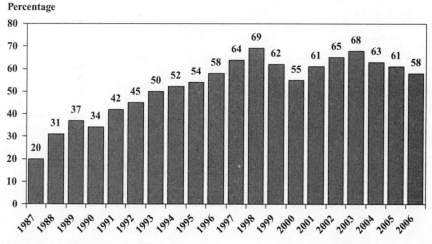

SOURCE: Wholesale Access.

Figure A.6 Surge in Amount and Diversity of Asset-Backed Securities Outstanding (1999–Q2 2008)

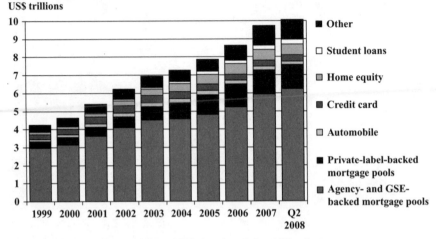

US$ trillions

- ■ Other
- □ Student loans
- ▨ Home equity
- ■ Credit card
- □ Automobile
- ■ Private-label-backed mortgage pools
- ▨ Agency- and GSE-backed mortgage pools

SOURCES: Securities Industry and Financial Markets Association, Milken Institute.
NOTE: "Agency" refers to Ginnie Mae. GSE refers to Fannie Mae and Freddie Mac.

Figure A.7 Foreign Share of Treasury Securities Outstanding (1952–Q2 2008)

Percentage of Treasury securities outstanding

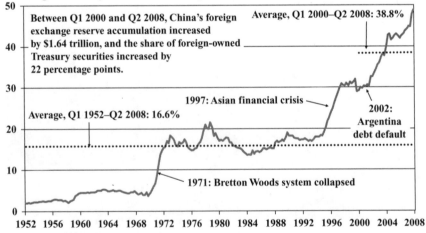

Between Q1 2000 and Q2 2008, China's foreign exchange reserve accumulation increased by $1.64 trillion, and the share of foreign-owned Treasury securities increased by 22 percentage points.

Average, Q1 2000–Q2 2008: 38.8%

1997: Asian financial crisis

Average, Q1 1952–Q2 2008: 16.6%

2002: Argentina debt default

1971: Bretton Woods system collapsed

SOURCES: Federal Reserve, Milken Institute.

Figure A.8 Foreign Share of Agency- and GSE-Backed Securities
Outstanding (1952–Q2 2008)

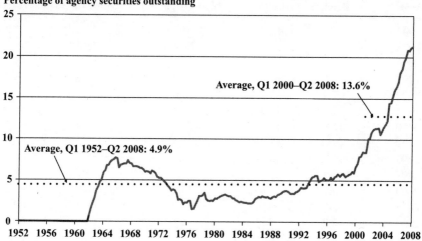

Percentage of agency securities outstanding

SOURCES: Federal Reserve, Milken Institute.
NOTE: Agency- and GSE-backed securities include issues of federal budget agencies, such as those for
the Tennessee Valley Authority; issues of government-sponsored enterprises, such as Fannie Mae,
Freddie Mac, and Federal Home Loan Banks; and agency- and GSE-backed mortgage pool securities
issued by Ginnie Mae, Fannie Mac, Freddie Mac, and the Farmers Home Administration.

Table A.14 Market Share of Adjustable vs. Fixed-Rate Home Mortgage
Originations (1983–2006)

Year	FRM Share (Percent)	ARM Share (Percent)	Year	FRM Share (Percent)	ARM Share (Percent)
1983	62.9	37.1	1995	67.0	33.0
1984	38.8	61.3	1996	73.0	37.6
1985	49.7	50.3	1997	77.9	22.1
1986	69.1	30.9	1998	87.9	12.1
1987	57.4	42.7	1999	78.1	21.9
1988	41.7	58.3	2000	75.4	24.6
1989	60.6	39.4	2001	87.7	12.3
1990	71.9	28.1	2002	82.8	17.2
1991	77.0	23.0	2003	81.2	18.8
1992	79.7	20.3	2004	65.7	34.3
1993	79.7	20.3	2005	70.0	30.0
1994	61.1	38.9	2006	78.3	21.7

SOURCES: Inside Mortgage Finance, Milken Institute.
NOTE: Shares for conventional mortgages.

Table A.15   Homeownership Rates by Race and Ethnicity (1994–Q3 2008)

Year	Black	Hispanic	White Non–Hispanic	Other Races	Total
1994	42.6	42.2	70.2	47.6	64.2
1995	44.3	41.1	71.2	48.4	65.1
1996	44.4	42.3	71.8	51.4	65.4
1997	45.1	44.0	71.9	52.5	65.7
1998	45.9	45.7	72.6	52.7	66.4
1999	46.8	45.5	73.3	54.3	66.9
2000	47.8	47.5	73.9	52.4	67.5
2001	48.1	48.8	74.4	53.2	68.3
2002	47.7	48.3	75.0	55.2	68.3
2003	49.4	47.7	75.5	56.6	68.6
2004	49.1	48.9	76.2	58.9	69.2
2005	48.0	50.0	76.0	60.1	69.0
2006	48.2	49.5	76.0	60.0	68.9
2007	47.7	48.5	74.9	58.6	67.8
Q3 2008	47.8	49.5	75.1	59.0	67.9

SOURCES: U.S. Census Bureau, Milken Institute.

Table A.16 Comparison of the Office of Federal Housing Enterprise Oversight and S&P/Case-Shiller Home Price Indexes

	Office of Federal Housing Enterprise Oversight	S&P/Case-Shiller
Period covered	Since 1975, quarterly	1. 10-metropolitan area composite: since 1987, monthly; 2. 20-metropolitan area composite: since 2000, monthly; 3. National index: since 1987, quarterly.
Geographic coverage	364 MSAs	1. Does not include house price data from 13 states.* Have incomplete coverage in another 29 states.** 2. Does not always align with the MSAs.
Refinance included	Includes refinance appraisals	Purchase only
Data filter used	1. Valuation pairs are dropped when they occur less than 90 days apart. Ten-year pairs receive about 75 percent less weight than two-quarter pairs.	1. Valuation pairs are dropped when they occur less than 6 months apart. Ten-year pairs receive 20 percent to 45 percent less weight than two-quarter pairs.
Conforming	1. Restricted to conforming mortgages. 2. Includes only valuation data for homes that have secondary market financing, based on securitized loan data provided by Fannie Mae and Freddie Mac	1. Include jumbo mortgages, subprime mortgages, VA, FHA, and other types of financing arrangements. 2. Valuation data also come from county assessor and recorder offices (source: DataQuick).
Weighting scheme	Equal weight regardless of home price	Weighted by home value
Data source Applications	Fannie Mae and Freddie Mac quarterly numbers are used in the Federal Reserve's estimates of household wealth	DataQuick Information System Basis for future contracts

SOURCES: S&P/Case-Shiller, Office of Federal Housing Enterprise Oversight, Milken Institute.
* Maine, Indiana, Wisconsin, North Dakota, South Dakota, South Carolina, West Virginia, Alabama, Mississippi, Idaho, Montana, Wyoming, and Alaska.
** New York, Pennsylvania, Illinois, Michigan, Ohio, Iowa, Kansas, Minnesota, Missouri, Nebraska, Delaware, Florida, Georgia, North Carolina, Virginia, Kentucky, Tennessee, Arkansas, Louisiana, Oklahoma, Texas, Arizona, Colorado, Nevada, New Mexico, Utah, California, Oregon, and Washington.

Table A.17 Average Annual Home Price Changes in Selected Metropolitan Areas (Percent)

	Dec. 2000–Dec. 2006, Cumulative	Dec. 2000–Dec. 2006, Annualized	August 2007–August 2008
Miami	157.9	17.1	−28.1
Los Angeles	145.2	16.1	−26.7
Las Vegas	119.8	14.0	−30.6
Washington	114.8	13.6	−15.4
Tampa	109.7	13.1	−18.1
Phoenix	109.2	13.1	−30.7
San Diego	104.7	12.7	−25.8
New York	91.1	11.4	−6.9
Portland	73.6	9.6	−7.6
Seattle	72.4	9.5	−8.8
San Francisco	65.0	8.7	−27.3
Chicago	55.4	7.6	−9.8
Minneapolis	50.4	7.0	−13.8
Boston	46.1	6.5	−4.7
Atlanta	26.0	3.9	−8.5
Charlotte	25.8	3.9	−2.8
Denver	20.0	3.1	−5.1
Dallas	16.5	2.6	−2.7
Cleveland	15.1	2.4	−6.6
Detroit	11.8	1.9	−17.2
Composite 10	95.8	11.9	−17.7
Composite 20	82.2	10.5	−16.6

SOURCES: S&P/Case-Shiller, Milken Institute.

Figure A.9   HUD Subprime and Manufactured Home Lender List
(1992–2005)

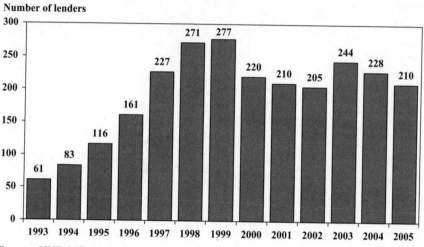

SOURCES: HUD, Milken Institute.
NOTE: The 2004 and 2005 HUD lists differ slightly from past lists. Since 2004, the HUD list is restricted to subprime lender specialists because HMDA analysts can now easily determine whether a lender specializes in manufactured home loans.

Table A.18 Prime Mortgage Originations by Year of Origination and Product Type (January 1999–July 2007)

									Hybrid															
		2/6 Hybrid		**2/1 Hybrid**		**3/6 Hybrid**		**3/1 Hybrid**		**5/6 Hybrid**		**5/1 Hybrid**		**7/6 Hybrid**		**7/1 Hybrid**		**10/6 Hybrid**		**10/1 Hybrid**		**15/6 Hybrid**		**Other Hybrid**
	Term	2 Years		2 Years		3 Years		3 Years		5 Years		5 Years		7 Years		7 Years		10 Years		10 Years		15 Years		n.a.
	Initial Fixed-Rate Period																							
Year of Origination	**Reset Frequency**	6 Months		1 Year		6 Months		1 Year		6 Months		1 Year		6 Months		1 Year		6 Months		1 Year		6 Months		n.a.
1999		3		357		194		3,206		0		7,594		0		3,968		0		1,199		0		58,509
2000		251		335		1,965		3,230		11		7,449		0		10,906		0		1,064		0		48,539
2001		407		114		5,373		23,725		511		43,676		0		8,504		0		2,275		0		52,242
2002		1,336		152		4,029		87,881		1,331		109,459		0		11,625		0		2,419		0		86,484
2003		1,132		13		3,547		131,778		3,112		189,653		50		51,061		3		18,327		0		91,396
2004		2,833		787		2,369		104,022		2,393		192,580		98		44,831		16		12,790		0		77,447
2005		5,867		488		3,932		36,758		31,592		187,948		319		50,922		57		37,839		0		55,341
2006		3,359		42		2,223		15,093		34,958		170,026		407		28,355		103		17,651		0		67,935
Jan.–July 2007		0		0		517		4,578		13,933		74,627		123		12,281		0		4,645		0		3,878
Total		15,188		2,288		24,149		410,271		87,841		983,012		997		222,453		179		98,209		0		541,771

	Adjustable Rate						
	ARM	ARM	ARM	ARM	ARM	ARM Balloon	Other ARM
Term	1 Month	6 Months	1 Year	3 Years	5 Years	n.a.	n.a.
Initial Fixed-Rate Period	1 Month	6 Months	1 Year	3 Years	5 Years	n.a.	n.a.
Year of Origination / Reset Frequency	1 Month	6 Months	1 Year	3 Years	5 Years	n.a.	n.a.
1999	56,255	4,467	186,313	5,342	10,818	58	79,797
2000	109,009	3,490	131,125	3,461	11,942	3	90,712
2001	64,473	5,396	170,529	10,250	33,509	1	84,126
2002	111,610	21,267	470,054	38,523	89,385	1	133,380
2003	147,815	18,477	627,653	78,069	165,788	0	161,926
2004	294,763	70,514	649,166	88,264	178,056	0	152,338
2005	436,350	57,443	410,926	39,989	132,751	69	149,705
2006	191,414	14,154	348,558	12,990	93,526	256	208,550
Jan.–July 2007	27,784	2,747	127,085	7,347	24,701	450	279,030
Total	1,439,473	197,955	3,121,409	284,235	740,476	838	1,339,564

(Continued)

Table A.18 (*Continued*)

Year of Origination	Fixed 10 10 Years	Fixed 15 15 Years	Fixed Rate Fixed 20 20 Years	Fixed 30 30 Years	Fixed 40 40 Years	Other Fixed
Term Initial Fixed-Rate Period Reset Frequency	n.a.	n.a.	n.a.	n.a.	n.a.	n.a.
1999	56,163	833,647	164,216	3,698,673	90	77,269
2000	15,852	244,880	60,142	2,144,634	146	765,054
2001	87,918	1,683,268	288,089	5,559,482	438	242,175
2002	167,783	2,868,283	506,547	6,517,075	84	161,862
2003	397,964	4,252,740	782,710	8,113,636	83	291,147
2004	146,812	1,188,737	302,979	4,180,370	348	131,541
2005	67,682	709,249	241,050	4,598,216	2,124	88,559
2006	34,216	423,685	144,223	4,459,747	20,775	46,557
Jan.–July 2007	19,244	213,281	84,071	2,833,615	33,407	26,109
Total	993,634	12,417,770	2,574,027	42,105,448	57,495	1,830,273

	Other							Grand Total of All Types of Originations
Term Initial Fixed-Rate Period	Balloon 3	Balloon 5	Balloon 7	Balloon 10	Balloon 15/30	Other Balloon	Other	
Reset Frequency	n.a.	n.a.	n.a.	n.a.	n.a.	n.a.	n.a.	
Year of Origination	n.a.	n.a.	n.a.	n.a.	n.a.	n.a.	n.a.	
1999	1	2,415	25,640	1,202	43	32,512	44,617	5,354,568
2000	6	1,509	7,410	468	489	24,322	45,194	3,733,598
2001	13	22,686	54,363	1,962	1,018	45,893	85,623	8,578,039
2002	1	55,294	95,426	947	301	80,744	11,092	11,634,375
2003	1	71,727	153,291	21	15	26,036	22,608	15,801,779
2004	0	22,093	39,436	2	36	19,274	26,822	7,931,717
2005	1	1,930	6,282	0	33	23,880	57,474	7,434,776
2006	0	459	1,693	0	70	1,633	104,094	6,446,752
Jan.–July 2007	0	14	213	11	84	1,010	91,494	3,886,279
Total	23	178,127	383,754	4,613	2,089	255,304	489,018	70,801,883

SOURCES: LoanPerformance, Milken Institute.

Table A.19 Subprime Mortgage Originations by Year of Origination and Product Type (January 1999–July 2007)

Year of Origination	2/6 Hybrid, 2 Years, 6 Months	2/1 Hybrid, 2 Years, 1 Year	3/6 Hybrid, 3 Years, 6 Months	3/1 Hybrid, 3 Years, 1 Year	5/6 Hybrid, 5 Years, 6 Months	5/1 Hybrid, 5 Years, 1 Year	7/6 Hybrid, 7 Years, 6 Months	7/1 Hybrid, 7 Years, 1 Year	10/6 Hybrid, 10 Years, 6 Months	10/1 Hybrid, 10 Years, 1 Year	15/6 Hybrid, 15 Years, 6 Months	Other Hybrid, n.a., n.a.
1999	26,730	20,909	64,426	32,869	840	8,650	0	0	0	0	0	1,708
2000	46,993	54,555	22,840	32,597	432	6,131	0	0	0	0	0	6,388
2001	71,823	78,935	18,310	13,237	2,337	411	0	0	0	0	0	7,903
2002	113,431	89,169	17,688	12,976	6,148	60	0	0	0	0	375	19,970
2003	217,490	71,642	31,426	29,642	5,379	747	0	13	0	0	733	40,229
2004	402,072	71,643	63,985	87,712	5,064	1,081	0	17	0	3	72	110,087
2005	342,930	121,945	73,950	79,700	9,733	1,880	6	1	9	1	150	127,894
2006	119,676	115,345	27,298	11,024	4,294	7,826	0	0	0	0	66	70,661
Jan.–July 2007	18,312	34,844	2,931	4,325	1,475	526	0	0	0	0	7	1,053
Total	1,359,457	658,987	322,854	304,082	35,702	27,312	6	31	9	4	1,403	385,893

	Adjustable Rate						
	ARM 1 Month	ARM 6 Months	ARM 1 Year	ARM 3 Years	ARM 5 Years	ARM Balloon	Other ARM
Term							
Initial Fixed-Rate Period	1 Month	6 Months	1 Year	3 Years	5 Years	n.a.	n.a.
Reset Frequency	1 Month	6 Months	1 Year	3 Years	5 Years	n.a.	n.a.
Year of Origination							
1999	190	19,669	3,193	0	0	1,155	10,425
2000	704	20,859	1,844	0	0	6	29,790
2001	932	24,333	338	25	0	1	58,428
2002	4,172	60,835	82	128	0	0	77,289
2003	8,626	98,595	4,342	233	3	0	55,846
2004	22,558	125,506	936	224	25	0	88,061
2005	44,972	162,941	941	103	136	1,931	123,089
2006	35,645	96,233	1,998	0	31	37,821	122,205
Jan.–July 2007	2,099	28,004	98	19	249	40,905	83,490
Total	119,898	636,975	13,772	732	444	81,819	648,623

(Continued)

Table A.19 (Continued)

Year of Origination	Term Initial Fixed-Rate Period Reset Frequency	Fixed Rate					
		Fixed 10	Fixed 15	Fixed 20	Fixed 30	Fixed 40	Other Fixed
		10 Years	15 Years	20 Years	30 Years	40 Years	n.a.
		n.a.	n.a.	n.a.	n.a.	n.a.	n.a.
1999		43,948	156,097	67,036	204,365	32	62,978
2000		39,731	112,513	61,548	197,946	25	59,358
2001		11,337	63,435	36,731	155,772	9	29,600
2002		10,669	70,353	47,253	188,905	0	41,423
2003		6,617	79,680	75,844	343,853	0	30,548
2004		5,421	76,349	66,615	460,004	0	7,876
2005		3,601	55,267	54,297	525,228	1,820	6,868
2006		2,140	56,369	29,140	389,376	20,346	5,925
Jan.–July 2007		612	12,234	4,633	139,173	11,974	3,736
Total		124,076	682,297	443,097	2,604,622	34,206	248,312

| | | | | Other | | | | |
Year of Origination	Balloon 3	Balloon 5	Balloon 7	Balloon 10	Balloon 15/30	Other Balloon	Other	Grand Total of All Types of Subprime Originations
Term Initial Fixed-Rate Period	n.a.	n.a.	n.a.	n.a.	n.a.	n.a.	n.a.	
Reset Frequency	n.a.	n.a.	n.a.	n.a.	n.a.	n.a.	n.a.	
1999	1,539	351	1,174	13,080	29,061	11,270	5,725	787,420
2000	861	326	138	728	18,722	9,155	15,559	739,749
2001	7	48	54	81	10,835	6,510	29,513	620,945
2002	0	6	4	0	4,056	11,095	21,538	797,625
2003	0	24	27	2	11,617	5,976	23,903	1,143,037
2004	0	43	3	2	28,404	21,232	71,146	1,716,141
2005	0	135	0	0	52,153	46,909	87,190	1,925,780
2006	0	0	0	1	64,016	58,348	92,922	1,368,706
Jan.–July 2007	0	0	0	0	13,924	22,433	13,878	440,934
Total	2,407	933	1,400	13,894	232,788	192,928	361,374	9,540,337

SOURCES: Loan Performance, Milken Institute.

Figure A.10 Mortgage-Backed Securities Issued by Issuer
(Quarterly, 1985–Q3 2008)

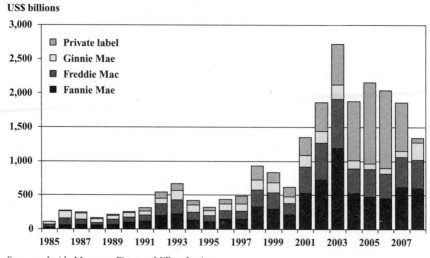

SOURCES: Inside Mortgage Finance, Milken Institute.
NOTE: 2008 data are annualized.

Figure A.11 Breakdown of Bank Home Loans

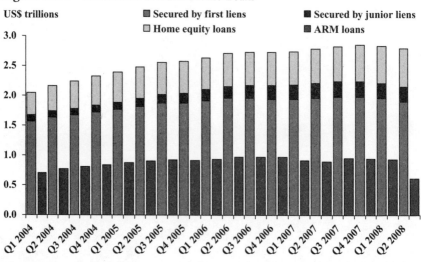

SOURCES: FDIC, Milken Institute.

Table A.20 Home Prices Have Dropped, But Are We at the Bottom Yet? Calculation Based on S&P/Case–Shiller Indices, as of August 2008

Price Change (Percentage From)

	12 Months	24 Months	36 Months	48 Months	60 Months	72 Months	84 Months	96 Months	108 Months	120 Months
Atlanta	−8.5	−7.7	−3.6	1.6	5.6	8.8	12.7	18.8	27.9	37.2
Boston	−4.7	−8.2	−10.4	−4.8	5.0	13.3	26.9	46.1	67.3	88.4
Charlotte	−2.8	2.6	10.2	16.3	20.7	23.0	25.6	28.2	32.5	39.0
Chicago	−9.8	−11.0	−5.2	3.3	12.4	21.1	28.7	39.2	52.4	60.8
Cleveland	−6.6	−10.4	−10.2	−7.5	−4.3	0.1	2.5	7.4	12.2	17.5
Dallas	−2.7	−2.2	1.4	4.9	6.5	7.4	10.3	17.0	–	–
Denver	−5.1	−5.4	−3.3	0.6	4.7	5.6	8.9	20.6	38.0	56.0
Detroit	−17.2	−24.8	−26.4	−24.4	−21.9	−19.6	−16.7	−11.7	−4.7	3.4
Las Vegas	−30.6	−35.9	−33.0	−25.4	14.2	27.2	34.7	45.1	52.8	59.0
Los Angeles	−26.7	−30.9	−24.7	−11.4	16.9	38.5	59.4	74.9	92.5	110.2
Miami	−28.1	−33.7	−25.2	−1.8	18.3	36.0	55.1	75.8	88.5	97.3
Minneapolis	−13.8	−17.0	−15.1	−10.5	−2.6	5.8	15.5	31.4	47.5	63.4
New York	−6.9	−10.0	−4.7	8.4	24.3	40.0	58.8	77.1	99.1	117.9
Phoenix	−30.7	−36.2	−29.3	4.4	17.9	25.0	31.2	38.0	49.0	60.0
Portland	−7.6	−5.0	10.9	31.4	43.3	52.2	58.0	66.4	70.8	77.6
San Diego	−25.8	−32.0	−32.3	−26.1	−1.8	14.2	32.3	49.1	73.6	93.3
San Francisco	−27.3	−30.3	−28.9	−13.9	1.8	6.7	17.2	26.2	59.2	79.4
Seattle	−8.8	−3.6	11.9	30.6	43.8	51.7	57.5	65.5	78.6	93.8
Tampa	−18.1	−26.4	−15.9	6.9	24.4	36.0	47.4	64.8	78.2	87.4
Washington	−15.4	−21.4	−19.5	−0.3	22.8	38.5	57.6	78.6	96.5	110.1
Composite-10	−17.7	−21.7	−17.5	−4.5	15.0	28.9	44.8	60.4	81.5	98.4
Composite-20	−16.6	−20.2	−15.6	−2.8	13.8	25.4	38.2	51.5	–	–

SOURCES: S&P/Case-Shiller, Milken Institute.

Table A.21 Home Prices Have Dropped, But Are We at the Bottom Yet?
Calculation Based on Office of Federal Housing Enterprise Oversight Data, as of Q2 2008

	Price Change (Percentage From)									
	12 Months	24 Months	36 Months	48 Months	60 Months	72 Months	84 Months	96 Months	108 Months	120 Months
Atlanta	0.0	4.0	7.8	13.4	17.4	22.1	27.4	37.5	46.4	56.5
Boston	−2.9	−5.1	−3.8	7.3	19.8	32.5	51.0	71.3	99.3	121.1
Charlotte	5.2	14.6	22.4	26.9	29.7	33.8	36.8	43.6	48.1	55.1
Chicago	−1.1	1.9	10.6	23.0	34.3	41.5	52.3	62.6	75.1	82.5
Cleveland	−1.8	−2.6	−1.9	1.9	5.6	9.0	12.9	19.0	22.1	26.8
Dallas	2.1	7.0	10.1	13.7	16.2	20.1	24.2	32.9	41.0	50.1
Denver	0.4	0.8	2.4	6.7	9.7	12.4	18.1	31.2	49.9	65.2
Detroit	−10.8	−14.4	−16.3	−14.1	−11.4	−8.6	−3.9	2.8	11.3	20.9
Las Vegas	−17.7	−18.1	−8.7	16.1	49.6	59.4	68.6	80.1	85.9	88.6
Los Angeles	−14.3	−12.8	4.4	31.4	63.1	84.0	106.8	127.4	143.6	162.4
Miami	−10.7	−4.2	19.5	49.7	75.4	100.0	126.0	151.5	166.9	172.7
Minneapolis	−3.5	−3.1	0.5	9.8	20.5	28.5	41.5	56.8	74.6	89.6
New York	−1.7	1.2	12.7	32.6	50.5	64.9	84.6	104.4	129.5	144.1
Phoenix	−11.1	−10.1	13.0	48.8	62.9	70.6	79.2	91.9	105.0	117.8
Portland	−0.2	7.8	29.1	49.0	61.0	67.4	73.7	83.3	87.0	93.0
San Diego	−14.5	−18.2	−14.2	4.1	27.6	45.6	65.9	88.0	115.7	136.6
San Francisco	−5.8	−6.3	2.1	24.0	36.7	43.2	47.9	68.5	109.5	134.6
Seattle	0.1	9.9	29.1	48.5	60.4	66.1	74.1	86.4	101.7	119.5
Tampa	−13.1	−12.1	7.0	30.6	48.9	61.1	75.4	94.1	108.7	121.0
Washington	−9.1	−8.3	5.3	33.0	56.4	71.0	91.6	113.4	132.2	140.1
United States	−1.7	1.6	10.4	23.9	34.8	43.0	51.8	63.8	74.1	82.8

Sources: Office of Federal Housing Enterprise Oversight, Milken Institute.

Figure A.12   One-Year Home Price Changes for Selected Metropolitan Areas
(Q2 2007–Q2 2008)

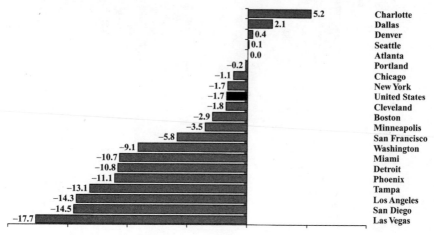

SOURCES: Office of Federal Housing Enterprise Oversight, Milken Institute.

Figure A.13   Two-Year Home Price Changes for Selected Metropolitan Areas
(Q2 2006–Q2 2008)

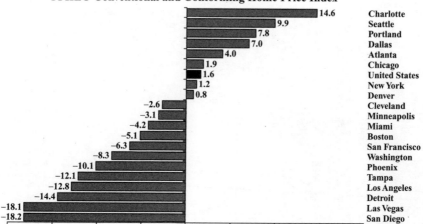

SOURCES: Office of Federal Housing Enterprise Oversight, Milken Institute.

Figure A.14   Four-Year Home Price Changes for Selected Metropolitan Areas (Q2 2004–Q2 2008)

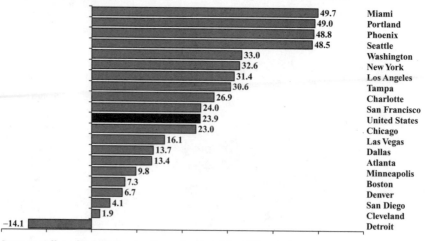

SOURCES: Office of Federal Housing Enterprise Oversight, Milken Institute.

Figure A.15   Five-Year Home Price Changes for Selected Metropolitan Areas (Q2 2003–Q2 2008)

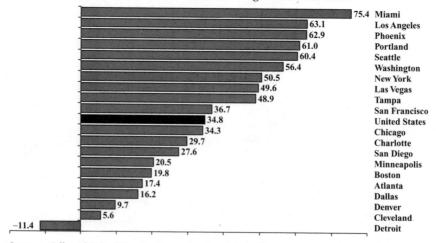

SOURCES: Office of Federal Housing Enterprise Oversight, Milken Institute.

Figure A.16 Housing Starts (Monthly, 1960–September 2008)

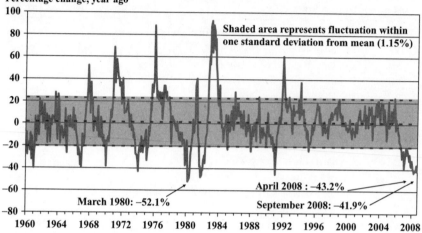

Percentage change, year ago

SOURCES: U.S. Census Bureau, Global Insight, Milken Institute.

Table A.22 Percentage of Homes Purchased between 2001 and 2006 That Now Have Negative Equity

	United States	44.8
1	Stockton, CA	94.7
2	Merced, CA	94.6
3	Modesto, CA	91.1
4	Vallejo-Fairfield, CA	90.7
5	Yuba City, CA	89.7
6	Riverside-San Bernardino-Ontario, CA	86.3
7	Madera, CA	84.3
8	El Centro, CA	84.1
9	Bakersfield, CA	82
10	Port St. Lucie-Fort Pierce, FL	80.5
11	Salinas, CA	80.2
12	Punta Gorda, FL	79.3
13	Fresno, CA	79.2
14	Cape Coral-Fort Myers, FL	78.5
15	Palm Bay-Melbourne-Titusville, FL	77.3

(Continued)

Table A.22 (*Continued*)

	United States	44.8
16	Miami–Fort Lauderdale–Miami Beach, FL	76.2
17	Phoenix–Mesa–Scottsdale, AZ	75.5
18	Sarasota–Bradenton–Venice, FL	75
19	Reno–Sparks, NV	73.1
20	Las Vegas–Paradise, NV	72.8
21	Orlando, FL	72.1
22	Tampa–St. Petersburg–Clearwater, FL	71.7
23	Los Angeles–Long Beach–Santa Ana, CA	71.1
24	Oxnard–Thousand Oaks–Ventura, CA	70.7
25	Visalia–Porterville, CA	69.6
26	Deltona–Daytona Beach–Ormond Beach, FL	69.2
27	Vero Beach, FL	68.7
28	San Diego–Carlsbad–San Marcos, CA	68.6
29	Naples–Marco Island, FL	66.7
30	Santa Barbara–Santa Maria–Goleta, CA	66.6
31	Santa Rosa–Petaluma, CA	65.9
32	Hanford–Corcoran, CA	65.2
33	Sacramento–Arden–Arcade–Roseville, CA	62.4
34	Ann Arbor, MI	60.8
35	Napa, CA	59.8
36	Bend, OR	59.3
37	Fort Walton Beach–Crestview–Destin, FL	58.4
38	Washington–Arlington–Alexandria, DC–VA–MD–WV	58.4
39	Lakeland, FL	57.6
40	Panama City–Lynn Haven, FL	57.6
41	San Francisco–Oakland–Fremont, CA	56.1
42	Carson City, NV	55.1
43	Ocala, FL	54.6
44	Detroit–Warren–Livonia, MI	53.8
45	Pensacola–Ferry Pass–Brent, FL	51.6
46	Jacksonville, FL	51
47	Santa Cruz–Watsonville, CA	50.5
48	Medford, OR	49.3
49	Yuma, AZ	47.4
50	Grand Rapids–Wyoming, MI	47.3

SOURCE: Zillow.com.

Table A.23 Percentage of Homes Sold for a Loss between Q3 2007 and Q2 2008

	United States	32.7
1	Merced, CA	74.9
2	Stockton, CA	72.5
3	Modesto, CA	70.8
4	Yuba City, CA	70.2
5	Las Vegas-Paradise, NV	69.0
6	Riverside-San Bernardino-Ontario, CA	65.1
7	Vallejo-Fairfield, CA	65.1
8	Sacramento-Arden-Arcade-Roseville, CA	63.8
9	Salinas, CA	63.5
10	Madera, CA	59.6
11	Bakersfield, CA	59.3
12	El Centro, CA	58.8
13	Muskegon-Norton Shores, MI	57.7
14	Detroit-Warren-Livonia, MI	56.4
15	Fresno, CA	54.6
16	Oxnard-Thousand Oaks-Ventura, CA	54.4
17	San Diego-Carlsbad-San Marcos, CA	54.4
18	Santa Rosa-Petaluma, CA	54.0
19	Ann Arbor, MI	52.3
20	Phoenix-Mesa-Scottsdale, AZ	52.1
21	Santa Barbara-Santa Maria-Goleta, CA	51.6
22	Los Angeles-Long Beach-Santa Ana, CA	51.1
23	San Francisco-Oakland-Fremont, CA	48.0
24	Napa, CA	46.8
25	Visalia-Porterville, CA	45.6
26	Grand Rapids-Wyoming, MI	45.3
27	Reno-Sparks, NV	44.7
28	Memphis, TN-MS-AR	43.8
29	Santa Cruz-Watsonville, CA	43.1
30	Washington-Arlington-Alexandria, DC-VA-MD-WV	42.7
31	Cleveland-Elyria-Mentor, OH	42.4
32	Denver-Aurora, CO	42.3
33	San Jose-Sunnyvale-Santa Clara, CA	41.6
34	Worcester, MA	39.4
35	Toledo, OH	38.8
36	Cape Coral-Fort Myers, FL	38.4

(Continued)

Table A.23   (*Continued*)

United States		32.7
37	Lansing–East Lansing, MI	38.3
38	Pueblo, CO	38.3
39	Hanford–Corcoran, CA	37.5
40	Columbus, OH	36.8
41	San Luis Obispo–Paso Robles, CA	36.4
42	Port St. Lucie–Fort Pierce, FL	36.2
43	Minneapolis–St. Paul–Bloomington, MN–WI	35.8
44	Redding, CA	35.6
45	Providence–New Bedford–Fall River, RI–MA	35.4
46	Akron, OH	35.3
47	Bay City, MI	35.2
48	Canton–Massillon, OH	35.0
49	Chico, CA	34.6
50	Battle Creek, MI	34.3

SOURCE: Zillow.com.

Table A.24   Percentage of Homes Sold between Q3 2007 and Q2 2008 That Were in Foreclosure

United States		18.6
1	Madera, CA	57.2
2	Merced, CA	55.6
3	Stockton, CA	53.9
4	Salinas, CA	53.8
5	Vallejo–Fairfield, CA	52.3
6	Riverside–San Bernardino–Ontario, CA	50.9
7	El Centro, CA	50.9
8	Modesto, CA	50.0
9	Las Vegas–Paradise, NV	48.3
10	Bakersfield, CA	46.5
11	Yuba City, CA	44.3
12	Fresno, CA	43.2
13	Sacramento–Arden–Arcade–Roseville, CA	39.0
14	Los Angeles–Long Beach–Santa Ana, CA	38.3
15	Phoenix–Mesa–Scottsdale, AZ	38.0

(*Continued*)

Table A.24   *(Continued)*

	United States	18.6
16	San Diego–Carlsbad–San Marcos, CA	37.3
17	Napa, CA	36.2
18	Santa Rosa–Petaluma, CA	35.8
19	Oxnard–Thousand Oaks–Ventura, CA	35.2
20	Visalia–Porterville, CA	35.0
21	Santa Barbara–Santa Maria–Goleta, CA	34.5
22	San Francisco–Oakland–Fremont, CA	34.3
23	Hanford–Corcoran, CA	31.1
24	Memphis, TN–MS–AR	30.2
25	Reno–Sparks, NV	28.8
26	Akron, OH	28.6
27	Santa Cruz–Watsonville, CA	28.6
28	Ann Arbor, MI	28.5
29	Detroit–Warren–Livonia, MI	27.5
30	San Jose–Sunnyvale–Santa Clara, CA	27.5
31	Grand Rapids–Wyoming, MI	27.3
32	Redding, CA	26.0
33	Cleveland–Elyria–Mentor, OH	25.6
34	Washington–Arlington–Alexandria, DC–VA–MD–WV	24.9
35	Toledo, OH	24.3
36	Springfield, OH	24.1
37	Dayton, OH	22.4
38	San Luis Obispo–Paso Robles, CA	22.2
39	Prescott, AZ	21.8
40	St. Louis, MO–IL	21.4
41	Medford, OR	20.2
42	Chico, CA	20.2
43	Tucson, AZ	20.0
44	Columbus, OH	19.9
45	Bend, OR	17.2
46	Yuma, AZ	16.5
47	Jackson, TN	16.4
48	Carson City, NV	15.0
49	Cleveland, TN	13.9
50	Winston-Salem, NC	13.3

Source: Zillow.com.

Table A.25 Delinquency and Foreclosure Start Rates for U.S. Residential Mortgage Loans

Period	All, Seriously Delinquent	Prime, Seriously Delinquent	Subprime, Seriously Delinquent	All, Foreclosure Starts	Prime, Foreclosure Starts	Subprime, Foreclosure Starts
Q1 1998	1.76	0.98	4.46	0.36	0.24	1.32
Q2 1998	1.71	0.89	4.54	0.37	0.21	1.54
Q3 1998	1.79	0.88	4.86	0.37	0.20	1.41
Q4 1998	1.81	0.87	5.81	0.39	0.22	1.57
Q1 1999	1.80	0.86	5.80	0.35	0.19	1.92
Q2 1999	1.73	0.78	6.25	0.41	0.16	1.73
Q3 1999	1.69	0.73	7.03	0.34	0.16	1.64
Q4 1999	1.76	0.72	7.68	0.36	0.16	1.71
Q1 2000	1.69	0.68	7.71	0.36	0.18	2.06
Q2 2000	1.55	0.62	6.41	0.31	0.14	1.20
Q3 2000	1.65	0.62	7.71	0.44	0.16	3.00
Q4 2000	1.82	0.64	12.08	0.41	0.14	2.99
Q1 2001	1.87	0.65	9.26	0.39	0.17	2.52
Q2 2001	1.95	0.67	10.52	0.48	0.19	2.53
Q3 2001	2.07	0.73	11.27	0.48	0.21	2.31
Q4 2001	2.24	0.81	12.08	0.44	0.21	2.00
Q1 2002	2.31	0.80	11.81	0.44	0.20	2.18
Q2 2002	2.31	0.78	11.63	0.50	0.19	2.67
Q3 2002	2.43	0.80	11.92	0.45	0.19	1.95
Q4 2002	2.40	0.86	11.49	0.41	0.19	1.70
Q1 2003	2.26	0.84	10.48	0.41	0.20	1.65
Q2 2003	2.27	0.82	10.35	0.36	0.19	1.18

Q3 2003	2.14	0.84	9.10	0.44	0.20	1.68
Q4 2003	2.18	0.87	8.33	0.45	0.20	2.10
Q1 2004	2.14	0.81	7.72	0.47	0.20	1.98
Q2 2004	2.03	0.77	7.05	0.40	0.19	1.18
Q3 2004	2.02	0.78	6.47	0.40	0.18	1.35
Q4 2004	2.07	0.80	6.52	0.46	0.20	1.47
Q1 2005	1.89	0.73	5.96	0.42	0.18	1.54
Q2 2005	1.83	0.69	5.81	0.39	0.18	1.26
Q3 2005	1.82	0.71	5.68	0.41	0.18	1.39
Q4 2005	2.08	0.86	6.32	0.42	0.18	1.47
Q1 2006	1.93	0.77	6.22	0.41	0.16	1.62
Q2 2006	1.89	0.75	6.24	0.43	0.18	1.79
Q3 2006	2.00	0.79	6.78	0.46	0.19	1.82
Q4 2006	2.21	0.86	7.78	0.54	0.24	2.00
Q1 2007	2.23	0.89	8.33	0.58	0.25	2.43
Q2 2007	2.47	0.98	9.27	0.65	0.27	2.72
Q3 2007	2.95	1.31	11.38	0.78	0.37	3.12
Q4 2007	3.62	1.67	14.44	0.83	0.41	3.44
Q1 2008	4.03	1.99	16.42	0.99	0.54	4.06
Q2 2008	4.50	2.35	17.85	1.19	0.67	4.70

Table A.26 Foreclosure Rates (1999–Q2 2008)

Period	Prime			Subprime			FHA			VA	Grand Total
	ARM	Fixed	Prime Total	ARM	Fixed	Subprime Total	ARM	Fixed	FHA Total	VA	
Q1 1999	0.35	0.15	0.19	1.83	1.5	1.92	n.a.	n.a.	0.62	0.48	0.35
Q2 1999	0.36	0.12	0.16	2.22	1.75	1.73	n.a.	n.a.	0.56	0.43	0.41
Q3 1999	0.28	0.12	0.16	1.88	1.58	1.64	n.a.	n.a.	0.57	0.42	0.34
Q4 1999	0.28	0.12	0.16	1.91	1.66	1.71	n.a.	n.a.	0.59	0.42	0.36
Q1 2000	0.32	0.12	0.18	1.78	1.65	2.06	n.a.	n.a.	0.58	0.41	0.36
Q2 2000	0.27	0.1	0.14	1.38	1.24	1.2	n.a.	n.a.	0.56	0.39	0.31
Q3 2000	0.25	0.11	0.16	2.62	3.41	3	0.68	0.36	0.54	0.37	0.44
Q4 2000	0.26	0.12	0.14	2.22	1.89	2.99	0.79	0.42	0.57	0.35	0.41
Q1 2001	0.35	0.13	0.17	2.21	2.03	2.52	0.88	0.44	0.59	0.37	0.39
Q2 2001	0.38	0.13	0.19	2.58	2.93	2.53	1.09	0.43	0.7	0.43	0.48
Q3 2001	0.36	0.16	0.21	2.13	2.6	2.31	1.19	0.64	0.75	0.46	0.48
Q4 2001	0.45	0.17	0.21	2.22	1.89	2	1.3	0.68	0.78	0.43	0.44
Q1 2002	0.36	0.16	0.2	2.14	1.53	2.18	1.2	0.71	0.81	0.47	0.44
Q2 2002	0.3	0.13	0.19	2.54	3.24	2.67	1	0.67	0.79	0.49	0.5
Q3 2002	0.25	0.14	0.19	1.99	2.03	1.95	0.8	0.63	0.81	0.46	0.45
Q4 2002	0.26	0.13	0.19	1.77	1.7	1.7	0.76	0.68	0.86	0.43	0.41
Q1 2003	0.24	0.15	0.2	1.52	1.28	1.65	0.78	0.7	0.87	0.48	0.41
Q2 2003	0.22	0.14	0.19	1.42	1.16	1.18	0.71	0.58	0.81	0.45	0.36
Q3 2003	0.24	0.15	0.2	1.86	1.62	1.68	0.78	0.73	1	0.5	0.44
Q4 2003	0.24	0.16	0.2	2.12	1.94	2.1	0.75	0.76	0.91	0.49	0.45
Q1 2004	0.19	0.16	0.2	1.68	1.62	1.98	0.76	0.75	0.93	0.48	0.47
Q2 2004	0.16	0.13	0.19	1.36	1.23	1.18	0.61	0.71	0.95	0.5	0.4
Q3 2004	0.16	0.15	0.18	1.45	1.33	1.35	0.75	0.85	0.98	0.51	0.4

Q4 2004	0.19	0.18	0.2	1.56	1.35	1.47	0.73	0.89	1.06	0.48	0.46
Q1 2005	0.18	0.16	0.18	1.44	1.12	1.54	0.81	0.78	0.86	0.4	0.42
Q2 2005	0.17	0.15	0.18	1.45	1.03	1.26	0.68	0.67	0.76	0.39	0.39
Q3 2005	0.18	0.15	0.18	1.57	1.12	1.39	0.84	0.76	0.88	0.39	0.41
Q4 2005	0.21	0.16	0.18	1.61	1.04	1.47	0.94	0.77	0.91	0.34	0.42
Q1 2006	0.22	0.14	0.16	1.84	1.1	1.62	0.88	0.63	0.83	0.39	0.41
Q2 2006	0.25	0.13	0.18	1.87	0.92	1.79	0.72	0.52	0.75	0.35	0.43
Q3 2006	0.29	0.13	0.19	2.23	1.02	1.82	0.81	0.55	0.79	0.32	0.46
Q4 2006	0.45	0.18	0.24	2.95	1.2	2	1.16	0.71	0.93	0.34	0.54
Q1 2007	0.53	0.17	0.25	3.13	1.21	2.43	1.06	0.67	0.9	0.41	0.58
Q2 2007	0.58	0.16	0.27	3.56	1.19	2.72	1.12	0.66	0.79	0.37	0.65
Q3 2007	0.97	0.21	0.37	4.78	1.43	3.12	1.49	0.81	0.95	0.39	0.78
Q4 2007	1.17	0.24	0.41	5.66	1.64	3.44	1.5	0.82	0.91	0.39	0.83
Q1 2008	1.56	0.29	0.54	6.32	1.8	4.06	1.54	0.82	0.87	0.5	0.99
Q2 2008	1.82	0.34	0.67	6.63	2.07	4.7	1.63	0.81	1.03	0.65	1.19

SOURCES: Mortgage Bankers Association, Milken Institute.

Table A.27 Subprime Originations and Foreclosure Start Rates by State (2006)

State	Subprime Loans (US$ Millions)	Subprime Market Share (Percent)	Total Originations (US$ Millions)	Subprime Origination of Total Origination (Percent)	Subprime FC Start Rate (Percent)	Total FC Start Rate (Percent)
Alabama	4,247	0.7	19,120	22.2	3.1	0.7
Alaska	886	0.1	4,446	19.9	4.0	1.1
Arizona	24,297	4.0	87,861	27.7	3.6	0.8
Arkansas	1,879	0.3	8,726	21.5	4.2	1.3
California	148,403	24.5	582,115	25.5	7.7	2.2
Colorado	9,176	1.5	49,408	18.6	5.5	1.3
Connecticut	6,646	1.1	30,590	21.7	4.7	1.3
Delaware	1,664	0.3	7,757	21.4	5.4	1.2
District of Columbia	1,876	0.3	8,323	22.5	3.2	0.8
Florida	72,775	12.0	223,632	32.5	5.3	2.0
Georgia	15,287	2.5	64,718	23.6	5.8	1.4
Hawaii	3,792	0.6	16,554	22.9	4.2	1.0
Idaho	2,558	0.4	12,205	21.0	4.2	1.0
Illinois	27,591	4.6	100,591	27.4	3.6	0.8
Indiana	5,996	1.0	24,422	24.6	5.0	1.5
Iowa	1,952	0.3	9,869	19.8	6.0	1.7
Kansas	2,019	0.3	10,367	19.5	3.9	0.9
Kentucky	2,872	0.5	13,696	21.0	5.0	1.2
Louisiana	3,795	0.6	15,407	24.6	3.5	1.0
Maine	1,703	0.3	7,268	23.4	6.0	1.3
Maryland	22,828	3.8	78,660	29.0	3.3	1.0
Massachusetts	13,042	2.2	59,469	21.9	3.8	1.1
Michigan	12,556	2.1	47,103	26.7	7.8	2.4
Minnesota	8,122	1.3	34,528	23.5	6.0	1.5
Mississippi	2,259	0.4	8,091	27.9	5.1	1.4

Missouri	7,492	1.2	29,935	25.0	5.0	1.4
Montana	808	0.1	4,757	17.0	3.3	0.5
Nebraska	1,110	0.2	5,636	19.7	3.4	0.8
Nevada	12,451	2.1	42,479	29.3	2.8	0.5
New Hampshire	2,065	0.3	9,560	21.6	3.9	0.8
New Jersey	23,038	3.8	89,893	25.6	4.2	1.0
New Mexico	2,592	0.4	12,025	21.6	4.2	1.2
New York	29,834	4.9	109,650	27.2	2.9	0.6
North Carolina	9,843	1.6	53,806	18.3	4.9	1.9
North Dakota	264	0.0	1,601	16.5	4.9	1.3
Ohio	10,501	1.7	44,584	23.6	6.3	1.5
Oklahoma	2,596	0.4	11,087	23.4	4.2	1.1
Oregon	6,857	1.1	33,684	20.4	3.2	0.6
Pennsylvania	12,142	2.0	57,107	21.3	2.6	0.7
Puerto Rico	578	0.1	7,172	8.1	n.a.	0.6
Rhode Island	2,567	0.4	8,955	28.7	6.1	2.0
South Carolina	5,407	0.9	27,634	19.6	3.9	0.9
South Dakota	395	0.1	2,570	15.4	4.1	0.8
Tennessee	6,804	1.1	29,094	23.4	4.6	1.2
Texas	22,878	3.8	91,994	24.9	3.7	1.0
Utah	5,573	0.9	25,288	22.0	2.5	0.6
Vermont	560	0.1	3,179	17.6	4.1	1.0
Virginia	18,674	3.1	84,909	22.0	3.5	0.7
Washington	14,796	2.4	73,022	20.3	3.5	0.7
West Virginia	1,215	0.2	5,447	22.3	3.9	1.0
Wisconsin	6,329	1.0	30,054	21.1	3.3	0.9
Wyoming	547	0.1	2,761	19.8	2.1	0.5
Total	606,133	100.0	2,422,804	25.0	5.1	1.4

SOURCES: Inside Mortgage Finance, LoanPerformance, Milken Institute.

Table A.28 U.S. Residential Mortgage Loans Delinquent or in Foreclosure (Percent of Total Number)

Period	All	Prime	Prime ARM	Prime FRM	Subprime	Subprime ARM	Subprime FRM	FHA and VA
Q2 1998	2.08	1.10	1.84	0.88	6.08	6.67	5.64	3.86
Q3 1998	2.16	1.08	1.80	0.88	6.27	7.04	5.51	4.29
Q4 1998	2.20	1.09	1.95	0.87	7.38	7.59	7.00	4.34
Q1 1999	2.15	1.05	1.77	0.83	7.72	8.11	7.03	4.24
Q2 1999	2.14	0.94	1.80	0.72	7.98	9.04	7.71	3.94
Q3 1999	2.03	0.89	1.50	0.70	8.67	9.39	8.33	3.84
Q4 1999	2.12	0.88	1.41	0.68	9.39	9.63	9.23	3.97
Q1 2000	2.05	0.86	1.55	0.65	9.77	9.27	9.37	3.70
Q2 2000	1.86	0.76	1.34	0.58	7.61	7.10	7.96	3.61
Q3 2000	2.09	0.78	1.30	0.61	10.71	9.70	11.50	3.57
Q4 2000	2.23	0.78	1.33	0.65	15.07	13.18	14.81	3.84
Q1 2001	2.26	0.82	1.47	0.66	11.78	11.16	11.46	3.81
Q2 2001	2.43	0.86	1.53	0.67	13.05	12.25	14.00	4.07
Q3 2001	2.55	0.94	1.63	0.76	13.58	11.97	15.05	4.48
Q4 2001	2.68	1.02	1.92	0.84	14.08	13.18	14.81	4.85
Q1 2002	2.75	1.00	1.83	0.81	13.99	12.77	14.30	4.68
Q2 2002	2.81	0.97	1.64	0.75	14.30	12.84	15.90	4.94
Q3 2002	2.88	0.99	1.57	0.79	13.87	12.51	15.09	5.26
Q4 2002	2.81	1.05	1.55	0.80	13.19	12.38	13.51	5.59
Q1 2003	2.67	1.04	1.49	0.85	12.13	11.13	11.90	5.37
Q2 2003	2.63	1.01	1.44	0.83	11.53	11.12	11.46	5.45
Q3 2003	2.58	1.04	1.41	0.83	10.78	11.35	11.34	5.95
Q4 2003	2.63	1.07	1.51	0.86	10.43	10.12	10.09	6.10

Q1 2004	2.61	1.01	1.18	0.83	9.70	8.58	9.50	5.52
Q2 2004	2.43	0.96	1.02	0.75	8.23	7.81	9.21	5.57
Q3 2004	2.42	0.96	0.99	0.84	7.82	7.38	8.88	5.75
Q4 2004	2.53	1.00	0.97	0.90	7.99	7.49	8.79	5.99
Q1 2005	2.31	0.91	0.88	0.82	7.50	6.67	7.36	5.29
Q2 2005	2.22	0.87	0.80	0.77	7.07	6.58	7.24	5.12
Q3 2005	2.23	0.89	0.85	0.78	7.07	6.72	6.84	5.47
Q4 2005	2.50	1.04	1.05	0.94	7.79	7.68	7.29	6.00
Q1 2006	2.34	0.93	1.04	0.82	7.84	8.12	7.10	5.47
Q2 2006	2.32	0.93	1.17	0.76	8.03	8.39	6.64	5.26
Q3 2006	2.46	0.98	1.43	0.78	8.60	9.95	6.67	5.52
Q4 2006	2.75	1.10	1.90	0.87	9.78	12.11	7.24	5.72
Q1 2007	2.81	1.14	2.19	0.83	10.76	13.26	7.10	5.26
Q2 2007	3.12	1.25	2.60	0.83	11.99	15.96	7.03	5.11
Q3 2007	3.73	1.68	4.09	1.04	14.50	20.41	8.04	5.55
Q4 2007	4.45	2.08	5.39	1.23	17.88	26.09	9.82	5.96
Q1 2008	5.02	2.53	6.99	1.40	20.48	30.43	10.53	5.68
Q2 2008	5.69	3.02	8.60	1.64	22.55	33.40	11.67	5.78

SOURCES: Mortgage Bankers Association, Milken Institute.

Table A.29 Number of Home Mortgage Loan Foreclosures Started
(Annualized Rate in Thousands)

	Percent of total			Total, Thousands
	Prime (Includes Alt–A)	FHA and VA	Subprime	
Q1 2000	0.40	0.47	0.13	386
Q2 2000	0.41	0.47	0.12	385
Q3 2000	0.40	0.45	0.15	401
Q4 2000	0.38	0.43	0.19	414
Q1 2001	0.37	0.42	0.21	430
Q2 2001	0.37	0.41	0.22	471
Q3 2001	0.38	0.42	0.20	504
Q4 2001	0.41	0.42	0.17	532
Q1 2002	0.41	0.43	0.16	558
Q2 2002	0.40	0.42	0.18	583
Q3 2002	0.40	0.42	0.19	586
Q4 2002	0.39	0.41	0.19	587
Q1 2003	0.40	0.40	0.20	589
Q2 2003	0.42	0.40	0.18	564
Q3 2003	0.42	0.40	0.18	572
Q4 2003	0.40	0.35	0.24	628
Q1 2004	0.37	0.31	0.32	699
Q2 2004	0.35	0.30	0.35	746
Q3 2004	0.33	0.28	0.39	779
Q4 2004	0.33	0.27	0.40	789
Q1 2005	0.33	0.27	0.40	770
Q2 2005	0.33	0.25	0.42	773
Q3 2005	0.33	0.23	0.44	779
Q4 2005	0.33	0.21	0.46	772
Q1 2006	0.33	0.20	0.47	777
Q2 2006	0.32	0.18	0.50	819
Q3 2006	0.31	0.17	0.52	855
Q4 2006	0.32	0.15	0.53	926
Q1 2007	0.33	0.14	0.54	1,029
Q2 2007	0.33	0.12	0.55	1,146
Q3 2007	0.34	0.11	0.55	1,329
Q4 2007	0.35	0.10	0.55	1,506
Q1 2008	0.38	0.09	0.53	1,730
Q2 2008	0.41	0.08	0.51	2,026

SOURCES: Mortgage Bankers Association, Milken Institute.
NOTE: Data are as of June 2008. Numbers are expanded to reflect 85 percent coverage.

Table A.30 National Subprime Foreclosure Rates by Origination Year (Percent, 1999–June 2007)

Foreclosure Rates in Origination Year and Subsequent Years		Origination Year*								Year to July 2007
		1999	2000	2001	2002	2003	2004	2005	2006	
Foreclosure year	Origination year	1.30	1.50	1.85	1.07	0.82	0.86	0.97	2.56	3.01
	1st year	6.33	6.86	7.17	5.51	4.14	3.93	6.38	7.69	
	2nd year	5.46	6.01	5.81	4.55	3.11	3.66	4.66		
	3rd year	4.85	3.35	4.23	2.37	2.23	1.85			
	4th year	2.29	2.49	1.88	1.56	0.83				
	5th year	2.05	1.19	1.17	0.59					
	6th year	0.79	0.71	0.48						
	7th year	0.56	0.30							
	8th year	0.24								
Total number of foreclosures from origination through September 2007		188,026	165,801	140,195	124,781	127,100	176,729	231,360	140,278	13,272
Total number of originations		787,420	739,749	620,945	797,625	1,143,037	1,716,141	1,925,780	1,368,706	440,934
Foreclosure rate through September 2007		23.88	22.41	22.58	15.64	11.12	10.30	12.01	10.25	3.01

SOURCES: LoanPerformance, Milken Institute.
*Foreclosure rates are based on the number of loans starting foreclosure.

Table A.31   California Subprime Foreclosure Rates by Origination Year (Percent, 1999–June 2007)

Foreclosure Rates in Origination Year and Subsequent Years		Origination Year*								
		1999	2000	2001	2002	2003	2004	2005	2006	Year to July 2007
Foreclosure period	Origination year	0.88	0.76	1.01	0.70	0.48	0.50	0.76	5.20	4.88
	1st year	4.03	3.72	4.29	3.18	2.08	2.04	5.97	14.10	
	2nd year	3.01	2.99	2.74	1.68	0.79	1.46	5.51		
	3rd year	2.66	1.26	1.17	0.36	0.34	0.85			
	4th year	0.93	0.49	0.22	0.16	0.12				
	5th year	0.46	0.11	0.12	0.06					
	6th year	0.12	0.07	0.04						
	7th year	0.06	0.02							
	8th year	0.03								
Total number of foreclosures from origination through September 2007		9,160	8,389	9,528	9,137	8,944	16,161	39,198	31,295	2,973
Total number of originations		75,224	88,915	99,412	148,796	235,065	333,327	320,200	162,134	60,871
Foreclosure rate through September 2007		12.18	9.43	9.58	6.14	3.80	4.85	12.24	19.30	4.88

SOURCES: LoanPerformance, Milken Institute.

*Foreclosure rates are based on the number of loans starting foreclosure.

Table A.32 Estimates of Losses from Mortgage and Credit Markets Crisis (June 30, 2007–October 7, 2008)

Date	Estimate	Source	Note	URL
6/30/2007	$250 billion	Institutional Risk Analytics	Subprime losses	http://www.safehaven.com/article–7870.htm
7/19/2007	$50–100 billion	Ben Bernanke, Chairman of Federal Reserve Board	Credit losses	http://www.reuters.com/article/ousiv/idUSN1933365020070719
10/9/2007	$100–150 billion	David Wyss, Standard and Poor's	Subprime losses	http://www.domain–b.com/industry/housing.finance/20071009_billion.html
10/17/2007	$100–200 billion	William C. Dudley, Federal Reserve of New York	Subprime losses	http://www.newyorkfed.org/newsevents/speeches/2007/dud071017.html
11/12/2007	$300–400 billion	Deutsche Bank AG analysts	Subprime losses	http://www.bloomberg.com/apps/news?pid=20601087&sid=a3fCFxLIgT2s&refer=worldwide
11/22/2007	$300 billion	Organization for Economic Cooperation and Development	Subprime losses	http://www.iht.com/articles/2007/11/22/business/oecd.php
1/17/2008	$100–500 billion	Ben Bernanke, Chairman of Federal Reserve Board	Subprime losses	http://www.reuters.com/article/businessNews/idUSL1786139420080117
1/31/2008	$265 billion	Standard & Poor's.	Subprime and CDO losses	http://uk.reuters.com/article/ousiv/idUKKIM1572692080131
2/11/2008	$400 billion	Peer Steinbruck, German finance minister at G7 meeting	Subprime losses	http://www.123jump.com/market-update/G7-Meeting-Slower-Growth-$400-B-Subprime-Loss/26279/
2/11/2008	$125–175 billion	Bear Stearns Cos. analyst	Credit losses	http://money.cnn.com/2008/02/11/news/companies/writedowns/index.htm

(*Continued*)

Table A.32 *(Continued)*

Date	Estimate	Source	Note	URL
2/29/2008	At least $600 billion	UBS AG analysts	Credit losses	http://www.bloomberg.com/apps/news?pid=20601087&sid=avwrGqojbJ3k&refer=home
3/3/2008	$600 billion	Geraud Charpin, head of European credit strategy at UBS in London	Credit losses	http://www.marketwatch.com/news/story/ubs-analysts-estimate-600-billion/story.aspx?guid=%7b29F30572-5D8A-40F5-92F9-C85E54A0FCF8%7d
3/8/2008	$325 billion	JPMorgan Chase & Co	Credit losses	http://www.reuters.com/article/bondsNews/idUSN0832645120080308
3/10/2008	$215 billion	Head of Japan's financial regulator, Japan's Financial Services Agency	Subprime losses	http://uk.reuters.com/article/gc06/idUKT2344622080310
3/13/2008	$285 billion	Standard & Poor's	Subprime losses	http://afp.google.com/article/ALeqM5gR3kk9fbsownAlzaCv91Q-n24Uow
3/25/2008	$460 billion	Goldman Sachs	Credit losses	http://www.bloomberg.com/apps/news?pid=20601087&sid=aIGeO4anykc&refer=worldwide
4/8/2008	$945 billion	International Monetary Fund	Credit losses	http://www.ft.com/cms/s/78249530-05a0-11dd-a9e0-0000779fd2ac,Authorised=false.html?i.location=http%3A%2F%2Fwww.ft.com%2Fcms%2Fs%2F0%2F78249530-05a0-11dd-a9e0-0000779fd2ac.html&i.referer=

Date	Amount	Source	Type	URL
4/15/2008	$350–420 billion	Organization for Economic Cooperation and Development	Credit losses	http://www.reuters.com/article/telecomm/idUSL15796842200080415
4/29/2008	$800 billion	Barclays Capital	Credit losses	http://www.bloomberg.com/apps/news?pid=20601087&sid=asPmMx3.HBrg&refer=home
5/14/2008	$400 billion	Krishnan Ramadurai, Fitch's Financial Institutions Group	Subprime losses	http://www.investmentexecutive.com/client/en/News/DetailNews.asp?id=44582&IdSection=147&cat=147
5/19/2008	$379 billion	Bloomberg	Credit losses	http://www.bloomberg.com/apps/news?pid=20601110&sid=a.dAvx5tof.o
5/20/2008	$170 billion	Oppenheimer & Co.	Credit losses	http://www.bloomberg.com/apps/news?pid=newsarchive&sid=ap5JLfJQyahs
8/4/2008	$1–2 trillion	Nouriel Roubini, New York University	Credit losses	http://online.barrons.com/article/SB121763156934206007.html?mod=9_0031_b_this_weeks_magazine_main
10/7/2008	$1.4 trillion	International Monetary Fund	Credit losses	International Monetary Fund

SOURCES: Various news media, Milken Institute.

Table A.33 Recent Losses/Write-Downs, Capital Raised and Jobs Cut by Financial Institutions Worldwide through October 31, 2008

	Total			Q3–Q4 2008			Q1–Q2 2008			Prior Quarters		
	Losses/ Write-downs (US$ B)	Capital Raised (US$ B)	Jobs Cut (number)	Losses/ Write-downs (US$ B)	Capital Raised (US$ B)	Jobs Cut (number)	Losses/ Write-downs (US$ B)	Capital Raised (US$ B)	Jobs Cut (number)	Losses/ Write-downs (US$ B)	Capital Raised (US$ B)	Jobs Cut (number)
Wachovia, United States	96.5	11	8,393	74	0	6,950	17	11	1,000	5.1	0	443
Citigroup, United States	68.1	74	23,660	13	29	9,760	31	33.2	13,900	23.8	11.8	0
Merrill Lynch, United States	58.1	29.9	5,720	12	11.7	500	19	11.5	3,000	27.4	6.7	2,220
Washington Mutual, United States	45.6	12.1	4,200	31	0	0	10	8.1	1,600	5.2	4	2,600
UBS, Switzerland	44.2	31.6	9,000	0	5.2	2,000	25	15.5	5,500	19.1	11.4	1,500
HSBC, United Kingdom	27.4	5	2,780	0	1	1,130	14	3.9	0	13.7	0	1,650

Bank of America, United States	27.4	55.7	11,150	6	35	0	12	19.7	8,150	9.2	1	3,000
National City, United States	26.2	8.9	4,900	21	0	4,000	4	8.9	900	1.6	0	0
JPMorgan Chase & Co., United States	20.5	44.7	4,100	8	36.8	0	8	7.9	4,000	4.5	0	100
Wells Fargo, United States	17.7	30.8	500	8	26.8	0	7	4.1	0	2.6	0	500
Morgan Stanley, United States	15.7	24.6	4,440	1	19	0	4	0	3,540	10.3	5.6	900
Lehman Brothers, United States	13.8	13.9	13,390	6	0	7,000	7	13.9	3,940	1.5	0	2,450
Credit Suisse, Switzerland	13.7	11.6	2,065	4	8.9	500	5	2.7	1,245	4.8	0	320

(Continued)

Table A.33 (*Continued*)

	Total			Q3-Q4 2008			Q1-Q2 2008			Prior Quarters		
	Losses/Write-downs (US$ B)	Capital Raised (US$ B)	Jobs Cut (number)	Losses/Write-downs (US$ B)	Capital Raised (US$ B)	Jobs Cut (number)	Losses/Write-downs (US$ B)	Capital Raised (US$ B)	Jobs Cut (number)	Losses/Write-downs (US$ B)	Capital Raised (US$ B)	Jobs Cut (number)
IKB Deutsche, Germany	13.1	10.8	0	0	0	0	13	2.9	0	0	7.9	0
Royal Bank of Scotland, United Kingdom	12.6	52.8	7,200	0	33	0	10	19.8	7,200	3	0	0
Deutsche Bank, Germany	11.7	5.8	1,570	3	2.6	1,100	6	3.3	470	2.9	0	0
Fortis, Netherlands	8.3	20.5	3,500	0	15.2	3,000	4	5.3	500	4.7	0	0
Other European Firms	8.2	3.8	2,870	1	2.6	870	4	1.3	2,000	3.4	0	0
ING Groep NV, Netherlands	8	17.1	0	2	12.8	0	6	4.3	0	0.2	0	0
Credit Agricole, France	7.8	11.4	500	0	3.8	500	3	7.5	0	5.3	0	0
Barclays, United Kingdom	7	28.2	3,900	0	12.2	3,000	4	11.9	100	2.6	4	800

Mizuho Financial Group, Japan	6.8	0	300	0	0	0	3	0	300	3.5	0	0
Bayerische Landesbank, Germany	6.2	8.1	350	0	8.1	0	2	0	350	4.1	0	0
Canadian Imperial, Canada	6.2	2.4	100	1	0	0	5	2.4	100	0.6	0	0
HBOS PLC, United Kingdom	6	24.9	615	0	24.9	525	5	0	90	1.2	0	0
Societe Generale, France	5.8	10.5	00	0	2.2	0	3	8.4	0	3.3	0	0
Other Asian Firms	4.9	9.2	00	1	1.9	0	1	7.2	0	2.9	0	0
IndyMac Bancor, United States	4.9	0	2,800	0	0	0	3	0	2,400	2.4	0	400
Goldman Sachs, United States	4.9	20.5	4,700	1	20	3,200	3	0.5	1,500	1	0	0

(Continued)

Table A.33 (Continued)

	Total			Q3–Q4 2008			Q1–Q2 2008			Prior Quarters		
	Losses/Write-downs (US$ B)	Capital Raised (US$ B)	Jobs Cut (number)	Losses/Write-downs (US$ B)	Capital Raised (US$ B)	Jobs Cut (number)	Losses/Write-downs (US$ B)	Capital Raised (US$ B)	Jobs Cut (number)	Losses/Write-downs (US$ B)	Capital Raised (US$ B)	Jobs Cut (number)
Lloyds TSB, United Kingdom	4.4	13.9	0	0	9.5	0	4	4.4	0	0.5	0	0
LB Baden-Wuerttemberg, Germany	4.2	0	0				2	0	0	1.9	0	0
WestLB, Germany	4.1	6.4	1,530	0	0	0	0	6.4	1,530	3.9	0	0
E*trade, United States	4.1	2.2	0	1	0.4	0	1	0	0	3.1	1.8	0
Bank of China, China	3.7	0	0	1	0	0	2	0	0	1.3	0	0
Natixis, France	3.6	7.4	850	0	6.6	0	3	0.8	850	1	0	0
Nomura Holdings, Japan	3.6	1.3	400	0	0	0	3	1.3	0	1.1	0	400
Other US Firms	3.6	1.8	2,914	1	15.7	0	2	1.9	2,914	0.7	0	0
Dresdner, Germany	3.5	0	0	0	0	0	2	0	0	1.7	0	0

BNP Paribas, France	3.4	3.3	0	0	3.3	0	1	0	0	1.3	0	0
Bear Stearns, United States	3.2	0	9,159	0	0	0	1	0	7,609	2.6	0	1,550
HSH Nordbank, Germany	3.1	1.6	750	1	1.6	750	1	0	0	1.7	0	0
Rabobank, the Netherlands	3.1	0	0	0	0	0	2	0	0	1.4	0	0
KBC Groep NV	2.9	4.5	0	2	4.5	0	1	0	0	0	0	0
Fifth Third Bancorp, United States	2.7	2.6	0	1	0	0	1	2.6	0	0.8	0	0
Sovereign Bancorp, United States	2.4	1.9	0	1	0	0	1	1.9	0	0	0	0
DZ Bank, Germany	2.3	0	0	0	0	0	1	0	0	1.7	0	0
LB Sachsen, Netherlands	2.2	0	0	0	0	0	0	0	0	2.2	0	0
U.S. Bancorp, United States	2.2	0	0	1	0	0	1	0	0	0.2	0	0
Commerzbank, Germany	2	0	9,000	0	0	9,000	1	0	0	0.8	0	0

(Continued)

Table A.33 *(Continued)*

	Total			Q3–Q4 2008			Q1–Q2 2008			Prior Quarters		
	Losses/ Write-downs (US$ B)	Capital Raised (US$ B)	Jobs Cut (number)	Losses/ Write-downs (US$ B)	Capital Raised (US$ B)	Jobs Cut (number)	Losses/ Write-downs (US$ B)	Capital Raised (US$ B)	Jobs Cut (number)	Losses/ Write-downs (US$ B)	Capital Raised (US$ B)	Jobs Cut (number)
ABN Amro, Netherlands	2	0	0	0	0	0	0	0	0	2	0	0
Royal Bank of Canada, Canada	1.9	0	64	1	0	24	1	0	0	0.3	0	40
Mitsubishi UFJ, Japan	1.7	11.8	90	0	11.7	90	1	0	0	0.5	0	0
Industrial and Commercial Bank of China	1.7	0	0	1	0	0	1	0	0	0.4	0	0
Keycorp, United States	1.6	4.2	740	0	2.5	0	1	1.7	0	0.5	0	740
Dexia SA, Belgium	1.5	8.1	0	0	8.1	0	1	0	0	0.7	0	0
Bank Hapoalim BM, Italy	1.5	2.3	0	0	0	0	1	2.3	0	0.5	0	0
Marshall & Ilsley, Unitd States	1.5	1.7	0	0	1.7	0	1	0	0	0.4	0	0

UniCredit, Italy	1.3	9.2	700	0	9.2	700	1	0	0	0	0	0
Alliance & Leicester, United Kingdom	1.2	0	0	0	0	0	1	0	0	0.5	0	0
Bank of Montreal, Canada	1	0	150	0	0	0	1	0	150	0.3	0	0
Group Caisse d'Epargne	1	0	0	0	0	0	0	0	0	1	0	0
Hypo Real Estate, Germany	1	0	0	0	0	0	0	0	0	0.6	0	0
Gulf International, Kingdom of Bahrain	1	1	0	0	0	0	0	1	0	1	0	0
Sumitomo Mitsui, Japan	1	4.9	0	0	1.8	0	1	3.2	0	0	0	0
Sumitomo Trust, Japan	0.8	1.1	0	0	0	0	1	1.1	0	0.2	0	0
National Bank of Canada, Canada	0.6	0.8	0	0	0	0	0	0.8	0	0.5	0	0
Other Canadian Firms	0.3	0	0	0	0	170	0	0	0	0.2	0	0
DBS, Singapore	0.2	1	0	0	0	0	0	1	0	0.1	0	0
Grand total	**684.8**	**688.3**	**149,220**	**201.1**	**389.2**	**54,769**	**276.2**	**245.2**	**74,838**	**207.6**	**53.9**	**19,613**

SOURCE: Bloomberg.

Table A.34 Top 25 Subprime Lenders in 2006 (for 12 Months, US\$ Millions)

Rank	Lender	Volume	Market Share	Status as of Sept. 2008
1	HSBC Finance, IL	\$52,800	8.80%	Decision One, HSBC Finance's subsidiary that originates mortgage loans, was closed
2	New Century Financial, CA	\$51,600	8.60%	Bankrupt
3	Countrywide Financial, CA	\$40,596	6.77%	Acquired
4	CitiMortgage, NY	\$38,040	6.34%	
5	WMC Mortgage, CA	\$33,157	5.53%	Bankrupt
6	Fremont Investment & Loan, CA	\$32,300	5.38%	Acquired
7	Ameriquest Mortgage, CA	\$29,500	4.92%	Bankrupt
8	Option One Mortgage, CA	\$28,792	4.80%	Acquired
9	Wells Fargo Home Mortgage, IA	\$27,869	4.64%	
10	First Franklin Financial Corp, CA	\$27,666	4.61%	Operations discontinued
11	Washington Mutual, WA	\$26,600	4.43%	Acquired
12	Residential Funding Corp., MN	\$21,200	3.53%	
13	Aegis Mortgage Corp., TX	\$17,000	2.83%	Bankrupt
14	American General Finance, IN	\$15,070	2.51%	
15	Accredited Home Lenders, CA	\$15,767	2.63%	
16	BNC Mortgage, CA	\$14,500	2.42%	Closed
17	Chase Home Finance, NJ	\$11,550	1.93%	
18	Equifirst, NC	\$10,750	1.79%	

(Continued)

Table A.34 (*Continued*)

Rank	Lender	Volume	Market Share	Status as of Sept. 2008
19	NovaStar Financial, KS	$10,233	1.71%	Lending operations discontinued
20	Ownit Mortgage Solutions, CA	$9,500	1.58%	Closed
21	ResMae Mortgage Corp., CA	$7,659	1.28%	Filed for bankruptcy
22	Mortgage Lenders Network USA, CT	$6,000	1.00%	Closed
23	ECC Capital Corp., CA	$5,485	0.91%	
24	Fieldstone Mortgage Company, MD	$4,991	0.83%	Bankrupt
25	Nationstar Mortgage (Centex), TX	$4,619	0.77%	
	Total for top 25 lenders:	**$543,243**	**90.5%**	
	Total subprime originations:	**$600,000**	**100.0%**	

SOURCES: Inside Mortgage Finance, Milken Institute.

Table A.35 Top Nonagency MBS Issuers in 2006 (for 12 Months, US$ Millions)

Rank	Issuer	2006	Number of Deals	Market Share	Status as of Sept. 2008
1	Countrywide Financial	$153,824	219	13.43%	Acquired
2	Washington Mutual	$72,843	81	6.36%	Acquired
3	Lehman Brothers	$69,413	116	6.06%	Bankrupt
4	Residential Funding Corp.	$66,187	111	5.78%	
5	Bear Stearns	$64,229	109	5.61%	Acquired
6	Wells Fargo	$60,436	61	5.28%	
7	Goldman Sachs	$46,078	75	4.02%	
8	IndyMac	$40,141	72	3.50%	Bankrupt
9	New Century	$35,318	49	3.08%	Bankrupt
10	JPMorgan Chase	$33,061	38	2.89%	
11	Option One	$31,260	40	2.73%	Acquired
12	Fremont	$29,826	46	2.60%	Acquired
13	Morgan Stanley	$29,775	38	2.60%	
14	Credit Suisse	$28,770	51	2.51%	
15	First Franklin	$28,257	40	2.47%	Operations discontinued
16	RBS Greenwich Capital	$28,085	45	2.45%	
17	Deutsche Bank	$25,328	57	2.21%	
18	Bank of America	$24,607	38	2.15%	
19	WMC Mortgage	$21,620	29	1.89%	Bankrupt
20	Ameriquest Mortgage	$21,610	24	1.89%	Bankrupt
21	Citigroup	$20,000	38	1.75%	
22	GreenPoint Mortgage	$17,525	20	1.53%	Closed
23	Merrill Lynch	$16,727	33	1.46%	Acquired
24	American Home Mortgage	$12,962	9	1.13%	Filed for bankruptcy
25	UBS Warburg	$12,848	42	1.12%	
	Total for top 25	**$990,731**	**1,481**	**86.5%**	
	Totals for all issuers	**$1,145,613**	**1,786**	**100.0%**	

SOURCES: Inside Mortgage Finance, Milken Institute.

Figure A.17 Credit Default Swap Index by Industry
(January 2004–October 31, 2008)

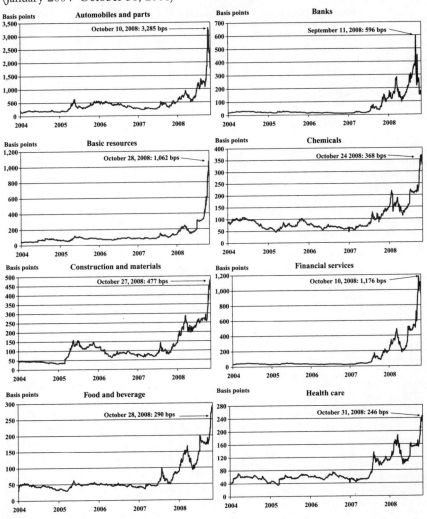

SOURCES: Datastream, Milken Institute.

Figure A.17   Credit Default Swap Index by Industry
(January 2004–October 31, 2008)

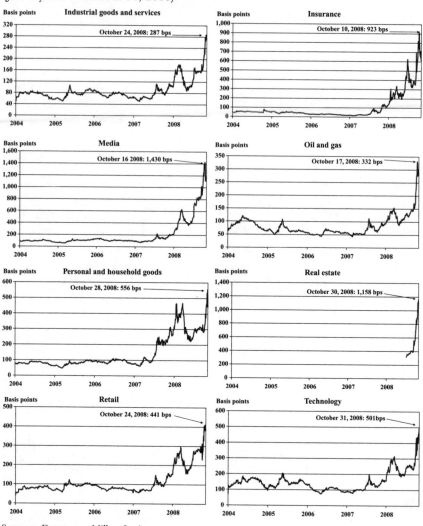

SOURCES: Datastream, Milken Institute.

Figure A.17   Credit Default Swap Index by Industry
(January 2004–October 31, 2008)

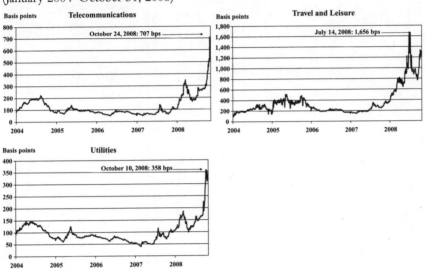

SOURCES: Datastream, Milken Institute.

Table A.36 Prime Mortgage Cumulative Foreclosure Starts through September 2007 by Year of Origination and Product Type (January 1999–July 2007)

	Hybrid											
Term Initial Fixed-Rate Period	2/6 Hybrid 2 Years	2/1 Hybrid 2 Years	3/6 Hybrid 3 Years	3/1 Hybrid 3 Years	5/6 Hybrid 5 Years	5/1 Hybrid 5 Years	7/6 Hybrid 7 Years	7/1 Hybrid 7 Years	10/6 Hybrid 10 Years	10/1 Hybrid 10 Years	15/6 Hybrid 15 Years	Other Hybrid n.a.
Reset Frequency	6 Months	1 Year	6 Months	1 Year	6 Months	1 Year	6 Months	1 Year	6 Months	1 Year	6 Months	n.a.
Year of Origination												
1999	13	8	15	306	1	395	0	65		56		1,338
2000	8	6	61	254	1	247		127		111		1,629
2001	110	20	124	343	1	405	0	104		187		774
2002	292	22	70	1,478	3	1,017	0	211		47		843
2003	233	15	44	1,555	25	1,954	0	508	0	128	0	959
2004	735	14	351	2,454	120	3,114	0	575	0	116	0	967
2005	1,507	4	326	1,258	1,814	4,362	10	1,099	4	818	0	1,380
2006	865	0	249	423	2,636	4,078	15	726	6	174	0	1,678
Jan.–July 2007	0	0	3	13	165	277	0	15	0	11	0	0
Total	3,763	89	1,240	8,071	4,601	15,572	25	3,415	10	1,637	0	9,568

		Adjustable Rate						
	Term **Initial Fixed-Rate** **Period**	**ARM** **1 Months**	**ARM** **6 Months**	**ARM** **1 Year**	**ARM** **3 Year**	**ARM** **5 Year**	**ARM** **Balloon**	**Other** **ARM**
Year of **Origination**	**Reset Frequency**	**1 Month**	**6 Months**	**1 Year**	**3 Years**	**5 Years**	**n.a.**	**n.a.**
1999		1,791	104	6,961	103	161	0	1,668
2000		2,708	222	3,267	68	205	0	1,930
2001		1,383	271	2,957	256	364	0	2,083
2002		1,464	298	7,183	666	601	0	1,797
2003		1,795	555	8,489	632	1,128	1	1,229
2004		4,057	2,090	8,133	1,104	1,832	4	1,536
2005		10,152	1,703	3,916	698	1,708	0	1,798
2006		5,331	2,840	2,817	277	1,611	13	4,478
Jan.–July 2007		127	121	368	56	30	3	934
Total		28,681	8,083	43,723	3,804	7,610	18	16,519

(Continued)

Table A.36 *(Continued)*

Term Initial Fixed-Rate Period	Fixed 10 10 Years	Fixed 15 15 Years	Fixed 20 20 Years	Fixed Rate Fixed 30 30 Years	Fixed 40 40 Years	Other Fixed
Reset Frequency	n.a.	n.a.	n.a.	n.a.	n.a.	n.a.
Year of Origination						
1999	725	12,292	3,471	166,415	125	9,106
2000	455	6,984	2,794	128,943	138	12,550
2001	667	16,709	7,047	218,082	217	11,692
2002	750	17,777	7,794	183,573	94	10,267
2003	875	17,713	7,082	165,024	61	9,598
2004	368	6,345	3,920	90,931	33	7,353
2005	218	2,724	1,348	67,406	31	3,966
2006	49	827	389	45,168	428	1,508
Jan.–July 2007	1	19	23	2,829	100	14
Total	4,107	81,371	33,845	1,065,542	1,127	66,040

Year of Origination	Other							Grand Total of FC Starts (All Types)
Term Initial Fixed-Rate Period	Balloon 3	Balloon 5	Balloon 7	Balloon 10	Balloon 15/30	Other Balloon	Other	
	n.a.	n.a.	n.a.	n.a.	n.a.	n.a.	n.a.	
Reset Frequency	n.a.	n.a.	n.a.	n.a.	n.a.	n.a.	n.a.	
1999	1	37	184	6	27	335	6,182	213,890
2000	0	15	38	1	41	413	5,387	170,603
2001	2	110	252	0	32	334	6,386	272,913
2002	1	248	419	2	14	301	3,031	242,265
2003	0	273	666	0	2	187	1,014	223,748
2004	0	90	191	0	4	58	459	138,958
2005	0	11	28	2	4	27	574	110,901
2006		1	5	0	43	88	1,342	80,071
Jan.–July 2007		0	0	0	0	5	254	5,368
Total	4	785	1,783	11	167	1,743	24,375	1,437,329

Sources: LoanPerformance, Milken Institute.

Table A.37 Subprime Mortgage Cumulative Foreclosure Starts through September 2007 by Year of Origination and Product Type (January 1999–July 2007)

							Hybrid						
Term	2/6 Hybrid	2/1 Hybrid	3/6 Hybrid	3/1 Hybrid	5/6 Hybrid	5/1 Hybrid	7/6 Hybrid	7/1 Hybrid	10/6 Hybrid	10/1 Hybrid	15/6 Hybrid	Other Hybrid
Initial Fixed-Rate Period	2 Years	2 Years	3 Years	3 Years	5 Years	5 Years	7 Years	7 Years	10 Years	10 Years	15 Years	n.a.
Reset Frequency	6 Months	1 Year	6 Months	1 Year	6 Months	1 Year	6 Months	1 Year	6 Months	1 Year	6 Months	n.a.
Year of Origination												
1999	7,285	9,326	11,672	4,952	459	1,279	0	3		0		842
2000	12,655	15,957	4,608	4,510	90	626		0		0		2,836
2001	13,744	15,658	2,120	2,565	305	43	0	0		0		3,158
2002	18,754	11,083	1,461	1,879	718	8	0	0	0	0	88	4,018
2003	32,665	5,212	4,182	4,302	509	10	0	2	0	0	162	6,662
2004	48,198	7,358	5,316	11,835	448	58	0	0	2	0	7	27,345
2005	47,646	20,783	6,415	12,675	620	194	0	0	0	0	3	29,902
2006	16,048	21,230	2,334	1,539	264	1,343	0	0	0	0	2	11,309
Jan.–July 2007	786	1,203	54	50	43	12	0	0		0	0	119
Total	196,995	106,607	38,108	44,257	3,413	3,561	0	5	2	0	262	86,072

		Adjustable Rate					
Term Initial Fixed- Rate Period	ARM 1 Months 1 Month	ARM 6 Months 6 Months	ARM 1 Year 1 Year	ARM 3 Year 3 Years	ARM 5 Year 5 Years	ARM Balloon n.a.	Other ARM n.a.
Year of Origination Reset Frequency	1 Month	6 Months	1 Year	3 Years	5 Years	n.a.	n.a.
1999	1,579	17,134	1,025	31	12	155	14,700
2000	824	21,031	680	18	19	5	13,159
2001	283	23,308	112	36	12	145	17,510
2002	193	21,509	85	33	4	0	21,699
2003	211	11,653	44	12	0	2	19,247
2004	432	12,078	40	8	0	1	20,360
2005	1,078	19,868	49	1	0	3,147	35,206
2006	422	13,073	516	0	1	11,751	22,173
Jan.–July 2007	29	1,099	10	0	1	2,801	4,369
Total	5,022	139,654	2,551	139	48	15,206	164,054

(Continued)

Table A.37 (Continued)

Term Initial Fixed-Rate Period		Fixed Rate					
		Fixed 10	Fixed 15	Fixed 20	Fixed 30	Fixed 40	Other fixed
	Reset Frequency	10 Years	15 Years	20 Years	30 Years	40 Years	n.a.
Year of Origination		n.a.	n.a.	n.a.	n.a.	n.a.	n.a.
1999		2,992	15,878	6,559	46,493	19	28,349
2000		1,434	9,092	4,993	41,246	12	17,685
2001		490	5,324	2,700	28,424	3	12,579
2002		282	3,777	2,510	23,519	0	5,706
2003		122	3,142	2,757	28,892	0	691
2004		128	2,612	2,529	29,346	0	412
2005		107	1,818	1,477	33,150	231	324
2006		18	885	298	23,423	1,473	108
Jan.–July 2007		5	49	8	1,612	135	19
Total		5,573	42,528	23,823	254,493	1,738	65,854

	Term Initial Fixed-Rate Period				Other				Grand Total of FC Storts (All Types)
Year of Origination	Reset Frequency	Balloon 3	Balloon 5	Balloon 7	Balloon 10	Balloon 15/30	Other Balloon	Other	
		n.a.	n.a.	n.a.	n.a.	n.a.	n.a.	n.a.	
		n.a.	n.a.	n.a.	n.a.	n.a.	n.a.	n.a.	
1999		91	48	200	2,312	6,765	4,525	3,910	190,594
2000		13	5	10	29	4,905	3,000	6,437	167,879
2001		1	3	2	20	2,162	2,182	7,333	142,223
2002		0	4	5	9	812	1,980	4,654	126,792
2003		0	2	3	1	593	708	5,339	129,126
2004		0	0	0	8	686	456	7,073	178,740
2005		0	0	0	2	2,154	2,583	11,929	233,369
2006			0	0	1	1,636	5,428	5,007	142,288
Jan.–July 2007			0	0	0	56	486	326	13,272
Total		105	62	220	2,382	19,713	20,862	51,682	1,294,991

SOURCES: LoanPerformance, Milken Institute.

Table A.38 Reset Dates for Adjustable-Rate First Mortgages Originated in 2004–2006

Year of First Reset

Initial Interest Rate	2004		2005		2006		2007		2008		2009		2010+	
	No. of Loans	US$ Millions	No. of Loans	US$ Millions	No. of Loans	US$ Millions	No. of Loans	US$ Millions	No. of Loans	US$ Millions	No. of Loans	US$ Millions	No. of Loans	US$ Millions
Below 2%	147,865	47,607	525,096	197,093	440,470	182,084	8,532	3,585	563	229	283	106	787	314
2%–3%	14,192	4,701	37,313	10,975	75,077	23,703	4,127	1,343	409	126	774	254	534	165
3%–4%	53,876	15,125	31,521	8,646	25,067	6,988	43,174	12,110	2,442	658	15,583	4,374	2,987	804
4.0%–4.5%	35,421	10,742	34,634	10,225	7,973	2,348	77,245	23,403	8,999	2,651	112,205	34,015	16,719	4,956
4.5%–5.0%	9,613	2,662	45,054	14,194	10,440	3,151	97,935	27,612	44,629	13,897	254,061	70,632	145,357	43,956
5.0%–5.5%	5,744	1,483	43,863	14,123	16,719	4,730	80,215	22,567	74,417	23,862	209,578	55,168	466,529	147,454
5.5%–6.0%	2,750	646	27,414	8,129	41,585	10,727	132,097	37,376	81,633	24,926	130,745	34,194	640,656	201,403
6.0%–6.5%	336	68	15,415	3,975	73,587	17,914	173,964	43,684	77,633	22,100	69,896	19,009	521,794	166,563
6.5%–7.0%	278	49	6,248	1,348	117,670	24,992	278,669	64,066	124,497	32,760	51,039	13,327	318,497	91,673
7.0%–7.5%	128	20	2,705	496	98,952	18,646	214,084	41,641	117,176	27,468	24,879	5,929	95,971	23,561
7.5%–8.0%	93	13	1,859	279	101,368	16,318	233,474	41,032	167,472	36,723	27,945	6,344	56,876	12,810
8.0%–8.5%	31	4	817	106	57,156	8,156	132,631	20,830	115,576	23,339	17,055	3,596	22,165	4,629
8.5%–9.0%	162	18	819	98	44,560	5,342	119,989	17,155	135,865	25,152	22,762	4,349	11,019	2,047
9.0%–9.5%	31	3	339	36	18,099	1,900	54,349	6,903	75,690	12,815	11,987	2,091	3,580	591
9.5%–10.0%	111	10	600	64	13,192	1,280	41,144	4,902	70,461	11,039	11,476	1,844	2,386	359
10.0%–10.5%	10	1	157	14	4,731	411	15,698	1,688	31,391	4,456	4,380	634	1,176	163
10.5%–11.0%	12	1	154	13	3,664	304	10,429	1,079	24,569	3,238	3,211	427	794	102
11.0%–11.5%	7	—	26	2	1,439	110	3,771	355	11,087	1,297	1,090	129	340	38
11.5%–12.0%	—	—	49	4	1,156	88	2,684	248	8,202	869	589	63	247	26
Total	270,660	$83,154	774,083	$269,820	1,152,905	$329,192	1,724,211	$371,579	1,172,711	$267,605	969,538	$256,485	2,308,414	$701,614

SOURCE: *Mortgage Payment Reset, The Issue and the Impact*, March 19, 2008.

NOTE: Many of the numbers are rounded for simplicity and space.

Table A.39 Mortgage Origination and Foreclosure Starts by FICO Scores Distribution (Percent of Total by FICO Score Distribution)

Mortgage Origination

Percentage of Total by FICO Score Distribution

	Below 460	460–479	480–499	500–519	520–539	540–559	560–579	580–599	600–619	620–639	640–659	660–679	680–699	700–719	720–739	740–759	760–779	780–799	Above 800	All FICO Scores
Prime	0.06	0.02	0.05	0.18	0.35	0.58	0.93	1.71	2.7	5.5	6.96	9.11	10.61	11.41	11.02	11.28	11.73	10.6	5.19	3,577,014
Subprime	0.05	0.11	0.25	2.78	4.47	5.81	7.69	11.18	13.62	14.7	12.75	9.1	6.5	4.04	2.77	1.9	1.25	0.74	0.27	1,175,464
All loans	2,783	1,964	4,810	39,216	65,207	89,137	123,509	192,575	256,856	369,571	398,983	432,934	455,858	455,539	426,752	425,857	434,156	387,971	188,800	4,752,478

Foreclosure Starts

Percentage of Total by FICO Score Distribution

	Below 460	460–479	480–499	500–519	520–539	540–559	560–579	580–599	600–619	620–639	640–659	660–679	680–699	700–719	720–739	740–759	760–779	780–799	Above 800	All FICO Scores
Prime	0.16	0.19	0.32	1.1	1.66	2.42	3.19	4.51	5.75	13	13.24	14.37	12.45	10.65	7.2	4.68	2.93	1.54	0.63	37,958
Subprime	0.32	0.55	0.9	4.49	6.57	7.67	8.83	12.3	13.6	15.15	11.62	7.28	4.54	2.61	1.62	1.03	0.57	0.28	0.08	117,721
All loans	437	719	1,186	5,705	8,361	9,950	11,606	16,185	18,199	22,767	18,702	14,019	10,069	7,113	4,643	2,987	1,783	913	337	155,679

SOURCES: LoanPerformance, Milken Institute.

413

Table A.40 Mortgage Origination and Foreclosure Starts: Loan Purpose by FICO Scores Distribution (Percent of Total by FICO Score Distribution)

Mortgage Origination: Loan Purpose

Percent of Total by FICO Score Distribution

	Below 460	460–479	480–499	500–519	520–539	540–559	560–579	580–599	600–619	620–639	640–659	660–679	680–699	700–719	720–739	740–759	760–779	780–799	Above 800	All FICO Scores
Prime: Purchase	0.01	0.01	0.03	0.09	0.18	0.32	0.51	0.87	1.33	2.31	2.91	3.93	4.97	5.75	5.72	6.12	6.69	6.42	3.26	1,839,461
Prime: Nonpurchase	0.05	0.01	0.03	0.1	0.17	0.26	0.41	0.84	1.38	3.19	4.06	5.19	5.63	5.65	5.3	5.16	5.04	4.18	1.93	1,737,402
All Prime Loans	2,191	694	1,859	6,583	12,665	20,808	33,101	61,114	96,722	196,754	249,070	325,998	379,407	408,055	394,138	403,518	419,456	379,283	185,598	3,577,014
Subprime: Purchase	0.01	0.02	0.05	0.67	1.29	1.89	3.04	5.37	6.86	7.72	6.95	5.15	3.77	2.41	1.7	1.16	0.74	0.43	0.15	578,962
Subprime: Nonpurchase	0.04	0.09	0.2	2.11	3.18	3.92	4.65	5.81	6.76	6.99	5.8	3.94	2.73	1.63	1.07	0.74	0.51	0.31	0.12	593,299
All Subprime Loans	592	1,270	2,951	32,633	52,542	68,329	90,408	131,461	160,134	172,817	149,913	106,936	76,451	47,484	32,614	22,339	14,700	8,688	0	1,172,262

Foreclosure Starts: Loan Purpose

Percent of Total by FICO Score Distribution

	Below 460	460–479	480–499	500–519	520–539	540–559	560–579	580–599	600–619	620–639	640–659	660–679	680–699	700–719	720–739	740–759	760–779	780–799	Above 800	All FICO Scores
Prime: Purchase	0.09	0.13	0.21	0.76	1.16	1.78	2.32	3.07	3.88	7.06	6.96	7.81	7.31	6.87	4.9	3.28	2.13	1.14	0.52	23,075
Prime: Nonpurchase	0.04	0.05	0.11	0.34	0.5	0.64	0.87	1.44	1.87	5.94	6.28	6.55	5.14	3.78	2.31	1.4	0.8	0.4	0.11	14,498
All Prime Loans	62	70	121	414	624	911	1,200	1,694	2,162	4,887	4,977	5,399	4,680	4,002	2,707	1,758	1,102	578	236	37,584
Subprime: Purchase	0.03	0.03	0.09	1.35	2.37	3.21	4.62	7.92	9.19	11.12	8.84	5.78	3.72	2.23	1.42	0.91	0.51	0.25	0.07	74,876
Subprime: Nonpurchase	0.29	0.52	0.82	3.14	4.2	4.46	4.21	4.38	4.42	4.03	2.77	1.49	0.82	0.38	0.2	0.12	0.06	0.03	0.01	42,745
All Subprime Loans	374	648	1,064	5,287	7,731	9,030	10,394	14,474	16,015	17,831	13,675	8,566	5,342	3,071	1,909	1,212	670	329	0	117,622

SOURCES: LoanPerformance, Milken Institute.

Table A.41 Mortgage Origination and Foreclosure Starts: Conforming and Nonconforming by FICO Score Distribution (Percent of Total by FICO Score Distribution)

| | Mortgage Origination: Conforming and Nonconforming | | | | | | | | | | | | | | | | | | | |
| | Percent of Total by FICO Score Distribution | | | | | | | | | | | | | | | | | | | |
	Below 460	460–479	480–499	500–519	520–539	540–559	560–579	580–599	600–619	620–639	640–659	660–679	680–699	700–719	720–739	740–759	760–779	780–799	Above 800	All FICO Scores
Prime:																				
Conforming	0.06	0.02	0.05	0.18	0.35	0.58	0.92	1.69	2.66	5.26	6.61	8.44	9.72	10.33	9.99	10.23	10.58	9.61	4.85	3,295,623
Prime: Nonconforming	0	0	0	0	0	0	0.01	0.02	0.04	0.24	0.36	0.67	0.89	1.07	1.03	1.06	1.15	1	0.34	281,388
All Prime Loans	2,191	694	1,859	6,583	12,665	20,808	33,101	61,114	96,722	196,754	249,070	325,998	379,407	408,055	394,138	403,518	419,456	379,283	185,598	3,577,014
Subprime:																				
Conforming	0.05	0.1	0.24	2.69	4.33	5.62	7.43	10.8	13.11	14.07	12.18	8.63	6.12	3.79	2.6	1.77	1.15	0.68	0.25	1,120,885
Subprime: Nonconforming	0	0	0.01	0.08	0.14	0.2	0.26	0.38	0.52	0.63	0.57	0.47	0.38	0.25	0.18	0.13	0.1	0.06	0.02	51,377
All Subprime Loans	592	1,270	2,951	32,633	52,542	68,329	90,408	131,461	160,134	172,817	149,913	106,936	76,451	47,484	32,614	22,339	14,700	8,688	0	1,172,262

(Continued)

Table A.41 (Continued)

| | Foreclosure Starts: Conforming and Nonconforming | | | | | | | | | | | | | | | | | | | |
| | Percent of Total by FICO Score Distribution | | | | | | | | | | | | | | | | | | | |
	Below 460	460–479	480–499	500–519	520–539	540–559	560–579	580–599	600–619	620–639	640–659	660–679	680–699	700–719	720–739	740–759	760–779	780–799	Above 800	All FICO Scores
Prime: Conforming	0.16	0.19	0.32	1.1	1.65	2.41	3.17	4.47	5.7	11.89	11.83	12.11	10.27	8.49	5.85	3.67	2.33	1.26	0.51	32,839
Prime: Nonconforming	0	0	0	0	0.01	0.01	0.03	0.04	0.05	1.11	1.41	2.26	2.18	2.16	1.35	1.01	0.61	0.27	0.11	4,745
All Prime Loans	62	70	121	414	624	911	1,200	1,694	2,162	4,887	4,977	5,399	4,680	4,002	2,707	1,758	1,102	578	236	37,584
Subprime: Conforming	0.31	0.52	0.86	4.27	6.23	7.27	8.37	11.47	12.62	13.78	10.45	6.45	3.99	2.27	1.41	0.89	0.48	0.24	0.07	108,170
Subprime: Nonconforming	0.01	0.03	0.04	0.22	0.34	0.4	0.46	0.83	0.98	1.37	1.17	0.83	0.55	0.34	0.21	0.14	0.09	0.04	0.02	9,452
All Subprime Loans	374	648	1,064	5,287	7,731	9,030	10,394	14,474	16,015	17,831	13,675	8,566	5,342	3,071	1,909	1,212	670	329	0	117,622

Sources: LoanPerformance Milken Institute.

Table A.42 Mortgage Origination and Foreclosure Starts: Documents by FICO Score Distribution (Percent of Total by FICO Score Distribution)

| | Mortgage Origination: Documents | | | | | | | | | | | | | | | | | | | |
| | Percent of Total by FICO Score Distribution | | | | | | | | | | | | | | | | | | | |
	Below 460	460–479	480–499	500–519	520–539	540–559	560–579	580–599	600–619	620–639	640–659	660–679	680–699	700–719	720–739	740–759	760–779	780–799	Above 800	All FICO Scores
Prime: Full Doc	0.02	0.01	0.03	0.11	0.2	0.34	0.52	0.93	1.42	2.7	3.24	3.59	3.68	3.41	3.11	3.2	3.38	3.04	1.42	1,228,590
Prime: Less-than-Full Doc	0.03	0.01	0.02	0.08	0.15	0.24	0.4	0.78	1.29	2.8	3.73	5.52	6.93	8	7.91	8.08	8.35	7.57	3.77	2,348,337
All Prime Loans	2,191	694	1,859	6,583	12,665	20,808	33,101	61,114	96,722	196,754	249,070	325,998	379,407	408,055	394,138	403,518	419,456	379,283	185,598	3,577,014
Subprime: Full Doc	0.03	0.07	0.18	2.15	3.41	4.47	6.01	8.89	10.35	9.23	7.07	4.64	3.09	1.84	1.26	0.9	0.64	0.41	0.17	762,268
Subprime: Less-than-Full Doc	0.02	0.03	0.07	0.63	1.06	1.35	1.69	2.29	3.28	5.47	5.68	4.46	3.42	2.2	1.51	1	0.61	0.33	0.11	414,190
All Subprime Loans	592	1,270	2,951	32,633	52,542	68,329	90,408	131,461	160,134	172,817	149,913	106,936	76,451	47,484	32,614	22,339	14,700	8,688	4,200	1,176,462

(*Continued*)

Table A.42 (Continued)

Foreclosure Starts: Documents

Percent of Total by FICO Score Distribution

	Below 460	460–479	480–499	500–519	520–539	540–559	560–579	580–599	600–619	620–639	640–659	660–679	680–699	700–719	720–739	740–759	760–779	780–799	Above 800	All FICO Scores
Prime: Full Doc	0.14	0.13	0.22	0.54	0.94	1.36	1.72	2.41	2.79	5.17	4.37	3.43	2.23	1.75	1.02	0.71	0.41	0.23	0.09	11,149
Prime: Less-than-Full Doc	0	0.05	0.1	0.56	0.72	1.07	1.47	2.1	2.96	7.84	8.87	10.94	10.22	8.9	6.18	3.97	2.52	1.31	0.54	26,428
All Prime Loans	62	70	121	414	624	911	1,200	1,694	2,162	4,887	4,977	5,399	4,680	4,002	2,707	1,758	1,102	578	236	37,584
Subprime: Full Doc	0.19	0.34	0.57	3.18	4.58	5.43	6.3	9.01	9.2	6.44	4.15	2.33	1.26	0.63	0.41	0.22	0.14	0.07	0.03	64,090
Subprime: Less-than-Full Doc	0.12	0.21	0.33	1.31	1.98	2.24	2.53	3.28	4.41	8.7	7.47	4.94	3.28	1.98	1.21	0.81	0.43	0.21	0.06	53,531
All Subprime Loans	374	648	1,064	5,287	7,731	9,030	10,394	14,474	16,015	17,831	13,675	8,566	5,342	3,071	1,909	1,212	670	329	0	117,622

SOURCES: LoanPerformance Milken Institute.

Table A.43 Mortgage Origination and Foreclosure Starts: LTV by FICO Score Distribution (Percent of Total by FICO Score Distribution)

	Below 460	460–479	480–499	500–519	520–539	540–559	560–579	580–599	600–619	620–639	640–659	660–679	680–699	700–719	720–739	740–759	760–779	780–799	Above 800	All FICO Scores
Mortgage Origination: LTV Percent of Total by FICO Score Distribution																				
Prime: LTV<=80	0.01	0	0.01	0.07	0.12	0.18	0.27	0.65	1.11	2.94	4.19	6.31	7.95	8.99	8.86	9.27	9.93	9.29	4.64	2,675,509
Prime: LTV>80	0.05	0.02	0.04	0.12	0.23	0.41	0.66	1.06	1.59	2.56	2.77	2.8	2.66	2.41	2.16	2.01	1.79	1.31	0.55	901,279
All Prime Loans	2,191	694	1,859	6,583	12,665	20,808	33,101	61,114	96,722	196,754	249,070	325,998	379,407	408,055	394,138	403,518	419,456	379,283	185,598	3,577,014
Subprime: LTV<=80	0.04	0.09	0.2	2.28	3.03	3.5	4.21	6.99	8.54	9.44	8.4	6.1	4.39	2.8	1.95	1.35	0.93	0.57	0.22	762,625
Subprime: LTV>80	0.01	0.02	0.05	0.49	1.43	2.31	3.48	4.19	5.08	5.26	4.35	2.99	2.11	1.24	0.82	0.55	0.32	0.17	0.06	409,637
All Subprime Loans	592	1,270	2,951	32,633	52,542	68,329	90,408	131,461	160,134	172,817	149,913	106,936	76,451	47,484	32,614	22,339	14,700	8,688	0	1,172,262

(*Continued*)

Table A.43 (Continued)

Foreclosure Starts: LTV

Percent of Total by FICO Score Distribution

	Below 460	460–479	480–499	500–519	520–539	540–559	560–579	580–599	600–619	620–639	640–659	660–679	680–699	700–719	720–739	740–759	760–779	780–799	Above 800	All FICO Scores
Prime: LTV<=80	0.02	0.01	0.04	0.2	0.29	0.36	0.43	1.02	1.56	5.68	7.7	9.73	8.86	8.15	5.7	3.51	2.24	1.14	0.45	21,459
Prime: LTV>80	0.06	0.18	0.28	0.9	1.37	2.06	2.76	3.49	4.19	7.32	5.54	4.64	3.6	2.49	1.5	1.17	0.7	0.4	0.18	16,093
All Prime Loans	62	70	121	414	624	911	1,200	1,694	2,162	4,887	4,977	5,399	4,680	4,002	2,707	1,758	1,102	578	236	37,584
Subprime: LTV<=80	0.24	0.41	0.7	3.44	4.11	3.88	3.73	6.57	7.69	9.87	7.83	5.1	3.26	1.89	1.18	0.76	0.45	0.21	0.06	72,196
Subprime: LTV>80	0.08	0.14	0.2	1.05	2.46	3.79	5.1	5.72	5.91	5.28	3.79	2.18	1.28	0.72	0.44	0.27	0.12	0.07	0.03	45,426
All Subprime Loans	374	648	1,064	5,287	7,731	9,030	10,394	14,474	16,015	17,831	13,675	8,566	5,342	3,071	1,909	1,212	670	329	0	117,622

SOURCES: LoanPerformance Milken Institute.

Table A.44 Mortgage Origination and Foreclosure Starts: Occupancy Status by FICO Score Distribution (Percent of Total by FICO Score Distribution)

| | Mortgage Origination: Occupancy Status | | | | | | | | | | | | | | | | | | | |
| | Percent of Total by FICO Score Distribution | | | | | | | | | | | | | | | | | | | |
	Below 460	460–479	480–499	500–519	520–539	540–559	560–579	580–599	600–619	620–639	640–659	660–679	680–699	700–719	720–739	740–759	760–779	780–799	Above 800	All FICO Scores
Prime:																				
Owner-Occupied	0.06	0.04	0.01	0.15	0.28	0.45	0.72	1.37	2.19	4.65	5.81	7.46	8.58	9.08	8.73	8.84	9.02	8.08	3.97	2,842,924
Prime: Non-owner-occupied	0	0.01	0.03	0.07	0.13	0.21	0.34	0.52	0.85	1.15	1.65	2.02	2.33	2.29	2.44	2.71	2.52		1.22	734,023
All Prime Loans	2,191	694	1,859	6,583	12,665	20,808	33,101	61,114	96,722	196,754	249,070	325,998	379,407	408,055	394,138	403,518	419,456	379,283	185,598	3,577,014
Subprime:																				
Owner-occupied	0.05	0.11	0.25	2.72	4.35	5.63	7.42	10.78	12.98	13.81	11.86	8.35	5.9	3.63	2.46	1.67	1.09	0.64	0.24	1,101,224
Subprime: Non-owner-occupied	0	0.01	0.05	0.12	0.18	0.27	0.41	0.64	0.89	0.9	0.74	0.6	0.4	0.31	0.23	0.16	0.09	0.03	0	71,038
All Subprime Loans	592	1,270	2,951	32,633	52,542	68,329	90,408	131,461	160,134	172,817	149,913	106,936	76,451	47,484	32,614	22,339	14,700	8,688	0	1,172,262

(Continued)

Table A.44 (Continued)

Foreclosure Starts: Occupancy Status

Percent of Total by FICO Score Distribution

	Below 460	460–479	480–499	500–519	520–539	540–559	560–579	580–599	600–619	620–639	640–659	660–679	680–699	700–719	720–739	740–759	760–779	780–799	Above 800	All FICO Scores
Prime: Owner-occupied	0.15	0.17	0.27	0.95	1.34	1.97	2.51	3.64	4.8	10.79	10.7	11.6	9.86	8.64	5.81	3.64	2.29	1.19	0.51	30,379
Prime: Non-owner-occupied	0	0.02	0.05	0.15	0.32	0.46	0.68	0.86	0.95	2.22	2.54	2.76	2.59	2.01	1.39	1.04	0.64	0.35	0.12	7199
All Prime Loans	62	70	121	414	624	911	1,200	1,694	2,162	4,887	4,977	5,399	4,680	4,002	2,707	1,758	1,102	578	236	37,584
Subprime: Owner-occupied	0.31	0.53	0.89	4.38	6.34	7.31	8.41	11.53	12.42	13.64	10.3	6.42	3.94	2.28	1.39	0.9	0.5	0.24	0.07	107,979
Subprime: Non-owner-occupied	0.01	0.02	0.02	0.11	0.22	0.36	0.42	0.77	1.18	1.5	1.32	0.86	0.6	0.33	0.23	0.13	0.07	0.04	0.01	9,643
All Subprime Loans	374	648	1,064	5,287	7,731	9,030	10,394	14,474	16,015	17,831	13,675	8,566	5,342	3,071	1,909	1,212	670	329	0	117,622

SOURCES: LoanPerformance Milken Institute.

Table A.45 Maximum Allowable Loan-to-Value Ratios for Fannie Mae

Transaction Type	Number of Units	Maximum LTV/CLTV/HCLTV	Minimum Credit Score	Maximum LTV/CLTV/HCLTV	Minimum Credit Score
		Fully Amortizing		With IO Feature	
Principal Residences					
Purchase money mortgage (PMM) and limited cash–out refinance (LCOR)	1–unit (no co–ops)	95%/95%/95%	660 if > 75% 620 if ≤ 75%	95%/95%/95%	720 if ≥ 90% 700 if 75.01 < 90% 660 if ≤ 75%
	1–unit co–op	PMM = 95%/(N/A)/(N/A) LCOR = 90%/(N/A)/(N/A)	660 if > 75% 620 if ≤ 75%	N/A	N/A
	2–units	95%/95%/95%	680 if > 75% 620 if ≤ 75%	90%/90%/90%	700 if > 75% 680 if ≤ 75%
	3–4 units	75%/75%/75%	640	75%/75%/75%	680
Cash–out refinance	1–2 units (no co–ops)	90%/90%/90%	700 if > 75% 620 if ≤ 75%	90%/90%/90%	740 if > 75% 700 if ≤ 75%
	1–unit co–op	85%/(N/A)/(N/A)	660 if > 75% 620 if ≤ 75%	N/A	N/A
	3–4 units	75%/75%/75%	680	75%/75%/75%	700

(Continued)

Table A.45 *(Continued)*

Transaction Type	Number of Units	Maximum LTV/ CLTV/HCLTV	Minimum Credit Score	Maximum LTV/ CLTV/HCLTV	Minimum Credit Score
Second Homes		**Fully Amortizing**		**With IO Feature**	
Purchase money mortgage and limited cash-out refinance	1-unit (no co-ops)	90%/90%/90%	660 if > 75% 620 if ≤ 75%	90%/90%/90%	740 if > 75% 680 if ≤ 75%
	1-unit co-op	PMM = 90%/ (N/A)/(N/A) LCOR = 75%/(N/A)/(N/A)	660 if > 75% 620 if ≤ 75% 620	N/A	N/A
Cash-out refinance	1-unit	85%/85%/85%	680	70%/70%/70%	680
Investment Properties		**Fully Amortizing**		**With IO Feature**	
Purchase money mortgage and limited cash-out refinance	1-2 units	90%/90%/90%	680 if > 75% 620 if ≤ 75%	90%/90%/90%	740 if > 75% 680 if ≤ 75%
	3-4 units	75%/75%/75%	660	N/A	N/A
Cash-out refinance	1-2 units	85%/85%/85%	700	70%/70%/70%	680
	3-4 units	70%/70%/70%	680	N/A	N/A

SOURCE: Fannie Mae.

Table A.46 Maximum Allowable Loan-to-Value Ratios for Freddie Mac

Purchase and Non-Cash-Out Refinance Mortgages (Fixed-Rate [Other Than 40-Year Mortgages], ARMs, and 5- or 7-Year Balloon/Reset Mortgages)

Property Type	Max. LTV w/o Sec. Fin. (%)	Max. LTV w/Sec. Fin. (%)	Max. TLTV w/Sec. Fin. (%)	Max. HTLTV w/Sec. Fin. (%)
1- to 2-unit primary residence or second home	95	90	95	95
1- to 2-unit investment property	85	80	85	90
3- to 4-unit primary residence	80	75	80	85
3- to 4-unit investment property	75	70	75	80

Cash-Out Refinance Mortgages (Fixed-Rate [Other Than 40-Year Mortgages], ARMs, and 5- or 7-Year Balloon/Reset Mortgages)

Property Type	Max. LTV w/o Sec. Fin. (%)	Max. LTV w/Sec. Fin. (%)	Max. TLTV w/Sec. Fin. (%)	Max. HTLTV w/Sec. Fin. (%)
1- to 2-unit primary residence or second home	85	80	85	90
1- to 2-unit investment property	85	80	85	90
3- to 4-unit primary residence	75	70	75	80
3- to 4-unit investment property	70	65	70	75

Streamlined Refinance Mortgages (Fixed-Rate, ARMs, and 5- or 7-Year Balloon/Reset Mortgages)

Property Type	Max. LTV w/o Sec. Fin. (%)	Max. LTV w/Sec. Fin. (%)	Max. TLTV w/Sec. Fin. (%)	Max. HTLTV w/Sec. Fin. (%)
1-unit primary residence	95	90	95	95
2-unit primary residence or second home	95	90	95	95

(Continued)

Table A.46 (Continued)

Streamlined Refinance Mortgages with Payoff of a Purchase Money Junior Lien

Property Type	Max. LTV w/o Sec. Fin. (%)	Max. LTV w/Sec. Fin. (%)	Max. TLTV w/Sec. Fin. (%)	Max. HTLTV w/Sec. Fin. (%)
1- to 2-unit primary residence or second home	90	85	90	90

Purchase and Non-Cash-Out Refinance Loan Prospector Mortgages (40-Year Fixed-Rate Mortgages)

Property Type	Max. LTV w/o Sec. Fin. (%)	Max. LTV w/Sec. Fin. (%)	Max. TLTV w/Sec. Fin. (%)	Max. HTLTV w/Sec. Fin. (%)
1- to 2-unit primary residence or second home	95	90	95	95
1- to 2-unit investment property	85	80	85	90
3- to 4-unit primary residence	80	75	80	85
3- to 4-unit investment property	75	70	75	80

Cash-Out Refinance Loan Prospector Mortgages (40-Year Fixed-Rate Mortgages)

Property Type	Max. LTV w/o Sec. Fin. (%)	Max. LTV w/Sec. Fin. (%)	Max. TLTV w/Sec. Fin. (%)	Max. HTLTV w/Sec. Fin. (%)
1- to 2-unit primary residence or second home	85	80	85	90
1- to 2-unit investment property	85	80	85	90
3- to 4-unit primary residence	75	70	75	80
3- to 4-unit investment property	70	65	70	75

Purchase and Non-Cash-Out Refinance Manually Underwritten Mortgages (40-Year Fixed-Rate Mortgages)

Property Type	Max. LTV w/o Sec. Fin. (%)	Max. LTV w/Sec. Fin. (%)	Max. TLTV w/Sec. Fin. (%)	Max. HTLTV w/Sec. Fin. (%)
1-unit primary residence	95	90	95	95
2-unit primary residence or second home	90	85	90	95
3- to 4-unit primary residence	80	75	80	85
1- to 4-unit investment property	75	70	75	80

Cash-out Refinance Manually Underwritten Mortgages (40-Year Fixed-Rate Mortgages)

Property Type	Max. LTV w/o Sec. Fin. (%)	Max. LTV w/Sec. Fin. (%)	Max. TLTV w/Sec. Fin. (%)	Max. HTLTV w/Sec. Fin. (%)
1- to 4-unit primary residence or second home	70	65	70	75
1- to 4-unit investment property	70	65	70	75

SOURCE: Freddie Mac.

NOTE: A minimum indicator score may be required for certain mortgages sold to Freddie Mac. The minimum indicator score requirements can be found in Exhibit 25, Mortgage Products with Risk Class and/or Minimum Indicator Score Requirements. Maximum LTV/TLTV/HTLTV ratios for certain mortgage products and property types that vary from those shown above may be found in other chapters of the Guide.

Table A.47   Historical Conventional Loan Limits, Fannie Mae and Freddie Mac (1980–2008)

	Historical Conventional Loan Limits					
	Single Family	Two Family	Three Family	Four Family	Second Loan	High-Cost Area, Single Family
1980	93,750	120,000	145,000	180,000	N/A*	140,625
1981	98,500	126,000	152,000	189,000	98,500	147,750
1982	107,000	136,800	165,100	205,300	107,000	160,500
1983	108,300	138,500	167,200	207,900	108,300	162,450
1984	114,000	145,800	176,100	218,900	57,000	171,000
1985	115,300	147,500	178,200	221,500	57,650	172,950
1986	133,250	170,450	205,950	256,000	66,625	199,875
1987	153,100	195,850	236,650	294,150	76,550	229,650
1988	168,700	215,800	260,800	324,150	84,350	253,050
1989	187,600	239,950	290,000	360,450	93,800	281,400
1990	187,450	239,750	289,750	360,150	93,725	281,175
1991	191,250	244,650	295,650	367,500	95,625	286,875
1992	202,300	258,800	312,800	388,800	101,150	303,450
1993	203,150	259,850	314,100	390,400	101,575	304,725
1994	203,150	259,850	314,100	390,400	101,575	304,725
1995	203,150	259,850	314,100	390,400	101,575	304,725
1996	207,000	264,750	320,050	397,800	103,500	310,500
1997	214,600	274,550	331,850	412,450	107,300	321,900
1998	227,150	290,650	351,300	436,600	113,575	340,725
1999	240,000	307,100	371,200	461,350	120,000	360,000
2000	252,700	323,400	390,900	485,800	126,350	379,050
2001	275,000	351,950	425,400	528,700	137,500	412,500
2002	300,700	384,900	465,200	578,150	150,350	451,050
2003	322,700	413,100	499,300	620,500	161,350	484,050
2004	333,700	427,150	516,300	641,650	166,850	500,550
2005	359,650	460,400	556,500	691,600	179,825	539,475
2006	417,000	533,850	645,300	801,950	208,500	625,500
2007	417,000	533,850	645,300	801,950	208,500	625,500
2008**	417,000	533,850	645,300	801,950	208,500	625,500

SOURCES: Fannie Mae, Milken Institute.

NOTE: Limits for Alaska, Hawaii, Virgin Islands, and Guam are 50 percent higher. The Virgin Islands were designated a high-cost area in 1992 and Guam in 2001.

*Prior to 1984, second mortgage limits were the same as first mortgage limits. Subsequent legislation reduced the limits to 50 percent of first mortgage limits. Fannie Mae had no second mortgage program before 1981.

**With passage of the economic stimulus package, Fannie Mae and Freddie Mac may temporarily increase purchase loans beyond the company's prevailing conventional loan limit in designated high-cost areas. The company may purchase loans with a maximum original principal obligation of up to 125 percent of the area median home price in high-cost areas, not to exceed $729,750, except in Alaska, Hawaii, Guam, and the U.S. Virgin Islands, where higher limits may apply.

Table A.48 Change in Governmental Mortgage Limits (1980–2008)

Year	Fannie/Freddie Loan Limit	Change	Goverment-Insured FHA	VA	Average House Prices Newly Built	Change	Existing	Change
1980	$93,751	0.00%	$90,000	$100,000	$76,400	6.41%	$72,800	13.40%
1981	$98,500	5.07%	$90,000	$110,000	$83,000	8.64%	$78,300	7.55%
1982	$107,000	8.63%	$90,000	$110,000	$83,900	1.08%	$80,500	2.81%
1983	$108,300	1.21%	$90,000	$110,000	$89,800	7.03%	$83,100	3.23%
1984	$114,000	5.26%	$90,000	$110,000	$97,600	8.69%	$86,000	3.49%
1985	$115,300	1.14%	$90,000	$110,000	$100,800	3.28%	$90,800	5.58%
1986	$133,250	15.57%	$90,000	$110,000	$111,900	11.01%	$98,500	8.48%
1987	$153,100	14.90%	$90,000	$110,000	$127,200	13.67%	$106,300	7.92%
1988	$168,700	10.19%	$101,250	$144,000	$138,300	8.73%	$112,800	6.11%
1989	$187,600	11.20%	$101,250	$144,000	$148,800	7.59%	$114,400	1.42%
1990	$187,450	−0.08%	$124,875	$184,000	$149,800	0.67%	$115,300	0.79%
1991	$191,250	2.03%	$124,875	$184,000	$147,200	−1.74%	$124,700	8.15%
1992	$202,300	5.78%	$124,875	$184,000	$144,100	−2.11%	$126,600	1.52%
1993	$203,150	0.42%	$151,725	$184,000	$147,700	2.50%	$129,300	2.13%
1994	$203,150	0.00%	$151,725	$184,000	$154,500	4.60%	$133,500	3.25%
1995	$203,150	0.00%	$152,362	$203,000	$158,700	2.72%	$135,800	1.72%
1996	$207,000	1.90%	$155,250	$203,000	$166,400	4.85%	$141,800	4.42%
1997	$214,600	3.67%	$160,950	$203,000	$176,200	5.89%	$150,500	6.14%
1998	$227,150	5.85%	$170,362	$203,000	$181,900	3.23%	$159,100	5.71%
1999	$240,000	5.66%	$208,800	$203,000	$195,600	7.53%	$168,300	5.78%
2000	$252,700	5.29%	$219,849	$203,000	$207,000	5.83%	$176,200	4.69%
2001	$275,000	8.82%	$239,250	$203,000	$213,200	3.00%	$185,300	5.16%
2002	$300,700	9.35%	$261,609	$240,000	$228,700	7.27%	$201,600	8.80%
2003	$322,700	7.32%	$280,749	$240,000	$246,300	7.70%	$216,200	7.24%
2004	$333,700	3.41%	$290,319	$240,000	$275,500	11.45%	$244,000	12.86%
2005	$359,650	7.78%	$312,896	$359,650	$297,000	8.20%	$266,600	9.26%
2006	$417,000	15.95%	$362,790	$417,000	$305,900	3.00%	$268,200	0.60%
2007	$417,000	0.00%	$362,790	$417,000	$311,600	1.86%	$266,000	−0.82%
2008*	$417,000	0.00%	$362,790	$417,000	n.a.	n.a.	n.a.	n.a.

SOURCES: Inside Mortgage Finance, Milken Institute.

NOTE: *With passage of the economic stimulus package, Fannie Mae and Freddie Mac may temporarily increase purchase loans beyond the company's prevailing conventional loan limit in designated high-cost areas. The company may purchase loans with a maximum original principal obligation of up to 125 percent of the area median home price in high-cost areas, not to exceed $729,750, except in Alaska, Hawaii, Guam, and the U.S. Virgin Islands, where higher limits may apply. Effective March 6, 2008, HUD will offer temporary FHA loan limits that will range from $271,050 to $729,750.

Table A.49 GSE Single-Family Mortgage Pool Characteristics (2005–Q3 2008)

Fannie Mae Pool Volume in US$ Millions	Total	Volume by Product Type			Weighted Averages				Purchase Share	
		FRM	ARM	IO	Loan Size	LTV	FICO		ARM	IO
2005	$488,357	$380,063	$108,294	$43,173	$192,604	71.7%	721.2		22.2%	8.8%
2006	$474,970	$393,637	$81,332	$70,940	$212,172	72.9%	720.1		17.1%	14.9%
2007	$609,815	$547,919	$61,897	$97,590	$219,552	75.1%	718.6		10.2%	16.0%
2007 Q1	$130,426	$114,099	$16,327	$24,520	$218,761	73.4%	720.9		12.5%	18.8%
2007 Q2	$146,165	$135,193	$10,972	$23,011	$219,041	74.6%	717.8		7.5%	15.7%
2007 Q3	$165,647	$147,345	$18,302	$26,086	$216,339	76.3%	717.7		11.0%	15.7%
2007 Q4	$167,578	$151,282	$16,296	$23,972	$223,790	75.5%	718.3		9.7%	14.3%
2008 Q1	$168,813	$156,908	$11,904	$13,078	$233,219	73.3%	727.2		7.1%	7.7%
2008 Q2	$174,918	$155,656	$19,262	$10,016	$232,535	71.3%	737.6		11.0%	5.7%
2008 Q3	$106,370	$96,865	$9,505	$4,215	$249,514	72.6%	743.5		8.9%	4.0%

2005	$387,989	$317,903	$70,090	$26,829	$190,994	71.5%	723.4	18.1%	6.9%
2006	$360,403	$285,058	$75,216	$60,042	$211,428	72.5%	725.6	20.9%	16.7%
2007	$446,087	$365,736	$80,352	$97,795	$223,220	74.3%	723.6	18.0%	21.9%
2007 Q1	$113,837	$84,570	$29,267	$29,267	$228,371	72.3%	725.4	25.7%	25.7%
2007 Q2	$119,149	$94,217	$24,932	$31,678	$224,211	73.9%	724.2	20.9%	26.6%
2007 Q3	$111,595	$96,464	$15,131	$22,439	$220,175	75.3%	722.9	13.6%	20.1%
2007 Q4	$101,507	$90,485	$11,021	$14,411	$219,628	75.8%	721.8	10.9%	14.2%
2008 Q1	$117,434	$106,991	$10,443	$12,237	$239,464	72.6%	734.3	8.9%	10.4%
2008 Q2	$126,620	$113,657	$12,963	$9,109	$229,888	70.5%	741.8	10.2%	7.2%
2008 Q3	$65,267	$57,275	$7,992	$5,091	$244,686	71.4%	745.2	12.2%	7.8%

SOURCE: Inside Mortgage Finance.

NOTE: Interest-only amounts are also included in FRM and ARM totals. Data include only conventional, single-family mortgages; megas and gants are not included. Weighted averages exclude pools for which data are not available.

Table A.50 Mortgage Originations by Source of Funding (US$ Billions)

| | Total Originations | Mortgage Securitization | | | | Portfolio Lending | | |
		All MBS	Nonagency	GSE	Ginnie Mae	All	Banks	Thrifts
2003	3,945	2,653.8	522.9	1,912.4	218.5	1,291.3	809.2	425.1
2004	2,920	1,825.0	806.3	892.3	126.4	1,094.6	613.2	376.4
2005	3,120	2,102.5	1,136.2	879.1	87.2	1,017.3	555.2	298.1
2006	2,980	2,017.4	1,115.8	821.9	82.7	962.0	526.0	318.0
2007	2,430	1,793.5	634.1	1,062.0	97.4	629.0	367.0	194.0
Q1 2007	680	523.9	259.5	246.8	17.6	154.0	97.0	42.0
Q2 2007	730	531.2	241.5	267.9	21.8	195.0	105.0	60.0
Q3 2007	570	399.6	90.8	282.7	26.1	169.0	90.0	60.0
Q4 2007	450	338.8	42.3	264.6	31.9	111.0	75.0	32.0
Q1 2008	480	324.2	7.7	284.6	31.9	176.0	95.0	55.0

SOURCES: Inside Mortgage Finance, Milken Institute.

NOTES: Nonagency MBS volume excludes NIMs, resecuritizations, and deals backed by seasoned mortgages. GSE MBS volume includes Fannie Mae MBS and Freddie Mac PC issuance. Other portfolio lenders include credit unions, finance companies, REITs, and other investors.

Table A.51 The Importance of Fannie Mae and Freddie Mac Compared to Commercial Banks and Savings Institutions for the Residential Real Estate Market (1971–Q2 2008; US$ Millions)

| | Fannie Mae | | Freddie Mac | | Residential Real Estate Assets | |
	Total Assets	Total MBS Outstanding	Total Assets	Total MBS Outstanding	Commercial Banks	Savings Institutions
1971	18,591	n.a.	1,038	64	51,863	n.a.
1972	20,346	n.a.	1,772	444	62,619	n.a.
1973	24,318	n.a.	2,873	791	74,725	n.a.
1974	29,671	n.a.	4,901	780	82,144	n.a.
1975	31,596	n.a.	5,899	1,643	82,934	n.a.
1976	32,393	n.a.	4,832	2,765	85,662	n.a.
1977	33,980	n.a.	3,501	6,765	101,676	n.a.
1978	43,506	n.a.	3,697	12,017	123,637	n.a.
1979	51,300	n.a.	4,648	15,316	143,057	n.a.
1980	57,879	n.a.	5,478	16,962	153,363	n.a.
1981	61,578	717	6,326	19,897	162,069	n.a.
1982	72,981	14,450	5,999	42,952	166,109	n.a.
1983	78,383	25,121	8,995	57,720	176,636	n.a.
1984	87,798	35,738	13,778	70,026	192,425	593,985
1985	99,076	54,552	16,587	99,909	211,341	630,828
1986	99,621	95,568	23,229	169,186	238,484	607,806
1987	103,459	135,734	25,674	212,635	280,903	650,391
1988	112,258	170,097	34,352	226,406	320,028	717,651
1989	124,315	216,512	35,462	272,870	370,823	676,171
1990	133,113	288,075	40,579	316,359	421,524	621,716
1991	147,072	355,284	46,860	359,163	454,574	577,017

(Continued)

Table A.51 (*Continued*)

	Fannie Mae		Freddie Mac		Residential Real Estate Assets	
	Total Assets	Total MBS Outstanding	Total Assets	Total MBS Outstanding	Commercial Banks	Savings Institutions
1992	180,978	424,444	59,502	407,514	490,707	535,360
1993	216,979	471,306	83,880	439,029	545,557	520,042
1994	272,508	486,345	106,199	460,656	600,883	530,566
1995	316,550	513,230	137,181	459,045	661,778	537,636
1996	351,041	548,173	173,866	473,065	693,584	561,593
1997	391,673	579,138	194,597	475,985	759,994	564,610
1998	485,146	637,143	321,421	478,351	808,594	572,720
1999	575,308	679,145	386,684	537,883	892,614	587,988
2000	675,224	706,722	459,297	576,101	978,129	629,618
2001	799,948	863,445	641,100	653,084	1,029,101	658,265
2002	904,739	1,040,439	752,249	729,809	1,232,497	672,057
2003	1,022,275	1,300,520	803,449	752,164	1,358,311	750,478
2004	1,020,934	1,408,047	795,284	852,270	1,565,912	926,404
2005	834,168	1,598,918	806,222	974,200	1,755,454	1,009,383
2006	843,936	1,777,550	804,910	1,122,761	2,012,806	915,349
2007	882,547	2,118,909	794,368	1,381,863	2,123,098	932,366
Q1 2008	843,227	2,374,033	802,992	1,437,227	2,107,822	939,941
Q2 2008	885,918	2,442,886	879,043	1,409,896	2,067,486	944,292

SOURCES: FDIC, Fannie Mae, Freddie Mac, Milken Institute.

434

Table A.52 Median Percentage Down Payment on Home Purchases
(Selected MSAs, 2006)

	United States	10.0
1	Bellingham, WA	20.0
2	Corvallis, OR	20.0
3	Bend, OR	20.0
4	Manchester-Nashua, NH	20.0
5	Pittsfield, MA	20.0
6	Springfield, MA	20.0
7	Boston-Cambridge-Quincy, MA-NH	20.0
8	Worcester, MA	20.0
9	Barnstable Town, MA	20.0
10	Hartford–West Hartford–East Hartford, CT	20.0
11	Norwich–New London, CT	20.0
12	Bridgeport-Stamford-Norwalk, CT	20.0
13	New Haven–Milford, CT	20.0
14	Providence–New Bedford–Fall River, RI-MA	20.0
15	Boulder, CO	20.0
16	Virginia Beach–Norfolk–Newport News, VA-NC	20.0
17	Flagstaff, AZ	20.0
18	San Luis Obispo–Paso Robles, CA	20.0
19	Prescott, AZ	20.0
20	Atlanta–Sandy Springs–Marietta, GA	20.0
21	New Orleans–Metairie-Kenner, LA	20.0
22	Naples–Marco Island, FL	19.0
23	Vero Beach, FL	17.1
24	Chico, CA	14.9
25	Champaign-Urbana, IL	14.4
26	Ann Arbor, MI	13.5
27	New York–Northern New Jersey–Long Island, NY-NJ-PA	13.3
28	Santa Cruz–Watsonville, CA	13.1
29	Myrtle Beach–Conway–North Myrtle Beach, SC	12.5
30	Punta Gorda, FL	12.1
31	Sarasota-Bradenton-Venice, FL	11.9
32	Mount Vernon–Anacortes, WA	10.1
33	Spokane, WA	10.1
34	Bremerton-Silverdale, WA	10.1
35	Medford, OR	10.1
36	Redding, CA	10.1
37	Sacramento-Arden-Arcade-Roseville, CA	10.1
38	Seattle-Tacoma-Bellevue, WA	10.0

(Continued)

Table A.52 (*Continued*)

	United States	10.0
39	Olympia, WA	10.0
40	Portland–Vancouver–Beaverton, OR–WA	10.0
41	Eugene–Springfield, OR	10.0
42	Detroit–Warren–Livonia, MI	10.0
43	Chicago–Naperville–Joliet, IL–IN–WI	10.0
44	Rockford, IL	10.0
45	Reno–Sparks, NV	10.0
46	Allentown–Bethlehem–Easton, PA–NJ	10.0
47	Fort Collins–Loveland, CO	10.0
48	Philadelphia–Camden–Wilmington, PA–NJ–DE–MD	10.0
49	Lancaster, PA	10.0
50	Atlantic City, NJ	10.0

SOURCE: Zillow.com.

Table A.53   Comparison of Home Mortgage Databases

LoanPerformance Database

- Time span: since 1998.
- Number of records: 4.3 million subprime loans reported by more than 20 subprime securitizers.
- Data items: loan amount, interest rate, borrower FICO scores, appraised value of the security property, borrower income and loan quality, information on delinquency and foreclosure, state of origins, and zip code. Does not include race, ethnicity, sex, or age.

Problems/known issues:

Tracks only loans that have been securitized.

American Financial Services Association (AFSA) Subprime Database

- Time span: July 1995–December 2004.
- Number of records: 5.4 million subprime loans from eight major subprime originators.
- Data items: APR, FICO score, borrower age, loan amount, property zip code, whether the loan is a first or subordinate lien, information on delinquency, foreclosure and write off, prepayment, etc.

Problems/known issues:

- Covers fewer lenders.
- Snapshots of loans outstanding, which makes it impossible to track a single loan across time.
- Subprime loans are identified using certain borrower characteristics.
- Most loans covered by AFSA database are also securitized.

HMDA Data

- Derived from reports by financial institutions to the government in compliance with the Home Mortgage Disclosure Act (HMDA).
- Who reports to HMDA: All depository institutions and banking holding companies subsidiaries, and some for-profit mortgage companies.
- Time span: since 1989.
- Number of records: 36.4 million loans reported by 8,848 institutions (2006).
- Data items: loan amount, the census tract where the secured property is located, whether the security property is owner occupied, whether the loan is a HOEPA loan, race/ethnicity of the borrowers. Does not include FICO scores, loan-to-value ratios, the value of the property, points, whether the loan was adjustable or fixed, and other pricing-related variables.

(Continued)

Table A.53 (*Continued*)

Problems/known issues:

- Methodology used to modify HMDA data changes year by year.
- HUD identifies lenders as "prime" or "subprime."
- Since 2004, the HUD list is restricted to subprime lender specialists.
- Only lenders that report under HMDA are included in HUD's subprime lender list.

Inside Mortgage Finance

- Most historical data go back at least 10 years, with some exceptions. The data are current through the end of 2006.
- Includes aggregate data on originations, purchases, sales, delinquencies, foreclosures, private mortgage insurance, top originators, and servicers.
- Covers mortgage-related securities markets, including ABS and MBS markets.

Problems/known issues

- Mostly aggregate level data. Limited data at state level.
- Data frequency: annual.
- Source of data unknown.

MBA National Delinquency Survey

- Based on a sample of more than 44 million mortgage loans serviced by mortgage companies, commercial banks, thrifts, credit unions, and others, NDS provides quarterly delinquency and foreclosure statistics at the national, regional, and state levels.
- Delinquency and foreclosure measures are broken out into loan type (prime, subprime, VA, and FHA) and fixed- and adjustable rate products.
- Seven measures: total delinquencies, delinquency by past due category (30–59 days, 60–89 days, and 90 days and over), new foreclosures, foreclosure inventory, and seriously delinquent. The total number of loans serviced each quarter is also included in the data.

MBA Weekly Applications Survey

- Contains 15 indices covering application activity for fixed-rate, adjustable rate, conventional, and government loans for home purchases and refinances.
- The weekly data dates back from 1990 through the most current week.
- Also includes percentage changes in number and dollar volume of applications from a week, a month, and a year; average loan size; average contract interest rates and corresponding points for six popular mortgage products; the refinance and ARM shares of applications (by application number and dollar amount).

Source: Milken Institute.

438

Table A.54 HOPE NOW Alliance Program: Accumulated Borrower
(Q3 2007–Q3 2008)

Number of Loans	2007 Q3	2007 Q4	2008 Q1	2008 Q2	2008 Q3	Total
Repayment plans	322,909	333,393	312,225	302,561	335,572	1,606,659
Prime	120,254	136,364	146,586	141,836	179,042	724,081
Subprime	202,656	197,029	165,639	160,725	156,530	882,578
Modifications	75,326	140,401	170,090	220,326	257,444	863,587
Prime	29,999	37,162	48,022	56,179	70,283	241,644
Subprime	45,327	103,239	122,068	164,147	187,161	621,943
Workout plans	398,236	473,794	482,315	522,887	593,016	2,470,246
Prime	150,253	173,526	194,607	198,015	249,325	965,725
Subprime	247,983	300,268	287,708	324,872	343,691	1,504,521

SOURCE: HOPE NOW Alliance.

Table A.55 HOPE NOW Alliance Program: Accumulated Foreclosure Sales
(Q3 2007–Q3 2008)

	2007 Q3	2007 Q4	2008 Q1	2008 Q2	2008 Q3	Total
Foreclosure sales	135,330	151,403	202,970	246,192	264,139	1,000,033
Prime	53,760	59,750	82,819	108,202	130,377	434,908
Subprime	81,570	91,653	120,151	137,990	133,762	565,125

SOURCE: HOPE NOW Alliance.

Table A.56 Countries with Single vs. Multiple Supervisory Authorities

Income Level	Single Supervisor					Multiple Supervisors	
High Income	Anguilla	Cyprus	Hong Kong, China	Liechtenstein	Singapore	Netherlands	Saudi Arabia
	Antigua and Barbuda	Czech Republic	Iceland	Luxembourg	Slovenia	South Korea	United States
	Australia	Denmark	Ireland	Macau, China	Spain		
	Austria	Estonia	Isle of Man	Malta	Switzerland		
	Bahrain	Finland	Israel	Montserrat	Taiwan, China		
	Belgium	France	Italy	New Zealand	Trinidad and Tobago		
	Canada	Germany	Japan	Norway	United Kingdom		
	Cayman Islands	Greece	Kuwait	Portugal	Sweden		
Upper Middle Income	Argentina	Costa Rica	Grenada	Lithuania	Seychelles	Malaysia	
	Belize	Croatia	Hungary	Mauritius	Slovak Republic		
	Botswana	Dominica	Kazakhstan	Mexico	St. Kitts and Nevis		
	Brazil	Equatorial Guinea	Latvia	Oman	St. Lucia		

Income group						
	Bulgaria	Romania	Lebanon	Poland	St. Vincent and the Grenadines	
	Chile	Gabon	South Africa	Russia	Uruguay	
	Panama					
Lower Middle Income	Guatemala	Bosnia and Herzegovina	Egypt	Lesotho	Peru	
	Algeria	Cameroon	El Salvador	Macedonia, FYR	Philippines	
	Angola	China	Fiji	Maldives	Sri Lanka	
	Armenia	Colombia	Guyana	Moldova	Suriname	
	Belarus	Jordan	Honduras	Morocco	Syrian	
	Bhutan	Congo	Indonesia	Nicaragua	Thailand	
	Bolivia	Dominican Republic	Jamaica			
Low Income	Bangladesh	Chad	India	Pakistan	Togo	Nigeria
	Benin	Côte d'Ivoire	Kenya	Senegal	Uganda	Zimbabwe
	Burkina Faso	Ethiopia	Kyrgyz Republic	Tajikistan	Mali	
	Burundi	Ghana	Malawi	Tanzania	Niger	
	Central African Republic	Guinea-Bissau	Mozambique			

SOURCES: Bank Regulation and Supervision Survey III from World Bank. Unless otherwise indicated, information is for 2005.
NOTE: Economies are classified according to 2007 GNI per capita, calculated using the World Bank Atlas method.

Table A.57 Countries with the Central Bank as a Supervisory Authority

Income Level	Central Bank Only					Central Bank among Multiple Supervisors		Central Bank Not a Supervisory Authority			
High Income	Anguilla	Estonia	Israel	Montserrat	Slovenia	Netherlands	South Korea	Australia	Denmark	Isle of Man	Norway
	Antigua and Barbuda	Germany	Italy	New Zealand	Spain	Saudi Arabia	United States	Bahrain	Finland	Japan	Sweden
	Austria	Greece	Kuwait	Portugal	Taiwan, China			Belgium	France	Luxembourg	Switzerland
	Cyprus	Hong Kong, China	Liechtenstein	Singapore	Trinidad & Tobago			Canada	Iceland	Macau, China	United Kingdom
	Czech Republic							Cayman Islands	Ireland	Malta	
Upper Middle Income	Argentina	Bulgaria	Lithuania	Russia	St. Kitts and Nevis	Malaysia		Chile	Gabon	Latvia	Panama
	Belize	Croatia	Mauritius	Seychelles	St. Lucia			Costa Rica	Hungary	Lebanon	Poland
	Botswana	Dominica	Oman	Slovak Republic	St. Vincent and the Grenadines			Equatorial Guinea	Kazakhstan	Mexico	
	Brazil	Grenada	Romania	South Africa	Uruguay						
	Algeria										
Lower Middle Income	Angola	Egypt	Jamaica	Maldives	Sri Lanka			Bolivia	China	Dominican Republic	Honduras
	Armenia	Fiji	Jordan	Moldova	Suriname			Bosnia and Herzegovina	Colombia	El Salvador	Nicaragua
	Belarus	Guyana	Lesotho	Morocco	Syrian			Cameroon	Congo	Guatemala	Peru
	Bhutan	Indonesia	Macedonia, FYR	Philippines	Thailand						
Low Income	Bangladesh	Ghana	Kyrgyz Republic	Tajikistan	Pakistan	Nigeria	Zimbabwe	Benin	Chad	Mali	Senegal
	Burundi	India	Malawi	Tanzania	Uganda			Burkina Faso	Côte d'Ivoire	Niger	Togo
	Ethiopia	Kenya	Mozambique					Central African Republic	Guinea-Bissau		

SOURCES: Bank Regulation and Supervision Survey III from World Bank. Unless otherwise indicated, information is for 2005.
NOTE: Economies are classified according to 2007 GNI per capita, calculated using the World Bank Atlas method.

Table A.58 Scope of Supervisory Authority for Countries

Income Level	Only Banks	All of the Main Financial Institutions
High Income	Anguilla, Antigua and Barbuda, Canada, Cyprus, Finland, France, Greece, Hong Kong, China, Isle of Man, Israel, Italy, Kuwait, Luxembourg, Montserrat, Netherlands, New Zealand, Portugal, Saudi Arabia, Slovenia, South Korea, Spain, Switzerland, United States	Australia, Austria, Bahrain, Belgium, Cayman Islands, Czech Republic, Denmark, Estonia, Germany, Iceland, Ireland, Japan, Liechtenstein, Macau, China, Malta, Norway, Singapore, Sweden, Taiwan, China, Trinidad & Tobago, United Kingdom
Upper Middle Income	Argentina, Belize, Botswana, Brazil, Bulgaria, Chile, Croatia, Dominica, Equatorial Guinea, Gabon, Grenada, Lebanon, Mauritius, Mexico, Oman, Panama, Poland, Romania, Seychelles, Slovak Republic, South Africa, St. Kitts and Nevis, St. Lucia, St. Vincent and the Grenadines	Hungary, Uruguay, Kazakhstan, Latvia, Malaysia
Lower Middle Income	Costa Rica, Algeria, Angola, Belarus, Lithuania, Congo, Dominican Republic, Egypt, Russia, Jamaica, Jordan, Macedonia, FYR, Sri Lanka, Suriname, Syrian	Armenia, Bhutan, Bosnia and Herzegovina, Colombia, Fiji, Guatemala, Honduras, Lesotho, Maldives, Nicaragua, Peru
Low Income	Bolivia, Cameroon, China, El Salvador, Guyana, Indonesia, Moldova, Morocco, Philippines, Thailand, Bangladesh, Benin, Burkina Faso, Burundi, Central African Republic, Chad, Côte d'Ivoire, Ethiopia, Ghana, Guinea-Bissau, India, Kenya, Kyrgyz Republic, Mali, Mozambique, Niger, Nigeria, Pakistan, Senegal, Tajikistan, Tanzania, Togo, Uganda, Zimbabwe	Malawi

SOURCES: Bank Regulation and Supervision Survey III from World Bank. Unless otherwise indicated, information is for 2005.

NOTE: Economies are classified according to 2007 GNI per capita, calculated using the World BankAtlas method.

Endnotes

Chapter 2   Overview of the Housing and Mortgage Markets

1. The United States is generally expected to gain between 1.2 million and 1.5 million households each year due to rising birth and immigration rates.

2. A housing unit is generally defined as a house, apartment, group of rooms, or single room occupied or intended for occupancy as separate living quarters. A more comprehensive definition can be found in the Glossary.

3. Throughout this report, the term *home* is used to refer to a single-family housing unit, in contrast to a single- and multifamily, or residential, housing unit.

4. The housing unit value, adjusted for inflation, increased nearly ninefold, whereas the U.S. population roughly doubled over the period.

5. In 1983, Freddie Mac and Fannie Mae issued the first collateralized mortgage obligation (CMO) with three separate tranches (categories organized by relative risk) of securities. Each successive lower tranche received payments only after the higher tranche had been paid off.

6. See Tables A.10 and A.11 in the Appendix for information on the importance of private-label securitizers in comparison to Ginnie Mae and the two government-sponsored enterprises (GSEs), Fannie Mae and Freddie Mac.

7. One way to provide an incentive for originators to be more selective with respect to borrowers is to require that representations and warrants be provided by them.

8. The real short-term federal funds rate was actually negative from the fall of 2002 to May 2005.

9. Of course, the movements between the one-year ARM rate and the target federal funds rates are far from perfect and contemporaneous, because the simple correlation between these two variables is −0.39.

Chapter 3 Buildup and Meltdown of the Mortgage and Credit Markets

1. Mark Doms, Frederick Furlong, and John Krainer, "House Prices and Subprime Mortgage Delinquencies," FRBSF Economic Letter, June 8, 2007.

2. A FICO score is a widely used numerical score developed by the Fair Isaac Corporation to express the quality of a consumer's credit history. It does not consider race, ethnicity, religion, national origin, sex, or marital status; age; salary, occupation, title, employer, date employed, or employment history; address; the interest rate being charged on a particular credit card or other account; items reported as child/family support obligations or rental agreements; certain types of inquiries (requests for credit report or score); any information not found in a credit report; and other information that has not been shown to be predictive of future credit performance. The three major credit bureaus are Equifax, Experian, and TransUnion, each of which creates its own version of the FICO score using its propriety information collected from credit reports.

3. Federal Register (2002). July 12, 2002. See Figure A.9 in the Appendix for the Department of Housing and Urban Development (HUD) subprime and manufactured home lender list from 1992 to 2005.

4. FDIC press release, "Statement on Subprime Mortgage Lending" (PR-55-2007), June 29, 2007.

5. Center for Responsible Lending, "Subprime Lending: A Net Drain on Home-ownership," March 27, 2007.

6. James Barth et al., "Despite Foreclosures, Subprime Lending Increases Home-ownership," *Perspectives on the Subprime Market* (Milken Institute, 2008).

7. Remarks by Federal Reserve Governor Edward M. Gramlich, Texas Association of Bank Counsel 27th Annual Convention, South Padre Island, Texas, October 9, 2003; available at http://www.federalreserve.gov/boarddocs/speeches/2003/20031009/default.htm (accessed December 2, 2008).

8. RealtyTrac press release, July 30, 2007, http://www.realtytrac.com/ContentManagement/pressrelease.aspx?ChannelID=9&ItemID=2932&accnt=64847 (accessed November 19, 2008).

9. It should be noted that foreclosures impose costs on individuals. Credit scores drop and as a result, getting future credit becomes more difficult and costly. The scores may also drop even when a lender agrees to allow a borrower to sell a home in a *short sale,* which means the house is sold at a price below the mortgage amount. In some states, moreover, lenders can go after borrowers for unpaid mortgage balances.

Chapter 4 When Will the Crisis End?

1. Testimony by Peter Orszag, director of the Congressional Budget Office, before the House Committee on Education and Labor, October 7, 2008,

http://www.cbo.gov/ftpdocs/98xx/doc9864/10-07-Retirement Security_
Testimony.1.1.shtml (accessed December 1, 2008). Also described at the CBO
director's blog, http://cboblog.cbo.gov/?p=176.

Chapter 5 What Went Wrong … ?

1. David C. Wheelock, "The Federal Response to Home Mortgage Distress:
   Lessons from the Great Depression," in *The Federal Reserve Bank of St. Louis
   Review* 90 (3): 133–48.

2. Panel discussion, "Recent Financial Market Disruptions: Implications for
   the Economy and American Families," The Brookings Institution, September 26, 2007 (transcript available at http://www.brookings.edu/events/2007/
   0926monetary-policy.aspx).

3. It should be noted that only six U.S. S&P 500 companies had a AAA rating in
   October 2008.

4. Helen Coster and Daniel Fisher, "Burnout: Does General Electric Deserve Its
   AAA Rating?," *Forbes,* October 27, 2008.

5. See http://securities.stanford.edu/news-archive/2004/20040428_Headline08_
   Drawbaugh.htm.

6. U.S. Securities and Exchange Commission, press release 2008-230, September
   26, 2008 (accessed at http://www.sec.gov/news/press/2008/2008-230.htm).

7. Lawrence Summers, "The Big Freeze, Part 4: A U.S. Recovery," *Financial
   Times,* August 6, 2008.

8. It is not clear that raising the limits on the size of the mortgage loans to $625,000
   in 2006 can be consistent with this goal, with temporary limits even higher at
   $729,750.

9. http://www.ofheo.gov/NewsRoom_Print.aspx?ID=388

10. FDIC press release, "FDIC Implements Loan Modification Program for Dis-
    tressed IndyMac Mortgage Loans," available at http://www.fdic.gov/news/
    news/press/2008/pr08067.html (accessed December 1, 2008).

11. It was reported that the FDIC has generally offered to reduce borrowers'
    interest rates or stretch the terms of their loans to as long as 40 years, but few
    offers have involved a reduction in principal (*The Wall Street Journal,* October
    8, 2008). A problem with principal-balance reductions is that they are likely
    to encourage nondefaulting homeowners to default in an attempt to secure
    similar reductions.

12. See, for example, Barr (2005) and Hyeton (2006).

13. The foreclosure start rate is defined as the number of loans originated in a given
    year that enter foreclosure proceedings during a certain time period, relative to
    the total number of same type of loans originated in the same year.

Chapter 6   So Far, Only Piecemeal Fixes

1. The advantage of deposits is that interest payments typically accrue in the accounts rather than being paid out as cash.

2. It should be noted that the actual federal funds rate has recently been lower than the target rate and even negative when adjusted for inflation.

3. Beginning March 7, 2008, funds provided through the Single-Tranche Open Market Operations (OMO) Program are made available weekly for a term of 28 days—longer than the overnight to 14-day term of conventional OMO. Also, on July 30, 2008, the Fed extended its emergency lending programs to Wall Street firms through January 2009, after policymakers judged that markets were still "fragile."

4. Note that state guaranty associations, which were established about 40 years ago, exist in all states and are funded by the insurers in each state. These associations cover claims up to the policy limits or limits set by state law in the event an insurance company fails.

5. Alison Vekshin and Alison Fitzgerald, "Bush Said to Tell Aides He Won't Seek Bailout Funds," *Bloomberg News*, November 17, 2008.

6. Justin Baer, "GE Tests Fed's New Commercial Paper Facility," *Financial Times,* October 28, 2008.

7. On November 7, 2008, *Bloomberg News* filed suit in the U.S. District Court, Southern District of New York (Manhattan), to force the Federal Reserve to disclose securities it is accepting as collateral for all the loans it has made to banks.

8. State and local governments are also taking steps to deal with the current crisis. For example, California passed enacted a new state law (SB1137) in July 2008 that prevents lenders from initiating foreclosure proceeding until 30 days after satisfying due diligence requirements to contact the borrower. (http://www.leginfo.ca.gov/pub/07-08/bill/sen/sb_1101-1150/sb_1137_bill_20080708_chaptered.html.)

9. See Mortgage Bankers Association, http://www.mortgagebankers.org/NewsandMedia/PressCenter/64098.htm.

10. Scott Reckard, "Government's Mortgage Relief Program Gets Few Takers," *Los Angeles Times,* November 5, 2008.

11. http://www.usdoj.gov/olc/esf2.htm

12. On June 13, 2007, the SEC removed Rule 10a-1, which provided that, subject to certain exceptions, a security may be sold short (A) at a price above the price at which the immediately preceding sale was effected (plus tick) or (B) at the last sale price if it is higher that the last different price (zero-plus tick). Short sales are not permitted on minus ticks or zero-minus ticks, subject to narrow

exceptions. It also removed any short sale price test of any self-regulatory organization. http://www.sec.gov/news/press/2007/2007-114.htm

13. "PNC Buys National City in Bank Shakeout," *The Wall Street Journal,* October 27, 2008, and http://pnc.mediaroom.com/index.php?s=43&item=591.

14. Evan Halper, "Bush's Tax Breaks for Banks Could Cost California $2 Billion," *Los Angeles Times,* November 11, 2008. See also Stephen Ohlemacher, "Banks Reap Big Tax Breaks Atop Bailout Billions," Associated Press, November 10, 2008, and Lynnley Browning, "Treasury to Review New Tax Break Plan," *The New York Times,* November 18, 2008.

15. In 1980, the U.S. Congress expanded deposit insurance to $100,000 from $40,000.

16. Statement by FDIC chairman Sheila Bair at U.S. Treasury, Federal Reserve, and FDIC joint press conference, October 14, 2008; available at http://www.fdic.gov/news/news/press/2008/pr08100a.html (accessed December 2, 2008).

17. It is interesting that in some years the FDIC set the rates that many banks pay for deposit insurance at zero. In 2006, for example, 95 percent of all the insured depository institutions paid no premiums. Clearly, providing coverage but yet charging no premiums is not typically a good business model. Furthermore, lowering premiums in good times and raising them in bad times result in procyclical assessments.

18. On November 12, 2008, the FDIC approved GE Capital to participate in the TLGP. Participants in this program benefit from lowering the cost of debt.

19. http://federalreserve.gov/newsevents/testimony/bernanke200810 20a.htm

Chapter 7 Where Should We Go from Here?

1. *IMF Survey,* Vol. 37, No. 10, October 2008, 151.

Glossary

125 loan   A loan program that allows homeowners to borrow up to 125 percent of their property's value, even if they hold little or no equity. These loans are typically used for home improvements or debt consolidation. Interest rates and loan amounts are sensitive to the borrower's credit score.

20-20 mortgage   A 40-year mortgage in which the interest rate resets after 20 years. The initial interest rate is likely to be lower than that of a traditional 30-year loan.

3/2 down payment   A program offered by some lenders allowing borrowers who secure a grant or gift equal to 2 percent of 'their down payment to provide only a 3 percent down payment from their own funds.

Abstract   See *Title search.*

Acceleration clause   A contractual provision that gives the lender the right to demand repayment of the entire loan balance if the borrower defaults or violates certain terms in the note.

Accrued interest   Interest that has accumulated but has yet to be paid.

A credit   The best credit rating. Consumers with A credit qualify for the lowest interest rates that lenders offer. Most lenders define this group as borrowers with FICO scores above 720. Consumers can pay a penalty for falling below this threshold.

Adjustable-rate mortgage (ARM)   A mortgage that allows the lender to change the interest rate after an introductory period. Most ARMs have limitations, or caps, on the frequency and/or magnitude of interest rate resets. There are several different categories of ARMs. In the United States, most ARM rates are pegged to a preselected benchmark index (e.g., LIBOR). These are commonly referred to as *indexed ARMs* (see definition). *Hybrid ARMs* (see definition) combine fixed and variable rates; an example of a hybrid is the 2/28 mortgage. For the first two years, its interest rate is fixed, but for the remaining life of the mortgage, rates float relative to an index, although caps may apply. In an *option ARM* (see definition), the borrower chooses which payment to make each month: a low specified minimum payment, an interest-only payment, or a 15- or 30-year fixed-rate payment. Choosing the minimum payment can add to the loan balance, resulting in *negative amortization* (see definition).

Adjustment interval   In an adjustable-rate mortgage, the time between changes (adjustments) in the interest rate or monthly payment. It is often displayed in "x/y" format, where "x" is the period until the first adjustment and "y" is the adjustment period thereafter. For example, in a 5/1 ARM, the initial rate holds for five years, after which the rate adjusts every year. The rate adjustment interval and the payment adjustment interval are the same on a fully amortizing ARM (see *Fully amortized payment*) but may differ on a negative amortization ARM (see *Negative amortization*).

Adverse selection   Asymmetry of information between buyers and sellers, with advantages realized by the better-informed party. Adverse selection problems can lead to market distortions. They arose in the mortgage market when lenders sold mortgage products to borrowers who did not comprehend the terms or when investors bought mortgage-backed securities without realizing the true composition or risk levels associated with these investment vehicles.

Affordability   A measurement of whether a home's price reasonably falls within a buyer's capacity to carry the required mortgage.

Alt-A   A category of mortgage risk that falls between prime and subprime; also referred to as A-minus.

Alternative documentation loans   Loans requiring documentation to back up the application but with simplified requirements that are designed to speed up the approval process. Instead of verifying with the applicant's employer, for example, a lender might accept paycheck stubs or W-2s. Though their requirements relaxed traditional standards, these transactions called for a higher level of vetting than *low-documentation or no-documentation loans* (see definition).

Amortization The process of paying off a loan in installments over time.

Amortization schedule A table showing each mortgage payment over the life of a loan, with the ratio of interest to principal decreasing over time until the balance is fully paid.

Amount financed On the "Truth in Lending" form, the amount financed is the actual loan amount minus finance charges (such as points) paid at or before closing. For example, if the loan is for $100,000 and the borrower prepays $4,000 in fees, the amount financed is $96,000.

Annual percentage rate (APR) The full cost of borrowing, calculated as a yearly rate across the full life of the loan and including all finance charges. This standardized measurement allows borrowers to compare different loan options, evaluating, for example, whether a mortgage with a higher interest rate but lower fees might be a better deal than a loan with a lower rate but high fees. The APR must be reported by lenders under "Truth in Lending" regulations.

Appraisal A written estimate of a property's current market value, prepared by a licensed professional. Lenders require appraisals as part of the loan approval process, and the fee is usually charged to the buyer at closing.

ARM See *Adjustable-rate mortgage.*

Asset-backed security (ABS) A bond or note backed by cash flow from a pool of loans or accounts receivable originated by banks, credit card companies, or other providers of credit (not first-lien mortgages).

Assignee liability Provisions in state and federal antipredatory lending laws that expressly hold purchasers or securitizers of loans liable for violations of the law committed by the originator and/or makes them party to lawsuits brought by borrowers who were victimized by predatory loans.

Assignment Document that shows which company has interest in a mortgage loan.

Assumable mortgage A mortgage contract that does not prohibit a creditworthy buyer from assuming the seller's ownership and obligations. Assuming a loan will save the buyer money if the rate on the existing loan is below the current market rate; closing costs are avoided as well. A loan with a "due-on-sale" clause stipulating that the mortgage must be repaid upon sale of the property is not assumable.

Balloon mortgage A mortgage that is payable in full after a specified period that is shorter than the term. In most cases, the balance due is then refinanced. On a 7-year balloon mortgage, for example, the monthly payment is usually calculated on a 30-year amortization schedule, but the balance remaining at the end of the seventh year comes due in a lump sum that must be repaid or refinanced at that time. Balloon mortgages are similar to ARMs in that the borrower benefits from a lower rate in the early years in exchange for assuming the risk of incurring a higher rate later. These loans are riskier than ARMs because there is no limit on the extent of the rate increase possible when the balloon payment comes due.

Bond covenants Legal restrictions in bond indentures that bind the issuer in various ways to prevent undercutting repayment ability.

Book value An accounting valuation of an asset, based on the price paid minus depreciation or amortization. This valuation is usually very different from the asset's market value.

Buy-down The payment of *points* (see definition) in exchange for a lower interest rate. A temporary buy-down concentrates the rate reduction in the early years of a mortgage's term.

Buy-up Payment at a higher interest rate in exchange for a rebate by the lender that reduces upfront costs.

Cash-out refinancing Refinancing for an amount that exceeds the balance on the existing loan plus settlement costs, allowing the borrower to take cash out of the transaction. This method of refinancing is an alternative to a home equity loan or a home equity line of credit.

CDO See *Collateralized debt obligation*.

CDO-squared A type of asset-backed security that is constructed from CDOs (see *Collateralized debt obligation*). A CDO-squared can be further combined into an asset called a "CDO-cubed."

CDR Counterparty Risk Index An index created by Credit Derivatives Research LLC to measures the default risk carried by the 15 major banks and brokers who are counterparties to most of the contracts traded in the credit default swap market.

COFI Cost of Funds Index. A regional interest rate index, one of many benchmarks that can be used to determine interest rate resets on an adjustable-rate mortgage.

Collateral An asset pledged as security to guarantee a loan or bond in case of default.

Collateralized debt obligation (CDO) A security constructed from a portfolio of fixed-income assets, such as mortgages. CDOs are unregulated and can have extremely complex structures. Rating firms often slice their risk associated with these investment vehicles into different classes or *tranches* (see definition): senior tranches (rated AAA), mezzanine tranches (AA to BB), and equity tranches (unrated). Investors in these different tranches absorb losses in reverse order of seniority; because equity tranches carry a higher risk of default, they offer higher "coupons" (interest rates) in return.

Collateralized mortgage obligation (CMO) A special-purpose entity set up as the legal owner of a portfolio of mortgages. CMOs issue bonds to investors (who buy into different *tranches* or categories of risk; see definition), with the mortgages themselves serving as collateral.

Commercial paper An unsecured promissory note that matures on a specified date within nine months of issuance. Typically issued by corporations to cover short-term debt such as operating expenses, commercial paper is not usually secured by collateral and is not regulated by the Securities and Exchange Commission.

Common stock Ownership shares in public corporations. Also called ordinary shares, they are the most widely held type of equity.

Conduit loans Commercial real estate loans specifically intended to be pooled with other loans to form an investment vehicle called a commercial mortgage-backed security (CMBS).

Conforming loan A mortgage loan that meets standards set by the Office of Federal Housing Enterprise Oversight (OFHEO) for purchase by Fannie Mae and Freddie Mac. These loans have debt-to-income ratio limits and documentation requirements and must fall below a specific maximum loan amount. Lenders offer their best interest rates on conforming loans, because the ability of Fannie Mae and Freddie Mac to buy these mortgages creates baseline demand in the secondary market. Loans that are larger than the maximum conforming amount are called *jumbo mortgages* (see definition).

Conventional mortgage   Although many sources use the term interchangeably with the *conforming loan* (see definition above), it has an additional meaning, which is used in this book; a conforming home mortgage that is not insured by the FHA or the VA.

Conversion option   The option to convert an adjustable-rate mortgage to a fixed-rate mortgage at a specific point in the life of the loan. These loans are likely to carry higher interest rates or points than ARMs without this option.

Convertible bond   A bond that can be converted into equity shares of a company under certain conditions.

Convertible preferred shares   Corporate fixed-income securities that can be converted into a predetermined number of shares of common stock at a specified interval. These investments combine steady income with the chance to benefit from a rising stock price.

Core capital   A measurement of a bank's financial soundness that includes common equity, preferred stock that cannot be redeemed, and retained earnings. Regulators set requirements for core capital, which is also called Tier 1 capital.

Corporate governance   The system of rules and processes that governs a corporation's operations. This structure ensures that the organization functions within applicable laws and regulations while also addressing issues of accountability, transparency, ethics, and conflicts of interest.

Cost of capital   The rate of return needed to make a capital investment worthwhile, taking into account opportunity cost.

Coverage ratio   A bank's ratio of loan–loss reserves to delinquent loans.

Credit default swap   A contract allowing an investor to hedge against defaults on debt payments. Credit default swaps are currently settled directly between the two parties to a contract, as opposed to handled by a central clearinghouse. The resulting lack of transparency in this market added to worries about the solvency of major investors.

Credit enhancements   Provisions that reduce the credit risk of an investment vehicle. These may include posting collaterals or obtaining loan guarantees or credit insurance. They may be provided by a third party (external credit enhancements) or by the originator (internal credit enhancements), and more than one type of provision may be associated with a given issuance.

Credit report   A report from a credit bureau containing detailed information on an individual's credit and bill-paying history. Mortgage lenders typically order a credit report for each borrower, and closing costs may include a fee for doing so. The three major U.S. credit reporting agencies are Equifax, TransUnion, and Experian.

Credit score   A single numerical score that expresses an individual consumer's creditworthiness, based on their credit history. A higher score carries a lower risk of default. The most widely used version is the FICO score, developed by the Fair Isaac Corporation.

Credit spread   The yield spread between similar securities with different credit quality; especially used to differentiate Treasury securities and non-Treasury securities.

Debt consolidation   Rolling existing debt (such as credit card or student loan balances) into a new loan (typically a home mortgage).

Debt-to-income ratio   A consumer's total monthly debt payments (including mortgage, credit cards, car loans, student loans, and other obligations) measured as a percentage of monthly gross income. Mortgage lenders typically prefer to keep debt-to-income ratios below 30 to 40 percent.

Deed in lieu of foreclosure   A mechanism for a borrower in default to transfer ownership of their property back to the lender while avoiding foreclosure. This process releases the borrower from all obligations while saving the lender the time and effort of a formal foreclosure proceeding.

Default   Failure of the borrower to honor the terms of the loan agreement. Lenders (and the law) usually view borrowers whose payments are more than 90 days delinquent as being in default.

Deleveraging   The act of reducing, or "unwinding," excessive leverage to lower risk and strengthen the balance sheet through selling assets and paying off debt. When many institutions and firms undertake deleveraging all at once, credit may be constrained and asset values may deflate rapidly.

Delinquency ratio (or rates)   The ratio of the number or value of loans with past due balances to the total number or value of loans outstanding.

Delinquency   A mortgage payment that is more than 30 days late.

Deposit Insurance Fund (DIF)   In 2006 the Bank Insurance Fund (BIF) and the Savings Association Insurance Fund (SAIF) were merged to form the Deposit Insurance Fund (DIF). Premiums paid by insured banks and savings institutions are pooled to form this reserve fund, which the Federal Deposit Insurance Corporation (FDIC) uses to guarantee deposits up to a certain size.

Derivatives, notional amount   The amounts used to calculate contractual cash flows to be exchanged; the total value of a leveraged position's assets.

Discount mortgage broker   A mortgage broker who claims to be compensated entirely by the lender rather than by the borrower for securing a loan.

Discretionary ARM   An adjustable-rate mortgage on which the lender has the right to change the interest rate at any time, subject only to advance notice. Discretionary ARMs are offered in Europe but not in the United States.

Down payment   An initial cash payment tendered as part of a home purchase, usually expressed as a percentage of the total purchase price. A 20 percent down payment was once the industry standard, but during the housing boom, lenders relaxed those requirements, offering some mortgage products with no down payment at all.

Due–on–sale clause   A provision in a mortgage loan contract stipulating that if the property is sold, the loan balance must be repaid at the time of sale. This bars the seller from transferring the remaining obligations of an existing loan to the buyer, protecting the lender from a situation in which the interest rate on the old loan is below current market rate. A loan agreement with a due–on–sale clause is not an *assumable mortgage* (see definition).

Equity   In connection with a home, the owner's level of ownership. It is calculated as the difference between the current market value of the home and the balance of outstanding mortgage loans.

Escrow   An agreement placing money with a third-party agent for safe keeping, pending the performance of some promised act by one of the parties to the agreement. Down payments may be held in escrow until a home sale closes. Some types of home mortgages include escrow agreements requiring borrowers to add specified amounts for taxes and insurance to their regular monthly mortgage payments. That money is held in an escrow account, from which the lender pays the taxes and insurance when they come due.

Estimated insured deposits   The FDIC states that, in general, insured deposits are total domestic deposits minus estimated uninsured deposits. Uninsured deposits are in accounts where balances exceed FDIC insurance limits.

Failed/assisted institutions   A bank or savings association is deemed to have failed when regulators seize control of the institution, placing its assets and liabilities into a bridge bank, conservatorship, receivership, or another healthy institution. This action may require the FDIC to provide funds to cover losses. An institution is defined as "assisted" when the institution remains open and receives some insurance funds to continue operating.

Fair value accounting   A method of accounting that calls for assets to be valued according to current market value rather than according to historical cost.

Fannie Mae   The Federal National Mortgage Association (FNMA), a publicly traded corporation founded during the Great Depression and chartered by Congress as a government-sponsored enterprise (GSE) in 1968. Fannie Mae does not directly issue home loans, but operates in the secondary mortgage market, buying and guaranteeing *conforming loans* (see definition). Its presence provides liquidity to mortgage originators, freeing up funds for mortgage companies, savings and loans, commercial banks, credit unions, and state and local housing finance agencies to increase lending to greater numbers of home buyers. Fannie Mae and *Freddie Mac* (see definition) held or backed approximately half of the $12 trillion U.S. mortgage market in 2008. After sustaining huge losses, the two GSEs were placed in conservatorship in September 2008, under the supervision of the Federal Housing Finance Agency.

Federal Deposit Insurance Corporation (FDIC)   An independent federal agency created in 1933 in response to a wave of bank failures. The FDIC provides insurance that guarantees the safety of deposits in thousands of member banks and thrifts. In October 2008, the coverage limit was temporarily raised from $100,000 to $250,000 per depositor, per institution; that limit is scheduled to return to $100,000 at the end of 2009.

Federal funds rate   The interest rate at which depository institutions lend balances to each other overnight. The Federal Open Market Committee establishes the target rate for trading in the federal funds market.

Federal Home Loan Bank System (FHLBanks)   A network of 12 regional banks that provide stable, low-cost funding to U.S. financial institutions for home mortgages; small business loans; and rural, agricultural, and economic development lending. The FHLBanks are the largest source of home mortgage and community credit in the United States; they providing funding to other banks, though not directly to individual borrowers. Equity stakes in the FHLBanks are privately held by thousands of member institutions.

Federal Housing Administration (FHA)   A federal agency within the U.S. Department of Housing and Urban Development (HUD) that provides mortgage insurance on loans made by FHA-approved lenders throughout the United States. It is the largest insurer of mortgages in the world, having insuring more than 34 million properties since its inception in 1934. FHA coverage protects lenders against losses from loan defaults, reducing the risk to lenders. Though it is a government agency, the FHA is fully funded by self-generated income. See also *FHA mortgage*.

Federal Housing Finance Agency   An independent federal agency formed by the merger of the Office of Federal Housing Enterprise Oversight (OFHEO) and Federal Housing Finance Board (FHFB). In September 2008, the agency became the conservator of Fannie Mae and Freddie Mac.

Fees   The sum of all upfront cash payments required by the lender for extending the loan. Origination fees and points are expressed as a percentage of the loan.

FHA mortgage   A mortgage issued by a lender that is approved by the *Federal Housing Administration* (see definition) and covered by FHA insurance. Loans must meet certain requirements to qualify for FHA insurance, and the cost of premiums is typically included in the borrower's monthly payments for at least the first five years of the loan. The major advantage of an FHA mortgage is that the required down payment is very low, but the maximum loan amount is also low.

FICO score   A *credit score* (see definition) created by the Fair Isaac Corporation and used by lenders to evaluate a potential borrower's creditworthiness and to determine a loan's interest rate.

Financing points   Rolling *points* (see definition) into the loan amount that is financed.

First mortgage   A mortgage that has a first-priority claim against the property in the event of default. It is generally the primary and often the largest mortgage on a home.

Fixed-income asset   Any type of investment that yields a regular (or fixed) return.

Fixed-rate mortgage (FRM)   A mortgage on which the interest rate and monthly payment is locked in throughout the term.

Float   Allowing the rate and points to vary with changes in market conditions. The borrower may elect to lock the rate and points at any time when securing a loan but must do so a few days before the closing. Allowing the rate to float exposes the borrower to market risk.

Float-down   A rate lock on a mortgage plus an option to reduce the interest rate if market rates decline during the lock period. It is also called a *rate-cap*. A float-down costs the borrower more than a lock because it is more costly to the lender. Float-downs may offer varying conditions regarding when and how often the borrower can exercise the option to reduce rates (usually only once).

Foreclosure   The legal process by which a lender takes possession of a property when the borrower defaults on a mortgage.

Freddie Mac   The Federal Home Loan Mortgage Corporation (FHLMC), created in 1970 to expand the secondary market for mortgages in the United States. This publicly traded corporation and government-sponsored enterprise (GSE) buys and guarantees conforming mortgage loans, pools them, and sells them to investors as mortgage backed securities, providing liquidity to lenders. In September 2008, federal regulators took over Freddie Mac and Fannie Mae (see definition), placing both GSEs under the conservatorship of the Federal Housing Finance Agency.

Fully amortizing payment   The monthly mortgage payment that will fully pay off a loan during its term, if maintained. On fixed-rate mortgages, the payment is always fully amortizing. (If the borrower makes prepayments, the monthly payment is more than fully amortizing.) On adjustable-rate mortgages, the payment may or may not be fully amortizing, depending on the terms of the loan.

Future and forward contracts   Derivative instruments in which the buyer agrees to purchase and the seller agrees to sell, at a specified future date, a specific quantity of an underlying variable or index at a specified price or yield. Both of these types of contracts are used to hedge risk and can be used with physical commodities as well as currencies and interest rates. Futures contracts are standardized and are traded on an organized exchange that sets limits on counterparty credit exposure. Forward contracts do not have standardized terms and are traded over the counter.

Ginnie Mae   The Government National Mortgage Association, a U.S. government-owned corporation created in 1968 and overseen by the U.S. Department of Housing and Urban Development. Ginnie Mae guarantees securities backed by federally insured loans, including those guaranteed by the Federal Housing Administration and the Department of Veterans Affairs. These are the only mortgage-backed securities guaranteed by the federal government.

Ginnie Mae I and II mortgage-backed securities   *Ginnie Mae* (see definition above) issues two types of income investment vehicles. Ginnie Mae I products pool together only similar mortgages into a single security (for example, only single-family home mortgages with comparable maturity dates and interest rates, all issued by the same lender). Ginnie Mae II securities are larger and more geographically diverse pools of mortgages from multiple issuers, with a wider range of coupons (returns).

Goodwill and other intangible assets   An accounting term, especially relevant in acquisitions and mergers, for those factors beyond book value that make companies or investments attractive beyond a strict examination of its assets and liabilities. Goodwill might encompass customer relationships, servicing rights, location, brand value, and similar items. Goodwill is the excess of the purchase price over the fair market value of the net assets acquired, less subsequent impairment adjustments. Other intangible assets are recorded at fair value, less subsequent quarterly amortization and impairment adjustments.

Government–sponsored enterprises (GSE)   Privately held financial service corporations with government charters and backing, such as *Fannie Mae, Freddie Mac,* and the *Federal Home Loan Banks* (see definitions), created to enhance U.S. capital markets. GSEs carry the *implicit* backing of the federal government.

Graduated payment mortgage (GPM)   A mortgage in which monthly payments are initially very low, later rising at a set rate over a set period after which they level out over the remaining term. Unlike an *option ARM* (see definition), a GPM clearly sets the monthly payment schedule, spelling out how it will change during the lifetime of the mortgage, because the interest rate remains fixed. The Federal Housing Administation offers a GPM loan program for home buyers who expect their earning potential to rise in the near future. A variation on the GPM is the *graduated payment adjustable-rate mortgage (GPARM),* which also starts out with very low monthly payments; with these loans, the initial low payment period may cause *negative amortization* (see definition). Adjustments to a GPARM are not set at signing, but as with other ARMs, interest rate resets are tied to a benchmark index.

Growing equity mortgage (GEM)   A loan product with a fixed interest rate and monthly payments that increase over time. Unlike a graduated payment mortgage, these loans begin with initial payments that are fully amortizing. Later increases are applied directly to principal, shorter the life of the loan and saving interest.

Home equity line of credit (HELOC)   An open-ended loan, usually recorded as a second mortgage, granting the borrower a cash advance against the equity in their home. The lender approves a maximum amount that is made available as a line of credit. Borrowers can access these funds in increments, and they pay back only the amount they withdraw, plus interest. Interest rates on HELOCs are typically variable.

Home equity loan   A loan with a second-priority claim against a property in the event of default. The lender who holds the second mortgage gets paid only after the lender holding the first mortgage is paid. Interest rates on home equity loans are generally fixed but at higher rates than first mortgages.

Home Ownership and Equity Protection Act (HOEPA) A federal law addressing deceptive, predatory, and unfair practices in home lending. HOEPA governs only certain high-rate home mortgages. It includes full disclosure requirements about interest rates and payment schedules and forbids practices such as balloon payments and negative amortization.

Homeownership rates The proportion of households that own, rather than rent, their homes. It is computed by dividing the number of owner households by the total number of households.

HOPE for Homeowners A program created by Congress in 2008 to help prevent foreclosures by refinancing troubled mortgages into more sustainable FHA-secured loans.

HOPE NOW An alliance of mortgage lenders and servicers, trade associations, nonprofit housing advocates, and debt counselors, formed in 2007 at the behest of the U.S. Department of Treasury and the Department of Housing and Urban Development. This coalition's counselors work directly with individual homeowners in distress, assisting them in efforts to obtain loan modifications and avoid foreclosure.

Householder A U.S. Census Bureau term for the person (or one of the persons) in whose name a particular housing unit is owned or rented. This term replaces "head of the household."

Housing unit According to the U.S. Census Bureau, a housing unit is a house, an apartment, a mobile home, a group of rooms, or a single room occupied or intended for occupancy as separate living quarters.

Hybrid ARM An adjustable-rate mortgage in which the initial rate is fixed (usually at a low rate) for an initial period and then resets at certain intervals.

Indexed ARM An adjustable-rate mortgage in which the interest rate adjustments are pegged to an agreed-on benchmark index (as opposed to a discretionary ARM, which allows the lender to change the rate at any time subject only to advance notice). All ARMs in the United States are indexed.

Initial interest rate The interest rate offered at the beginning of the life of an adjustable-rate mortgage. The initial rate is often a low "teaser" rate set below the fully indexed interest rate.

Initial rate period The period of time during which the initial rate on a mortgage holds.

Inspection An examination of the structure and mechanical systems of a home by a licensed professional. Before a home purchase closes, borrowers typically commission a home inspection and receive a full report evaluating the home's soundness and safety and listing any needed repairs. Buyers typically pay a fee for this service. Most home sale transactions are contingent on the buyer's satisfaction with the results of the report, and in some cases, the terms of the deal may be renegotiated based on the inspector's findings.

Interest rate adjustment period The frequency of rate adjustments on an adjustable rate mortgage after the initial rate period ends. For example, a 3/1 ARM has an initial rate period of three years, after which the rate adjusts every year.

Interest rate ceiling The highest interest rate possible under an adjustable-rate mortgage contract; also called a "lifetime cap." It is often expressed as a specified number of percentage points above the initial interest rate.

Interest rate decrease cap The maximum allowable decrease in the interest rate on an adjustable-rate mortgage each time the rate resets. It is usually 1 or 2 percentage points.

Interest rate floor The lowest interest rate possible under an adjustable-rate mortgage contract. Floors are less common than ceilings.

Interest rate increase cap The maximum allowable increase in the interest rate on an adjustable-rate mortgage each time the rate resets. It is usually 1 or 2 percentage points but may be 5 points if the initial rate period is five years or longer.

Interest rate index The specific benchmark to which the interest rate on an adjustable-rate mortgage is tied. All of the commonly used indices are regularly and widely published.

Interest-only mortgage A loan agreement under which the monthly payment consists of interest only for a specific interval. During that period, the principal balance remains unchanged and the borrower's equity does not grow unless the home's market value increases. These loans are also called "deferred amortization mortgages." After the interest-only period ends, the monthly payment jumps to cover both the interest owed and the principal. If the loan is an interest-only ARM, the interest rate may also adjust based on a particular index.

Jumbo mortgage   A nonconforming mortgage loan larger than the maximum amount eligible for purchase by Fannie Mae or Freddie Mac. However, some lenders use the term to refer to programs for even larger loans, such as those exceeding $500,000. A loan in excess of $650,000 is referred to as a "super-jumbo mortgage." The average interest rates on jumbo mortgages are typically higher than those on conforming mortgages and vary depending on property types and mortgage amounts.

Jumbo pools   *Ginnie Mae II mortgage-backed securities* (see definition) are collateralized by pools that may include *jumbo mortgages* (see definition above). Mortgage loans in Ginnie Mae jumbo pools may vary in terms of the interest rate within one percentage point.

Leverage   Using debt so that a smaller but riskier equity investment controls a larger asset base. A common measure of leverage is the asset-to-equity ratio (also called the leverage ratio).

Leveraged buyout (LBO)   The acquisition of a company using a significant amount of borrowed money (bonds or loans) to finance the purchase. Often, the assets of the company being acquired are used as collateral for the loans in addition to the assets of the acquiring company. Leveraged buyouts allow investors to make large acquisitions with smaller capital commitments.

Liar loans   Low-documentation or no-documentation mortgages that have been abused through misrepresentation or fraud by borrowers, mortgage brokers, or lenders. Certain loan programs, such as stated income/stated asset (SISA) loans, were particularly susceptible to unethical behavior.

LIBOR (London Interbank Offered Rate)   An interest rate index, published daily, reflecting the rates banks offer when lending unsecured funds to other banks in the London wholesale money market (or interbank market). Some mortgage products peg their interest rate adjustments to movement in the LIBOR.

Lien   The lender's right to claim the borrower's property if the borrower defaults. If there is more than one lien, the claim of the lender holding the first lien will be satisfied before the claim of the lender holding the second lien.

Limited liability   A legal concept limiting an investor's losses to a specific sum (often the amount of the initial investment).

Loan amount   The amount the borrower promises to repay, as set forth in the mortgage contract. It differs from the amount of cash disbursed by the lender by the amount of points and other upfront costs included in the loan.

Loan modification   A permanent change in the terms of an existing mortgage agreement. Modifications are generally designed to make monthly payments more affordable, helping borrowers avoid foreclosure. These may include extending the term of the loan or lowering the interest rate. Also known as a *workout*.

Loan servicing   The administrative handling of a loan after it is initially provided. A company that "services" a loan processes payments, sends statements, manages any escrow/impound accounts, provides collection efforts on delinquent loans, handles pay-offs, and more.

Loan-to-value (LTV) ratio   The loan amount expressed as a percentage of the lesser of the selling price or the appraised value.

Lock period   The number of days during which any interest rate lock or float-down holds before the loan's rate is finalized. Ordinarily, the longer the period, the higher the price to the borrower.

Lock   An option exercised by the borrower during the loan application process to "lock in" the interest rates and points prevailing in the market at that time. The lender and borrower are then committed to those terms, regardless of what happens in the market between that point and the closing date.

Low-documentation or no-documentation (low-doc or no-doc) loans   Loans in which the application process required minimal or no verification from third-party sources to confirm representations made regarding the borrower's income, employment, and assets. See also *Liar loans*.

Mark-to-market accounting   See *Fair value accounting.*

Master servicer   The entity that is contractually responsible for overseeing the primary and subservicers who administer all mortgage loans in a securitization pool. The master servicer handles reporting and remittances to investors.

Mezzanine CDO The medium-risk/medium-yield portion, or *tranche* (see definition), of a *collateralized debt obligation* (see definition). If there are defaults on the underlying portfolio of assets, the mezzanine tranche is more insulated from risk than the higher-yielding junior or equity tranche. The senior tranche carries the lowest risk but also the lowest yield. The size of the equity tranche may determine how much risk protection the mezzanine tranche will actually enjoy.

Monoline insurers Insurance companies that function solely in the capital markets, guaranteeing the payment of bond principal and interest in case of default and providing no other types of insurance.

Moral hazard A concept positing that when parties are insulated from the full consequences of their actions, they will be more likely to take undue risks.

Mortgage A written legal document evidencing the lien on a property taken by a lender as security for the repayment of a loan. The terms *mortgage* and *mortgage loan* are often used loosely to refer both to the actual lien and the loan. In most cases, they are defined in two separate documents: a mortgage and a note.

Mortgage-backed security (MBS) An investment instrument secured by a mortgage loan or a pool of mortgage loans. When these investments are securitized, they are rated by a rating agency. Income from the underlying mortgages is used to pay interest and principal to the investors. Commercial mortgage-backed securities (CMBS) are secured by mortgages on commercial, retail, or multifamily properties, while residential mortgage-backed securities are secured by residential real estate loans.

Mortgage banker A lender that both initiates and funds mortgage loans. A mortgage banker will offer borrowers only the loan programs from their own institution.

Mortgage broker A firm or individual who, for a commission, matches borrowers with lenders. A mortgage broker takes loan applications and qualifies borrowers and may counsel borrowers on the offerings available from multiple lenders. But unlike a mortgage banker, the broker does not fund loans and thus does not assume the risk of default.

Mortgage insurance   See *PMI*.

Mortgage lender   The party who disburses funds to the borrower at closing. The lender receives the note evidencing the borrower's indebtedness and obligation to repay and the mortgage, which is the lien on the subject property.

Mortgage loan   A real estate loan secured by a mortgage.

Mortgage payment   The monthly payment of interest and principal made by the borrower.

Mortgage price   The interest rate, points, and fees paid by the borrowers. On adjustable-rate mortgages, the price also includes the fully indexed rate and the maximum rate.

Mortgage servicing rights   A contract to perform the administrative services surrounding the fulfillment of an existing mortgage, such as collecting and transmitting monthly payments, mailing statements, and administering taxes and insurance premiums held in escrow. Lenders may retain ownership of a loan but sell its servicing rights to an outside firm that receives a fee for these services.

Negative amortization   A process that occurs when a loan payment is less than the interest due, raising the total loan balance. Sometimes called *deferred interest*. Negative amortization arises most frequently on adjustable rate mortgages.

Negative amortization cap   The maximum amount of negative amortization permitted on an adjustable-rate mortgage, usually expressed as a percentage of the original loan amount (e.g., 110 percent). Reaching the cap triggers an automatic increase in the monthly payment, usually to the fully amortizing payment level, overriding any payment increase cap.

Negative equity   The condition of owing more on a property than the property is currently worth. When homeowners have negative equity, they are said to be "under water" or "upside down."

Negative points   Points paid by a lender for a loan with a higher interest rate. When this fee goes to the borrower, it is often called a *rebate* and is used to offset settlement costs. When negative points are retained by a mortgage broker, they are called a *yield spread premium* and represent the broker's compensation for selling a loan with better terms for the lender.

Net charge-offs   Total loans and leases charged off (purged from a balance sheet because they cannot be collected) less amounts recovered on loans and leases previously charged off.

NINA loan   A no income/no asset loan, a type of low-documentation loan that does not require verification of income or assets but does verify employment.

NINJA loan   A no income/no job/no asset loan, which had even more lax underwriting standards than a NINA loan (see definition above). More than simply an acronym, the term is also a tongue-in-cheek reference to the mysteries on the loan application and the likelihood that the borrower would eventually disappear.

Nominal interest rate   The rate of interest with no adjustment for inflation or compounding.

Nominal price   A price given in current price levels, with no adjustment for inflation. Also, an estimated price used to initiate a transaction, often used when a true market price cannot be established.

Nonconforming loan   A mortgage loan that does not meet the requirements for purchase by Fannie Mae and Freddie Mac, either because it is too large or for other reasons such as poor credit or high loan-to-value ratio. See also *Conforming loan*.

Nonprime loan   See *Subprime loan*.

Note   A legal document that evidences a debt and a promise to repay. A mortgage loan transaction always includes both a note evidencing the debt and a mortgage evidencing the lien on the property, usually in two documents.

Option ARM   An *adjustable-rate mortgage* (see definition) that offers the borrower flexible payment options during the initial period. Each month the borrower can choose a low minimum payment, an interest-only payment, or a fully amortizing 15- or 30-year fixed-rate payment. Because the minimum payment is actually less than the interest due, it can add to the loan balance on the back end, resulting in *negative amortization* (see definition). These loans, also called "pick-a-payment" or "pay-option" ARMs, carry the risk of very large monthly payments in later years. Many option ARMs have defaulted.

Option contracts Contracts in which the buyer acquires the right to buy from or sell to another party some specified amount of an underlying variable or index at a stated price (strike price) during a period or on a specified future date, in return for compensation (such as a fee or premium). The seller is obligated to purchase or sell the variable or index at the discretion of the buyer of the contract.

Originate-to-distribute model A business model for lenders in which loans are granted but then securitized and sold in the secondary market. It represents a departure from the previous *originate-to-hold model* (see definition below). Because risk is passed along to the investor who buys the loan, the incentive to maintain high credit standards was eroded.

Originate-to-hold model The dominant business model among mortgage lenders prior to the 1970s and 1980s. Lenders (mostly savings and loans at that time) would write loans, service them, and hold them in portfolio throughout their term. This business model created incentive for the lender to carefully scrutinize the creditworthiness of the borrower, because any defaults directly created losses.

Origination fee An upfront fee charged by some lenders, usually expressed as a percentage of the loan amount. It should be added to points in determining the total fees charged by the lender that are expressed as a percentage of the loan amount. Unlike points, however, an origination fee does not vary with the interest rate. It covers the lender's administrative costs in processing the loan and varies among lenders.

Pass-through securities A security granting the holder an interest in a pool of mortgages. All payments of principal and interest are "passed through" to investors each month, providing a flow of fixed income. Issued by Ginnie Mae, Freddie Mac, and others.

Payment decrease cap The maximum percentage decrease allowed in the payment on an adjustable-rate mortgage at a payment adjustment date.

Payment increase cap The maximum percentage increase allowed in the payment on an adjustable-rate mortgage at a payment adjustment date. A 7.5 percent cap is common.

Pay-option mortgage See *Option ARM*.

Piggyback loans   A second mortgage taken at the same time as a first mortgage as a way of borrowing a larger total amount while avoiding the need to purchase mortgage insurance (typically required on loans where the loan-to-value ratio is greater than 80 percent). Piggybacks were common among borrowers who could not purchase with 20 percent down payments. The interest rate on the second loan is typically higher than the rate on the primary mortgage.

PMI (private mortgage insurance)   Mortgage insurance provided by nongovernment insurers, protecting a lender against loss if the borrower defaults. In most cases, the borrower pays the premiums, which can be rolled into the monthly loan payments. Mortgage insurance is typically required on loans with down payments of less than 20 percent. The insurance can be dropped once the principal balance is reduced to 80 percent of the home's value.

Points   An upfront cash payment to the lender as part of the charge for the loan, expressed as a percentage of the loan amount; e.g., "three points" means a charge equal to 3 percent of the loan balance. Borrowers sometimes opt to pay points in exchange for receiving a better interest rate. It is common for lenders to offer a wide range of rate/point combinations, especially on fixed-rate mortgages, including combinations with *negative points* (see definition).

Pool   A collection or portfolio of mortgage loans assembled by an originator or master servicer as the basis for a security.

Portfolio lender   A lender that originates loans and holds them on its own balance sheet rather than selling its loans to investors in the secondary market. Instead of relying on secondary market sales for income, their business model is built around a flow of income from borrowers' interest payments throughout the life of the loan.

Predatory lending   Lending practices that employ fraud, pressure, or misrepresentation to lure borrowers into mortgage loans that are inappropriate, overpriced, or too risky. Predatory lenders often target low-income or minority consumers.

Preferred equity   A claim with both debt and equity characteristics. Preferred dividends, usually paid as a fixed dollar amount per calendar quarter per share, are usually higher than common dividends and have priority over any common dividend payments in bankruptcy.

Prepayment The unscheduled partial or complete payment of the principal amount outstanding on a debt obligation before it is due.

Prepayment penalty A charge imposed by the lender if the borrower pays off a loan early. The charge is usually expressed as a percentage of the loan balance at the time of prepayment or as a specified number of months' interest. A large prepayment penalty in a loan agreement may make it difficult for a borrower to refinance.

Principal The face amount of a loan, exclusive of interest. The portion of the monthly payment that is used to reduce the loan balance rather to pay interest is called the "principal payment."

Principal-agent problem A concept in economics that arises when a party or investor hires an agent but their interests and incentives are not aligned. Asymmetry of information can worsen this problem.

"Problem" institutions A designation applied by the FDIC to banks that have weak capital cushions and have been placed under greater regulatory scrutiny. The FDIC periodically releases a count of problem institutions but does not reveal their names to avoid causing bank runs.

Rate-spread reportable loans Any mortgage with an annual percentage rate exceeding the yield on U.S. treasuries of comparable maturity by a certain level (3 percent on a first mortgage or 5 percent on a secondary mortgage). As of 2004, these loans must be reported in the lender's annual Home Mortgage Disclosure Act (HMDA) reporting.

Real estate investment trust (REIT) An investment vehicle that holds title to real estate assets that are managed by one or more trustees who control acquisitions and investments. These investments can be bought and sold like mutual funds.

Real estate mortgage investment conduit (REMIC) A special purpose vehicle for pooling mortgages and issuing varying classes of mortgage-backed securities.

Real interest rate The *nominal interest rate* (see definition) minus the inflation rate.

Refinancing Paying off an old loan while simultaneously taking a new one. This may be done to reduce costs by obtaining a better interest rate, to reduce risk by converting an adjustable-rate mortgage to a fixed-rate mortgage, or to cash out equity.

Reverse mortgage A loan available to homeowners over age 62 that allows borrowers to convert their home equity into cash. The proceeds can be paid out as a lump sum or in multiple regular payments. The loan does not have to be paid back as long as the borrower remains in the home, but equity is depleted.

Risk-based pricing Setting the interest rate on a loan higher or lower to account for the likelihood of default.

Seasonal vacant units Seasonal housing units are those intended for occupancy only during certain seasons of the year; found primarily in resort areas.

Second mortgage A loan with a second-priority claim against a property in the event that the borrower defaults. The lender who holds the second mortgage gets paid only after the lender holding the first mortgage is paid. Second mortgages (often home equity loans) generally have higher interest rates than primary mortgages.

Secondary mortgage market The market in which mortgage loans and servicing rights are bought and sold. Most loans in the secondary market are packaged into mortgage-backed securities and sold to investors. This process provides lenders with liquidity.

Securitization The process of combining assets and creating a financial instrument that is repackaged and sold to investors as a "security."

Servicing See *Loan servicing.*

Servicing outstanding The unpaid portion or remaining principal of serviced loans.

Shared appreciation mortgage (SAM) A mortgage in which the lender offers the borrower a lower interest rate in exchange for a share of future price appreciation.

Short sale A real estate sale in which the proceeds fall short of the outstanding balance owed on the property by the seller. Lenders must give their approval to short sales; many do so to avoid the larger losses that may be incurred if the property falls into foreclosure. A short sale will harm the seller's credit score, but its impact is less severe than a foreclosure. The forgiven mortgage debt was once taxed as income, but the Mortgage Forgiveness Debt Relief Act of 2007 removed this tax burden through 2009. The Emergency Economic Stabilization Act of 2008 later extended this tax relief through 2012.

Special-purpose entity (SPE) A corporation, limited partnership, or other type of legally sanctioned body formed specifically to fulfill a narrow objective, such as isolating risk, realizing tax benefits, or acquiring and holding certain assets; also called a *special-purpose vehicle.*

Stated asset loan A loan in which the borrower discloses his or her assets on the application but the lender does not verify the borrower's statements.

Stated income loan A loan in which the borrower discloses his or her income but the lender does not verify the borrower's statements. These applications may or may not include lender verification of employment.

Stripped mortgage-backed securities (SMBS) Securities created by "stripping" or separating the principal and interest payments from the underlying pool of mortgages into distinct classes of securities.

Subprime borrower Borrowers who do not qualify for the lowest, or "prime," interest rates because of poor credit histories, high debt burdens relative to income, high loan-to-value ratios, or other risk factors.

Subprime lender A lender who specializes in lending to subprime borrowers.

Subprime loans Subprime mortgages are loans that in some way exceed the level of credit risk that government-sponsored enterprises are willing to accept for purchase. Lenders charge higher interest rates on these loans to compensate the higher risk of borrower default.

Subprime market The network of subprime lenders, mortgage brokers, warehouse lenders, and investment bankers who market, originate, and service loans to subprime borrowers.

Swaps A derivative in which two parties agree to exchange a series of cash flows at agreed-on intervals (settlement dates). The cash flows of a swap are either fixed or determined for each settlement date by multiplying the quantity (notional principal) of the underlying variable or index by specified reference rates or prices. Except in currency swaps, the notional principal is used to calculate each payment but is not exchanged.

Tax-related service fee During the life of a loan, borrowers will be making property tax payments, either on their own or through an escrow account with the lender. Because property tax liens can sometimes take precedence over a first mortgage, the lender may pay an independent service to monitor property tax payments. The fee for this service may be charged to borrowers as a closing cost.

Teaser rate   The initial, low-interest rate on an adjustable-rate mortgage, generally below the fully indexed rate.

TED spread   The gap between the three-month *LIBOR* (see definition) rate for interbank lending and the three-month Treasury bill rate. A widening TED spread indicates an increased risk of credit defaults in the marketplace.

Title search   A detailed examination of public documents regarding the property's ownership history. The search, which may turn up issues such as liens or easements, confirms that the seller is the property's true owner and has the legal right to make the sale. There may be separate fees to the borrower for compiling the documents (creating an "abstract") and for title examination.

Tranche   A slice or portion of a collateralized debt obligation. Used to denote different levels or classes of investment with varying levels of risk and yield.

Two-step mortgage   A loan that offers a low interest rate for the first five to seven years and then adjusts to a higher interest rate for the remaining life of the mortgage. During the "first step," the interest rate is fixed; during the "second step," it can be either fixed or adjustable but is based on current market rates.

Under water   Describes a mortgage or a homeowner with negative equity (that is, the borrower owes more on the property than the property is currently worth). Also known as being "upside down."

Underwriting standards   Standards and requirements imposed by lenders as conditions for granting loans, such as credit history, maximum ratio of expenses to income, maximum loan amounts, maximum loan-to-value ratios, and more.

VA loan   A mortgage loan available only to U.S. military veterans and insured by the Department of Veterans Affairs. No down payment is required.

Vacant housing units   A housing unit is vacant if no one is living in it, unless its occupants are only temporarily absent. In addition, a vacant unit may be one which is entirely occupied by persons who have a usual residence elsewhere. New units not yet occupied are classified as vacant housing units if construction is largely complete.

Warehouse lender   A short-term lender for mortgage bankers. Using the note as collateral, the warehouse lender provides interim financing from the time a loan is originated until it is sold in the secondary market.

Wholesale origination   A loan origination strategy by which loans are purchased from mortgage brokers, mortgage bankers, or other lenders. This process enables a lender to acquire servicing rights without incurring the costs associated with running a retail origination operation.

Workout   See *Loan modification*.

Wrap-around mortgage   A form of direct seller financing in which the buyer assumes the payment obligations on the old mortgage while also taking out a junior mortgage. A due-on-sale clause would discourage a seller from opting for a wrap-around mortgage.

Year-round vacant units   Units intended for occupancy at any time of the year, even though they may not be in use the year round. In resort areas, a housing unit that is usually occupied on a year-round basis is considered a year-round unit. Year-round vacant units may be for sale, for rent, or both.

References

Adelson, Mark, and David Jacob. 2008. *The sub-prime problem: Causes and lessons.* Adelson & Jacob Consulting. http://www.securitization.net/pdf/Publications/Sub-prime_Problem_8Jan08.pdf (accessed October 8, 2008).

Adrian, Tobias, and Hyun Song Shin. 2008. Liquidity and financial contagion. [Special issue on liquidity.] Banque de France, *Financial Stability Review*, no. 11: 1–7.

Aglietta, Michel, and Laurence Scialom. 2008. Permanence and innovation in central banking policy for financial stability. Working paper series 2008–12, Economix, University of Paris X and National Center for Scientific Research, Paris, France.

Agarwal, Sumit, and Calvin T. Ho. 2007. Comparing the prime and subprime mortgage markets. *Chicago Fed Letter*, no. 241.

Ahearne, Alan G., William L. Griever, and Francis E. Warnock. 2004. Information costs and home bias: An analysis of U.S. holdings of foreign equities. *Journal of International Economics* 62 (2): 313–36.

Aizcorbe, Ana M., Arthur B. Kennickell, and Kevin B. Moore. 2003. Recent changes in U.S. family finances: Evidence from the 1998 and 2001 Survey of Consumer Finances. *Federal Reserve Bulletin*, January: 1–32.

Aizenman, Joshua, and Yothin Jinjarak. 2008. Current account patterns and national real estate markets. NBER Working paper series 13921, National Bureau of Economic Research, Cambridge, Massachusetts.

Allen, Franklin, and Douglas Gale. 2000. Financial contagion. *Journal of Political Economy* 108: 1–33.

———. 2004a. Financial fragility, liquidity, and asset prices. *Journal of the European Economic Association* 2: 1015–1048.

———. 2004b. Financial intermediaries and markets. *Econometrica* 72: 1023–1061.

———. 2007. *Understanding financial crises: Clarendon lectures in finance.* New York: Oxford University Press.

Allen, Franklin, and Elena Carletti. 2006. Mark-to-market accounting and liquidity pricing. CFS working paper series 2006/17, Center for Financial Studies, University of Frankfurt, Germany.

———. 2008. The role of liquidity in financial crises. Working paper series 08–33, Wharton Financial Institutions Center, University of Pennsylvania, Philadelphia.

Allen, Franklin, Elena Carletti, and Douglas Gale. 2008. Interbank market liquidity and central bank intervention. Working paper, Wharton School, University of Pennsylvania, Philadelphia.

Anderson, Charles D., Dennis R. Capozza, and Robert Van Order. 2008. *Deconstructing the subprime debacle using new indices of underwriting quality and economic conditions: A first look.* July. University Financial Associates, Ann Arbor, MI. http://papers.ssrn.com/sol3/papers.cfm? abstract_id=1160073 (accessed October 9, 2008).

Anshasy, Amany El, Gregory Elliehausen, and Yoshiaki Shimazaki. 2006. The pricing of subprime mortgages by mortgage brokers and lenders. Working paper 70, Credit Research Center, Georgetown University, Washington, D.C.

Apgar, William, Amal Bendimerad, and Ren S. Essene. 2007. *Mortgage market channels and fair lending: An analysis of HMDA data.* Cambridge: Joint Center for Housing Studies, Harvard University.

Ashcraft, Adam B., and Til Schuermann. 2008. *Understanding the securitization of subprime mortgage credit.* Staff report 318, Federal Reserve Bank of New York.

Avery, Robert B., Kenneth P. Brevoort, and Glenn B. Canner. 2007. The 2006 HMDA Data. *Federal Reserve Bulletin* 93: A73–A109.

Azarchs, Tanya, Scott Bugie, and Nick Hill. 2008. *More subprime write-downs to come, but the end is now in sight for large financial institutions.* March. RatingsDirect. http://www2.standardandpoors.com/portal/site/sp/en/us/page.article_print/4,5,5,1,1204834028416.html (accessed September 23, 2008).

Baily, Martin Neil, Douglas W. Elmendorf, and Robert E. Litan. 2008. *The great credit squeeze: How it happened, how to prevent another.* Washington, D.C.: The Brookings Institution.

Baily, Martin Neil, and Robert E. Litan. 2008. *A brief guide to fixing finance.* September 22. The Brookings Institution, http://www.brookings.edu/papers/2008/0922_fixing_finance_baily_litan.aspx (accessed October 10, 2008).

Bair, Sheila C. 2007. Recent events in the credit and mortgage markets and possible implications for U.S. consumers and the global economy: Hearing before the Financial Services Committee on September 5. House. 110th Cong., 1st sess.

Baker, Dean. 2007. *Midsummer meltdown: Prospects for the stock and housing markets.* Washington, D.C.: Center for Economic and Policy Research.

Baker, Dean, and Andrew Samwick. 2007. Save the homeowners, not the hedge funds. *Providence Journal,* August 31. http://www.projo.com/opinion/ contributors/content/CT_baker31_08-31-07_8G6SA6I.1c1d9dc.html (accessed January 21, 2009).

Bardhan, Ashok, and Dwight Jaffee. 2007. *The impact of global capital flows and foreign financing on U.S. mortgage and Treasury interest rates.* Washington, D.C.: Research Institute for Housing America, Mortgage Bankers Association.

Barr, Michael. 2005. Credit where it counts: The Community Reinvestment Act and its critics. *New York University Law Review* 8: 513–653.

Barr, Michael, Sendhil Mullainathan, and Eldar Shafir. 2007. A one-size-fits-all solution. *The New York Times,* December 26.

Barth, James R. 1991. *The great savings and loan debacle.* Washington, D.C.: American Enterprise Institute.

Barth, James R., and Anthony M. J. Yezer. 1983. Default risk on home mortgages: A further test of competing hypotheses. *Journal of Risk and Insurance* 50 (3): 500–5.

Barth, James R., and Martin Regalia. 1988. The evolving role of regulation in the savings and loan industry. In *The financial services revolution: Policy directions for the future,* edited by Catherine England and Thomas F. Huertas. New York: Kluwer Academic.

Barth, James R., and Michael G. Bradley. 1989. Thrift deregulation and federal deposit insurance. *Journal of Financial Services Research* 2 (3): 231–59.

Barth, James R., and Peter Passell. 2007. In defense of hybrids. *The Wall Street Journal,* December 6.

Barth, James R., and R. Dan Brumbaugh, Jr. 1992. Turmoil among depository institutions: Implications for the U.S. real estate market. *Housing Policy Debate* 3 (4): 901–26.

———, eds. 1992. *The reform of federal deposit insurance: Disciplining the government and protecting taxpayers.* New York: HarperCollins.

Barth, James R., and R. Dan Brumbaugh, Jr. 1994a. Moral hazard and agency problems: Understanding depository institution failure costs. In *Research in financial services,* edited by George G. Kaufman. Greenwich: JAI Press.

———. 1994b. Risk-based capital requirements: Informational and political implications, vol. 1. In *Global risk based capital regulations,* edited by Charles A. Stone and Anne Zissu. New York: Irwin Professional.

———. 1996. The condition and regulation of Madison Guaranty Savings and Loan Association in the 1980s: A case study of regulatory failure. In *Research in financial services: Private and public policy*, edited by George G. Kaufman. Greenwich: JAI Press.

———, 1997. Development and evolution of national financial systems: An international perspective. Paper presented at the meeting of the Latin American Studies Association, April 17–19, Guadalajara, Mexico.

Barth, James R., and Robert E. Litan. 1998. Lessons from bank failures in the United States. In *Preventing bank crises: Lessons from recent global bank failures*, edited by Gerard Caprio, Jr., William C. Hunter, George G. Kaufman, and Danny M. Leipziger. Washington, D.C.: World Bank Publications.

Barth, James R., and Robert Keleher. 1984. Financial crises and the role of the lender of last resort. *Federal Reserve of Atlanta Economic Review*, January: 58–67.

Barth, James R., Daniel E. Nolle, Triphon Phumiwasana, and Glenn Yago. 2003. A cross-country analysis of the bank supervisory framework and bank performance. *Financial Markets, Institutions and Instruments* 12 (1): 67–120.

Barth, James R., Gerard Caprio, Jr., and Ross Levine. 2001. Banking systems around the globe: Do regulations and ownership affect performance and stability? In *Prudential supervision: What works and what doesn't*, edited by Frederic S.. Mishkin. Chicago: University of Chicago Press.

———, 2006. *Rethinking bank regulation: Till angels govern*. New York: Cambridge University Press.

———, 2007. Bank regulations are changing, but for better or worse? Paper presented at the 13th Annual Dubrovnik Economic Conference, June 27–30, Dubrovnik, Croatia.

———, 2008a. Reassessing the rationale and practice of bank regulation and supervision. *Current Developments in Monetary and Financial Law* 5: 41–67.

———, 2008b. The microeconomic effects of different approaches to bank supervision. In *Political institutions and financial development*, edited by Stephen Haber, Douglass North, and Barry Weingast. Palo Alto: Stanford University Press.

Barth, James R., Jie Gan, and Daniel E. Nolle. 2005. Global banking regulation and supervision: What are the issues and what are the practices? In *Reforms and innovations in bank management*, edited by Duk-Hoon Lee and Gill-Chin Lim. Seoul, Korea: NANAM Publishing House.

Barth, James R., John Feid, Gabriel Riedel, and M. Hampton Tunis. 1989. *Alternative federal deposit insurance regimes*. Research paper 152. Federal Home Loan Bank Board.

Barth, James R., Joseph Cordes, and Anthony M. J. Yezer. 1980. Financial institution regulations, redlining and mortgage markets. In *The regulation of financial institutions*, Conference Series 21, pp. 101–43. Boston: Federal Reserve Bank of Boston.

———. 1981. Federal government attempts to influence the allocation of mortgage credit: FHA mortgage insurance and government regulations. U.S. Congressional Budget Office, *The Economics of Federal Credit Activity*, October.

———. 1983a. An analysis of information restrictions on the lending decisions of financial institution. *Economic Inquiry* 21 (3): 349–60.

———. 1983b. FHA mortgage insurance and high risk mortgage lending: Some lessons for policy. *Housing Finance Review* 2: 93–107.

———. 1986. Benefits and costs of legal restrictions on personal loan markets. *Journal of Law and Economics* 29 (2): 357–80.

Barth, James R., Lawrence Goldberg, Daniel E. Nolle, and Glenn Yago. 2006. Financial supervision and crisis management: U.S. experience and lessons for emerging market economies. In *Regulatory reforms in the age of financial consolidation: Emerging market economy and advanced countries*, edited by Lee-Jay Cho and Joon-Kyung Kim. Seoul and Honolulu: Korea Development Institute and East-West Center.

Barth, James R., Luis G. Dopico, Daniel E. Nolle, and James A. Wilcox. 2002. Bank safety and soundness and the structure of bank supervision: A cross-country analysis. *International Review of Finance* 3 (3–4): 163–88.

Barth, James R., Mark J. Bertus, Valentina Hartarska, Hai Jason Jiang, and Triphon Phumiwasana. 2007. A cross-country analysis of bank performance: The role of external governance. In *Corporate governance in banking: A global perspective*, edited by Benton E. Gup. Cheltenham, U.K.: Edward Elgar.

Barth, James R., Michael G. Bradley, and John Feid. 1989. How deposit insurance went awry. *Federal Home Loan Bank Board Journal*, February: 15–21.

Barth, James R., Padma Gotur, Neela Manage, and Anthony M. J. Yezer. 1983. The effect of government regulations on the lending loan markets: A Tobit estimation of a microeconomic model. *Journal of Finance* 38 (4): 1233–51.

Barth, James R., Philip Bartholomew, and Carol Labich. 1989. Moral hazard and the thrift crisis: An analysis of 1988 resolutions. *Federal Reserve Bank of Chicago Proceedings* 344–84.

Barth, James R., Philip Bartholomew, and Michael G. Bradley. 1989. The determinants of thrift institution resolution costs. *Journal of Finance* 45 (3): 731–54.

Barth, James R., R. Dan Brumbaugh, Jr., and Glenn Yago, eds. 2000. *Restructuring regulation and financial institutions*. Norwell: Kluwer Academic.

Barth, James R., R. Dan Brumbaugh, Jr., Lalita Ramesh, and Glenn Yago. 1998. The role of governments and markets in international banking crisis: The case of East Asia. In *Bank crisis: Causes, analysis and prevention*, edited by George Kaufman. Greenwich: JAI Press.

Barth, James R., Susanne Trimbath, and Glenn Yago, eds. 2004. *The savings and loan crisis: Lessons from a regulatory failure.* Norwell: Kluwer Academic.

Barth, James R., Tong Li, Sangeetha Malaiyandi, Donald McCarthy, Triphon Phumiwasana, and Glenn Yago. 2005. *Capital access index 2005: Securitization in financing economic activities.* Santa Monica: Milken Institute.

Barth, James R., Tong Li, Triphon Phumiwasana, and Glenn Yago. 2007. Inverted yield curves and financial institutions: Is the United States headed for a repeat of the 1980s crisis? *Banks and Banking Systems* 2 (3).

Barth, James R., Tong Li, and Triphon Phumiwasana. 2009. The U.S. financial crisis: Credit crunch and yield spreads. *RBS Reserve Management Trends 2009.* London: Central Banking Publications.

Barth, James R., Triphon Phumiwasana, and Wenling Lu. 2008. Bank regulation in the United States. *CESifo DICE Report* 6 (3): 3–8.

Benner, Katie. 2008. *The $5 trillion mess.* July 14. CNNMoney.com.http://money.cnn.com/2008/07/11/news/economy/fannie_freddie.fortune/index.htm (accessed September 8, 2008).

Berger, Allen N., and Christa H. S. Bouwman. Forthcoming. Bank liquidity creation. *Review of Financial Studies* (RFS Advance Access published on January 8, 2009).

Bernanke, Ben S. 2005. The global saving glut and the U.S. current account deficit. Remarks at the Sandridge Lecture, Virginia Association of Economics, March 10, Richmond, Virginia.

———. 2006. Community development financial institutions: Promoting economic growth and opportunity. Speech at the Opportunity Finance Network's annual conference, November 1, Washington, D.C.

———. 2007. The subprime mortgage market. Speech at the Federal Reserve Bank of Chicago's 43rd Annual Conference on Bank Structure and Competition, May 17, Chicago.

Berry, John. 2007. *Subprime losses are big, exaggerated by some.* December 27. Bloomberg.com. http://www.bloomberg.com/apps/news?pid=20601039&sid=am4LxWcQQbPQ (accessed September 7, 2008).

Bertaut, Carol C., and William L. Griever. 2004. Recent developments in cross-border investment in securities. *Federal Reserve Bulletin,* Winter: 19–31.

Bloomberg News. 2008. Paulson says no plan is afoot to rescue mortgage agencies. *The New York Times,* August 11.

Blundell-Wignall, Adrian. 2008. The subprime crisis: Size, deleveraging and some policy options. *Financial Market Trend* 1: 21–45.

Bocian, Debbie Gruenstein, Keith S. Ernst, and Wei Li. 2006. *Unfair lending: The effect of race and ethnicity on the price of subprime mortgages.* Durham, NC: Center for Responsible Lending.

Bond, Philip, David K. Musto, and Bilge Yılmaz. 2006. Predatory lending in a rational world. Working paper 06–2, Federal Reserve Bank of Philadelphia.

Bond Market Association. 2004. *The secondary market for subprime mortgages: A common sense approach to addressing assignee liability through federal legislation.* New York: Bond Market Association.

Bramley, Glen, and Kathleen Dunmore. 1996. Shared ownership: Short-term expedient or long-term major tenure? *Housing Studies* 11 (1): 105–31.

Brewer III, Elijah, and Julapa Jagtiani. 2007. How much would banks be willing to pay to become "too-big-to-fail" and to capture other benefits? Research working paper RWP 07–05, Federal Reserve Bank of Kansas City.

Browning, E.S. 2008. Bond market flashes caution signals for stocks. *The Wall Street Journal*, August 25.

Brumbaugh, R. Dan, Jr.. 1987. *Thrifts under siege.* Cambridge, MA: Ballinger Publishing.

Brumbaugh, R. Dan, Jr., and Andrew S. Carron. 1987. Thrift industry crisis: Causes and solutions. *Brookings Papers on Economic Activities* 2: 349–88.

Brumbaugh, R. Dan, Jr., Andrew S. Carron, and Robert E. Litan. 1989. Cleaning up the depository institutions mess. *Brookings Papers on Economic Activities* 1: 243–95.

Brumbaugh, R. Dan, Jr., and Robert E. Litan. 1989. The S&L crisis: How to get out and stay out. *Brookings Review*, Spring, 3–15.

Brunnermeier, Markus K. Forthcoming. Deciphering the 2007–08 liquidity and credit crunch. *Journal of Economic Perspectives* (earlier version available at http://www.princeton.edu/~markus/).

Bucks, Brian K, Arthur B. Kennickell, and Kevin B. Moore. 2006. Recent changes in U.S. family finances: Evidence from the 2001 and 2004 survey of consumer finances. *Federal Reserve Bulletin* 92: A1–A38.

Bucks, Brian, and Karen Pence. 2006. *Do homeowners know their house values and mortgage terms?* Finance and economics discussion series 2006–03, The Federal Reserve Board, Washington, D.C.

Buiter, Willem H. 2008. Central banks and financial crises. Paper presented at the 2008 Jackson Hole Symposium on Maintaining Stability in a Changing Financial System, August 21–23, Jackson Hole, Wyoming.

Cagan, Christopher L. 2007. *Mortgage payment reset: The issue and the impact.* Santa Ana: First American CoreLogic.

Calhoun, Michael D. 2006. *Calculated risk: Assessing non-traditional mortgage products*: Hearing before Subcommittee on Housing and Transportation and Subcommittee on Economic Policy on September 20. House. 109th Cong., 2nd sess.

Calomiris, Charles W. 2008. Subprime turmoil: What's old, what's new, and what's next. Paper presented at the 2008 Jackson Hole Symposium on

Maintaining Stability in a Changing Financial System, August 21–23, Jackson Hole, Wyoming.

Calomiris, Charles W., Stanley D. Longhofer, and William Miles. 2008. The foreclosure-house price nexus: Lessons from the 2007–2008 housing turmoil. NBER working paper series 14294, National Bureau of Economic Research, Cambridge, Massachusetts.

Campello, Murillo. 2006. Debt financing: Does it boost or hurt firm performance in product markets? *Journal of Financial Economics* 82: 135–72.

Canfield, Anne C. 2007a. Letter to the Board of Governors of the Federal Reserve System on the Home Equity and Ownership Protection Act and on the adequacy of existing regulatory and legislative provisions in protecting the interests of consumers, August 14, Consumer Mortgage Coalition, Washington, D.C.

———. 2007b. Letter to Office of the Comptroller of the Currency, Office of Thrift Supervision, Federal Deposit Insurance Corporation, Board of Governors of the Federal Reserve System, and National Credit Union Administration on Statement on Subprime Mortgage Lending proposed by the agencies, May 7, Consumer Mortgage Coalition, Washington, D.C.

Canner, Glenn B., Wayne Passmore, and Elizabeth Laderman. 1999. The role of specialized lenders in extending mortgages to lower-income and minority homebuyers. *Federal Reserve Bulletin* November: 709–726.

Caplin, Andrew, Noel Cunningham, Mitchell Engler, and Frederick Pollock. 2008. *Facilitating shared appreciation mortgages to prevent housing crashes and affordability crisis.* Hamilton Project discussion paper 2008–12, The Brookings Institution, Washington, D.C.

Capozza, Dennis R., and Thomas A. Thomson. 2006. Subprime transitions: Lingering or malingering in default? *Journal of Real Estate Financial Economics* 33: 241–58.

Caprio, Jr., Gerard, Asli Demirguc-Kunt, and Edward J. Kane. 2008. The 2007 meltdown in structured securitization: Searching for lessons not scapegoats. Paper presented at Conference on Risk Analysis and Management, October 2–3, Washington, D.C.

Carasso, Adam, Elizabeth Bell, Edgar O. Olsen, and C. Eugene Steuerle. 2005. *Improving homeownership among poor and moderate-income households.* Opportunity and Ownership Project Series 2. Washington, D.C.: The Urban Institute.

Cardarelli, Roberto, Deniz Igan, and Alessandro Rebucci. 2008. The changing housing cycle and the implications for monetary policy. International Monetary Fund, *World Economic Outlook*, April.

Carlson, Mark. 2007. A brief history of the 1987 stock market crash with a discussion of the Federal Reserve response. Finance and economics discussion series 2007–13, The Federal Reserve Board, Washington, D.C.

Carlson, Mark, and Jason Steinman. 2008. Market conditions and hedge fund survival. Finance and economics discussion series 2008–28, The Federal Reserve Board, Washington, D.C.

Carow, Kenneth A., Edward J. Kane, and Rajesh P. Narayanan. 2006. How have borrowers fared in banking mega-mergers? *Journal of Money, Credit and Banking* 38 (3): 821–36.

Carr, Jack L., and Lawrence B. Smith. 1975. Public land banking and the price of land. *Land Economics* 51 (4): 316–30.

Carr, James H., and Lopa Kolluri. 2001. *Predatory lending: An overview.* Washington, D.C.: Fannie Mae Foundation.

Center for Responsible Lending. 2007a. *Case study in subprime hybrid ARM refinance outcomes.* Durham, NC: Center for Responsible Lending.

———. 2007b. *Subprime lending: A net drain on homeownership.* CRL issue paper 14, Center for Responsible Lending, Durham, North Carolina.

———. 2007c. *The Center for Responsible Lending's losing ground foreclosure study.* Alexandria: Center for Statistical Research.

———. 2007d. *U.S. mortgage borrowing: Providing Americans with opportunity, or imposing excessive risk? An empirical analysis of recent foreclosure experience in U.S. mortgage lending and particularly subprime lending.* Alexandria, VA: Center for Statistical Research.

Chambers, Matthew, Carlos Garriga, and Don E. Schlagenhauf. 2007. Accounting for changes in the homeownership rate. Working paper series 2007–034A, Federal Reserve Bank of St. Louis.

———. 2008. Mortgage innovation, mortgage choice, and housing decisions. *Federal Reserve Bank of St. Louis Review* 90 (6): 585–608.

Chan, Sewin. 2001. Spatial lock-in: Do falling house prices constrain residential mobility? *Journal of Urban Economics* 49 (3): 567–86.

Chang, Yan, Amy Crews Cutts, and Richard Green. 2005. Did changing rents explain changing house prices during the 1990s? Working paper. School of Business, George Washington University, Washington, D.C.

Charles, Kerwin Kofi, and Erik Hurst. 2002. The transition to home ownership and the black-white wealth gap. *Review of Economics and Statistics* 84 (2): 281–97.

Chasan, Emily, and John Poirier. 2007. Lifting the lid: Wall Street poses subprime obstacles. *The Washington Post,* June 1.

Chaudry, Sharad. 2007. *An introduction to the subprime mortgage sector.* Bank of America. RMBS Trading Desk Strategy. June 27.

Chomsisengphet, Souphala, and Anthony Pennington-Cross. 2006a. Subprime refinancing: Equity extraction and mortgage termination. Working paper series 2006–023, Federal Reserve Bank of St. Louis.

———. 2006b. The evolution of the subprime mortgage market. *Federal Reserve Bank of St. Louis Review* 88 (1): 31–56.

Cirasino, Massimo, and Mario Guadamillas. 2004. Reforming payments and securities settlement systems: A key element of financial infrastructure. *AccessFinance* 2: 1–3.

Citi Smith Barney. 2007. *Bond market roundup: Strategy—MBS and real estate ABS.* September. Citi Smith Barney.

Clark, Ellen H. 2006. Developments in derivatives and synthetic securitization following the US bankruptcy reform of 2005. In *Innovations in securitisation, yearbook 2006,* edited by Jan Job de Vries Robbe, and Paul U Ali, pp. 85–110. Leiden: Kluwer Law International.

CNBC.com with wire services. 2007. Mortgage crisis may slash lending up to $2 trillion. November 16. CNBC. http://www.cnbc.com/id/21832463/ (accessed September 16, 2008).

Cole, Roger T. 2007a. Subprime mortgage market: Hearing before Committee on Banking, Housing, and Urban Affairs on March 22. Senate. 110th Cong., 1st sess.

———. 2007b. Subprime mortgages: Hearing before Subcommittee on Financial Institutions and Consumer Credit on March 27. House. 110th Cong., 1st sess.

Collins, Michael, Eric Belsky, and Karl E. Case. 2004. Exploring the welfare effects of risk-based pricing in the subprime mortgage market. Working paper series BABC 04–8, Joint Center for Housing Studies, Harvard University. Cambridge, Massachusetts.

Comptroller of the Currency, Federal Reserve System, Federal Deposit Insurance Corporation, and Office of Thrift Supervision. 2002. Agency information collection activities: Proposed collection. *Federal Register* 67 (134).

Council of the District of Columbia. 2007. Committee on Public Services and Consumer Affairs 17th Council. Testimony by Peter A. Tatian on subprime mortgage lending in Washington, D.C.

Coy, Peter. 2008. Covered bonds, exposed taxpayers. *BusinessWeek,* August 11.

Crossney, Kristen B., and David W. Bartelt. 2005. The legacy of the home owners' loan corporation. *Housing Policy Debate* 16 (3–4): 547–74.

Cutts, Amy Crews, and Robert A. Van Order. 2005. On the economics of subprime lending. *Journal of Real Estate Finance and Economics* 30 (2): 167–96.

Cutts, Amy Crews, and William A. Merrill. 2008. *Interventions in mortgage default: Policies and practices to prevent home loss and lower costs.* Cambridge: Joint Center for Housing Studies, Harvard University.

Danis, Michelle A., and Anthony Pennington-Cross. 2005a. A dynamic look at subprime loan performance. Working paper series 2005–029A, Federal Reserve Bank of St. Louis.

————. 2005b. The delinquency of subprime mortgages. Working paper series 2005–022A. Federal Reserve Bank of St. Louis.

Davis, John Emmeus. 2006. *Shared equity homeownership the changing landscape of resale-restricted, owner-occupied housing.* Montclair, NJ: National Housing Institute.

Davis, Morris A., Andreas Lehnert, and Robert F. Martin. 2008. The rent-price ratio for the aggregate stock of owner-occupied housing. *Review of Income and Wealth* 54 (2): 279–84.

Davis, Morris A., François Ortalo-Magné, and Peter Rupert. 2007. *What's really going on in housing markets?* July. Economic Commentary. Federal Reserve Bank of Cleveland. http://www.clevelandfed.org/research/Commentary/2007/0707.cfm (accessed January 21, 2009).

Dell'Ariccia, Giovanni, Deniz Igan, and Luc Laeven. 2008. Credit booms and lending standards: Evidence from the subprime mortgage market. IMF working paper WP/08/106, International Monetary Fund, Washington, D.C.

Dell'Ariccia, Giovanni, Enrica Detragiache, and Raghuram Rajan. 2005. The real effect of banking crises. IMF working paper WP/05/63. International Monetary Fund, Washington, D.C.

Demyanyk, Yuliya, and Otto VanHemert. 2008. Understanding the subprime mortgage crisis. Supervisory policy analysis working paper series 2007–05, Federal Reserve Bank of St. Louis.

Deng, Yongheng, John M. Quigley, and Robert Van Order. 1996. Mortgage default and low down payment loans: The costs of public subsidy. *Regional Science and Urban Economics* 26 (3–4): 263–85.

DiMartino, Danielle, and John Duca. 2007. The rise and fall of subprime mortgages. *Economic Letter: Insights from the Federal Reserve Bank of Dallas* 2 (11).

Doherty, Jacqueline. 2008. Closer to the bottom. *Barron's*, October 13.

Doms, Mark, Fred Furlong, and John Krainer. 2007a. House prices and subprime mortgage delinquencies. *FRBSF Economic Letter*, 14 (June 8). http://www.frbsf.org/publications/economics/letter/2007/el2007-14.html (accessed January 21, 2009)

————. 2007b. Subprime mortgage delinquency rates. FRBSF working paper series 2007–33, Federal Reserve Bank of San Francisco.

Downes, John, and Jordan Elliot Goodman. 2002. *Barron's finance and investment handbook.* 6th ed. Hauppauge: Barron's Educational Series Inc.

Dudley, William C. 2007. May you live in interesting times. Lecture presented at the Federal Reserve Bank of Philadelphia, October 17, Philadelphia.

Duffie, Darrell. 2008. Innovations in credit risk transfer: Implications for financial stability. BIS working paper 255, Bank for International Settlements, Basel, Switzerland.

Dugan, John C. 2007. Testimony before the House Committee on Financial Services on September 5. 110th Cong., 1st sess.

Eavis, Peter, and David Reilly. 2008. Deflating mortgage rates: Moves to bolster Fannie, Freddie could lower costs. *The Wall Street Journal*, August 20.

Ebrahim, M. Shahid, and Ike Mathur. 2007. Pricing home mortgages and bank collateral: A rational expectations approach. *Journal of Economic Dynamics and Control* 31 (4): 1217–44.

Erbas, S. Nuri, and Frank E. Nothaft. 2005. Mortgage markets in Middle East and North African countries: Market development, poverty reduction, and growth. *Journal of Housing Economics* 14: 212–41.

Economist. 2007. *Mortgage industry lawsuits: The finger of suspicion.* December 19. http://www.economist.com/finance/displaystory.cfm?story_id=10337884 (accessed October 8, 2008).

———. 2008. *Pressure gauge: Are credit-default swaps living up to the hype?* August 21. http://www.economist.com/finance/displaystory.cfm?story_id=11985964 (accessed October 8, 2008).

Eichengreen, Barry. 2008. *What the Fed can learn from history's blunders.* August 18. *Financial Times.* http://www.ft.com/cms/s/0/bd13f3e8-6d38-11dd-857b-0000779fd18c.html (accessed October 8, 2008).

Elliehausen, Gregory, Michael E. Staten, and Jevgenijs Steinbuks. 2006. The effects of state predatory lending laws on the availability of subprime mortgage credit. Washington, D.C.: Credit Research Center, Georgetown University.

Elmendorf, Douglas W. 2007. *Notes on policy responses to the subprime mortgage unraveling.* Washington, D.C.: The Brookings Institution.

———. 2008. *Concerns about the treasury rescue plan.* September 19. The Brookings Institution. http://www.brookings.edu/opinions/2008/0919_treasury_plan_elmendorf.aspx (accessed October 10, 2008)

Essene, Ren S., and William Apgar. 2007. *Understanding mortgage market behavior: Creating good mortgage options for all Americans.* Cambridge: Joint Center for Housing Studies, Harvard University.

European Mortgage Federation. 2004. *Covered bonds and mortgage-backed securities in the European Union.* Brussels, Belgium: European Mortgage Federation.

European Shadow Financial Regulatory Committee. 2007. *Lessons from recent financial turmoil. Statement 26.* Center for European Policy Studies. http://www.ceps.eu/wp.php?article_id=568 (accessed September 16, 2008).

Evans, David. 2007. The poison in your pension. *Bloomberg Markets*, July, 64–9.

Experian. 2007. *VantageScore addresses deficiencies in traditional scores in the subprime consumer sector.* Costa Mesa: Experian.

Federal Deposit Insurance Corporation. 2006a. Accessing capital markets and managing market risk. *FDIC Outlook*, fall.

——. 2006b. Economic conditions and emerging risks in banking: A report to the FDIC Board of Directors.

——. 2006c. Looking ahead at banking conditions in 2007. *FDIC Outlook*, winter.

——. 2006d. The evolution of the credit cycle. *FDIC Outlook*, summer.

——. 2008. *Fact sheet: FHFA conservatorship*. September. Federal Housing Finance Board and Office of Federal Housing Enterprise Oversight. http://www.treas.gov/press/releases/reports/fhfa_ consrv_faq_090708hp1128. pdf (accessed October 8, 2008).

Federal Housing Administration. *FHA home loans for purchasers with rising incomes*. http://www.fha.com/graduated_payment.cfm (accessed September 8, 2008).

Federal Reserve Board. 2002. Division of Banking Supervision and Regulation. Subprime lending (risk management and internal controls). In *Bank holding company supervision manual*. Section 2128.08. Washington, D.C.: Federal Reserve Board.

——. 2008. *Distribution to respondents of a national summary of the July Senior Loan Officer Opinion Survey on Bank Lending Practices*. Washington, D.C.: Federal Reserve Board.

Feldstein, Martin. 2007. Housing, housing finance, and monetary policy. *Financial Times*, September 13.

Ferreira, Fernando, Joseph Gyourko, and Joseph Tracy. 2008. Housing busts and household mobility. NBER working paper series 14310, National Bureau of Economic Research. Cambridge, Massachusetts

First American CoreLogic. 2008a. *Core Mortgage Risk Monitor* Q2.

——. 2008b. Latest U.S. residential mortgage and price performance maps. *Core Mortgage Risk Monitor* Q1. Supplement.

Fishbein, Allen J., and Patrick Woodall. 2006. *Subprime locations: Patterns of geographic disparity in subprime lending*. Washington, D.C.: Consumer Federation of America.

Fitch Ratings. 2007. *Fitch ratings 1991–2006 U.S. structured finance transition study*. New York: Fitch Ratings.

Foote, Christopher L., Kristopher Gerardi, and Paul S. Willen. 2008. Negative equity and foreclosure: Theory and evidence. Public Policy discussion papers 08–3, Federal Reserve Bank of Boston.

Frame, W. Scott. 2003. Federal Home Loan Bank mortgage purchases: Implications for mortgage markets. *Federal Reserve Bank of Atlanta Economic Review* 88 (3): 17–31.

Frankel, Allen, Jacob Gyntelberg, Kristian Kjeldsen, and Mattias Persson. 2004. The Danish mortgage market. *BIS Quarterly Review*, March: 95–109.

Fratantoni, Michael, Douglas G. Duncan, Jay Brinkmann, and Orawin Velz. 2007. *The residential mortgage market and its economic context in 2007*. MBA Research Monograph Series. Washington, D.C.: Mortgage Bankers Association.

French, Dan W., and Richard L. Haney. 1984. Pricing the shared-appreciation mortgage in a stochastic environment. *Housing Finance Review* 3 (4): 431–43.

Fuchs, Karlo, and Karen Naylor. 2007. *All covered bonds are not created equal.* RatingsDirect. http://www.hypverband.de/d/internet.nsf/0/267B351573A49934C12574010053128C/$FILE/S&P_Rating_All%20Covered%20Bonds%20Are%20Not%20Created%20Equal.pdf?OpenElement (accessed September 23, 2008).

Garriga, Carlos, William T. Gavin, and Don Schlagenhauf. 2006. Recent trends in homeownership. *Federal Reserve Bank of St. Louis Review* 88 (5): 397–411.

Gerardi, Kristopher, Adam Hale Shapiro, and Paul S. Willen. 2007. Subprime outcomes: Risky mortgages, homeownership experiences, and foreclosures. Working paper 07–15, Federal Reserve Bank of Boston.

Gerardi, Kristopher, Harvey S. Rosen, and Paul Willen. 2007. Do households benefit from financial deregulation and innovation? The case of the mortgage market. CEPS working paper series 141, Center for Economic Policy Studies, Princeton, New Jersey.

Glaeser, Edward. 2007. Sensible solutions to the lending mess. *Boston Globe*, September 7. http://www.boston.com/news/globe/editorial_opinion/oped/articles/2007/09/07/sensible_solutions_to_the_lending_mess/ (accessed January 21, 2009).

Goolsbee, Austan. 2007. "Irresponsible" mortgages have opened doors to many of the excluded. *New York Times*, March 29. http://www.nytimes.com/2007/03/29/business/29scene.html (accessed January 21, 2009).

Gorton, Gary. 2008. The panic of 2007. Paper presented at the 2008 Jackson Hole Symposium on Maintaining Stability in a Changing Financial System, August 21–23, Jackson Hole, Wyoming.

Gramlich, Edward M. 2000. Predatory lending. Speech at the Fair Housing Council of New York, April 14, Syracuse, New York.

———. 2003. An update on the predatory lending issue. Speech at the Texas Association of Bank Counsel 27th Annual Convention, October 9, South Padre Island, Texas.

———. 2007a. *America's second housing boom*. Opportunity and Ownership Project Series 7. Washington, D.C.: The Urban Institute.

———. 2007b. Booms and busts: The case of subprime mortgages. *Economic Review*, Fourth Quarter: 105–13.

———. 2007c. *Subprime Mortgages: America's Latest Boom and Bust*. Washington, D.C.: The Urban Institute Press.

Green, Richard, and Susan Wachter. 2005. The American mortgage in historical and international context. *Journal of Economic Perspectives* 19 (4): 93–114.

———. 2007. The housing finance revolution. Paper presented at the 31st Economic Policy Symposium: Housing, Housing Finance and Monetary Policy, August 31–September 1, Jackson Hole, Wyoming.

Greenlaw, David, Jan Hatzius, Anil K Kashyap, and Hyun Song Shin. 2008. Leveraged losses: Lessons from the mortgage market meltdown. Paper presented at the U.S. Monetary Policy Forum, February 29, New York.

Greenspan, Alan. 2002. Issues for monetary policy. Remarks before the Economic Club of New York, December 19, New York.

———. 2003. Home mortgage market. Speech at the annual convention of the Independent Community Bankers of America, March 4, Orlando.

Greenspan, Alan, and James Kennedy. 2007. *Sources and uses of equity extracted from homes*. Finance and Economics Discussion Paper 2007–20. Washington, D.C.: Board of Governors of the Federal Reserve System.

Gross, Bill. 2007. Where's Waldo? Where's W? *Investment Outlook*, September. http://www.pimco.com/LeftNav/Featured+Market+Commentary/IO/2007/IO+September+2007.htm (accessed January 21, 2009).

Gunther, Jeffery W., and Anna Zhang. 2007. Hedge fund investors more rational than rash. *Economic Letter: Insights from the Federal Reserve Bank of Dallas* 2 (8). Available for download at http://www.dallasfed.org/research/eclett/2007/index.html (accessed January 21, 2009).

Guttentag, Jack M. 2007. *Upheaval in the sub-prime mortgage market*. Mortgage Professor's Web Site. http://www.mtgprofessor.com/A% 20-%20Public%20 Policy%20Issues/upheaval_in_the_sub-prime_mortgage_market.htm (accessed September 8, 2008).

Hagerty, James R., and Serena Ng. 2008. Banks take a hit as Fannie and Freddie are downgraded. *The Wall Street Journal*, August 23.

Hamilton, James. 2007. Comments on "Housing and the Monetary Transmission Mechanism." Paper presented at the Symposium on Housing, Housing Finance, and Monetary Policy, September 1, Jackson Hole, Wyoming.

Harvey, Paul. 2007. If "pro" is the opposite of "con" what is the opposite of "progress"? *CFC Economic Outlook*, July.

Hassett, Kevin A. 2007. *Bust and boom*. Washington, D.C.: American Enterprise Institute for Public Policy Research.

Haughwout, Andrew, Richard Peach, and Joseph Tracy. 2008. Juvenile delinquent mortgages: Bad credit or bad economy? Staff report 341, Federal Reserve Bank of New York.

Henry, David, and Matthew Goldstein. 2008. How bad will it get on Wall Street? *BusinessWeek*, July 28.

Ho, Giang, and Anthony Pennington-Cross. 2005. The impact of local predatory lending laws. Working paper series 2005–049B, Federal Reserve Bank of St. Louis.

———. 2006a. Predatory lending laws and the cost of credit. Working paper series 2006–022A, Federal Reserve Bank of St. Louis.

———. 2006b. States fight predatory lending. *Regional Economist*, January: 12–13.

———. 2006c. The impact of local predatory lending laws on the flow of subprime credit: North Carolina and beyond. Working paper series 2006–009A, Federal Reserve Bank of St. Louis.

———. 2007. The varying effects of predatory lending laws on high-cost mortgage applications. *Federal Reserve Bank of St. Louis Review* 89 (1): 39–59.

Honohan, Patrick. 2008. Discussion of "Financial Innovation and European Housing and Mortgage Markets" by David Miles and Vladimir Pillonca. *Oxford Review of Economic Policy* 24 (1): 176–79.

Hurd, Maude. 2007. Letter to Federal Reserve System regarding the Proposed Statement on Subprime Lending, May 7. New Orleans: Association of Community Organizations for Reform Now.

Hylton, Keith. 2006. Development lending and the Community Reinvestment Act. Law and economic working paper series 06–07, School of Law, Boston University, Bostons

Inside Mortgage Finance. 2007a. Democrats looking to increase regulation of subprime market. *Inside B&C Lending*, September.

———. 2007b. Subprime MBS declines, GSE classes gain greater share. *Inside B&C Lending* 12 (20).

———. 2007c. Subprime originations volume continues to decline in 3Q. *Inside B&C Lending* 12 (22).

Integrated Financial Engineering Inc. 2007. *Mortgage securitization: Lessons for emerging markets*. Rockville: Integrated Financial Engineering Inc.

International Monetary Fund. 2007. *Global financial stability report: Financial market turbulence—causes, consequences, and policies*. Washington, D.C.: International Monetary Fund.

———. 2008. *Global financial stability report: Containing systematic risks and restoring financial soundness*. Washington, D.C.: International Monetary Fund.

International Swaps and Derivatives Association. 2008a. *ISDA mid-year 2008 market survey shows credit derivatives at $54.6 trillion.* September 24. http://www.isda. org/press/press092508.html (accessed October 7, 2008).

———. 2008b. *ISDA publishes year-end 2007 market survey.* April 16. http://www.isda.org/press/press 041608market.html (accessed October 7, 2008).

Johnson, Simon. 2007. The rise of sovereign wealth funds. *Finance and Development* 44 (3).

Jones, Stephanie K. 2007. The blame game and the subprime mortgage lending meltdown. *Insurance Journal*, August 22.

Kahn, James A. 2008. What drives housing prices? Staff report 345, Federal Reserve Bank of New York.

Kane, Edward J. 1977. Good intentions and unintended evil: The case against selective credit allocation. *Journal of Money, Credit and Banking* 9 (1): 55–69.

———. 1989. Changing incentives facing financial-services regulators. *Journal of Financial Services Research* 2 (3): 263–272.

———. 1998. Interaction of financial and regulatory innovation. *American Economic Review* 78 (2): 328–334.

———. 2003. What kind of multinational arrangements might best enhance world welfare? *Pacific Basin Finance Journal* 11 (4): 413–428.

———. 2005. Impediments to fair and efficient resolution of large banks and banking crises. In *Systematic Financial Crises: Resolving Large Bank Insolvencies*, edited by Douglas Evanoff and George G. Kaufman, pp. 123–140. Singapore: World Scientific.

———. 2008a. *Ethical failures in regulating and supervising the pursuit of safety-net subsidies.* Boston College. http://www2.bc.edu/%7Ekaneeb/Ethical %20Failure%20in%20Regulating-8-8-08.doc (accessed September 23, 2008).

———. 2008b. *Who should bear responsibility for mistakes made in assigning credit ratings to securitized debt?* Boston College. http://www2.bc.edu/ %7Ekaneeb/Who%20Should%20Bear%20Responsibility%20for%20Mistakes %20Made%20in%20Assigning%20Credit%20Ratings.doc (accessed September 23, 2008).

———. Forthcoming. Regulation and supervision: An ethical perspective. In *Oxford handbook of banking*, edited by Allen Berger, Phil Molyneux, and John Wilson. London: Oxford University Press.

———. 1999. Housing finance GSEs: Who gets the subsidy? *Journal of Financial Services Research* 15 (3): 197–209.

Kane, Edward J., and Klingebiel, Daniela. 2004. Alternatives to blanket guarantees for containing a systemic crisis. *Journal of Financial Stability* 1 (1): 31–63.

Kashyap, Anil K., Raghuram G. Rajan, and Jeremy C. Stein. 2008. Rethinking capital regulation. Paper presented at the 2008 Jackson Hole Symposium on Maintaining Stability in a Changing Financial System, August 21–23, Jackson Hole, Wyoming.

Kiff, John, and Paul Mills. 2007. Money for nothing and checks for free: Recent developments in U.S. subprime mortgage markets. IMF working paper WP/07/188, International Monetary Fund, Washington, D.C.

Kim, Anne. 2002. *Taken for a ride: Subprime lenders, automobility, and the working poor.* Policy report, Progressive Policy Institute, Washington, D.C.

Knowledge@Wharton. 2007. *Could tremors in the subprime mortgage market be the first signs of an earthquake?* February 21. http://knowledge.wharton.upenn .edu/article.cfm?articleid=1664 (accessed September 23, 2008).

Koijen, Ralph S. J., Otto Van Hemert, and Stijn Van Nieuwerburgh. 2007. Mortgage timing. Paper presented at the 34th European Finance Association annual meeting, August 22–25, Ljubljana, Slovenia.

Koons, Cynthia. 2008. Risk-taking hits investors in leveraged-loan market. *Wall Street Journal*, August 23.

Kovacevich, Richard M., James Dimon, Thomas A. James, and Thomas A. Renyi. 2007. *The blueprint for U.S. financial competitiveness.* Washington, D.C.: The Financial Services Roundtable.

Lachman, Desmond. 2007a. Subprime blues sound familiar. *Financial Times*, August 2.

———. 2007b. The U.S. housing bust is a big deal. *TCS Daily*, August 10. http://www.tcsdaily.com/article.aspx?id=080907B (accessed January 21, 2009).

———. 2007c. What Congress should—and shouldn't—do about the housing crisis. *TCS Daily*, August 29. http://www.tcsdaily .com/article.aspx?id=082907A (accessed January 21, 2009).

Lacko, James M., and Janis K. Pappalardo. 2007. *Improving consumer mortgage disclosures: An empirical assessment of current and prototype disclosure forms.* Washington, D.C.: Federal Trade Commission.

Larson, Michael D. 2007. How federal regulators, lenders, and Wall Street created America's housing crisis: Nine proposals for a long-term recovery. July. Weiss Research.

Lea, Michael J. 1994. Efficiency and stability of housing finance systems: A comparison of the United Kingdom and the United States. *Housing Policy Debate* 5 (3): 361–79.

Lehnert, Andreas, Wayne Passmore, and Shane M. Sherlund. 2005. *GSEs, mortgage rates, and secondary market activities.* Finance and Economics Discussion Series 2005–07. Washington, D.C.: Federal Reserve Board.

Levitin, Adam J., and Joshua S. Goodman. 2008. Resolving the foreclosure crisis: Modification of mortgages in bankruptcy. Business, economics and regulatory policy working paper series 1071931, Law Center, Georgetown University, Washington, D.C.

Li, Wei, and Keith S. Ernst. 2006. *The best value in the subprime market: State predatory lending reforms*. Durham: Center for Responsible Lending.

Liu, David, and Shumin Li. 2006. Alt-A credit: The other shoe drops? *MarketPulse*, December.

Lockhart, James B. 2008a. Lessons learned from mortgage Market Turmoil. Paper presented at the 44th Annual Conference on Bank Structure and Competition, May 14–16, Chicago.

———. 2008b. Statement of James B. Lockhart, director of Federal Housing Enterprise Oversight, at a news conference, March 19.

———. 2008c. Statement of James B. Lockhart, director of Federal Housing Finance Agency, on the conservatorship of Fannie Mae and Freddie Mac on September 7. Federal Housing Finance Board and Office of Federal Housing Enterprise Oversight.

Makin, John. 2007. Recession 2008? *The Wall Street Journal*, September 8.

Mason, Joseph R. 2007, The role of credit rating agencies in the structured finance market: Hearing before Subcommittee on Capital Markets, Insurance, and Government Sponsored Enterprises on September 27. House. 110th Cong., 1st sess.

Mason, Joseph R., and Joshua Rosner. 2007. *Where did the risk go? How misapplied bond ratings cause mortgage backed securities and collateralized debt obligation market disruptions*. May. http://papers.ssrn.com/sol3/papers.cfm?abstract_id=1027475 (accessed September 23, 2008).

Mason, Joseph R., Kolari, James W. and Anari, Ali. 2005. Bank asset liquidation and the propagation of the great depression. *Journal of Money, Credit, and Banking* 37 (4): 753–73.

Mayer, Christopher J., and Karen Pence. 2008. Subprime mortgages: What, where and to whom? NBER working paper series 14083, National Bureau of Economic Research, Cambridge, Massachusetts.

McCue, Daniel, and Eric S. Belsky. 2007. Why do house prices fall? Perspectives on the historical drivers of large nominal house price declines. Working paper W07–3, Joint Center for Housing Studies, Harvard University, Cambridge, Massachusetts.

McDonald, Daniel J., and Daniel L. Thornton. 2008. A primer on the mortgage market and mortgage finance. *Federal Reserve Bank of St. Louis Review* 90 (1): 31–45.

Mian, Atif, and Amir Sufi. 2008. The consequences of mortgage credit expansion: Evidence from the 2007 mortgage default crisis. NBER working paper series 13936, National Bureau of Economic Research, Cambridge, Massachusetts.

Mihm, Stephen. 2008. *Dr. Doom. The New York Times Magazine,* August 17. http://www .nytimes.com/2008/08/17/magazine/17pessimist-t.html (accessed January 21, 2009).

Miles, David. 1992. Housing markets, consumption and financial liberalisation in the major economies. *European Economic Review* 36 (5): 1093–127.

Miles, David, and Vladimir Pillonca. 2008. Financial innovation and European housing and mortgage markets. *Oxford Review of Economic Policy* 24 (1): 145–75.

Mishkin, Frederic S. 2007. Housing and the monetary transmission mechanism. NBER working paper series 13518, National Bureau of Economic Research, Cambridge, Massachusetts.

Modukuri, Srinivas, Prasanth Subramanian, Vikas Reddy Shilpiekandula, Akhil Mago, and Rahul Sabarwal. 2007. *Will subprime woes spill over to the broad markets v2.0.* July. Lehman Brothers.

Morgan, Donald P. 2007. Defining and detecting predatory lending. Staff report 273, Federal Reserve Bank of New York.

Mortgage Bankers Association. 2006. *National delinquency survey.* Mortgage Bankers Association, First Quarter.

———. 2007. *Suitability: Don't turn back the clock on fair lending and homeownership gains.* MBA Policy Paper Series 2007–1, Washington, D.C.: Mortgage Bankers Association.

Mudd, Daniel H. 2008, Reforming the regulation of the government sponsored enterprises: Hearing before Committee on Banking, Housing and Urban Affairs on February 7. Senate. 110th Cong., 1st sess.

Muellbauer, John. 2007. Housing, credit and consumer expenditure. Paper presented at the 31st Economic Policy Symposium: Housing, Housing Finance and Monetary Policy on 30 August –1 September, at Jackson Hole, Wyoming.

Murai, Reiji. 2008. *Global subprime losses hit $215 billion: Japan's FSA.* March 10. Reuters. http://www.reuters.com/article/ousiv/idUST23446220080310 (accessed September 23, 2008).

Murphy, J. Austin. 1991. A practical analysis of shared-appreciation mortgages. *Housing Policy Debate* 2 (1): 43–8.

Murphy, Robert P. 2007. *The worst recession in 25 years?* Ludwig von Mises Institute. http://mises.org/story/2728 (accessed October 8, 2008).

MyFICO. 2007. *Understanding your FICO score.* October. Fair Isaac Corporation. http://www.nasfaa.org/subhomes/annualconference2006/handouts2006/s065 privateloansandcreditscores2.pdf (accessed September 23, 2008).

National Association of Consumer Bankruptcy Attorneys, Consumer Federation of America, and Center for Responsible Lending. 2007. *Consumer groups: Fix bankruptcy laws so hundreds of thousands of Americans can avoid home foreclosures in subprime mortgage crisis.* April. National Association of Consumer Bankruptcy Attorneys, Consumer Federation of America, and Center for Responsible Lending. http://www.consumerfed.org/pdfs/bankruptcy_press _release041207.pdf (accessed September 23, 2008).

Nothaft, Frank E., and James L. Freund. 2003. The evolution of securitization in multifamily mortgage markets and its effect on lending rates. *Journal of Real Estate Research* 25 (2): 91–112.

Nothaft, Frank E. 2004. The contribution of home value appreciation to U.S. economic growth. *Urban Policy and Research* 22 (1): 23–34.

———. 2007. The rise and fall of subprime: The subprime mortgage meltdown of 2007. *Research Review* 14 (3): 7–11.

Odell, Anne Moore. 2007. *Subprime lending hurts homeowners.* April. Social Funds. April 5. http://www.socialfunds.com/news/print.cgi?sfArticleId=2266 (accessed September 23, 2008).

Office of the Comptroller of the Currency, Board of Governors of the Federal Reserve System, Federal Deposit Insurance Corporation, Office of Thrift Supervision, and National Credit Union Administration. 2007. Statement on subprime mortgage lending. http://www.federalreserve.gov/newsevents/ press/bcreg/20070629a.htm (accessed January 21, 2009).

Office of Thrift Supervision. 2007. *2006 fact book: A statistical profile of the thrift industry.* Washington, D.C. Office of Thrift Supervision.

Packer, Frank, Ryan Stever, and Christian Upper. 2007. The covered bond market. *BIS Quarterly Review*, September: 43–55.

Page, Frank H., and Anthony B. Sanders. 1986. On the pricing of shared-appreciation mortgages. *Housing Finance Review* 5 (1): 49–57.

Paulson, Jr., Henry M. 2008a. Statement before House Committee on Financial Services on Regulatory Reform on July 10. House. 110th Cong., 2nd sess.

———. 2008. Statement on Treasury and Federal Housing Finance Agency Action to protect financial markets and taxpayers. Press release, United States Treasury, Washington, D.C.

Pavlov, Andrey, and Susan Wachter. 2007. *Aggressive lending and real estate markets.* Philadelphia: The Wharton School, University of Pennsylvania.

Pence, Karen M. 2006. Foreclosing on opportunity: State laws and mortgage credit. *Review of Economics and Statistics* 88 (1): 177–82.

Pennington-Cross, Anthony. 2002. Subprime lending in the primary and secondary markets. *Journal of Housing Research* 13 (1): 31–50.

———. 2004. The value of foreclosed property. Working paper series 2004–022A, Federal Reserve Bank of St. Louis.

———. 2006. The duration of foreclosures in the subprime mortgage market: A competing risks model with mixing. Working paper series 2006–027A, Federal Reserve Bank of St. Louis.

Pennington-Cross, Anthony, and Giang Ho. 2006a. Loan servicer heterogeneity and the termination of subprime mortgages. Working paper series 2006–024A, Federal Reserve Bank of St. Louis.

———. 2006b. The termination of subprime hybrid and fixed rate mortgages. Working paper series 2006–042A, Federal Reserve Bank of St. Louis.

Pollock, Alex J. 2007a. Evolution of an economic crisis?: The subprime lending disaster and the threat to the broader economy: Hearing before the Senate Joint Economic Committee on September 19. 110th Cong., 1st sess.

———. 2007b. Legislative and regulatory options regarding mortgage foreclosures: Hearing before the House Committee on Financial Services on September 20. 110th Cong., 1st sess.

———. 2007c. Subprime and predatory mortgage lending: New regulatory guidance, current market conditions and effects on regulated financial institutions: Hearing before the House Subcommittee on Financial Institutions and Consumer Credit of the Committee on Financial Services on March 27. 110th Cong., 1st sess.

———. 2007. *Subprime bust expands.* August 6. American.com. http://american.com/archive/2007/august-0807/subprime-bust-expands (accessed September 25, 2008).

Puryear, Paul D., Buck Horne, Kevin Ross, and Jeremy VanScoyoc. 2008. *Housing quarterly.* June. Raymond James & Associates Inc., St. Petersburg, FL.

Qi, Min, and Xiaolong Yang. 2007. Loss given default of high loan-to-value residential mortgages. Economics and policy analysis working paper 2007–4, U.S. Office of the Comptroller of the Currency, Washington, D.C.

Quercia, Roberto G., and Michael A. Stegman. 2002. Residential mortgage default: A review of the literature. *Journal of Housing Research* 3 (2): 341–79.

Quercia, Roberto G., Michael A. Stegman, and Walter R. Davis. 2003. *The impact of North Carolina's anti-predatory lending law: A descriptive assessment.* Chapel Hill: University of North Carolina.

———. 2005. *The impact of predatory loan terms on subprime foreclosures: The special case of prepayment penalties and balloon payments.* Chapel Hill: Center for Community Capitalism, University of North Carolina.

Reiss, David. 2005. Subprime standardization: How rating agencies allow predatory lending to flourish in the secondary mortgage market. *Florida State University Law Review* 33: 985–1066.

Renuart, Elizabeth. 2004. An overview of the predatory mortgage lending process. *Housing Policy Debate* 15 (3): 467–99.

Robbins, John. 2007. Letter to Board of Governors of the Federal Reserve System on the Home Ownership and Equity Protection Act, 15 August.

Rose, Morgan J. 2008. Predatory lending practices and subprime foreclosures: Distinguishing impacts by loan category. *Journal of Economics and Business* 60 (1–2): 13–32.

Roubini, Nouriel. 2007. *I was way too optimistic on the housing recession.* September 25. RGE Monitor. http://www.rgemonitor.com/blog/roubini/216854 (accessed September 25, 2008).

———. 2008. *The forthcoming "Jingle Mail" tsunami: 10 to 15 million households likely to walk away from their homes/mortgages leading to a systemic banking crisis.* February 19. RGE Monitor. http://www.rgemonitor.com/roubini-monitor/ 244768/the_forthcoming_jingle_mail_tsunami_10_to_15_million_households_ likely_to_walk_away_from_their_homesmortgages_leading_to_a_systemic_banking_crisis/ (accessed September 25, 2008).

Rutherford, Reid. 1995. Securitizing small-business loans: A banker's action plan. *Commercial Lending Review* 10 (1): 62–74.

Sanders, Anthony B., and V. Carlos Slawson. 2005. Shared appreciation mortgages: Lessons from the UK. *Journal of Housing Economics* 14 (3): 178–93.

Sayeed, Almas. 2007. *From boom to bust: Helping families prepare for the rise in subprime mortgage foreclosures.* March 12. Center for American Progress. http://www.americanprogress.org/issues/2007/03/foreclosure_paper.html (accessed September 25, 2008).

Schloemer, Ellen, Wei Li, Keith Ernst, and Kathleen Keest. 2006. *Losing ground: Foreclosures in the subprime market and their cost to homeowners.* Durham: Center for Responsible Lending.

Schmitt, Richard B. 2008. FBI saw threat of loan crisis. *Los Angeles Times*, August 25. http://articles.latimes.com/2008/aug/25/business/fi-mortgagefraud25 (accessed January 21, 2009).

Schultz, Glenn M., John McElravey, and Shane Whitworth. 2007. Implications for ABX valuations in an uncertain market. Wachovia. Slide.

Schumer, Charles E. 2007. *Sheltering neighborhoods from the subprime foreclosure storm.* Washington, D.C.: U.S. Congress Joint Economic Committee.

Shiller, Robert J. 2001. *Irrational exuberance.* 2nd ed. Princeton: Princeton University Press.

———. 2008a. Crisis averted. What of the next one? *The New York Times*, August 9. http://www.nytimes.com/2008/08/10/business/economy/10view.html (accessed January 21, 2009).

———. 2008b. *The subprime solution: How today's global financial crisis happened and what to do about it.* Princeton: Princeton University Press.

Showalter, Tom. 2006. Mortgage servicing: An apples to apples comparison with billions at stake. LoanPerformance *MarketPulse*, 2.

Shultz, George, and John Taylor. 2007. The silver lining in America's subprime cloud. *Financial Times*, November 5.

Snook, Randolph C., and George P. Miller. 2007. Letter to Federal Reserve System (the Board) regarding the Board's authority to address certain abusive or unfair lending practices on August 3.

Speakes, Jeff. 2007. Derivatives: Financial WMD? *CFC Economic Outlook*, April.

Sperling, Gene. 2007. *Subprime market: Isolated or a tipping point?* March 14. Bloomberg.com. http://www.bloomberg.com/apps/news?pid= 20601039&sid=a2mHr9ol.GUs&refer=columnist_sperling (accessed September 25, 2008).

Spillenkothen, Richard. 1999. Letter to the officer in charge of supervision, appropriate supervisory and examination staff at each Federal Reserve Bank, and to each domestic banking organization supervised by the Federal Reserve on subprime lending, SR 99-6, March 5. http://www.federalreserve.gov/boarddocs/ SRLetters/1999/SR9906.HTM (accessed January 21, 2009).

Stegman, Michael A., Roberto G. Quercia, and Walter R. Davis. 2003. North Carolina's anti-predatory lending law: Doing what it's supposed to do: A reply. November. AEI–Brookings Joint Center for Regulatory Studies.

Summers, Lawrence. 2007. *Recent financial market disruptions: Implications for the economy and American families.* Washington, D.C.: The Hamilton Project, The Brookings Institution.

Taleb, Nasseem. 2007. History doesn't evolve, it jumps. *CFC Economic Outlook*, August.

Tatom, John. 2008a. The continuing foreclosure crisis: New institutions and risks. *ResearchBuzz* 4 (7).

———. 2008b. The U.S. foreclosure crisis: A two-pronged assault on the U.S. economy. Working paper 2008–WP–10, Networks Financial Institute, Indiana State University, Terre Haute, Indiana.

Taylor, John B. 2007. Housing and monetary policy. NBER working paper series 13682, National Bureau of Economic Research, Washington, D.C.

Temkin, Kenneth, Jennifer E. H. Johnson, and Diane Levy. 2002. *Subprime markets, the role of GSEs, and risk-based pricing.* Washington, D.C.: U.S. Department of Housing and Urban Development/Office of Policy Development and Research.

Tenhundfeld, Mark, and Robert Davis. 2007. Letter to Federal Reserve System (Board) on whether the Board should use its rulemaking authority to address concerns about certain loan terms or practice, August 15.

Thornton, Daniel L. 2008. In response to recent financial market turmoil, the Federal Reserve has introduced an alphabet soup of programs (TAF, TSLF, PDCF, etc.). What are these, and how do they work? *Regional Economist*, July. http://www.stls.frb.org/publications/re/2008/c/pages/reader-exchange.html (accessed January 21, 2009).

Timiraos, Nick. 2008. FBI probes unusual incentives for home buyers: Investigators ask whether payments misled lenders. *The Wall Street Journal*, August 16.

Tong, Hui, and Shang-Jin Wei. 2008. Real effects of the subprime mortgage crisis: Is it a demand or a finance shock?NBER working paper series 14205, National Bureau of Economic Research, Washinton, D.C.

U.S. Bureau of the Census. 1960. *Historical statistics of the United States, colonial times to 1957*. Washington, D.C.: U.S. Bureau of the Census.

U.S. Department of Housing and Urban Development. 2000a. *Unequal burden in Baltimore: Income and racial disparities in subprime lending*. Washington, D.C.: U.S. Department of Housing and Urban Development.

———. 2000b. *Unequal burden: Income and racial disparities in subprime lending in America*. April. Washington, D.C.: U.S. Department of Housing and Urban Development.

U.S. General Accountability Office. 2004. *Consumer protection: Federal and state agencies face challenges in combating predatory lending*. Washington, D.C.: U.S. General Accountability Office.

U.S. House. 2007a. Committee on Banking, Housing, and Urban Affairs. *Borrower's Protection Act of 2007*. 110th Cong., 1st sess.

———. 2007b. House. House Financial Services Committee. *Mortgage Reform and Anti-Predatory Lending Act of 2007*. 110th Cong., 1st sess.

———. 2007c. House Financial Services Committee. *Mortgage Reform and Anti-Predatory Lending Act of 2007*. 110th Cong., 1st sess.

———. 2007d. Subcommittee on Capital Markets, Insurance, and Government Sponsored Enterprises. *The Role of Credit Rating Agencies in the Structured Finance Market*. 110th Cong., 1st sess. September 27.

U.S. Senate. 2008. Committee on Banking, Housing and Urban Affairs. *Reforming the Regulation of the Government-Sponsored Enterprises*. 110th Cong., 1st sess., 7 February.

U.S. Treasury. 2008a. *Fact Sheet: Government Sponsored Enterprise Credit Facility*. Washington, D.C.: Department Office of Public Affairs, U.S. Treasury.

———. 2008b. *Fact Sheet: GSE Mortgage Backed Securities Purchase Program.* Washington, D.C.: Department Office of Public Affairs, U.S. Treasury.

———. 2008c. Fact Sheet: Treasury Senior Preferred Stock Purchase Agreement. Washington, D.C.: Department Office of Public Affairs, U.S. Treasury.

Utt, Ronald D., and David C. John. 2007. *The subprime mortgage situation: Bailout not the right solution.* Heritage Foundation, WebMemo no. 1604. http://www. heritage.org/Research/Economy/wm1604.cfm (accessed October 8, 2008).

Van Order, Robert. 2000. The U.S. mortgage market: A model of dueling charters. *Journal of Housing Research* 11 (2): 233–55.

Wallace, George, Gregory Elliehausen, and Michael Staten. 2005. Are legislative solutions to abusive mortgage lending practices throwing out the baby with the bath? Guidance from empirical research. Draft presented at the 41st Annual Conference on Bank Structure and Competition at Federal Reserve Bank of Chicago, May 4–6, Chicago.

Weaver, Karen, and Katie Reeves. 2007. The impact of underwriting subprime ARMs at the fully indexed rate: An analysis of debt-to-income ratios. *MarketPulse*, March.

Wheaton, William C., and Gleb Nechayev. 2008. The 1998–2005 housing "bubble" and the current "correction": What's different this time? *Journal of Real Estate Research* 30 (1): 1–26.

Wheelock, David C. 2008. The Federal response to home mortgage distress: Lessons from the Great Depression. *The Federal Reserve Bank of St. Louis Review* 90 (3): 133–48.

White, Lawrence J. 2003. Focusing on Fannie and Freddie: The dilemmas of reforming housing finance. *Journal of Financial Services Research* 23 (1): 43–58.

Whitehead, Christine, and Judy Yates. 2007. Increasing affordability problems: A role for shared equity products? Experience in Australia and UK. *Housing Finance International* 21 (5): 16–20.

Youngblood, Michael. 2006. Explaining the higher default rates of the 2005 origination year. *MarketPulse*, 3.

Zandi, Mark. 2008. *Financial shock: A 360° look at the subprime mortgage implosion, and how to avoid the next financial crisis.* Upper Saddle River: Financial Times Press.

Zelman, Ivy L., Dennis McGill, Justin Speer, and Alan Ratner. 2007. *Mortgage liquidity du jour: Underestimated no more.* March. Credit Suisse.

Zeng, Min. 2008. Despite fuss, mortgage-backed bonds have fans. *The Wall Street Journal*, August 22.

Zimmerman, Thomas. 2007a. *The deflating mortgage and housing bubble: Part II*. Slide presentation at The Deflating Mortgage and Housing Bubble, Part II: The Financial and Political Risks, October 11, Washington, D.C.

———. 2007b. *The U.S. subprime market: An industry in turmoil*. Slide presentation at Mortgage Credit and Subprime Lending: Implications of a Deflating Bubble, March 28, Washington, D.C.

About the
Milken Institute and
General Disclaimer

The Milken Institute is an independent economic think tank whose mission is to improve the lives and economic conditions of diverse populations in the United States and around the world by helping business and public policy leaders identify and implement innovative ideas for creating broad-based prosperity. We put research to work with the goal of revitalizing regions and finding new ways to generate capital for people with original ideas.

By creating ways to spread the benefits of human, financial, and social capital to as many people as possible—by *democratizing* capital—we hope to contribute to prosperity and freedom in all corners of the globe.

As a nonprofit, charitable organization, the Milken Institute receives financial support from many sources, a number of which have had interests in the mortgage market. None of our sponsors, however, were involved in the writing of this book.

About the Authors

James R. Barth is a Senior Fellow at the Milken Institute and the Lowder Eminent Scholar in Finance at Auburn University. His research focuses on financial institutions and capital markets, both domestic and global, with special emphasis on regulatory issues. He recently served as leader of an international team advising the People's Bank of China on banking reform. Barth was an appointee of Presidents Ronald Reagan and George H. W. Bush as chief economist of the Federal Home Loan Bank Board and later of the Office of Thrift Supervision. He has also been a professor of economics at George Washington University, associate director of the economics program at the National Science Foundation, and the Shaw Foundation Professor of Banking and Finance at Nanyang Technological University. He has been a visiting scholar at the U.S. Congressional Budget Office, the Federal Reserve Bank of Atlanta, the Office of the Comptroller of the Currency, and the World Bank. He is a member of the Advisory Council of George Washington University's Financial Services Research Program. Barth is the coauthor of *Rethinking Bank Regulation: Till Angels Govern*, coeditor of *Financial Restructuring and Reform in Post-WTO China*, coeditor of *China's Emerging Financial Markets: Challenges and Opportunities*, and overseas associate editor of *The Chinese Banker*.

Tong (Cindy) Li is a Senior Research Analyst at the Milken Institute, where her research topics include international financial markets, the U.S. mortgage market, banking regulation, and the Chinese economy.

Li has coauthored many Milken Institute research papers and policy briefs. Her research work has been published in academic journals and presented at international conferences, and she is also a freelance columnist for several newspapers. Li earned her Ph.D. in economics with a concentration in development economics and econometrics from the University of California, Riverside. She received her bachelor's degree in international finance from Peking University.

Wenling (Carol) Lu is a Research Analyst in the Capital Studies Group at the Milken Institute, focusing on financial institutions and mergers and acquisitions. Prior to joining the Institute, she worked as a research assistant at Auburn University, providing support to projects related to corporate governance, IPOs, and bankruptcies. Lu previously held positions with ACE Group and Dresdner Asset Management Corporation in Taipei, Taiwan. She received her MBA with a concentration in finance from Auburn University and a bachelor's degree in business from National Taiwan University of Science and Technology, Taiwan.

Triphon (Ed) Phumiwasana is a Research Economist at the Milken Institute. His research focuses on financial institutions, capital markets, banking regulation, corporate governance, and economic development, with special emphasis on global issues. Phumiwasana has coauthored a number of Milken Institute publications, including policy briefs and articles in *The Milken Institute Review*. His research has also been featured in *Financial Markets, Institutions and Instruments Journal*, *MIT Sloan Management Review*, and *Regulation of Financial Intermediaries in Emerging Markets*. Phumiwasana earned his Ph.D. in economics with a concentration in international money and finance from Claremont Graduate University.

Glenn Yago is Director of Capital Studies at the Milken Institute and an authority on financial innovations, capital markets, emerging markets, and environmental finance. He focuses on the innovative use of financial instruments to solve long-standing economic development, social, and environmental challenges. Prior to joining the Institute, Yago served as a professor at the State University of New York–Stony Brook and City University of New York Graduate Center. He has also taught at Tel Aviv University and is a visiting professor at the Hebrew University of Jerusalem, where he directs the Koret–Milken Institute Fellows program. He is the author of five books, including *Global Edge* and *Beyond Junk Bonds*, and coeditor of the Milken Institute Series on Financial Innovation and Economic Growth. Yago created the Milken Institute's Capital Access Index, an annual survey measuring access to capital for entrepreneurs across countries, and cocreated the Opacity Index, measuring financial risks associated with corruption, legal, enforcement, accounting, and regulatory practices internationally. His opinions appear regularly in the *Los Angeles Times* and *The Wall Street Journal*. Yago is a recipient of the 2002 Gleitsman Foundation Award of Achievement for social change. He earned a Ph.D. at the University of Wisconsin–Madison.

Index